Covert Investigation

Covert Investigation

Clive Harfield

MSc, LLM, MPhil, PhD
John Grieve Centre for Policing and Community Safety

and

Karen Harfield

BSc (Hons)
Superintendent, Warwickshire Police

OXFORD
UNIVERSITY PRESS

OXFORD
UNIVERSITY PRESS

Great Clarendon Street, Oxford OX2 6DP

Oxford University Press is a department of the University of Oxford.
It furthers the University's objective of excellence in research, scholarship,
and education by publishing worldwide in

Oxford New York

Auckland Cape Town Dar es Salaam Hong Kong Karachi
Kuala Lumpur Madrid Melbourne Mexico City Nairobi
New Delhi Shanghai Taipei Toronto

With offices in

Argentina Austria Brazil Chile Czech Republic France Greece
Guatemala Hungary Italy Japan Poland Portugal Singapore
South Korea Switzerland Thailand Turkey Ukraine Vietnam

Oxford is a registered trademark of Oxford University Press
in the UK and in certain other countries

Published in the United States
by Oxford University Press Inc., New York

The moral rights of the authors have been asserted
Database right Oxford University Press (maker)

Crown copyright material is reproduced under Class Licence
Number C01P0000148 with the permission of OPSI
and the Queen's Printer for Scotland

Cover photos: © Brand X Pictures / Punchstock; StockDisc / Punchstock; Brand X Pictures /
Punchstock; ImageState / Punchstock; Photodisc / Punchstock; Brand X Pictures / Punchstock;
Stocksearch / Alamy; Stockbyte / Punchstock; DigitalVision / Punchstock; Dominic Harrison /
Alamy; Up The Resolution (uptheres) / Alamy; Photodisc / Punchstock

First published 2005

British Library Cataloguing in Publication Data

Data available

Library of Congress Cataloging in Publication Data

Harfield, Clive.
  Covert investigation : a practitioners' guide / Clive Harfield, Karen
Harfield.
    p. cm.
  Includes Index.
  ISBN-13: 978-0-19-928377-4 (alk. paper)
  ISBN-10: 0-19-928377-X (alk. paper)
  1. Undercover operations–Law and legislation–Great Britain.
2. Police patrol–Great Britain–Surveillance operations.   I. Harfield,
Karen. II. Title.
KD8335.H37 2005
344.4105'232–dc22

                                                    2005031874

Typeset by Laserwords Private Limited, Chennai, India
Printed in Great Britain
on acid-free paper by
Antony Rowe Ltd, Chippenham

ISBN 0–19–928377–X   978–0–19–928377–4

10 9 8 7 6 5 4 3 2

For Bryn

Foreword

As a Detective Sergeant in 1974, I was part of the team that reviewed the cases of Mealey and Sheridan. As a Detective Inspector in 1978, I inherited a team of investigators who had been involved in the Malone case. By the time that case reached the European Court of Human Rights in 1984, I was a Detective Chief Inspector member of the team that reorganized covert policing and, in particular, wrote the first editions of the *Informants Handling Guidelines*, now called *Covert Human Intelligence Sources*. A decade later, as Director of Intelligence at New Scotland Yard, I was again involved in the reorganisation of the intelligence function and its covert arm in particular. Another decade on, I am a recipient of all the dedicated, hard-developed products of RIPA as an independent Commissioner on the Independent Monitoring Commission in Belfast and Dublin. In any one of those task arenas, and in many others, I would have welcomed this valuable book into my toolkit.

Clive and Karen Harfield have done a remarkable job in distilling a vast amount of complex law and practice into this guide. Modestly, they told me their target readers were not the experienced SIOs on the specialist squads, but the practitioners in everyday policing. There are many who will benefit from the material gathered here.

The next generation of investigators gaining their initial experiences, the new team leaders, and those tasked with wider leadership and decision making are other groups where sensitive reasoning is required to acquire the resources needed for a successful investigation and the survival of that investigation in a court or courts of trial and appeal. Who would not benefit from over 80 cases described by the authors before facing a team of barristers who each have their chosen specialist field in the covert arena and are out to challenge every twist and turn of the investigation?

It is not just the police investigators who face that white knuckle ride in the witness box. Besides the 43 police services, another 900 agencies and authorities are now beneficiaries of the act, there have been 30 statutory instruments directly connected to RIPA since 2000, supplementing the act which has been amended 89 times since then. The Police Act 1997 has itself been amended 92 times but not all relate to Part III. Here is a complex world described.

It is as much a neglect of duty not to use every lawful endeavour, not to be legally audacious in seeking every investigative tool to bring offenders to justice. In years to come, I hope to see heavily annotated copies of this book in offices, from crime squads to ACPO, on desks, hidden under the seats in surveillance vehicles, in briefcases and in any number of locations for ready reference, sprouting updating Times Law Reports. It is a valuable addition to the hunter/gatherer's toolkit. It is an honour to write this foreword. Good hunting.

John G D Grieve CBE QPM
Centre for Policing and Community Safety
Buckinghamshire Chilterns University College
September 2005

Acknowledgements

The authors wish to express their appreciation to colleagues in a number of organizations investigations and discussions with whom inspired and informed this book, many of whom have subsequently commented on early drafts. Others have provided material for study. In particular we thank: Sue Biddle, Cara Airey, Jackie Griffin, Glynis Hooper, Tony Hutchings, Kingsley Hyland, Mick Ives, Louise Pierpoint, Phil Swinburne, Debbie Tedds, Dave Whordley, and Katie Whiting.

Organizations as well as individuals have provided practical assistance and access to information, as well as permission to reproduce copyright material: Bramshill Police Library (Centrex), the House of Commons Information Office, the National Specialist Law Enforcement Centre (Centrex), and University of Warwick Library.

At Oxford University Press we are grateful to Katie Allan and Andrea Oliver for their help and guidance during the writing of this work.

Contents

Tables of Cases   xv

Tables of Legislation   xix

Abbreviations   xxv

Special Features   xxvii

Introduction   xxix

1   Covert Investigation in Context   1

1.1   Introduction   2
1.2   Why Investigate Covertly?   2
1.3   What Are the Issues Arising from Covert Investigation?   4
1.4   Why Have Covert Investigation Powers Only Recently Been
       Enacted?   6
1.5   What Benefits and Disadvantages Arise from the UK Regulatory
       Regime?   9
1.6   What Do the Article 8 Tests Mean?   12
1.7   What Issues Have Arisen from Independent Inspections of Covert
       Investigation?   17
1.8   What Are the Consequences of Investigator Malpractice?   19
1.9   Protecting Covert Investigation Methodology   21

2   Directed Surveillance   27

2.1   Introduction   28
2.2   Which Public Authorities May Deploy Directed Surveillance?   29
2.3   What Powers Does the Law Provide in Relation to Directed
       Surveillance?   31
2.4   What Authority Regime Is Required for Directed Surveillance?   33
2.5   Cancellation of Authorities   34
2.6   What Significant Case Law Has Been Decided in Relation to Directed
       Surveillance?   36

3   Intrusive Surveillance   47

3.1   Introduction   48
3.2   Which Public Authorities May Deploy Intrusive Surveillance?   49
3.3   What Powers Does the Law Provide in Relation to Intrusive
       Surveillance?   49
3.4   What Authority Regime Is Required for Intrusive Surveillance?   51

3.5   The Need for Prior Approval from the Office of Surveillance
       Commissioners   52
3.6   Cancellation of Authorities   53
3.7   What Significant Case Law Has Been Decided in Relation to
       Intrusive Surveillance?   54

**4   Interference with Property or Wireless Telegraphy
       and Entry onto Land   67**
4.1   Introduction   68
4.2   Which Public Authorities May Interfere with Property or Wireless
       Telegraphy and Enter onto Land?   68
4.3   What Powers Does the Law Provide in Relation to Interference with
       Property or Wireless Telegraphy and Entry onto Land?   69
4.4   What Authority Regime Is Required for Interference with Property
       or Wireless Telegraphy and Entry onto Land?   70
4.5   The Need for Prior Approval from the Office of Surveillance
       Commissioners   72
4.6   Cancellation of Authorities   72
4.7   What Significant Case Law Has Been Decided in Relation to Property
       or Wireless Telegraphy Interference and Entry onto Land?   73

5   Covert Investigation and Computers   83
5.1   Introduction   84
5.2   Which Public Authorities Can Investigate Computers Covertly and
       Which Legal Authorities Are Required?   84
5.3   What Action Requires a Directed Surveillance Authority in Relation
       to the Investigation of Computers?   87
5.4   What Action Requires an Intrusive Surveillance Authority in
       Relation to the Investigation of Computers?   88
5.5   What Action Requires a Property Interference Authority in Relation
       to the Investigation of Computers?   88
5.6   What Action Requires an Interception Authority in Relation to the
       Investigation of Computers?   89
5.7   What Action Requires a CHIS Authority in Relation to the
       Investigation of Computers or Using Computers?   89
5.8   What Is the Appropriate Authority for Accessing Data Stored
       on a Computer?   90
5.9   Good Practice for the Covert Investigation of Computers   90
5.10   Issues for Consideration Regarding the Investigation of Computers 91

6   Examining Mobile Phones   97
6.1   Introduction   98
6.2   Which Public Authorities Can Examine Mobile Phones?   98

6.3	What Powers Does the Law Provide in Relation to the Examination of Mobile Phones?	99
6.4	What Authority Regime Is Required for the Examination of Mobile Phones?	99
6.5	What Significant Case Law Has Been Decided in Relation to the Examination of Mobile Phones?	100

7	**Communications Data**	**105**
7.1	Introduction	106
7.2	Which Public Authorities Can Investigate Communications Data?	106
7.3	What Powers Does the Law Provide in Relation to Communications Data?	107
7.4	What Authority Regime Is Prescribed for the Acquisition of Communications Data?	109
7.5	What Significant Case Law Has Been Decided in Relation to Communications Data?	111

8	**Interception of Communications**	**115**
8.1	Introduction	116
8.2	Which Public Authorities Can Intercept Communications?	117
8.3	What Powers Does the Law Provide in Relation to Interception of Communications?	118
8.4	What Authority Regime Is Required for Interception of Communications?	118
8.5	What Are the Procedures for Intercepting Legal Privilege Communications?	123
8.6	What Are the Procedures for Intercepting Communications Containing Confidential Personal Information?	123
8.7	What Are the Procedures for Intercepting Communications Containing Confidential Journalistic Material?	124
8.8	What Are the Interception Provisions of s 83 Postal Services Act 2000?	124
8.9	What Are the Procedures for Handling Intercept Products?	124
8.10	How Is Disclosure of an Intercept Product Addressed?	125
8.11	What Is a 'Preston' Briefing?	125
8.12	What Significant Case Law Has Been Decided in Relation to Interception of Communications?	126

9	**Covert Human Intelligence Sources**	**131**
9.1	Introduction	132
9.2	Which Public Authorities May Deploy CHISs?	132
9.3	What Is a CHIS?	133
9.4	What Is a 'Confidential Source' or 'Confidential Contact'?	134

9.5   What Powers Does the Law Provide in Relation to CHISs?   134
9.6   What Authority Regime Is Required for a CHIS?   135
9.7   Juveniles and Vulnerable Persons as CHISs   136
9.8   Acquisition of Confidential Information by a CHIS   136
9.9   What Management Regime Is Required for a CHIS?   137
9.10   What Significant Case Law Applies to CHISs?   137
9.11   Good Practice in Light of the Above Case Law   142

10   Covert Investigation Abroad   151
10.1   Introduction   152
10.2   Which Public Authorities May Conduct Covert Investigation
       Abroad?   153
10.3   What Powers Does the Law Provide in Relation to Covert
       Investigation Abroad?   153
10.4   What Authority Regime Is Required for Covert Investigation Abroad?   156
10.5   What Significant Case Law Has Been Decided in Relation to Covert
       Investigation Abroad?   157
10.6   Sources of Advice   159

11   Risk Management   165
11.1   Introduction   166
11.2   What Positive Obligations Are Imposed on Investigators?   166
11.3   The Benefits of Good Risk Assessment   167
11.4   Identifying Risks and How to Manage Them: The Model Approach   168
11.5   The PPPLEM Model   169
11.6   Vulnerability and RARA   169
11.7   Conclusion   172

APPENDICES
A   Relevant Extracts of Part III Police Act 1997 as Amended   175
B   Extracts from the Regulation of Investigatory Powers Act 2000 as Amended 191
C   Extracts from Statutory Instruments Issued Pursuant to RIPA 2000   249
D   The Covert Surveillance Code of Practice   285
E   Covert Human Intelligence Sources (CHIS) Code of Practice   313
F   Interception of Communications Code of Practice   331

Index   349

Tables of Cases

United Kingdom

Attorney-General v Bryant (1846) 15 M&W 169 142
Attorney-General's Reference (No. 3 of 1999) [2001] 2 AC 91 5
B v SSHD [2000] 2 CMLR 1086 16
Blake and Austin v DPP (1993) 97 Cr App R 169 .... 37, 56
Borough of Ealing v Woolworths PLC [1998] Crim LR 58 139
D v NSPCC [1978] AC 171 142
DPP v Marshall and Downes [1988] Crim LR 750 139
Hardy's Case (1794) 24 St Tr 199 142
Marks and Beyfus (1890) 25 QBD 494 142
Nottingham City Council v Amin [2000] Crim LR 174 140
NTL Group Ltd v Ipswich Crown Court [2002] EWHC 1585 .... 89, 99, 100, 120
R v Agar [1990] 2 All ER 442 142
R v Ameer and Lucas [1977] Crim LR 104 139
R v Aujla [1998] 2 Cr App R 16 .... 126, 158
R v Bailey and Smith [1993] 3 All ER 513 54
R v Birtles [1969] 1 WLR 1047 .... 137, 138
R v Brown and Daley (1988) 87 Cr App R 52 .... 37, 56
R v Bryce [1992] 4 All ER 567 141
R v Chalkley and Jeffries [1998] 2 All ER 155 20
R v Christou [1992] 4 All ER 559 .... 140, 141
R v Clarke (1984) 80 Cr App R 344 138
R v E [2004] EWCA Crim 1243 126
R v Edwards [1991] Crim LR 45 138
R v Gooch (No. 1) [1999] 1 Cr App R (s) 283 157
R v Governor of Pentonville Prison, ex p Chinoy [1992] 1 All ER 317 158
R v Grimes [1994] Crim LR 213 .... 37, 55
R v H [1987] Crim LR 47 119
R v H and C [2004] 2 AC 134 .... 22, 142
R v Hallett [1986] Crim LR 462 142
R v Hardy and Hardy [2002] EWCA Crim 3012 .... 38, 56
R v Hennessy (1979) 68 Cr App R 419 142
R v Hewitt and Davis (1992) 95 Cr App R 81 .... 37, 55
R v Horseferry Road Magistrates Court, ex p Bennett (No. 1) (1994) 98 Cr App
    R 114 ....138, 141
R v Johnson [1988] 1 WLR 1377 .... 37, 39, 55
R v Khan [1997] AC 558 ....5, 68, 73, 158
R v Lawrence [2002] Crim LR 584 10
R v Loosley [2002] Crim LR 301 140

R v Mann and Dixon [1995] Crim LR 647 141
R v Mason [2002] 2 Cr App R 38 .... 19, 54
R v Mealey and Sheridan [1974] 60 Cr App R 59 138
R v P (Telephone Intercepts: Admissibility of Evidence) [2001] 2 WLR 463 .... 126, 159
R v Pattemore [1994] Crim LR 836 .... 139, 142
R v Preston [1994] 2 AC 130 .... 125, 126
R v Rankine [1986] 1 QB 861 .... 37, 55
R v Roberts (Stephen Paul) [1997] 1 Cr App R 217 54
R v Sang (1979) 69 Cr App R 282, [1980] AC 402 .... 139, 140, 158
R v Secretary of State, ex p Finninvest SpA [1997] 1 WLR 743 158
R v Smurthwaite and Gill (1994) 1 All ER 898 .... 140, 141
R v Sutherland (Unreported, Nottingham Crown Court, 29 January 2002) 19, 54, 59
R v Turner (Paul) [1995] 2 Cr App R 94 142
R v W, Attorney-General's Reference (No. 5 of 2002), [2003] EWCA Crim 1632
Savage v Chief Constable of Hampshire [1997] 2 All ER 631 142
Swinney v Chief Constable of Northumbria [1996] 3 All ER 449 142
Williams v DPP [1993] 3 All ER 365 140

European Court of Human Rights

Barthold v Germany (1985) 7 EHRR 383 14
Buckley v UK (1997) 23 EHRR 101 17
Campbell v UK (1993) 15 EHRR 137 17
Christie v UK (1993) 78-A DR 119 10
Costello-Roberts v UK (1995) 19 EHRR 112 .... 36, 54
Esbester v UK (1994) 18 EHRR CD72 10
Friedl v Austria (1996) 21 EHRR 83 .... 36, 54
Govell v UK (1997) 23 EHRR CD101 73
Halford v UK (1997) 24 EHRR 523 .... 36, 54, 126
Harman and Hewitt v UK (1992) 14 EHRR 657 7
Huvig v France (1990) 12 EHRR 528 15
Jersild v Denmark (1995) 19 EHRR 1 17
Khan v UK (2001) 31 EHRR 45 .... 20, 68, 73, 158
Klass v Germany (1979–80) 2 EHRR 214 .... 10, 17
Kopp v Switzerland (1999) 27 EHRR 91 10
Lewis v UK (2004) 39 EHRR 9 73
McMichael v UK (1995) 20 EHRR 205 17
Malone v UK [1984] EHRR 14 .... 7, 15, 116, 126
Neimitz v Austria (1993) 16 EHRR 97 .... 36, 54
Osman v UK (2000) 29 EHRR 245 166
Perry v UK (2004) 39 EHRR 3 .... 13, 36, 54
PG v UK [2002] Crim LR 308 20
Schenk v Switzerland (1991) 13 EHRR 242 20
Silver v UK (1983) 5 EHRR 347 15
Sunday Times v UK (No. 1) (1979–1980) 2 EHRR 245 15

Teixeira de Castro v Portugal (1999) 28 EHRR 101 138
W v UK (1988) 10 EHRR 29 17

Foreign

Kamal Jain, Appeal Court of Aix en Provence 4 May 1992, Cour de Cassation, Paris
    7 October 1993, case no. M92-83.707D 158

Tables of Legislation

United Kingdom

Air Force Act 1955
Part I 179
Part II 179
s 209 179
Army Act 1955
Part II 179
s 209 179
Company Directors Disqualification
Act 1986 176
s 7 176
s 8 176
Computer Misuse Act 1990 90
Constitutional Reform Act 2005 175
Part 2 175
Part 3 175
Sched. 17 175
Crime and Disorder Act 1998
s 5 12
s 6 12
Crime (International Co-Operation)
Act 2003
s 9 157
s 18(2) 155
s 26(2)(b) 155
s 26(4)(b) 155
s 27(1) 155
s 83 154
Criminal Justice and Court Services
Act 2000
Sched. 7 178
Criminal Procedures and Investigations
Act 1996 .... 38, 56, 158
s 3(7) 125
s 8(6) 125
s 9(9) 125
s 23(6) 125
Customs and Excise Management
Act 1979
s 1(1) 50, 178
Enterprise Act 2002
s 188 177
Fire Services Act 1947 .... 29, 86, 133
Harbours, Docks and Piers Clauses
Act 1847

s 79 .... 29, 85, 132
Human Rights Act 1998 .... 5, 7, 8, 9
s 6 .... 5, 6, 14
s 6(3)(a) 14
s 6(3)(b) 5, 14
s 7 21
s 8 21
Insolvency Act 1986
s 429(2)(b) 176
Intelligence Service Act 1994 7
s 5 .... 28, 48, 69, 71, 85, 98
Interception of Communications Act
1985 .... 7, 8, 10, 116, 117, 126
s 9 158
Interpretation Act (Northern Ireland)
1954
s 44 .... 30, 87, 133
Local Government Act 1985
Sched. 11 .... 29, 86, 133
National Health Service Act 1977
s 8 .... 30, 86
s 11 .... 30, 86
National Health Service and Community
Care Act 1990
s 5 .... 30, 86
National Health Service Reform and
Health Care Professions Act 2002
s 6 .... 30, 86
Naval Discipline Act 1957
Part I 179
Part II 179
s 118 179
Police Act 1996
s 2 .... 49, 68, 84, 85, 98, 178
Police Act 1997 .... 7, 10, 11, 15, 19, 98
Part III 7, 8, 17, 28, 48, 68, 73, 77,
78, 79, 88, 90, 91, 99, 153, 175
s 91 175
s 92 176
s 93 .... 14, 16, 17, 50, 153, 176, 180
s 93(1) 69
s 93(1)(b) 91
s 93(2) 69, 72
s 93(2)(a) 7
s 93(3) 71

Police Act 1997 (*cont.*):
  Part III (*cont.*):
    s 93(4) 50, 70, 77, 78, 79
    s 93(5) 69, 70, 85, 98, 179
    s 93(6) 72, 91
    s 94 ....70, 179
    s 95 ....71, 181
    s 95(5) 73
    s 96 ....72, 181
    s 97 182
    s 97(2) 72
    s 98 .... 72, 123, 183
    s 99 .... 72, 123, 183
    s 100 .... 72, 124, 184
    s 101 184
    s 102 184
    s 103 184
    s 104 .... 72, 176, 186
    s 105 187
    s 106 ....176, 187
    s 107 187
    s 108 188
Police and Criminal Evidence Act
  1984 .... 4, 11, 34, 54, 90, 98
  s 9 ....89, 100, 120
  s 78 .... 19, 35, 119, 140, 143, 156, 158
  Sched. 1.. 120
Police Reform Act 2002
  s 97 12
  s 103 155
  s 104 155
  Sched. 2.. 181
  Sched. 3.. 177
Police (Scotland) Act 1967
  s 1 .... 49, 68, 84, 85, 98, 178
Postal Services Act 2000 .... 30, 86, 133
  s 83 .... 115, 119, 124
Regulation of Investigatory Powers Act
  2000 .... 3, 8, 10, 11, 15, 18, 19, 34,
      54, 68, 77, 78, 79, 116, 138, 139
  Chap. I 106
  Chap. II 21, 99, 106, 111
  Part I 21, 99, 106, 111, 117, 124
  Part II 21, 119, 176, 177
  Part IV 17
  s 1 191
  s 1(1).. 118
  s 1(2).. 118
  s 1(3).. 118
  s 1(4)..155, 157
  s 1(5)...............................89, 100, 120
  s 1(6).. 118

s 2 192
s 2(1).. 120
s 2(2)..117, 126
s 2(4).. 117
s 2(5).. 117
s 2(7).. 117
s 3 195
s 3(1).. 119
s 3(2)..87, 119
s 3(3).. 119
s 3(4).. 120
s 3(5).. 120
s 4 196
s 4(2)..118, 119
s 4(4) 118, 122, 123
s 5 ....89, 100, 118, 120, 121, 122,
                            123, 125, 197
s 5(1)(c).. 156
s 5(2)... 120
s 5(3)........................... 120, 124, 127
s 6 ....118, 120, 124, 198
s 7 199
s 8 ....121, 200
s 8(1).. 120
s 8(4)..120, 121
s 8(5).. 121
s 9 ....121, 200
s 10 ....121, 201
s 11 203
s 12 204
s 13 206
s 14 206
s 15 ....124, 207
s 15(3)......................................124, 125
s 15(4)......................................124, 125
s 16 ....124, 208
s 17 .... 21, 106, 117, 125, 126,
                            155, 159, 209
s 17(1).. 121
s 18 210
s 18(4) 89, 100, 119, 120, 123
s 18(5) 89, 100, 119, 120
s 18(7).. 125
s 19 ....117, 212
s 20 214
s 21 214
s 21(1).. 110
s 21(4)(c) 108, 110
s 21(4)(a) 108, 110
s 21(4)(b) 108, 110
s 21(6) 108
s 22 216

Regulation of Investigatory Powers Act
 2000 (*cont.*):
 Part IV (*cont.*):
  s 22(2) 107, 110
  s 22(3) 109, 110
  s 22(4) 109, 110
  s 22(5) 107
  s 23 217
  s 23(3) 110
  s 23(4) 110
  s 23(5) 110
  s 24 218
  s 24(4) 107
  s 24(4)(C) 107
  s 24(4)(b) 107
  s 25 218
  s 25(1) 106
  s 26 .... 153, 219
  s 26(2) 31, 50, 87
  s 26(3) 49
  s 26(4)(a) 50
  s 26(8) 132, 133
  s 26(9) 148
  s 26(10) 33
  s 27 221
  s 27(3) 153, 156
  s 28 .... 14, 16, 17, 87, 221
  s 28(2) 35
  s 28(3) 31, 35
  s 28(4) 35
  s 28(9) 133
  s 29 .... 14, 16, 17, 222
  s 29(2) 135, 148
  s 29(3) 135
  s 29(4) 134
  s 29(5) 135, 137
  s 30 224
  s 31 224
  s 32 226
  s 32(3) 50, 52
  s 32(6) 49
  s 33 227
  s 33(5) 50, 51, 71
  s 34 228
  s 35 .... 52, 230
  s 36 232
  s 36(2) 52
  s 36(3) 52
  s 37 233
  s 38 235
  s 39 236
  s 40 236
  s 41 236
  s 42 .... 49, 85, 237
  s 43 238
  s 44 239
  s 45 .... 53, 241
  s 46 242
  s 47 243
  s 48 243
  s 48(2) 28, 48
  s 48(3) 28, 48
  s 48(7)(a) 32
  s 49 21
  s 63 176
  s 65 20
  s 67(2) 20
  s 67(3)(c) 20
  s 67(3)(b) 21
  s 68(6) 21
  s 68(7) 21
  s 71 117
  s 76A 154
  s 81 50
  s 81(1) 29, 85, 132
  s 81(2) 31
  s 81(2)(b) 50
  s 81(3) 50, 121, 122, 127
  s 81(5) 31, 50, 107, 124
  Sched. 1 .... 14, 29, 132
Security Service Act 1989 7
Serious Organized Crime and Police Act
 2005 .... 116, 121, 154, 175
 Part II 179
 Sched. 4 .... 177, 178, 179, 180
 Sched. 17 179
Wireless Telegraphy Act 1949
 s 5 120

UK Statutory Instruments

Communications Act 2003
 (Commencement No. 1) Order 2003
 (SI 2003/1900) 283
Companies (Northern Ireland) Order 1989
 Part II 176
Copyright and Related Rights Regulations
 2003 (SI 2003/2498) 283
Criminal Procedure Rules 2005
 (SI 2005/384) 283
Crown Court (Amendment No. 3) Rules
 2004 (SI 2004/2991) 283
Enterprise Act 2002 (Commencement
 No. 3 Transitional and Transitory

Provisions and Savings) Order 2003
(SI 2003/1397) 283
Financial Services and Markets Tribunal
Rules 2001 (SI 2001/2476) 282
Health and Personal Social Services
(Northern Ireland) Order 1972
Art 10 .... 30, 87
Art 16 .... 30, 87
Independent Police Complaints
Commission (Investigatory Powers)
Order 2004 (SI 2004/815) 283
Intervention Board for Agricultural
Produce (Abolition) Regulations 2001
(SI 2001/3686) 282
Investigatory Powers Tribunal Rules 2000
(SI 2000/2665) 282
Magistrates Court (Amendment) Rules
2004 (SI 2004/2993) 283
Mersey Docks and Harbour (Police) Order
1975
Art 3 ....29, 85, 132
Ministry of Agriculture, Fisheries and Food
(Dissolution) Order 2002 (SI 2002/
794) 282
Official Secrets Act (Prescription)
(Amendment) Order 2003 (SI 2003/
1918) 283
Police and Criminal Evidence (Northern
Ireland) Order 1989
Art 12 123
Postal Services Act 2000 (Disclosure of
Information) Order 2001 (SI 2001/
3617) 282
Prison (Amendment) Rules 2000 122
Prison Rules 1999 122
r 35A-35D 122
Proceeds of Crime Act 2002 (Disclosure of
Information) Order 2003 (SI 2003/
335) 282
Proscribed Organisation Appeal
Commission (Procedure) Rules 2001
(SI 2001/443) 282
Regulation of Investigatory Powers Act
2000 (Commencement No. 1 and
Transitional Provisions) Order 2000 (SI
2000/2543) 281
Regulation of Investigatory Powers Act
2000 (Commencement No. 2) Order
2001 (SI 2001/2727) 282
Regulation of Investigatory Powers Act
2000 (Commencement No. 3) Order
2003 (SI 2003/3140) 283

Regulation of Investigatory Powers
(Authorizations Extending to
Scotland) Order 2000 (SI 2000/
2418) 281
Regulation of Investigatory Powers
(British Broadcasting Corporation)
Order 2001 (SI 2001/
1057) 278, 282
reg 1 278
reg 2 278
reg 3 279
reg 4 279
reg 5 280
Regulation of Investigatory Powers
(Cancellation of Authorisations)
Regulations 2000 (SI 2000/
2794) 53, 282
Regulation of Investigatory Powers
(Communications Data)
(Amendment) Order 2005 (SI 2005/
1083) 106, 111, 283
reg 1 267
reg 2 267
Regulation of Investigatory Powers
(Communications Data) Order
2003 (SI 2003/
3172) 106, 107, 108, 109,
111, 262, 283
reg 1 263
reg 2 ....263, 265
reg 3 263
reg 4 263
reg 5 263
reg 6 263
reg 7 263
reg 8 264
reg 9 264
reg 10 264
reg 11 264
Sched. 1 110
Regulation of Investigatory Powers
(Conditions for Lawful Interception of
Persons outside the United Kingdom)
Regulations 2004 (SI 2004/
157) 126, 155, 283
reg 1 273
reg 2 273
reg 3 273
Regulation of Investigatory Powers (Covert
Human Intelligence Sources: Code of
Practice) Order 2002 (SI 2002/
1932) 282

Regulation of Investigatory Powers
(Covert Surveillance: Code of Practice)
Order 2002 (SI 2002/
1933) 282

Regulation of Investigatory Powers
(Designation of an International
Agreement) Order 2004 (SI 2004/
158) 155, 283

Regulation of Investigatory Powers
(Designation of Public Authorities
for the Purposes of Intrusive
Surveillance) Order 2001 (SI 2001/
1126) 282

Regulation of Investigatory Powers
(Directed Surveillance and Covert
Human Intelligence Sources)
(Amendment) Order 2005 (SI 2005/
1084) 33, 34, 38, 146
reg 1.. 260
reg 2.. 260
reg 3.. 260

Regulation of Investigatory Powers
(Directed Surveillance and Covert
Human Intelligence Sources)
(Amendment) Order 2005 (SI
2005/1085) 283

Regulation of Investigatory Powers
(Directed Surveillance and Covert
Human Intelligence Sources) Order
2003 (SI 2003/3171) 33, 34, 38,
56, 283
reg 1.. 251
reg 2.. 252
reg 3.. 252
reg 4...252, 254
reg 5.. 253
reg 6.. 253
reg 7.. 253
reg 8.. 253
reg 9.. 253
reg 10.. 253
reg 11.. 254

Regulation of Investigatory Powers
(Foreign Surveillance Operations)
Order 2004 (SI 2004/1128) 283

Regulation of Investigatory Powers
(Interception of Communications:
Code of Practice) Order 2002 (SI 2002/
1693) 282

Regulation of Investigatory Powers
(Intrusive Surveillance) Order 2003 (SI
2003/3174) 283

Regulation of Investigatory Powers
(Juveniles) Order 2000 (SI 2000/
2793) 136, 146, 282
reg 1.. 276
reg 2.. 276
reg 3.. 276
reg 4.. 276
reg 5.. 277
reg 6.. 277

Regulation of Investigatory Powers
(Maintenance of Interception
Capability) Order 2002 (SI 2002/
1931) 282

Regulation of Investigatory Powers
(Notification of Authorizations etc)
Order 2000 (SI 2000/
2563) 38, 53, 56, 249, 281
reg 1.. 250
reg 2.. 250
reg 3.. 250
reg 4.. 250
reg 5.. 250

Regulation of Investigatory Powers
(Prescription of Offices, Ranks and
Positions) (Amendment) Order 2002
(SI 2002/1298) 33, 282

Regulation of Investigatory Powers
(Prescription of Offices, Ranks and
Positions) Order 2000 (SI 2000/
2417) 33, 135

Regulation of Investigatory Powers (Source
Records) Regulations 2000 (SI 2000/
2725) 146, 282
reg 1.. 274
reg 2.. 274
reg 3.. 275

Regulation of Investigatory Powers
(Technical Advisory Board) Order
2001 (SI 2001/3734) 282

Road Vehicles (Construction and Use)
(Amendment) (No. 3) Regulations
2003 (SI 2002/2126) 282

Scotland Act 1998 (Modifications of
Schedule 5) (No. 2) Order 2005 (SI
2005/866) 283

Scotland Act 1998 (Transfer of Functions
to the Scottish Ministers etc) (No. 2)
Order 2003 (SI 2003/2617) 283

Scotland Act (Transfer of Functions
to the Scottish Ministers etc) (No. 2)
Order 2000 (SI 2000/
3252) 282

Scottish Parliament (Disqualification)
Order 2003 (SI 2003/
409)...282
Secretaries of State for Education and
Skills and for Work and Pensions
Order 2002 (SI 2002/
1397)...282
Secretaries of State for Transport, Local
Government and the Regions and
for Environment, Food and Rural
Affairs Order 2001 (SI 2001/
2568)...282
Telecommunications (Lawful Business
Practice) (Interception of
Communications) Regulations 2000
(SI 2000/2699) 118, 119, 126,
269, 282
    reg 1................................ 270
    reg 2................................ 270
    reg 3................................ 270
Transfer of Functions (Transport, Local
Government and the Regions)
Order 2002 (SI 2002/
2626)...282
Wireless Telegraphy (Interception and
Disclosure of Messages) (Designation)
Regulations 2000 (SI 2000/
2409)...281
Wireless Telegraphy (Interception and
Disclosure of Messages) (Designation)
Regulations 2003 (SI 2003/
3104)...283

European

Decision of 13 June 2002 on Joint
Investigation Teams OJ 2002/
L 162/1 155
Directive 97/66/EC............................. 107

Treaties and Conventions

EU Convention on Mutual Assistance in
Criminal Matters 2000 153
    Art 13.. 154
    Art 14.. 154
European Convention on Human
Rights 5, 6, 9, 17
    Art 1 of the First Protocol....................5
    Art 2... 166
    Art 6...143, 156
    Art 8..........6, 12, 13, 14, 20, 21, 31, 143,
156, 158, 168
    Art 8(1)......... 5, 6, 12, 14, 15, 17, 22, 60,
101, 111, 127, 146, 161
    Art 8(2)......5, 6, 7, 10, 15, 22, 60, 68, 73,
101, 111, 127, 146, 161
    Art 18.. 15
    Protocol 1...6
    Protocol 11 5
Schengen Convention 1990 153
    Art 40........................153, 154, 156, 159
    Art 40(1).. 154
    Art 40(3)(f) 154
    Art 40(7).. 153
    Art 41.. 154

Abbreviations

AC	Appeal Court
ACPO	Association of Chief Police Officers
All ER	All England Law Reports
ANPR	automatic number plate recognition
CCTV	closed circuit television
CDRP	Crime and Disorder Reduction Partnerships
CHIS	covert human intelligence source
CMLR	Common Market Law Reports
CPIA	Criminal Procedure and Investigations Act 1996
CPS	Crown Prosecution Service
CSP	communication service provider
Cr App R	Criminal Appeal Reports
Crim LR	Criminal Law Review
ECHR	European Convention on Human Rights 1959
ECtHR	European Court of Human Rights, Strasbourg
EHRR	European Human Rights Reports
EHRLR	European Human Rights Law Reports
EWHC	England and Wales High Court
GCHQ	Government Communications Headquarters
Hansard HC	Official Record of the House of Commons
Hansard HL	Official Record of the House of Lords
HMCE	HM Customs and Excise (now HM Revenue and Customs)
HRA	Human Rights Act 1998
IOCA	Interception of Communications Act 1985 (repealed)
ISP	internet service provider
JIT	joint investigation team
MI5	Security Service
MI6	Secret Intelligence Service
MOD	Ministry of Defence
NCIS	National Criminal Intelligence Service
NCS	National Crime Squad
NHS	National Health Service
NIM	National Intelligence Model
NOMS	National Offender Management Service
NSLEC	National Specialist Law Enforcement Centre
OFT	Office of Fair Trading

OSC	Office of Surveillance Commissioners
PA97	Police Act 1997
PACE	Police and Criminal Evidence Act 1984
PII	Public Interest Immunity
PSNI	Police Service of Northern Ireland
QB	Queens Bench
RIPA	Regulation of Investigatory Powers Act 2000
SI	Statutory Instrument (secondary legislation supplementing Acts)
SOCA	Serious Organized Crime Agency
SOCAPA	Serious Organised Crime and Police Act 2005
SPOC	single point of contact
UKCA	UK Central Authority (department of the Home Office)
WLR	Weekly Law Reports
WTA	Wireless Telegraphy Act 1949

Special Features

This book contains several special features that it is hoped will make it more helpful to the reader. These are defined and explained below.

Case law criteria

Where case law has defined certain tests or criteria to be met in given situations or when considering certain determinations, these are highlighted in case law criteria features.

Checklists of key issues

Where appropriate, chapters conclude with a checklist of key issues that invest-igators and authorizing officers might usefully consider when planning or man-aging covert investigations.

Definitions

Definitions of specific terms are provided where this is useful.

Further information and reading

These boxes provide the reader with additional information and direct the reader towards additional reading that will elaborate upon points discussed in the text.

Hints and tips

Good-practice advice is offered where it has developed over time.

Key points

Information requiring particular emphasis is summarized in key points.

PLAN

Supporting the concluding checklists is the pneumonic PLAN, which provides a structure for investigators to use in their policy-books and for authorizing officers to use when structuring their authorizations or refusals.

Scenarios

To illustrate some of the issues discussed in the chapters, example scenarios are presented.

Tables

Some information or concepts have been tabulated for ease of illustration and presentation.

Introduction

This is the book that the authors themselves needed when, as either covert investigation managers, covert human intelligence source (CHIS) controllers or authorizing officers, they had, in their various professional police roles at local and national levels, daily responsibilities under the Police Act 1997 (PA97) and Regulation of Investigatory Powers Act 2000 (RIPA) for managing covert investigation. As no one else had yet written it, they decided to do so themselves on the premise that others performing similar roles would probably also appreciate such a book. Market research would appear to support this assertion. The intention is to provide those responsible for planning, executing, and overseeing covert investigations with introductory basic guidance about covert investigation law and practical considerations that follow on from it when trying to conduct or supervise such operations. For obvious reasons discussion will stop short of disclosing specific sensitive tactics and techniques. For reasons of space, the complex arena of covert financial investigation, a specialist field in its own right, has not been addressed in this edition.

Covert investigation law in the UK is nothing if not complicated. Besides statute law, certain aspects of covert investigation, the use of informants for example, have a long history of case law. Other aspects have very little or as yet no significant case law to provide additional illumination. There are arguments to suggest that this whole body of law is incomplete and inconsistent. The implications of this for investigators will at least be highlighted even though the issues may be beyond resolution here. Interpretations of the various statutory powers vary from one expert to another and from one organization policy to another, indicating that covert investigation law is far from being the precise and unambiguous instrument that all criminal justice practitioners need it to be. Clarke LJ described RIPA as a 'very puzzling statute' (*R v W*, Attorney-General's Reference (No. 5 of 2002), [2003] EWCA Crim 1632 at para 98).

Notwithstanding that it is difficult to disagree with this analysis, the ambitious objective of this book is to provide an introduction to this arena that contributes to making these statutory powers less puzzling for investigators to understand and use.

The principal audience for this book, then, are the investigators and authorizing officers of the approximately 950 public authorities (Office of Surveillance Commissioners estimate) empowered to deploy some or all of the covert investigation powers provided for in both the PA97 and RIPA. The book has been structured with these readers in mind: plain English explanations cross-referenced against original texts; case law citation and interpretation; operational considerations; and extracts of the relevant legislation, both primary and secondary, together with relevant Codes of Practice, all between two covers. But it is anticipated that others will also find this work of value.

Trainee investigators and an academic audience (in the fields of law, criminology, police studies, politics, and social administration, for instance) will also find this a useful introduction to the statutory framework underpinning the use of covert investigation methods. With this audience in mind, further information references have been included to guide readers towards detailed academic arguments that practitioners may not necessarily wish to follow up. Expert commentary on covert investigation law and policy ranges from the broadly supportive to arguments that suggest the law not only fails to give sufficient effect to human rights principles, but even undermines long-established protections in procedural law governing more conventional methods of investigation (D Ormerod, 'ECHR and the exclusion of evidence: trial remedies for Article 8 breaches?' Crim LR [2003] 61, 62). It is not the purpose of this book to contribute to this legal commentary but where such secondary literature helps elucidate points of guidance, reference will be made to it.

The chapter structure is thematic. The statutory context is presented as an introduction before different aspects of covert investigation are considered in turn. Investigators are required to use the least intrusive means of investigation that will achieve their objective. Accordingly the chapters are arranged in order of increasing intrusion. The volume ends with a discussion on risk assessment and management which, based on the authors' operational supervisory experience, is an area often overlooked by investigators.

Chapters are structured around questions that have been frequently debated by colleagues. Because each chapter is intended to be a self-sufficient reference guide, readers of the entire volume will notice that repetition of some points has been preferred to cross-referencing within this volume; an approach consistent with the preference of the publishers. Various features (definition boxes, bullet point lists, key points, scenarios) have been included in the chapters to render the information more readily accessible and digestible. In researching these, the authors have found that RIPA, in particular, has generated different interpretations and whilst guidance will be offered here, definitive judgment is properly the role of the courts. Where scenarios have been used, these are based on actual issues encountered by the authors and other colleagues. Those selected for inclusion here focus not on the ordinary and mundane but upon those episodes that have, through case law or as a result of external independent inspection, illustrated the subtle nuances of covert investigation law. In some cases answers are offered. In others ongoing debates are highlighted. The information is up to date as of July 2005. This arena continues to develop both through case law and statute.

Government and Parliament have striven, and continue to strive, to facilitate the more effective investigation of crime, within the context of perceived new criminal threats and trends, whilst at the same time eliminating abuses of power by investigators. The ever-increasing sophistication and scale of the criminal threat to society is argued as the justification for enacting enhanced investigation powers (Home Secretary Jack Straw MP, opening the Second Reading Debate on the Regulation of Investigatory Powers Bill, *Hansard* HC (series 6) vol 345 col 768 (6 March 2000)). The investigation methods given parliamentary authority in 1997 and 2000 were not new; what was new was their statutory foundation to ensure investigators had a legal basis for their work and regulation as a means to protect the citizen against abuse of power. Parliament enacted the powers within the British tradition of investigator autonomy. In other words, the role of the Procurator-Fiscal in Scotland aside, there is no British equivalent to the European investigating magistrate or American District Attorney overseeing criminal investigations (although in practice early consultation between investigators and the relevant prosecuting authority will benefit British investigators). British public authorities trusted and empowered with investigation and enforcement responsibilities are expected to regulate their own behaviour, only the application for search warrants and the continued detention of suspects being subject to judicial authority. Such autonomy is a privilege vulnerable to abuse, either through deliberate act or lack of awareness and competence.

Covert investigation methods often provide incontrovertible evidence because of the level of intrusion by investigators into the private lives of citizens. Such intrusion is only permitted within strict statutory and procedural frameworks and, for a defendant faced with incontrovertible evidence, the only defence strategy left available in the adversarial trial system is to attack investigation procedure and seek exclusion of the incontrovertible evidence on the basis that it was unfairly obtained and prejudicial to the defendant.

It is hoped that this volume will increase investigator awareness in order to minimize the risk of unwitting abuse of these powers and to minimize the misuse of procedure leading to technical acquittals of defendants against whom the evidence is strong enough to convict. The latter will fail society by not protecting citizens from crime and the former will fail society by not protecting citizens from abuse of authority. This consequence could persuade Parliament to reconsider the powers invested in investigators.

At the time of writing this book, the statutory framework of covert investigation is under review by the Home Office. The particular focus of the review is on the perceived bureaucracy associated with the procedures for authorizing covert investigation that engages human rights issues. The outcome is awaited with interest. It is not certain to what extent, if any, the review will result in legislative changes.

During the preparation of this book the Association of Chief Police Officers (ACPO), in association with the National Centre for Policing Excellence, have published their *Practice Advice on Core Investigative Doctrine* (2005), the first time that the police service has defined investigative doctrine. The principles outlined on page 103 of the doctrine, regarding covert policing, are equally applicable to non-police investigators undertaking covert investigation. They bear quotation here, providing the doctrinal context within which this book should be read and to which this book seeks to make a contribution.

Principles underpinning a covert investigation strategy which investigators should consider:

- Have a good working knowledge of intelligence processes and the National Intelligence Model.
- Become fully cognizant of all current, pertinent intelligence material prior to the instigation of an operation.
- Anticipate the need for covert policing and make early and timely bids for such resources (failure to make an early request may undermine the investigation and valuable material may be lost).
- Ensure that the covert policing strategy is proportionate to the overall objectives of the investigation.
- Know how to obtain advice and guidance for covert options.
- Have a thorough understanding of RIPA and the relevant aspects of the Police Act 1997.
- Understand Public Interest Immunity procedures and legislation, and the Criminal Procedures and Investigations Act.
- Ensure that operations are run on a 'need-to-know basis' and that operational security is maintained at all times.
- Consult the Crown Prosecution Service at the earliest opportunity (in more complex cases this may be prior to the commencement of the operation).
- Establish a review mechanism if necessary. In serious or complex investigations which involve a high degree of risk, a senior officer must authorize and/or review all operations.

1

Covert Investigation
in Context

1.1	Introduction	2
1.2	Why Investigate Covertly?	2
1.3	What Are the Issues Arising from Covert Investigation?	4
1.4	Why Have Covert Investigation Powers Only Recently Been Enacted?	6
1.5	What Benefits and Disadvantages Arise from the UK Regulatory Regime?	9
1.6	What Do the Article 8 Tests Mean?	12
1.7	What Issues Have Arisen from Independent Inspections of Covert Investigation?	17
1.8	What Are the Consequences of Investigator Malpractice?	19
1.9	Protecting Covert Investigation Methodology	21

1.1 Introduction

This chapter outlines the political and statutory context within which covert investigation law has developed in the UK. Covert investigation for the purpose of this book is investigation of which the suspect is assumed to be unaware and which infringes upon the private life of the suspect. Primarily this means some form of active surveillance. Whilst this will usually be proactive investigation into crimes in progress or incomplete offences, there will be occasions when covert methods are used during a reactive investigation into reported or discovered crime. Covert investigation methods can also be deployed to acquire intelligence to inform crime management (including investigation) within the National Intelligence Model (for information on the NIM, see <http://www.policereform.gov.uk/implementation/natintellmodel.html>). The use of surveillance to gather information that may prove useful in the future is not uncontroversial. Equally of concern to some is the fact that 'covert surveillance may be used as much to prevent civil disorder and disobedience, or to effect public compliance in respect of the payment of government taxes and duties, as to deal with criminal conduct' (S Sharpe, 'Covert surveillance and the use of informants' in M McConville and G Wilson (eds), *The Handbook of the Criminal Justice Process* (OUP, Oxford, 2002) 59–73, 65).

1.2 Why Investigate Covertly?

Prevention is argued to be better (and cheaper) than cure. Crime prevention is, and always has been, as much if not more of a priority for UK enforcement authorities than is the investigation of offences committed (see, for instance, C Emsley, *The English Police: A Political and Social History* (2nd edn, Longman, London, 1996) 25). Overt, high-visibility policing, in its widest sense whether undertaken by police officers, community support officers, local authority wardens, customs officers or private sector security firms for instance, is premised upon the prevention of crime and reassuring the public: the deterrence and disruption of disorder by means of physical presence. Such overt activity engages the first and basic level of accountability since it takes place in the public arena, open to witness by the average citizen whose perception of reasonableness is what the law seeks to represent and what the courts seek to interpret.

By definition, a priority with such a visible objective cannot be achieved by covert means, but covert investigation has both a preventative and evidential role. It is the means by which evidence that would not otherwise be open to third-party witnesses can be gathered by investigators in order to support a prosecution. In investigations involving serious and/or organized crimes as yet incomplete, it can be the means by which investigators can gather sufficient evidence to prosecute for preliminary offences, whilst at the same time being able to intervene before a more serious offence is committed or at a time before the harmful consequences of an offence take effect.

For example, the trafficking or manufacture of illicit drugs are offences in which the immediate victims, drug users, are very unlikely to report the matter to enforcement authorities voluntarily because in possessing illegal drugs they are themselves committing an offence. The extent to which they can provide evidence against the organized crime syndicates supplying the drugs is limited because the street dealer who deals to the user is likely to be far removed in the criminal commercial chain from the importer profiting by trafficking. Prosecuting minor actors in the criminal chain will neither disrupt nor prevent the drug importation or manufacture nor reduce the harm to wider society. Covert investigation methods can be used to secure evidence of manufacture, importation, and distribution that would not otherwise be available to prosecuting authorities. The ideal outcome for investigators in such instances would be to intervene at the point at which they had acquired sufficient evidence to prosecute, but before the imported or manufactured narcotics had been made available to users who would suffer harm from such use, and who might themselves commit acquisitive crime (so creating more, indirect victims, thus increasing the overall harm caused) in order to fund their drug dependency. Covert investigation is considered the means by which such a successful outcome, evidential and preventative, can be achieved.

In this example, whereas overt policing as described above might deter or disrupt street dealing of illicit drugs, covert investigation is the only realistic means of prosecuting and preventing, through network disruption and dismantling, the manufacture or importation and distribution that precedes the street dealing and end-user harm.

Whilst not normally deployed in the reactive investigation of reported crimes, covert investigation methods can occasionally provide useful supporting evidence or intelligence that generates opportunities to secure such evidence. Because the crime has already occurred, subsequent proactive covert investigation is unlikely to produce direct evidence of the crime itself, but it can provide evidence in relation to the suspect that could support the main contention of the prosecution.

Covert investigation is necessary to prosecute any criminal activity evidence of which cannot be secured by normal, overt means. Covert investigation might also be required to identify or confirm the true nature of a defendant's assets for asset recovery purposes where it is suspected that criminal profits were being laundered.

Amongst non-police agencies empowered to conduct covert surveillance, local authority use of CCTV, if targeted at particular individuals for the purpose of an investigation, constitutes activity requiring a RIPA authority. Close liaison with police forces in connection with the use of CCTV can complicate matters with circumstances arising in which both the police and the local authority require individual RIPA authorities for one given act of surveillance. Partnership protocols are a useful means of identifying issues of responsibility and liability in given circumstances.

Nineteen Special Health Authorities, 270 NHS Trusts, and twenty-two Local Health Boards are also empowered to conduct directed surveillance for the purpose of protecting public health, or for preventing or detecting crime or disorder. Figures of the year 2003–2004 indicate that relatively few health authorities have used their surveillance powers, prompting concerns from the Office of Surveillance Commissioners (OSC) (whose role it is to inspect public authorities and their use of covert investigation powers) that health authorities will not develop sufficient familiarity and expertise ever to conduct such operations without there being a high risk of unauthorized activity taking place through a lack of competence. Matters investigated by health authorities using their surveillance powers include issues of fraud and security.

1.3 What Are the Issues Arising from Covert Investigation?

The significant advantage of covert investigation is that it produces evidence that is often considered to be incontrovertible. Although additional evidence might be necessary to prove the relevance of any given observed event or meeting, the fact that the participants were observed doing what they were doing cannot be contradicted. Investigation subjects incriminate themselves without realizing it, severely compromising their right to non-self-incrimination at trial. In regulating overt investigation, the Police and Criminal Evidence Act 1984 (PACE) ensures that subjects, even if they do not co-operate, are aware of investigative actions that are happening or have taken place. Such due process ensures that investigators do not act unlawfully, or provide protections if they do (Sharpe, 'Covert surveillance', 59–73, 65).

Within the context of due process protection, preserving the integrity of the criminal justice system is the key issue arising from the use of covert investigation. Investigators, because they are acting outside the public arena, must be capable of being held to account for their actions by other means. As much as the citizen wishes to be protected from being harmed by crime, agents within the criminal justice system must not abuse their powers and authority in providing that protection. The secrecy of covert investigation limits the ways in which investigators can be managed and held to account. Equally important in protecting the integrity of the criminal justice system is protecting investigators from malicious allegations that they have acted improperly.

The management and regulation of covert investigation thus seeks to meet three criteria:

- the rights of the suspect must not be breached except where there is statutory provision to do so,

- the rights of other citizens not suspected of criminal involvement must be protected,
- the integrity of the investigator must be demonstrated (or, if necessary, its absence exposed).

Covert investigation intrudes upon the private lives of individuals. Respect for private life is an obligation imposed upon UK public authorities by virtue of two legal instruments, the 1950 European Convention for the Protection of Human Rights and Fundamental Freedoms (hereafter ECHR; opened for signature at Rome, 4 November 1950; TS 71 (1953); Cmd 8969, as amended by Protocol Number 11, which entered into force on 1 November 1998) and s 6 Human Rights Act 1998 (HRA) which makes it unlawful for UK public authorities (including those who act on their behalf, s 6(3)(b)) 'to act in a way which is incompatible with a Convention right'. The right in question is outlined in Article 8(1) ECHR:

> Everyone has the right to respect for his private and family life, his home and his correspondence.

This is reinforced by Article 1 of the First Protocol to the ECHR done at Paris, 20 November 1952:

> Every natural and legal person is entitled to the peaceful enjoyment of his possessions.

'It would be a strange reflection on our law if a man who had admitted his participation in the illegal importation of a large quantity of heroin should have his conviction set aside on the grounds that his privacy has been invaded', observed Lord Nolan (*R v Khan* [1997] AC 558); see also Attorney-General's Reference (No. 3 of 1999) [2001] 2 AC 91, which asserted that the interests of crime victims and the public should be taken into account.

And indeed that is not the intention of the ECHR because the right to respect for private life is qualified by Article 8(2). In certain circumstances public authorities can breach the Article 8(1) right:

> There shall be no interference by a public authority with the exercise of this right except such as is in accordance with the law and is necessary in a democratic society in the interests of national security, public safety or the economic well-being of the country, for the prevention of disorder or crime, for the protection of health and morals, or for the protection of the rights and freedoms of others.

Article 1, Protocol 1, ECHR is similarly qualified:

> No one shall be deprived of his possessions except in the public interest and subject to the conditions provided for by law and by the general principles of international law.

Further information and reading

Protocol 1 provides 'public interest' as grounds justifying deprivation of property. There is no similar justification for intrusion into private life in Article 8. A Ashworth, *Human Rights, Serious Crime and Criminal Procedure* (Sweet & Maxwell, London, 2002), particularly chs 2 and 3, provides a comprehensive discussion of 'public interest' in the context of covert investigation.

Thus investigators planning covert operations or managers supervising or authorizing such activity know from the outset that such investigation is likely to breach Article 8(1), given domestic effect in UK law by s 6 HRA, and that they can only proceed in certain prescribed circumstances which have come to be considered by the European Court of Human Rights at Strasbourg (hereafter ECtHR) in a framework of sequential tests:

(1) Does the investigative act fall within the scope of Article 8? (1.6.1)
(2) If yes, has the Article 8 right been interfered with by a Public Authority? (1.6.2)
(3) If it has, was this interference in accordance with the law? (1.6.3)
(4) If it was lawful, was the interference pursuant to a legitimate aim as identified in Article 8(2)? (1.6.4)
(5) Even if it was both lawful and pursuant to a legitimate aim, was it still necessary, and no more than necessary (i.e. proportionate), in a democratic society? (1.6.5)

Investigators must comply with these tests, which are discussed in detail later in this chapter, and defendants will seek to disrupt a prosecution by arguing that tests 1 and 2 have been met but that one or more of tests 3, 4, and 5 have not.

1.4 Why Have Covert Investigation Powers Only Recently Been Enacted?

Covert investigation techniques are not new, as the then Home Secretary, Jack Straw MP, stressed when opening the Second Reading debate on the Regulation of Investigatory Powers Bill in Parliament: 'None of the law enforcement activities specified in the Bill is new. What is new is that, for the first time, the use of these techniques will be properly regulated by law and externally supervised' (*Hansard* HC (series 6) vol 345 col 768 (6 March 2000)). So what prompted this legislation? Why was there, in 2000, a perceived need to legislate where previously no need had been identified?

Arguably the need for legislation to regulate covert investigation had been extant from the moment the UK signed the ECHR in 1950, even though the UK did not give domestic statutory effect to the Convention for forty-eight years, and the momentum for change had become unstoppable by the 1980s when the first covert investigation legislation was enacted in response to external stimuli. Up until that first statute, however, UK authorities relied upon the principle that which was not specifically prohibited by law was implicitly permitted.

Investigators were not left entirely to their own devices. In lieu of statute came official guidelines; for instance from the Home Office in 1969 (Circular 97 of that year) in relation to the use of participating informants (subsequently replaced by a joint ACPO/HM Customs and Excise (HMCE) Voluntary Code of Practice); from the Home Office in 1984 in relation to the use of equipment in police surveillance operations; from the Home Office in relation to the interception of communications; and also an ACPO Voluntary Code Of Practice regarding surveillance prior to RIPA. Such guidelines are no substitute for statute.

The move to statute, when it came, arose from an investigation involving covert interception of communications. In 1957 a Privy Council review, the Birkett Report, recommended consideration of legislation to clarify the authority to intercept communications (Cmnd 283; see also D Ormerod and S McKay, 'Telephone intercepts and their admissibility' Crim LR [2004] 15, 18). In 1981 the Royal Commission on Criminal Procedure recommended legislation and judicial oversight (Cmnd 8092). In 1984 the ECtHR held, amongst other issues, that official guidelines, no matter how closely adhered to, did not constitute publicly accessible law and so actions undertaken pursuant to such guidelines (and in the absence of any other statute) would not be 'in accordance with law' as prescribed by the ECHR Art 8(2) (*Malone v UK* (1984) 7 EHRR 14). In 1985 Parliament enacted the Interception of Communications Act (IOCA) precisely so that future interceptions by investigating authorities would be in accordance with law. And as a result of *Harman and Hewitt v UK* [1989] 67 DR 88, the Security Service Act 1989 and the Intelligence Service Act 1994 were enacted to ensure that the Security Service (MI5), the Secret Intelligence Service (MI6), and the Government Communications Headquarters (GCHQ) were able to operate within the context of statutory authority.

The lacuna in relation to other methods of covert investigation was exposed. One surveillance technique was authorized by statutory provision; others were not. Potentially it was only a matter of time before another case was brought before Strasbourg that would result in forcing the UK's hand. In the event a change of political administration in 1997 brought in a government committed to ratifying the ECHR and giving it domestic effect in what was to become the 1998 HRA.

The consequences of enacting the HRA included the need to update existing legislation to ensure it was ECHR-compliant. Anticipating this development, Part III of the Police Act 1997 provided for 'Authorization of Action in Respect of Property', which established an authority regime within which investigators could take action that would otherwise constitute trespass or criminal damage pursuant to the investigation of 'serious crime' by covert means (s 93(2)(a)).

This, however, was but one small part of covert investigation and the entry into force of the HRA 1998 was delayed until October 2000 to allow other legislation to be drafted to provide for statutory authority covering the remaining aspects of covert investigation.

In the summer of 1999 a review of IOCA was already under way because 1990s telecommunications technology had by then far outstripped the parameters of 1980s legislation. Without statutory revision a number of communication methods now lay outside the regime for lawful interception. At the same time an Electronic Commerce Bill was being drafted which contained regulatory provisions regarding the investigation of encrypted digital data, potentially a major obstacle to investigators. Separately, the issues of regulating surveillance and informants were being discussed at policy level in order to be able to instruct Treasury Counsel to draft appropriate legislation. In the autumn of 1999 these separate pieces of work were brought together to comprise the individual parts of what was to become the Regulation of Investigatory Powers Bill. Arguably the end result was more a collision than a collaboration of these various efforts. For the legislative draftsmen, the consequence of bringing together for a common purpose policy strands from such diverse origins, some of which built of existing legislation, was an unavoidable, but to the legal draftsman's eye ugly, inconsistency of definition within a single Act.

Given that Part III of the Police Act 1997 was already enacted, it also meant that there were now two separate Acts covering various aspects of covert investigation. Both PA97 and RIPA 2000 have been subject to substantive and consequential amendments in subsequent legislation, which begs the question, where will an investigator find an up-to-date version of the legislation from which to work? The appendices for this volume, giving consolidated texts as of July 2005, have been compiled from a number of sources. UK statutes made available on-line at <http://www.opsi.gov.uk/legislation/index.htm> are the versions of laws as originally enacted prior to any amendment. (At time of writing the House of Commons Information Office advised the authors that there are plans to provide consolidated texts on-line in due course.)

Further information and reading

To discover via the internet amendments to any legislation the following procedure must be carried out:

- Access <http://www.legislation.opsi.gov.uk/legislation/index.htm> (formerly the HMSO website)
- Select the *Advanced Search* facility
- Type in the title of the Act along with the year
- Select *exact phrase*

- Select *Acts* and *Statutory Instruments*
- Select *UK* and click on *Search*.

This will produce a list of all the instruments subsequent to a piece of original legislation that amend the original legislation. These must then be searched to identify what changes have been made.

Statutory Instruments can be accessed at http://www.opsi.gov.uk/stat.htm.

Two standard hard-copy reference works, regularly updated, also provide amended texts or references to amendments up to the point of their publication, namely *Halsbury's Statutes of England and Wales* (4th edn, Lexis Nexis, London, 2003, revised), vol 33 p 1516 for Part III PA97, vol 45 p 790 for RIPA and *Archbold's Criminal Pleading, Evidence and Practice* (revd edn, Sweet & Maxwell, London, 2005) arranged thematically with relevant statute extracts.

Relevant legislation and case law can also be accessed via the following subscription websites: http://www.westlaw.co.uk or http://www.lexisnexis. co.uk; or via the following free (at time of writing) website: http://www. bailii.org.

Covert investigation statute law in the UK has been derived from external stimuli such as adverse case law from Strasbourg and a political desire to plug legislative gaps when implementing the HRA 1998.

1.5 What Benefits and Disadvantages Arise from the UK Regulatory Regime?

The role played by continental prosecutors (usually a branch of the judiciary or else trained as judges) and investigating magistrates (where such a role exists) means that continental investigators nearly always have some form of judicial supervision, particularly for methods likely to engage ECHR rights. The advantage of judicial oversight is that it is considered to be a guarantor of the integrity of the criminal justice system and a means of ensuring that investigators do not act unfairly or unlawfully. Many have argued for judicial oversight of covert investigation within the UK, which would put covert investigation on a par with overt coercive investigation methods such as the execution of production orders and search warrants which require judicial authority and which, so it is argued, is necessary in order to comply with ECHR. Self-regulation by investigators is seen as a mechanism vulnerable to abuse.

Parliament has established a number of different supervisory regimes tailored to different aspects of covert investigation. These will be detailed in turn in subsequent chapters. It is sufficient to say here that an Office of Surveillance Commissioners (OSC), headed by a Chief Surveillance Commissioner assisted by a number of Assistant Commissioners and Inspectors, has been set up to oversee the use of covert investigation in the UK. Oversight is managed by annual inspections, notification of authorities, and in certain types of investigation prior approval for proposed actions.

This approach has its critics. Whilst declaring a preference for judicial supervision, the ECtHR nevertheless found that parliamentary oversight and independent scrutiny of investigator self-regulation, particularly if undertaken by persons with judicial experience, to be an acceptable alternative to direct judicial supervision and therefore such a regime is therefore compliant with Article 8(2). This principle, applied by the ECtHR in *Klass v Germany* (1979–80) 2 EHRR 214, 235, was reinforced in respect of the inspection and review regime for IOCA 1985, and subsequently reproduced with slight variations in the PA97 and RIPA 2000, by *Esbester v UK* (1994) 18 EHRR CD72 (see also *Christie v UK* (1993) 78-A DR 119; *R v Lawrence* [2002] Crim LR 584; and G Ferguson and J Wadham, 103), although elsewhere differently structured internal authorization regimes have been found to be inconsistent with the rule of law (*Kopp v Switzerland* (1999) 27 EHRR 91).

Further information and reading

- A Ashworth, *Human Rights, Serious Crime and Criminal Procedure* (Sweet & Maxwell, London, 2002) ch 2, for a discussion of the debate and various authorities.

- G Ferguson and J Wadham, 'Privacy and surveillance: a review of the Regulation of the Investigatory Powers Act 2000' [sic] EHRLR [2003] Special Issue 101, for a further general introductory discussion of the issues.

- M Seneviratne, 'Policing the police in the United Kingdom' *Policing and Society* 14(4) [2004] 329–347, for discussion about the pitfalls of self-regulation and how these can be overcome.

The regulatory regime, if not judicial, should be independent from the investigating authorities and must be seen to be guarding against the abuse of powers by investigators. This has translated itself into what many investigators regard as a bureaucratic nightmare of form-filling.

The process of seeking written authority:

- helps investigators structure their operations appropriately
- enables authorizing officers to demonstrate how they have considered the issues of legitimacy, necessity, and proportionality
- records the decision-making process throughout an investigation
- is a substitute for alternative methods of due process control.

It is a means by which not only are the justifications for breaching ECHR qualified rights recorded in a transparent form, but also by which the investigator can be protected from subsequent allegations of abuse of authority and malpractice.

Self-regulation subject to scrutiny arguably is a more flexible authority regime, from the operational perspective, than one requiring investigators to go to court on a regular basis, perhaps as often as several times a day, to seek a judicial warrant for the investigative activity to be employed, which for many would provide a greater guarantee of rights protection. The current authority regime seeks to balance the need for operational flexibility and responsiveness against the obligation to protect citizens' rights. It gives investigators a flexibility they would certainly miss if it was withdrawn, and being asked to account for their actions in writing could be seen as a small price to pay for such an operational advantage.

But there are practical problems that should be acknowledged by investigators, authorizing officers, their senior executives, and by external commentators. To use a police example: authorizing officers in the National Crime Squad deal with covert investigation daily, are very experienced in considering the human rights issues, and have become very familiar with the provisions of the PA97 and RIPA 2000. Their opposite numbers in territorial local policing, by and large, do not have the same daily operational familiarity with covert investigation and not infrequently have additional authorizing duties under PACE 1984 as well as a wider range of managerial and community issues to deal with, all of which place demands on their time in addition to their RIPA obligations. It is not unknown for a Superintendent to find him- or herself in a position in which the demands of the authorizing officer role protecting human rights and ensuring the integrity of an investigation appear to conflict with the demands of their performance management role meeting monthly targets. Authorizing officers in other public-sector organizations similarly have other duties competing with their RIPA obligations for attention and time.

All of this appears to reinforce the jurist argument that supervision of covert investigation should be confined to the courts. But there are a number of wider issues that militate against such a move. Leaving aside the overarching issue of how much surveillance is desirable in any given society, the amount currently being undertaken in the UK, based on the annual reports of the Office of Surveillance Commissioners, could fundamentally alter the relationship of the judiciary to the trial process. For instance, instead of issuing a search warrant for a specific item or items, which tends to be a single event, because a covert investigation operation is an entire sequence of related events judicial oversight would involve a greater degree of investigation management. To some this might be desirable, but it would reduce the independence of the judiciary from the pre-trial process.

The second wider consideration concerns promotion of the rights culture and integrity of the criminal justice system. Why confine to the judiciary pre-trial consideration (as well as final determination at trial) of how the rights of an individual suspect should be balanced against the rights of the wider community? Investigators who daily might take actions that engage the ECHR rights of an individual should themselves be engaged in identifying how those rights should be protected and how necessary breaches of qualified rights can be minimized. Rather than abdicating such decision-making to others, self-regulation

11

(subject to external scrutiny) affords the opportunity to increase the profession-alism of investigators and helps to instil in state agents the very values that the ECHR seeks to protect. It forces investigators and authorizing officers to confront the ECHR daily. The concepts, which would otherwise remain remote arguments at *voir dire* become ingrained in the daily thinking of investigation practitioners. Within such an approach the trial process, adjudicated by the judiciary, remains the final guarantee of individual rights, independent from the investigation process.

1.6 What Do the Article 8 Tests Mean?

So, working on the presumption that the status quo will remain undisturbed for some time, subject to any future statutory revision in the event of serious miscarriages of justice or significant change in policy, what do the ECHR Art 8 tests mean for investigators and authorizing officers?

1.6.1 Does the investigative act fall within the scope of Article 8?

If the proposed investigative activity *is intended* or *is likely* to gather information about the private life of an individual (whether or not that individual is the sub-ject of the investigation) then such activity will fall within the scope of Article 8. If the plan is physically to watch an individual in order to observe their move-ments or associations, or to listen to their conversations, or to photograph or video what they do, or to deploy a third party to interact with the subject in such a way as to acquire information, or to monitor their movements by technical tracking devices, then whether the desired product is to be used for evidential or intelligence purposes, the subject's rights protected by Article 8(1) will be viol-ated as will the rights of any third parties present in the surveillance arena.

A particular issue of concern to police forces and local authorities seeking to prevent crime or detect volume crime offenders is the policing of crime hot-spots, particularly as the policing of such hotspots is a priority action derived from application of the National Intelligence Model. Agencies working in part-nerships such as the Crime and Disorder Reduction Partnerships (CDRP), estab-lished by s 97 Police Reform Act 2002 within the context of ss 5 and 6 Crime and Disorder Act 1998, will be working with police forces using the NIM (which all police forces had to implement fully by April 2004 pursuant to the statutory National Policing Plan 2004–2007) to identify and respond to crime hotspots. An oft-quoted and surprisingly controversial example is the public car park vul-nerable to regular thefts from unattended motor vehicles.

One traditional approach to resolving such a problem has been to deploy police officers or security staff employed by the local authority to maintain ob-servations of such areas with the express intention of catching offenders in the act of committing crime. Since in such cases the identity of the offender is likely to be unknown, even if there are a number of likely suspects, it has been the practice to make such deployments without recourse to a surveillance authority. *Perry v UK* ((2004) 39 EHRR 3), a case that actually centred on incorrect application of PACE Code D, coincidentally had implications for surveillance of hotspots because of the very broad interpretation that the ECtHR applied to the likelihood that private information might be obtained: 'the respect for private life under Article 8 of the Convention brings with it decades of developing jurisprudence' (see N Taylor, 'Policing, privacy and proportionality' EHRLR [2003] Special Issue 86).

Even when the purpose of a surveillance operation is to identify a hitherto unknown suspect for thefts at a public car park, it is argued that the fact that private information about anyone present in the car park is likely to be obtained during such an operation dictates that a surveillance authority should be sought because the issues below will be engaged. The point, although strongly disputed by some investigators and senior police officers, has been reiterated by the Chief Surveillance Commissioner: when conducting surveillance 'at a crime hotspot for the prevention or detection of crime, an authorisation for directed surveillance should be sought, if there is any likelihood that "private information" will be obtained' (*Annual Report of the Chief Surveillance Commissioner to the Prime Minister and to Scottish Ministers for 2003–2004*, HC 688, SE/2004/109, 8).

The contrary has recently been suggested in *The Sharp End*, a journalism magazine aimed at police officers published for the Home Office by Square One Group. On page 7 of issue 4, four brief scenarios are presented. One of these suggests that a car park which is a crime hotspot may be surveilled without authorization where the purpose is to identify persons currently unknown who are regularly committing crime at the location. Clarification of the status of this advice was sought from the Home Office for the purpose of this book. The scenario published in *The Sharp End* was described as having 'been prepared in consultation with the Home Office', although 'it is not strictly Home Office advice'. The purpose of the piece was to provoke thought and encourage investigators to consider whether authorization was properly needed because of the infringement of human rights or whether it is sometimes routinely provided in order to remain within an organizational comfort zone (email correspondence between the authors and the Home Office dated 21–23 June 2005), although this more philosophical purpose may have been obscured through the constraints of journalism. This is an example of one of the issues that case law would help resolve (although the OSC might argue that *Perry v UK* has already given the steer in these circumstances). Until investigators in collaboration with their respective prosecuting authorities test such parameters at court, no case law will be forthcoming.

1.6.2 If yes, has the Article 8 right been interfered with by a public authority?

The HRA 1998 applies to public authorities. 'It is unlawful for a public authority to act in a way which is incompatible with a Convention right' prescribes s 6. A public authority is defined in HRA as a public body including 'a court or tribunal' (s 6(3)(a)) and 'any person certain of whose functions are functions of a public nature' (s 6(3)(b)), which includes not only public authorities but private contractors carrying out a public function on behalf of the authority.

Public authorities empowered to undertake surveillance under ss 28 and 29 of RIPA are identified in Schedule 1 to that Act (see Chapters 2 and 3) whilst those authorities permitted in law to interfere with property are identified in s 93 PA97 (see Chapter 4). The Schedule as published at <http://www.opsi.gov.uk/legislation/index.htm> is that as originally enacted. A number of amendments have been made as organizations and government departments have been added or deleted. The lists used in the following chapters and the Schedule 1 reproduced in Appendix B are as amended up to July 2005.

1.6.3 If a public authority has so interfered with Article 8(1) rights, was this interference in accordance with the law?

The ECHR makes reference to 'in accordance with the law', 'prescribed by law', and 'lawful'. Starmer identifies three criteria as a test to ensure compliance with the principle of legality thus established (K Starmer, *European Human Rights Law* (Legal Action Group, London, 1999) 166):

(1) domestic law must identify the legal basis for any restriction on an ECHR right;
(2) persons likely to be affected by such a restriction must be able to access the relevant domestic law; and
(3) the relevant domestic law must be clear and comprehensible so that anyone should be reasonably able to identify or foresee whether or not their behaviour is breaking or might break the law.

The principle of legality is considered to be satisfied by the following categories of law:

• statute
• delegated legislation such as Codes of Practice
• common (or case) law
• European Community law.

The extent to which these categories are truly accessible to the layperson is debatable. The potential difficulty in identifying the latest consolidated text of any given statute as amended has already been referred to. Codes of practice, held to satisfy the principle of legality, *Barthold v Germany* (1985) 7 EHRR 383, are certainly intended to make the law more comprehensible to the non-lawyer. The layperson is unlikely to be sufficiently familiar with stated cases for common law for them to be regarded as properly accessible, but through professional legal representation a layperson may be considered to have sufficient access to common law decisions. The common law was held to meet the principle of legality in *Sunday Times v UK (No. 1)* (1979–80) 2 EHRR 245, reinforced by the decision in *Huvig v France* (1990) 12 EHRR 528, that 'law' could be understood in a substantive sense rather than just in a statutory sense.

As was demonstrated in *Malone v UK* (1984) 7 EHRR 14, following *Silver v UK* (1983) 5 EHRR 347, internal or official guidelines are not sufficient to constitute being in accordance with law, even where published, particularly where the criteria for interpretation of such guidelines remains unpublished.

The PA97 and RIPA make provision for certain covert investigation tactics. Public authorities complying with such provisions will therefore be doing so in accordance with statute law supported by codes of practice.

1.6.4 If it was lawful, was the interference pursuant to a legitimate aim as identified in Article 8(2)?

If the actions of the public authority pass the legality test, they must then be considered within the context of the legitimacy test. The legitimate reasons for interfering with an Article 8(1) ECHR right are prescribed in Article 8(2).

For public officials engaged in law enforcement the legitimate reason provided by Article 8(2) is

- the prevention of disorder or crime.

For state agents undertaking other forms of regulatory function or public protection, other legitimate reasons apply:

- the interests of national security
- the interests of public safety
- the interests of the economic well-being of the country
- the protection of health or morals
- the protection of the rights and freedoms of others.

There is no scope for adding to this list of reasons and they should be interpreted strictly within the ordinary meaning of the language. Article 18 ECHR prescribes that none of the restrictions permitted should be applied for any reason other than for the reasons prescribed (Starmer, *European Human Rights Law*, 177).

1.6.5 Even if it was both lawful and pursuant to a legitimate aim, was it still necessary and proportionate in a democratic society?

The final test is that of necessity in a democratic society. This test incorporates the concept of proportionality which is concerned with balancing the often conflicting interests of the individual and the wider community. Thus Sedley LJ in *B v SSHD* [2000] 2 CMLR 1086:

> a measure which interferes with a human right must not only be authorised by law but must correspond to a pressing social need and go no further than is strictly necessary in a pluralistic society to achieve its permitted purpose; or, more shortly, must be appropriate and necessary to its legitimate aim.

(The authors are grateful to Kingsley Hyland, CPS, for drawing their attention to this dictum. See also Starmer, *European Human Rights Law*, 170.)

Section 28 RIPA imposes the specific obligation upon authorizing officers to consider proportionality in a twofold test in relation to directed surveillance. Firstly, authorizing officers must ensure that the surveillance is necessary for the purpose of preventing or detecting crime or that it is necessary for preventing disorder. Secondly, they must believe that the proposed investigation method is proportionate to what is sought to be achieved by it. A similar obligation is imposed in relation to s 29 RIPA and the authorizing of CHIS deployments.

The phrasing of the proportionality test in s 93 PA97 is slightly different but essentially amounts to providing the same protection for suspects. For property interference to be authorized the officer must believe that it is necessary because it is likely to be of substantial value in the prevention or detection of serious crime (a higher threshold than for directed surveillance) and that the desired objective cannot be reasonably achieved by other means.

Further guidance is provided by the *Covert Surveillance: Codes of Practice* (paras 2.4 and 2.5) and the *Covert Human Intelligence Sources: Codes of Practice* (paras 2.4 and 2.5) which are reproduced in the appendices at the end of this book. The *National Intelligence Model: Code of Practice* (para 5.5.1) supplements these provisions.

Further information and reading

The Codes of Practice are available on-line from the following websites (as of July 2005):

- Covert Surveillance Code of Practice
  <http://www.homeoffice.gov.uk/docs3/surveillcodeofpractice.doc>
- CHIS Code of Practice
  <http://www.homeoffice.gov.uk/docs3/chiscodeofpractice.doc>
- Interception Code of Practice
  <http://www.homeoffice.gov.uk/docs/ioccop.html>
- NIM Code of Practice
  <http://www.policereform.gov.uk/nim_codeprac.html>

Investigators and authorizing officers, resisting the urge to find an objective that justifies a technique, must be clear from the outset what evidence or intelligence it is that is sought and how it relates to the investigation as a whole. When reviewing existing authorities and considering applications for renewal, invest-igators and authorizing officers must consider whether the proportionality has changed and if so how. It may be that as a result of the evidence or intelligence gained the continued use of surveillance is proportionate. But it may equally be possible that surveillance has in fact produced evidence or intelligence that militates against continued intrusion.

Once again a five-part checklist exists to help investigators and authorizing officers to assess proportionality, and will aid authorizing officers in particular to undertake their statutory obligations under ss 28 and 29 RIPA or s 93 PA97:

KEY POINTS ON PROPORTIONALITY

(1) Have relevant and sufficient reasons based on reliable information been put forward for conducting the proposed covert investigation in that particular way? *Jersild v Denmark* (1995) 19 EHRR 1.

(2) Could the same evidence or intelligence be gained by a less intrusive method? *Campbell v UK* (1993) 15 EHRR 137.

(3) Is the decision-making process by which the application is made and the authorization given demonstrably fair? *W v UK* (1988) 10 EHRR 29; *McMichael v UK* (1995) 20 EHRR 205; *Buckley v UK* (1997) 23 EHRR 101.

(4) What safeguards have been put in place to prevent abuse of the technique? *Klass v Germany* (1979–80) 2 EHRR 214. See para 59 in which it is argued safeguards represent the compromise between defending democratic society and individual rights.

(5) Does the proposed infringement in fact destroy the 'very essence' of the ECHR right engaged?

(Based on Starmer, *European Human Rights Law*, 171, 175–176)

If there is no information or evidence to support the deployment of investig-ation methods that will infringe Article 8(1), then an unjustifiable breach will take place.

1.7 What Issues Have Arisen from Independent Inspections of Covert Investigation?

Part III PA97 established the Office of Surveillance Commissioners and the role of Chief Surveillance Commissioner to oversee property interference. Part IV RIPA 2000 extends the functions of the Chief Surveillance Commissioner to include oversight of directed and intrusive surveillance. (Separate Commission-ers have been appointed for interception and for the intelligence services.) Part of the Chief Surveillance Commissioner's duties includes reporting annually to the Prime Minister and to Scottish Ministers. Such reports are laid before the respective Parliaments and so are publicly available. They contain an insight into how well or otherwise public authorities are handling their statutory obligations in respect of these covert investigation methods and are a source of guidance to investigators and authorizing officers alike.

The annual reports for 2000–2001 (presented in January 2002) and for 2003–2004 (presented in June 2004) demonstrate improved understanding over time amongst public authorities using covert investigation methods (*Annual Report 2000–2001* Cm 5360 (SE/2002/5 in Scotland); *Annual Report 2003–2004* HC668 (SE/2004/109 in Scotland)).

But there are recurring deficiencies. In 2001 the Chief Surveillance Commissioner had felt it necessary to highlight the 'poor wording' in the applications for property interference submitted by police chief officers. 'There have been examples where Chief Officers have authorized the removal of property to attach surveillance equipment to it but have failed to authorize the entry on to property necessary to do so or even the return of a vehicle after the device has been fitted' (OSC *Annual Report 2000–2001*, para 15.9). 'Insufficiently specific applications and authorizations' were still an issue in 2004 (OSC *Annual Report 2003–2004*, 11).

The need for comprehensive precision in both applications and authorizations cannot be overemphasized. Actions that have not been specifically authorized will not be lawful.

Deficiencies identified by the OSC have included:

- confusion about the statutory definitions of directed and intrusive surveillance
- confusion about the definition of a CHIS
- errors in detail such as car registration numbers and incorrect addresses
- lateness in notification, renewal, and cancellation
- commencement of operations requiring a Commissioner's prior approval before such had been granted
- failure to explain urgency in oral authorizations
- authorizations given by staff without power to do so
- authorizing more than was sought on an application (there may, of course, be very good reasons for authorizing officers authorizing less than an applicant had applied for once proportionality and necessity had been considered)
- delegation of reviews by authorizing officers
- Codes of practice not readily available to practitioners.

Overall, the OSC has repeatedly identified the lack of adequate training in RIPA and covert investigation management as a theme common to all the public authorities empowered to undertake covert investigation. Such deficiencies heighten the risks of improperly authorized or unauthorized investigations taking place. Such investigations will, by definition, be unlawful, thus undermining the integrity of the criminal justice and other public regulatory systems.

On the frequent complaint about the bureaucracy of self-regulation under RIPA and PA97, the OSC offers this palliative: 'conscientious completion of the application form will incline the judge, if the authorization is called into question, to uphold it, if he can. But for routine policing this is a tiresome exercise, because, instead of being able to apply a rule-of-thumb solution, each case must be separately assessed on its own facts' (OSC *Annual Report 2003–2004*, 8).

1.8 What Are the Consequences of Investigator Malpractice?

There are three possible adverse consequences for investigators who have not acted properly during a covert investigation: a stay of proceedings (where investigators are considered to have unfairly entrapped an offender or enticed an offence that would not otherwise have been committed); exclusion of evidence from trial; and becoming the subject of a complaint.

Proceedings were stayed in *R v Sutherland* (Unreported, Nottingham Crown Court, 29 January 2002). Police, acting in bad faith, covertly recorded legal privilege conversations in the exercise yard at the police station between suspects and their solicitors (3.7.2 below). (See also *Archbold* 2005, para 15-532 and *R v Mason* [2002] 2 Cr App R 38.)

Section 78 PACE 1984 provides for the exclusion from trial of unfair evidence as follows:

> A court may refuse to allow evidence on which the prosecution proposes to rely to be given if it appears to the court that, having regard to all the circumstances, including the circumstances in which the evidence was obtained, the admission of the evidence would have such an adverse effect on the fairness of the proceedings that the court ought not to admit it.

PACE does not impose an absolute duty upon courts to exclude unfairly obtained evidence. The power to do so is discretionary. Section 78 PACE ensures that a court is competent to consider whether or not, in the interest of ensuring fair trial, evidence obtained by unlawful covert investigation should be adduced. If the court decides that it would be unfair to admit evidence that had been unlawfully obtained, for instance through improperly authorized or unauthorized surveillance, then such evidence should be excluded. Since PACE came into force 'there have been many such cases under section 78' (M Zander, *The Police and Criminal Evidence Act 1984* (3rd edn, Sweet & Maxwell, London, 1996), 171).

Neither Europe nor the UK has followed New Zealand's example in automatically excluding any evidence that has been secured in breach of the New Zealand Bill of Rights Act (Starmer, *European Human Rights Law*, 298–299). When considering whether to not to admit evidence that has been unfairly obtained, both UK and Strasbourg courts have taken a broad view when having regard to all the circumstances and apply a standard test: what would be the effect on the fairness of the trial if evidence that had been obtained unlawfully is admitted?

The ECtHR has held that rules of evidence regarding admissibility are primarily the preserve of domestic courts, Strasbourg's role being to determine the fairness of a trial as a whole (*Schenk v Switzerland* (1991) 13 EHRR 242). It would appear that the requirements of a fair trial do not necessarily demand the exclusion of evidence unlawfully obtained. But as *Schenk v Switzerland* illustrates, careful consideration will be given to the probative weight of the evidence, and the opportunities available to the defence to challenge the evidence and any other relevant factors in a given case before unlawfully obtained evidence will be admitted by the court. In both *Khan v UK* ((2000) 31 EHRR 1016) and *PG v UK* ((2002) Crim LR 308), the ECtHR found unanimous breaches of Article 8 yet no unfairness arising from the evidence adduced therefrom. 'Technical breaches especially of qualified rights might not impact on fairness' (Ormerod, 'ECHR and the exclusion of evidence', 61, 66). Unattractive though the unlawful activities of investigators might be, the courts have held that there are circumstances in which it is undesirable for 'guilty' people to go free. The Court of Appeal has held that exclusionary rules cannot be employed merely to express disapproval of the manner in which investigators have secured relevant evidence (*R v Chalkley and Jeffries* [1998] 2 All ER 155). Critics have argued that 'the courts routinely admit covert surveillance evidence owing to its reliability, despite acknowledged breaches of Article 8' (Ormerod, 'ECHR and the exclusion of evidence', 66 and 67). 'A problem with this approach is that it does nothing to encourage or exhort police officers to uphold the law and to conduct ethical investigations' (Sharpe, 'Covert surveillance', 70). The same could be said in relation to other investigators.

The unlawful conduct of investigators, whether deliberate or unwitting, can never be condoned. The fact that courts have not always excluded evidence unlawfully obtained as a result of covert investigation does not excuse investigators from always complying with procedural law. Admission of the evidence notwithstanding, such judgments are damning indictments of the investigators concerned for acting unlawfully thereby compromising their integrity, that of the organization for which they work, and the integrity of the criminal justice and public regulatory systems as a whole.

Up until October 2000 the OSC investigated complaints from the public relating to the exercise of investigation powers to interfere with property. From that date such complaints, together with complaints arising against any public authority empowered under RIPA, have been investigated by an independent tribunal established pursuant to s 65 RIPA for that purpose. The tribunal shall determine its findings according to the same principles that are applied in judicial review, ss 67(2) and 67(3)(c) RIPA.

The tribunal shall first determine whether or not the individual against whom the complaint has been made has, in relation to the complaint made, engaged in:

(1) conduct by or on behalf of any of the intelligence services
(2) conduct for or in connection with the interception of communications in the course of their transmission by means of a postal service or telecommunications system
(3) conduct to which RIPA Part I Chapter II applies (access to communications data)
(4) conduct to which RIPA Part II applies (directed and intrusive surveillance or CHISs)
(5) the giving of a notice under s 49 or any disclosure or use of an encryption key to protect information
(6) any entry on or interference with property or any interference with wireless telegraphy.

The tribunal shall then investigate the authority under which the individual concerned acted, pursuant to s 67(3)(b) RIPA. No frivolous or vexatious complaint will be entertained. Complaints will not normally be investigated if they are made more than a year after the date of the alleged incident. The tribunal has the power to award compensation or make such other order as they see fit and their decisions are final, not being subject to appeal. By virtue of s 68(6) and (7) anyone working for an organization empowered with covert investigation powers under RIPA shall provide the tribunal with such documents or other information as is required.

For complaints arising out of conduct relating to covert investigation which does not fall within the specific remit outlined and (1) to (6) above, the normal complaints procedures relating to the investigator's organization apply.

Complainants also have recourse to civil suit against investigators who are alleged to have breached Article 8 rights, pursuant to ss 7 and 8 HRA 1998.

1.9 **Protecting Covert Investigation Methodology**

Covert investigation methods will only remain effective to the extent that criminals remain ignorant of them. Every trial represents an opportunity for those accused to learn about the methods that brought them before the court (see, for instance, T Barnes, R Elias, and P Walsh, *Cocky: The Rise and Fall of Curtis Warren, Britain's Biggest Drug Baron* (Milo Books, Bury, 2000)). It is important therefore for investigators and prosecutors to avoid exposing sensitive techniques or CHISs in court. In the case of interception, statute provides the protection: s 17 RIPA prohibits trial reference to interception and the information obtained by it (see Chapter 8). The protection of CHISs and other sensitive techniques will require application to the judge for Public Interest Immunity (PII) exemption.

Investigators will need to liaise with their prosecuting authorities in respect of information which they wish the judge to withhold subject to a PII order, as prosecutors have a continuing duty to review all material to ascertain whether it undermines the prosecution case or assists the defence case.

....

Case law criteria: *R v H and C* [2004] 2 AC 134—Public Interest Immunity

Full disclosure should be made of all material held by the Crown that weakens its case or assists the defence. An exception from this rule may be justified if an important public interest has to be protected. If material does not undermine the Crown case or assist the defence, there is no requirement to disclose it or apply for PII. Sensitive/unused neutral material or sensitive/unused material damaging to the defence need not be disclosed and should not be brought to the attention of the court. PII should be sought only where absolutely necessary.

See also A Choo, *Evidence: Text and Materials* (Longman, Harlow, 1998) 537–538, 548–563.

....

Checklist of key issues when considering whether or not to deploy covert investigation techniques

- What evidence or intelligence is being sought?

- How is it relevant to the operation under consideration?

- What is the least intrusive means of securing such evidence or information?

- What are the risks to the organization of such tactics? (Chapter 11)

- What are the risks to the organization's staff of such tactics? (Chapter 11)

- What are the risks to the public or specific third parties when such tactics are deployed? (Chapter 11)

- What are the risks to the subject of the investigation? (Chapter 11)

- Will such methods breach Article 8(1)? (1.6.1)

- Is there justification for doing so provided by Article 8(2)? (1.6.4)

- How is the legality test met? (1.6.3)

- How is the legitimacy test met? (1.6.4)

- How is the necessity test met? (1.6.5)

- How is the proportionality test met? (1.6.5)

- Are the arguments justifying the application to use covert investigation based on reliable information/intelligence, or has the applicant adopted a 'tick-the-box' approach to completing the application without giving full consideration to the facts of the case and the issues arising?

- Have the arguments justifying the granting of authorization to use covert investigation been fully articulated, or has the authorizing officer merely paid lip service to the pro forma authorization template via which authority is granted?

- How are the methods by which the evidence/intelligence will be obtained to be protected at trial? (1.9)

SPACE FOR NOTES

SPACE FOR NOTES

SPACE FOR NOTES

SPACE FOR NOTES

2

Directed Surveillance

2.1 Introduction   28

2.2 Which Public Authorities May Deploy Directed Surveillance?   29

2.3 What Powers Does the Law Provide in Relation to Directed
    Surveillance?   31

2.4 What Authority Regime Is Required for Directed Surveillance?   33

2.5 Cancellation of Authorities   34

2.6 What Significant Case Law Has Been Decided in Relation
    to Directed Surveillance?   36

2.1 **Introduction**

Surveillance is defined at s 48(2) RIPA.

Definition of surveillance

Surveillance 'includes

(a) monitoring, observing or listening to persons, their movements, their conversations or their other activities or communications

(b) recording anything monitored, observed or listened to in the course of surveillance; and

(c) surveillance by or with the assistance of a surveillance device.'

Because they are subject to their own specific authority regimes (as will be discussed in later chapters), the conduct of covert human intelligence sources and interference with property under either Part III PA97 or s 5 Intelligence Services Act 1994 are not included in this definition (s 48(3) RIPA), notwithstanding that these tactics are deployed for exactly the same purposes.

A two-part hierarchy of surveillance is prescribed by law: directed and intrusive. Chapters 2 and 3 consider directed and intrusive surveillance separately because

* not all public authorities empowered to conduct directed surveillance may also conduct intrusive surveillance, and
* the circumstances in which intrusive surveillance may be conducted are more restricted than those in which directed surveillance may take place.

Applications to conduct either type of surveillance may only be made to, and considered by, investigators and authorizing officers working in the same organization. Thus a police officer may only seek authority from, or grant authority to, a member of the same force. Similarly, a member of a local authority or other empowered organization may only seek authority from, or grant authority to, a member of the same organization. That does not preclude staff from more than one agency collaborating under the auspices of a single authority, in circumstances for instance in which specialist skills have to be brought in from another agency, provided applicant and authorizing officer belong to the same agency and the authority specifies the collaboration.

A Code of Practice for Covert Surveillance has been published. It is reproduced in the appendices below and is available on-line at <http://www.homeoffice.gov.uk/docs3/surveillcodeofpractice.doc>. 'Code' in this chapter refers to this Code.

2.2 **Which Public Authorities May Deploy Directed Surveillance?**

Public authorities empowered to utilize directed surveillance are defined in Schedule 1 RIPA. They are:

- Any police force as defined by s 81(1) RIPA: essentially the forty-three police forces of England and Wales, the Scottish police forces, the Police Service of Northern Ireland, British Transport Police, the MOD police, and the military police forces
- The Civil Nuclear Constabulary
- The Force comprising the special constables appointed under s 79 of the Harbours, Docks and Piers Clauses Act 1847 on the nomination of the Dover Harbour Board
- The force comprising the constables appointed under Article 3 of the Mersey Docks and Harbour (Police) Order 1975 on the nomination of the Mersey Docks and Harbour Board
- The Royal Parks Constabulary
- The National Criminal Intelligence Service (until the SOCA becomes operational)
- The National Crime Squad (until the SOCA becomes operational)
- The Serious Organized Crime Agency (SOCA) (date of becoming operational to be announced, likely to be 1 April 2006)
- The Serious Fraud Office
- The Independent Police Complaints Commission
- The Office of the Police Ombudsman of Northern Ireland
- MI5, MI6, and GCHQ
- The Army, Royal Navy, Royal Marines, Royal Air Force
- The Commissioners of Customs and Excise
- The Commissioners of Inland Revenue
- Any local, county, or district council in England, a London borough council, the Common Council of the City of London in its capacity as a local authority, the Council of the Isles of Scilly, and any county council or county borough council in Wales
- Any fire authority within the meaning of the Fire Services Act 1947 (read with para 2 of Schedule 11 to the Local Government Act 1985)
- The Ministry of Defence
- Office of the Deputy Prime Minister
- The Department for Environment, Food and Rural Affairs
- The Department of Health
- The Home Office
- The Northern Ireland Office
- The Department of Trade and Industry
- Department for Work and Pensions

- Department for Transport
- The National Assembly for Wales
- A universal service provider (within the meaning of the *Postal Services Act 2000*) acting in connection with the provision of a universal postal service (within the meaning of that Act)
- The Postal Services Commission
- The Charity Commission
- The Environment Agency
- The Financial Services Authority
- The Food Standards Agency
- The Gambling Commission
- The Office of Fair Trading
- The Health and Safety Executive
- A Health Authority established under s 8 of the National Health Service Act 1977
- A Special Health Authority established under s 11 of the National Health Service Act 1977
- A National Heath Service trust established under s 5 of the National Health Service and Community Care Act 1990
- Local Health Boards in Wales established under s 6 of the National Health Service Reform and Health Care Professions Act 2002
- Her Majesty's Chief Inspector of Schools in England
- The Information Commissioner
- The Royal Pharmaceutical Society of Great Britain
- The Department of Health, Social Services and Public Safety (Northern Ireland)
- The Department of Agriculture and Rural Development (Northern Ireland)
- The Department of Enterprise, Trade and Investment (Northern Ireland)
- The Department of the Environment (Northern Ireland)
- Any district council (within the meaning of s 44 of the Interpretation Act (Northern Ireland) 1954)
- The Department of Regional Development (Northern Ireland)
- The Department of Social Development (Northern Ireland)
- The Department of Culture, Arts and Leisure (Northern Ireland)
- The Foyle, Carlingford and Irish Lights Commission (Northern Ireland)
- The Fisheries Conservancy Board for Northern Ireland (Northern Ireland)
- A Health and Social Services trust established under Article 10 of the Health and Personal Social Services (Northern Ireland) Order 1972
- A Health and Social Services Board established under Article 16 of the Health and Personal Social Services (Northern Ireland) Order 1972
- A Health and Safety Executive for Northern Ireland
- The Northern Ireland Central Services Agency for the Health and Social Services

- The Fire Authority for Northern Ireland
- The Northern Ireland Housing Executive.

2.3 **What Powers Does the Law Provide in Relation to Directed Surveillance?**

Directed surveillance, subject to it being authorized, can be conducted for the purpose of preventing or detecting crime or of preventing disorder. This means establishing by whom, for what purpose, by what means and generally in what circumstances any criminal offence was committed. It may also be conducted in order to apprehend the suspected offender (s 28(3), s 81(2), and s 81(5) RIPA).

Other purposes for which directed surveillance is permitted are (s 28(3) RIPA):

- in the interests of national security
- in the interests of the economic well-being of the UK
- in the interests of public safety
- for the purpose of protecting public health
- for the purpose of assessing or collecting certain fiscal levies.

Definition of directed surveillance

Perhaps a little confusingly, directed surveillance is defined (s 26(2) RIPA) both by what it is not as well as what it is. Surveillance will require a directed surveillance authority if:

- it comprises covert observation or monitoring by whatever means
- it is for the purpose of a specific investigation or specific operation (any crime or any other offence)
- it will or is likely to obtain private information about *any* person, not just the subject of the operation (this is the key element that engages Article 8 ECHR)

but

- it does not include observations conducted in an immediate response to spontaneous events.

Directed surveillance scenario

On patrol, investigators see a person acting suspiciously near a house. In order to maintain a view of the individual without raising their suspicions, the investigators conceal themselves behind a nearby wall.

An authority is not required to carry out as this is a response to immediate events or circumstances.

Such surveillance may be authorized as directed surveillance and can take place anywhere *except*:

- inside any premises at the time being used as a residence, no matter how temporary, including hotel accommodation, tents, caravans, a prison cell, or even railway arches
- in any vehicle which is primarily used as a private vehicle either by the owner or the person having the right to use it (taxis are specifically excluded from this definition, s 48(7)(a) RIPA)
- outside such premises or vehicles if conducted by remote technical means (for instance a long-range microphone) which enables events and conversations inside residential premises and private vehicles to be monitored from outside, producing a surveillance product of the same quality as would be obtained by devices or persons inside such premises or vehicles.

In these three circumstances such surveillance is considered to be intrusive and may be carried out only by certain public authorities (see Chapter 3).

Scenario illustrating action that goes beyond directed surveillance

Investigators wish to confirm whether a benefit claimant lives at a particular address identified to the social security department. At the address investigators are unable to get an answer to a knock at the door. They consider whether it would be appropriate to push open a window that is slightly ajar at the front of the house in order to look inside.

By opening the window investigators would be engaged in surveillance that is carried out on private premises, i.e. a dwelling house. This would constitute intrusive surveillance and property interference and therefore would not be lawful in these circumstances unless it was carried out by an investigating authority with such powers in circumstances that met the criteria for conducting intrusive surveillance and property interference.

(OSC *Annual Report 2005*, 4.18)

Surveillance conducted in offices or in business vehicles (including taxis) requires a directed surveillance authority, not an intrusive surveillance authority.

If surveillance is conducted as an immediate response to a spontaneous event, for instance searching for suspects who have made off from a car park where they have broken into cars and are believed to be in the vicinity of the offence still trying to avoid arrest, then this would not constitute surveillance requiring authority because it would not have been reasonably practicable to seek authority before conducting the spontaneous surveillance. Given the urgency provisions for oral authority from an authorizing officer, the period during which investigators might avail themselves of this exception will be immediately after the event in question and not very long.

To continue this example, the offenders have made good their escape. The witnesses have provided only vague descriptions. The local council or police suspect that the offenders will return to the car park the next day to repeat their crimes. The authorities determine to mount surveillance to try to catch the offenders in the act. Such surveillance requires a directed surveillance authority. The operation will inevitably, and collaterally, gather information about who uses the car park for legitimate purposes and this is private information. It will no longer be an immediate response to spontaneous events. Such reasoning is founded upon the OSC interpretation of the implications for RIPA of Strasbourg case law regarding private information and collateral intrusion. As was seen above (1.6), there is an alternative interpretation which argues no authority will be needed. Investigators and prosecutors must test the matter in court to secure a UK case law determination. English courts must take Strasbourg case law into consideration and are likely to be guided by it.

Definition of private information

Private information is defined (s 26(10) RIPA; Code para 4.3) as being:

- any information relating to a person's private or family life or personal relationships with others.

The fact that an individual happens to be located in a public space, for instance a car park, does not negate the obligation on public authorities to respect that individual's right to privacy and conduct surveillance only if duly authorized. It is not only the rights of the investigation subject that have to be respected. There will be collateral intrusion into the privacy of third parties present in the surveillance arena and so investigators and authorizing officers must be able to demonstrate why it is proportionate and necessary to violate their Article 8 rights and what steps are to be taken to minimize the intrusion and the consequences thereof.

2.4 What Authority Regime Is Required for Directed Surveillance?

Individuals empowered within each public authority to grant authorities for directed surveillance have been defined in Statutory Instruments 2000/2417 and 2002/1298, as amended and consolidated by 2003/3171 and 2005/1084 (these latter two are reproduced in Appendix C).

Thus authorizing officers include, amongst others, police superintendents, military Provosts Marshal, Lieutenant Colonels, Wing Commanders, or Commanders (Royal Navy), Band 9 customs officers, assistant directors of the SFO, prison service area managers, local authority assistant chief officers and senior investigation managers in Royal Mail.

2.5 Cancellation of Authorities

The authorizing officer who granted or last renewed the authorization (or, if no longer available, the person who has succeeded him in that role) must cancel it if he is satisfied that the directed surveillance no longer meets the criteria upon which it was authorized (Code paras 4.28 and 4.29).

Definition of urgent circumstances

Urgent circumstances are defined as instances in which to wait for an authorizing officer to become available to consider a written application would either

• endanger life

or

• jeopardize the investigation concerned (Code para 4.13)

Hint and tip: Negligence on the part of an applicant or conduct of the authorizing officer's own making does not constitute urgency.

Thus where an investigator forgets to apply for authorization until just before the operation is due to begin or where the authorizing officer does not or cannot attend to the application before the operation is due to start, the operation will have to be postponed until the full written application procedure is carried out (Code para 4.13).

There are two types of urgent authority procedure: one where an authorizing officer is available, and one where such an officer is unavailable.

In genuinely urgent cases an available authorizing officer may issue an *oral authority* (Code para 4.12), recording the fact that this has been done as soon as practicable. In the police service it is almost unheard of now for there not to be a duty on-call superintendent to deal with urgent PACE and RIPA authorities.

In urgent cases in which there is no authorizing officer immediately available, specified individuals entitled to act in urgent cases (SI 2003/3171, SI 2005/1084; both reproduced in Appendix C) may give a *written authorization* for directed surveillance for a period of seventy-two hours. Such individuals cannot issue oral authorities. The current edition of the Code can be interpreted ambiguously on this point but the clarification will be found in Code para 4.20. Police inspectors, for instance, have fallen foul of issuing urgent oral authorities in the absence of a superintendent when in fact they had no alternative but to require the applicant to submit a full written application (see scenario below).

Scenario illustrating issues around urgent authorization for directed surveillance

Intelligence came to light at 0300 one night about a burglary being planned for immediate execution. Police desired to maintain surveillance on the offender's house. Having tried unsuccessfully several times to contact the duty superintendent, officers thought it expedient to seek an urgent authority from the night duty inspector on the basis of an oral application. The inspector gave verbal authority for the surveillance to be conducted. However, the OSC confirmed that, absent an authorizing officer, an inspector could only consider a full written application upon which to base an authorization. In this particular instance circumstances were such that there would not have been time to complete and submit such an application to the inspector before the burglary had been committed and the burglar had returned home. Thus alternative intervention strategies not involving surveillance, including perhaps disruption such as the presence of marked police vehicles in the immediate vicinity, should have been considered.

Authorizing officers should not authorize covert surveillance in investigations in which they have direct involvement, although this may sometimes be unavoidable (Code para 4.14).

Authorizing officers must apply two tests when considering whether to grant an authorization. These are set out in s 28(2) RIPA and are explained in the OSC *Annual Report 2000–2001*, para 4.13: 'When giving an authorization for directed surveillance ... the authorizing officer must *believe* that the authorized surveillance is *proportionate* to what is sought to be achieved by carrying it out, and that the action is *necessary* for' one of the purposes defined in s 28(3) RIPA (emphasis added).

Section 28(4) makes it clear that only conduct and circumstances specified in the authority will be authorized and therefore lawful. This important subsection obliges investigators and authorizing officers to be very precise in the wording of their applications and authorities.

For example, investigators conducting surveillance decide to secure photographic and video evidence. If the use of still photography and video cameras is not specified in the authority, then any evidence so secured will have been unlawfully obtained and therefore vulnerable to exclusion under s 78 PACE. Lack of precision in the wording of authorities, resulting in unlawful activity by investigators, is a recurring deficiency identified by the OSC (*Annual Report 2003–2004*, 12).

Thus investigators must seek detailed authority for all the conduct they wish to engage in, and authorizing officers must ensure that their authorities specify in detail all conduct that they are content to authorize. Where authorizing officers authorize more than has been applied for they must state their reasons for doing so (OSC *Annual Report* 2005, 3.5). Similarly they must record their reasons for not authorizing all or any of the conduct detailed in an application.

Authorizations last for three months and can be renewed. They should be reviewed at monthly intervals or whenever there is a material change in circumstances affecting the validity of the authority.

In relation to town centre CCTV systems, the Covert Surveillance codes (para 1.4) provide that, *except when used for preplanned surveillance operations*, the use of such systems do not require a directed surveillance authority.

2.6 What Significant Case Law Has Been Decided in Relation to Directed Surveillance?

Unsurprisingly, given the relatively recent enactment of the legislation, the body of case law relating to RIPA is still small. Nevertheless some key principles have been established or confirmed, in some cases drawing upon pre-RIPA case law.

2.6.1 Private life

An initial issue for investigators and authorizing officers is the determination of whether surveillance will or is likely to obtain information about anyone's private life. This has proved particularly vexing in dealing with crime hotspots in the absence of known offenders. Strasbourg has interpreted 'private life' and what might constitute information about private life very broadly; consequently it is difficult to envisage circumstances in which the surveillance of a crime hotspot will not require a directed surveillance authority (see 1.6 for further discussion).

Further information and reading

For a fuller discussion around the case law enforcement interpreting private life see K Starmer, *European Human Rights Law* (Legal Action Group, London, 1999) paras 3.109–3.111; *Neimitz v Austria* (1993) 16 EHRR 97; *Costello-Roberts v UK* (1995) 19 EHRR 112; *Friedl v Austria* (1996) 21 EHRR 83; *Halford v UK* (1997) 24 EHRR 523; *Perry v UK* (2004) 39 EHRR 3 (although a case involving a breach of PACE, it has been applied by OSC inspectors when interpreting private life). See also OSC *Annual Report 2003–2004*, 8.

2.6.2 **Protection of observation posts**

Recognizing that failure to secure observation posts from which to conduct surveillance could seriously impede legitimate investigations, the Appeal Court applied, in *R v Rankine* [1986] 1 QB 861, the same presumption of protection applied to human sources of information, namely that the identity of locations used should be protected unless doing so would lead to a miscarriage of justice. Minimum evidential standards were applied to this principle in *R v Johnson* [1988] 1 WLR 1377, confirmed by *R v Hewitt and Davis* (1992) 95 Cr App R 81 and *R v Grimes* [1994] Crim LR 213.

Case law criteria: *R v Johnson* [1988] 1 WLR 1377

The criteria set out in *R v Johnson* are reproduced in the ACPO *Practice Advice on Core Investigative Doctrine* (2005) 104:

The police officer in charge of observations of a rank not lower than sergeant must be able to testify that beforehand he/she visited all the observation places to be used and ascertained the attitude of the occupiers of the premises:

- as to the use of the premises;
- to the disclosure of the use of the premises;
- to the possible identification of the premises or the occupiers.

The difficulties, if any are encountered, in obtaining observation posts in the area.

In addition, immediately prior to the trial, an officer of a rank not lower than chief inspector must be able to testify that he visited the premises used for observations and ascertained if the occupiers are the same as when the observations were conducted and, whether they are or not, what their attitude is to:

- the possible disclosure of the use made of the premises;
- the disclosure of facts which would lead to the identification of those premises and their occupiers.

This evidence will be given in the absence of the jury when the application to exclude the material evidence is made. The judge should explain to the jury the effect of his or her ruling regarding the disclosure of the premises.

Because exposure of unmarked police vehicles would not necessarily involve the same threat of harassment or fear of violence for members of the public (*Blake and Austin v DPP* (1993) 97 Cr App R 169), the presumption of protection for private premises used as observation points would not, as a matter of policy, be applied to police vehicles from which observations were conducted (*R v Brown and Daley* (1988) 87 Cr App R 52).

2.6.3 Disclosure of surveillance authorizations

The statutory presumption of disclosure is founded in the CPIA 1996. Because surveillance authorities may contain sensitive detail which it would be against the public interest to expose, such authorities will normally be scheduled as sensitive unused material. If the prosecutor recognizes contentious issues regarding the authorization process, a redacted version of the authority should be disclosed and an unedited version supplied to the judge for determination that the defendant is not vulnerable to a miscarriage arising from non-disclosure (*R v Hardy and Hardy* [2002] EWCA Crim 3012).

Further information and reading

- SI 2000/2563
  The Regulation of Investigatory Powers (Notification of Authorizations etc.) Order 2000

- SI 2003/3171
  The Regulation of Investigatory Powers (Directed Surveillance and Covert Human Intelligence Sources) Order 2003

- SI 2005/1084
  The Regulation of Investigatory Powers (Directed Surveillance and Covert Human Intelligence Sources) (Amendment) Order 2005

                                                    (Reproduced in Appendix C)

Directed surveillance scenario

A uniformed police officer wishes to record covertly a conversation with a member of the public in order to have an accurate record of the meeting which is due to take place at the police station.

A directed surveillance authority is required even though the officer is in uniform, as a member of the public would not be aware of the recording. This is considered a higher level of intrusion than would normally be expected.

Directed surveillance scenario

There have been a number of repeated problems at a parade of shops on a local estate including offences of criminal damage. Intelligence suggests that these offences are being carried out by a group of local youths mainly on Friday and Saturday evenings. The local authority has already installed CCTV in the area and two cameras cover the parade of shops. Investigators intend to carry out an operation where operators in CCTV identify those responsible for committing offences so that officers can attend and make arrests.

As this is a preplanned covert operation in a public place it will require a directed surveillance authority. This would still apply even if the presence of CCTV was clearly signposted in the area around the parade of shops.

Directed surveillance scenario

Intelligence suggests an enclosed compound is being used in order to exchange counterfeit goods for sale at local markets. The vehicles being used to transport these goods are left in the secure compound overnight. The intention is to use an unmarked helicopter to obtain images to identify the vehicles being used in the commission of the offences.

This will require a directed surveillance authority as it is a preplanned operation in which private information will be obtained (i.e. the vehicle registration numbers and any trade markings).

If a marked police helicopter were used the surveillance would cease to be covert and therefore no authority would be required.

Directed surveillance scenario

A commercial catering premises has been the subject of early morning thefts of its milk supply. The thefts occur in the early hours after the milk delivery but before the premises open. An officer wishes to set up an observation point in premises opposite where the thefts occur. Investigators intend to arrest the suspects should any theft occur.

This is a preplanned operation for directed surveillance and therefore an authority should be obtained. Investigators must comply with *R v Johnson*.

Directed surveillance scenario

Local residents are complaining about the number of young people drinking alcohol in the park in the evenings. It is believed that those drinking in the park are obtaining their alcohol from a local shop which has previously been visited by officers outlining the problems in the local area. The shop owner denies selling alcohol to anyone under age. Investigators wish to set up surveillance to establish a pattern of business in the store and identify anyone under age being sold alcohol.

This will be covert observation and therefore directed surveillance authority is required.

Directed surveillance scenario

As part of an operational order in which a search warrant is to be executed on a premises, investigators wish to set up observations in order to establish who is on the premises prior to the execution of the warrant. This is required as intelligence suggests a number of potentially violent individuals use and stay at the address and the intention is to execute the warrant when such persons are away from the premises in order to minimize risk.

A directed surveillance authority will be required in order to carry out the covert observations of the premises. If the visual equipment being used by the officers were to give information on activities inside the dwelling that will have the same quality as if they were inside the dwelling, then an intrusive surveillance authority would be required.

Directed surveillance scenario

Ed Collins has breached his bail conditions having been released from prison to a bail hostel only recently. He contacted the bail hostel stating his intention not to return and is therefore wanted. Information suggests that Collins is using a number of known vehicles. He is also known to have family and associates in towns close by. Investigators intend to deploy the automatic number plate recognition (ANPR) device on the main route between these towns in order to arrest Collins.

As this is a preplanned operation involving covert observation a directed surveillance authority will be required. A known subject is being targeted. Routine ANPR operations do not normally require a surveillance authority.

Directed surveillance scenario

Environmental health officers wish to covertly record the noise levels at a domestic property, by use of noise monitoring equipment.

A directed surveillance authority will be required only if 'private information' is acquired. As long as the monitoring equipment is only recording noise levels the surveillance will not be intrusive and will therefore not require authorization.

If reconnaissance was required prior to the noise measurement operation, perhaps to confirm the identity of premises being used or to establish a pattern of noise disturbance, then this should be authorized as directed surveillance.

Directed surveillance scenario

Information suggests an individual is operating a business from her home address unlawfully. Investigators wish to carry out covert surveillance which does not amount to intrusive surveillance on the address.

A directed surveillance authority will be required.

Directed surveillance scenario

Information suggests that an employee who is currently on sick leave from work with a bad back has been seen working in their garden without any difficulty. Investigators wish to carry out surveillance in order to establish if the employee is claiming sickness benefit inappropriately.

As long as the surveillance is not intrusive, in other words if it is confined to the areas outside the dwelling such as the garden, then a directed surveillance authority is all that is required.

Checklist of key issues when considering whether or not to deploy covert investigation techniques

- What evidence or intelligence is being sought?
- How is it relevant to the operation under consideration?
- What is the least intrusive means of securing such evidence or information?
- What are the risks to the organization of such tactics? (Chapter 11)
- What are the risks to the organization's staff of such tactics? (Chapter 11)
- What are the risks to the public or specific third parties when such tactics are deployed? (Chapter 11)
- What are the risks to the subject of the investigation? (Chapter 11)
- Will such methods breach Article 8(1)? (1.6.1)
- Is there justification for doing so provided by Article 8(2)? (1.6.4)

- How is the legality test met? (1.6.3)

- How is the legitimacy test met? (1.6.4)

- How is the necessity test met? (1.6.5)

- How is the proportionality test met? (1.6.5)

- Are the arguments justifying the application to use covert investigation based on reliable information/intelligence, or has the applicant adopted a 'tick-the-box' approach to completing the application without giving full consideration to the facts of the case and the issues arising?

- Have the arguments justifying the granting of authorization to use covert investigation been fully articulated, or has the authorizing officer merely paid lip service to the pro forma authorization template via which authority is granted?

- How are the methods by which the evidence/intelligence will be obtained to be protected at trial?

Planning covert investigation actions

Remember to include the PLAN for covert investigation tactics in all investigation policy-book entries relating to covert investigation considerations and decisions.

P   PROPORTIONALITY
Why is it proportionate to obtain the intended product of this surveillance in the manner proposed? (1.6.5)

L   LEGITIMACY
What is the legitimate purpose of the proposed action: the prevention of disorder or crime; the interests of national security; the interests of public safety; the interests of the economic well-being of the country; the protection of health or morals; the protection of the rights and freedoms of others? (1.6.4)

A   AUTHORITY TO UNDERTAKE PROPOSED ACTION
What is the lawful foundation and authority for the proposed action? From whom must authorization be sought? (1.6.3)

N   NECESSITY OF PROPOSED ACTION
Why is the proposed action necessary? (1.6.5)

Flowchart for Authorizing a Directed Surveillance Operation

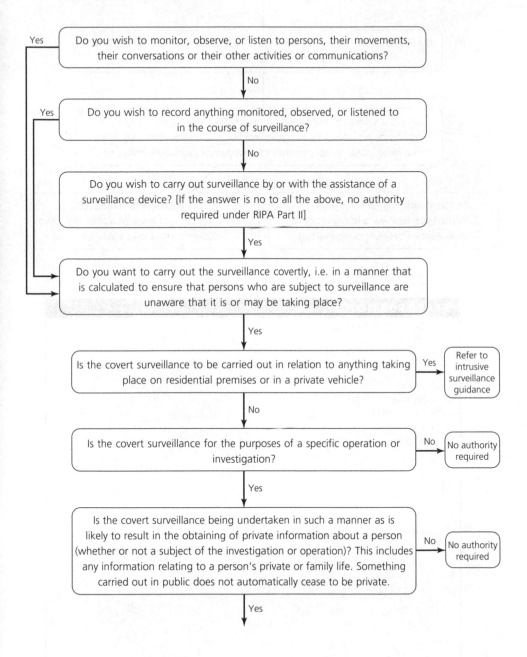

Yes — Do you wish to monitor, observe, or listen to persons, their movements, their conversations or their other activities or communications?

No ↓

Yes — Do you wish to record anything monitored, observed, or listened to in the course of surveillance?

No ↓

Do you wish to carry out surveillance by or with the assistance of a surveillance device? [If the answer is no to all the above, no authority required under RIPA Part II]

Yes ↓

Do you want to carry out the surveillance covertly, i.e. in a manner that is calculated to ensure that persons who are subject to surveillance are unaware that it is or may be taking place?

Yes ↓

Is the covert surveillance to be carried out in relation to anything taking place on residential premises or in a private vehicle? — Yes → Refer to intrusive surveillance guidance

No ↓

Is the covert surveillance for the purposes of a specific operation or investigation? — No → No authority required

Yes ↓

Is the covert surveillance being undertaken in such a manner as is likely to result in the obtaining of private information about a person (whether or not a subject of the investigation or operation)? This includes any information relating to a person's private or family life. Something carried out in public does not automatically cease to be private. — No → No authority required

Yes ↓

Flowchart for Authorizing a Directed Surveillance Operation *continued*

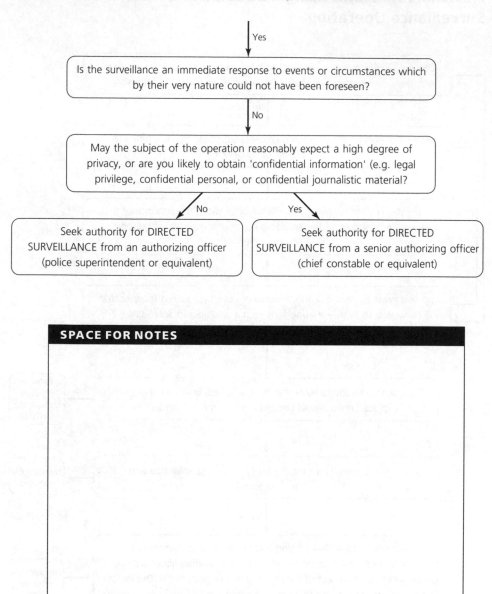

Yes

Is the surveillance an immediate response to events or circumstances which by their very nature could not have been foreseen?

No

May the subject of the operation reasonably expect a high degree of privacy, or are you likely to obtain 'confidential information' (e.g. legal privilege, confidential personal, or confidential journalistic material?

No

Yes

Seek authority for DIRECTED SURVEILLANCE from an authorizing officer (police superintendent or equivalent)

Seek authority for DIRECTED SURVEILLANCE from a senior authorizing officer (chief constable or equivalent)

SPACE FOR NOTES

SPACE FOR NOTES

SPACE FOR NOTES

3

Intrusive Surveillance

3.1	Introduction	48
3.2	Which Public Authorities May Deploy Intrusive Surveillance?	49
3.3	What Powers Does the Law Provide in Relation to Intrusive Surveillance?	49
3.4	What Authority Regime Is Required for Intrusive Surveillance?	51
3.5	The Need for Prior Approval from the Office of Surveillance Commissioners	52
3.6	Cancellation of Authorities	53
3.7	What Significant Case Law Has Been Decided in Relation to Intrusive Surveillance?	54

3.1 **Introduction**

Surveillance is defined at s 48(2) RIPA.

Definition of surveillance

Surveillance 'includes

(a) monitoring, observing or listening to persons, their movements, their conversations or their other activities or communications;

(b) recording anything monitored, observed or listened to in the course of surveillance; and

(c) surveillance by or with the assistance of a surveillance device.'

Because they are subject to their own specific authority regimes (as will be discussed in later chapters), the conduct of CHISs and interference with property under either Part III PA97 or s 5 Intelligence Services Act 1994 are not included in this definition (s 48(3) RIPA), notwithstanding that these tactics are deployed for exactly the same purposes.

A two-part hierarchy of surveillance is prescribed by law: directed and intrusive. Chapters 2 and 3 consider directed and intrusive surveillance separately because:

- not all public authorities empowered to conduct directed surveillance may also conduct intrusive surveillance, and
- the circumstances in which intrusive surveillance may be conducted are more restricted than those in which directed surveillance may take place.

Applications to conduct either type of surveillance may only be made to, and considered by, investigators and authorizing officers working in the same organization. Thus a police officer may only seek authority from, or grant authority to, a member of the same force. Similarly, a member of a local authority or other empowered organization may only seek authority from, or grant authority to, a member of the same organization. That does not preclude staff from more than one agency collaborating under the auspices of a single authority, in circumstances for instance in which specialist skills have to be brought in from another agency, provided applicant and authorizing officer belong to the same agency and the authority specifies the collaboration.

A Code of Practice for Covert Surveillance has been published. It is reproduced in the Appendices below and is online at <http://www.homeoffice.gov.uk/docs3/surveillcodeofpractice.doc>. 'Code' in this chapter refers to this Code.

3.2 Which Public Authorities May Deploy Intrusive Surveillance?

Public authorities empowered to utilize intrusive surveillance are defined by reference to senior authorizing officers within each organization able to grant an intrusive surveillance authority (s 32(6) RIPA). Fewer organizations may conduct intrusive surveillance than those empowered to conduct directed surveillance. Those organizations are:

- Any police force maintained under s 2 Police Act 1996
- Any police force maintained under s 1 Police (Scotland) Act 1967
- The Metropolitan Police Service
- The City of London Police
- The Police Service of Northern Ireland
- The Ministry of Defence Police
- The British Transport Police
- The National Criminal Intelligence Service (until SOCA becomes operational)
- The National Crime Squad (until SOCA becomes operational)
- The Serious Organized Crime Agency (when it becomes operational, likely to be 1 April 2006)
- The Army, Royal Navy, and Royal Air Force
- HM Customs and Excise
- Office of Fair Trading
- MI5, MI6, and GCHQ (by virtue of s 42 RIPA).

3.3 What Powers Does the Law Provide in Relation to Intrusive Surveillance?

Definition of intrusive surveillance

Intrusive surveillance is (s 26(3) RIPA):

- covert surveillance
- carried out on any residential premises or in any private vehicle

and which involves

- the presence of an individual on the premises or in the vehicle

or

- the use of a surveillance device (i.e. audio or visual probe).

Hint and tip: a stolen vehicle is not a private vehicle for the purposes of RIPA authorization as the necessity for authorization relates to the rightful owner or user of the vehicle.

If a technical device deployed outside the premises or the vehicle neverthe- less produces a product of the same quality as would have been obtained by a device inside the premises or vehicle, then this also requires authority for intrusive surveillance; for instance, a long-range microphone capable of hearing conversations inside a building.

A device attached to a vehicle merely to reveal its location does not constitute intrusive surveillance (s 26(4)(a) RIPA), but will comprise directed surveillance and interference with property (s 26(2) RIPA in conjunction with s 93 PA97). Where both a surveillance authority and a property interference authority is required, a combined authority may be issued (s 33(5) RIPA). The relevant provisions of each Act apply in a combined authority and so in practice the different authority levels mean that whoever is the senior appropriate authorizing officer under the two regimes will consider combined applications.

Surveillance conducted in offices or in business vehicles (including taxis) requires a directed surveillance authority, not an intrusive surveillance authority.

Intrusive surveillance, subject to it being authorized, may be conducted for the purpose of *preventing or detecting serious crime*. Which means establishing by whom, for what purpose, by what means and generally in what circumstances any *serious crime* was committed and apprehending the suspected offender (s 32(3) and s 81(5) RIPA). Note that there is a higher threshold for intrusive surveillance—serious crime—than for directed surveillance (any crime or offence).

Other purposes for which intrusive surveillance is permitted are (s 32(3) RIPA):

- in the interests of national security
- in the interests of the economic well-being of the UK.

Definition of serious crime

Serious crime is defined as (s 81(2)(b) RIPA, s 81(3) RIPA following s 93(4) PA97):

(a) An offence for which, on first conviction, a person aged twenty-one years or over with no previous convictions might receive three years imprisonment,

or

(b) The conduct
  - involves the use of violence;
  - results in substantial financial gain; or
  - is engaged in by a large number of persons for a common purpose.

(Section 81 RIPA does not reproduce that part of s 93(4) PA97 which refers to matters assigned under 1(1) Custom and Excise Management Act 1979)

3.4 **What Authority Regime Is Required for Intrusive Surveillance?**

Authorizations for intrusive surveillance may be given by:

- Chief Constable or Commissioner of a police force as defined at 3.2 above, including the Ministry of Defence Police and British Transport Police
- Director General or a designated deputy National Crime Squad (until SOCA becomes operational)
- Director General National Criminal Intelligence Service (until SOCA becomes operational)
- Director General SOCA (when SOCA becomes operational, likely to be 1 April 2006)
- The Chief Constable and Deputy Chief Constable, Police Service of Northern Ireland
- Any Assistant Commissioner of the Metropolitan Police Service
- A designated senior officer of HM Customs and Excise
- A Provost Marshal in the Army, Royal Air Force or Royal Navy.

Authorizations last for three months and can be renewed. They should be reviewed at monthly intervals or whenever there is a material change in circumstances affecting the validity of the authority.

KEY POINTS FOR APPLICANTS

When considering combined authorities (s 33(5) RIPA) first identify whether this will lead to complications as a result of disclosure requirements.

To ensure precision of applications (and therefore lawful authority), be careful to use words that are not ambiguous (for instance 'monitor' is open to varied interpretation, 'listen' and 'watch' are more precise; use both if both are required).

KEY POINTS FOR AUTHORIZING OFFICERS

- Do not use the term 'subject' without identifying the person.
- If an authorization is no longer necessary it must be cancelled and notice given to the OSC within four hours of signing the cancellation.
- Rank or position of the authorizing officer must be indicated on the authority and if the authorizing officer is a designated deputy, this must also be indicated on the authority, as must the reason why the deputy has given the authority.
- Designated deputies can only authorize if the authorizing officer is too ill, on annual leave, absent from their office or home and not able to access a secure telephone or fax machine within a reasonable time. The reason for the absence of the authorizing officer must be included in the application.

> - The scope of an authority may not be expanded on renewal but it may be reduced. A new authority is required if the scope of the surveillance is to increase.
>
> Authorizing officers must review and renew the authorities they gave.
>
> OSC *Annual Report 2005*, section 4

3.5 The Need for Prior Approval from the Office of Surveillance Commissioners

Before any investigative action pursuant to the authority can be carried out, the authorizing officer must notify the OSC in writing (s 35 RIPA). To make the authorization effective *prior approval* is required from the OSC *and* written notice of the OSC approval has to be given to the person who granted the authorization (s 36(2) RIPA).

Surveillance cannot commence until the authorizing officer has received written approval from the OSC.

If the authorizing officer considers the matter to be so urgent that prior approval cannot be sought, the authority will be effective upon written notification to the OSC (s 36(3) RIPA), subject to the OSC confirming or quashing the authority having considered both whether it is an authority that would have received prior approval in normal circumstances *and* whether the circumstances in this case were really urgent.

Where the OSC decides not to approve an authority or to quash an authority, the decision will be conveyed to the most senior relevant person in the organization concerned.

Prior approval has been withheld in cases where the matter under investigation failed to meet the serious crime criteria, where the proposed action was not necessary, and where the proposed action would not have been of substantial value to the investigation (OSC *Annual Report 2002*, 8–9).

Further information and reading

Applications should be in writing and describe the conduct to be authorized and the purpose of the investigation or operation. The following matters must be covered in an application:

- an explanation of the *information or evidence* which it is desired to obtain as a result of the surveillance;
- the reasons why the authorization is *necessary* in the particular case and on the grounds listed in s 32(3) RIPA;

- the reasons why the surveillance is considered *proportionate* to what it seeks to achieve;

- an explanation as to why the information sought cannot reasonably be acquired by other means;

- the nature of the surveillance (i.e. precisely what actions investigators intend to take);

- precise details of the residential premises or private vehicle in relation to which the surveillance will take place;

- details of any potential *collateral intrusion* and why the intrusion is justified;

- details of any *confidential information* that is likely to be obtained as a consequence of the surveillance.

A subsequent record should be made of whether authority was given or refused, by whom and the time and date.

(Based on Code para 5.16)

Hint and tip: In relation to confidential information *(communications subject to legal privilege; confidential personal information; or confidential journalistic material), special rules of authorization exist when such material is likely to be gathered by a CHIS or as a consequence of property interference (including variously the need for authorization by more senior staff and OSC prior approval). These rules are not reproduced for intrusive surveillance because such actions must have OSC prior approval, regardless of whether confidential information is likely to be acquired. Nevertheless the likelihood of doing so must be brought to the attention of the OSC in the application and authority.*

3.6 **Cancellation of Authorities**

'The senor authorizing officer who granted or last renewed the authorization must cancel it, or the person who made the application to the Secretary of State must apply for its cancellation, if he is satisfied that the authorization no longer meets the criteria upon which it was authorised'. If this individual is no longer available, this statutory duty will fall to the person who has succeeded them in the relevant role (s 45 RIPA; Code para 5.41; SI 2000/2794).

The OSC must be notified where police, NCS, NCIS, or HMCE authorities are cancelled (SI 2000/2563 reproduced in Appendix C).

KEY POINTS FOR AUTHORITIES

Authorities and renewals last for a period of *three months* from when authorization is given. For *prior approval* this means authority from the Commissioner; thus if an authority was given at 0900 hours on 10 May, it expires at 2359 hours on 9 August. Authorities given under the urgency provisions last only *seventy-two hours*.

3.7 What Significant Case Law Has Been Decided in Relation to Intrusive Surveillance?

Unsurprisingly, given the relatively recent enactment of the legislation, the body . of case law relating to RIPA is still small. Nevertheless some key principles have been established or confirmed, in some cases drawing upon pre-RIPA case law.

3.7.1 Private life

An initial issue for investigators and authorizing officers is the determination of whether surveillance will or is likely to obtain information about anyone's private life. This has proved particularly vexing in dealing with crime hotspots in the absence of known offenders. Strasbourg has interpreted 'private life' and what might constitute information about private life very broadly.

Further information and reading

For a fuller discussion around the case law enforcement interpreting private life, see Starmer, *European Human Rights Law* (Legal Action Group, London) paras 3.109–3.111; *Neimitz v Austria* (1993) 16 EHRR 97; *Costello-Roberts v UK* (1995) 19 EHRR 112; *Friedl v Austria* (1996) 21 EHRR 83; *Halford v UK* (1997) 24 EHRR 523; *Perry v UK* (2004) 39 EHRR 3 (although a case involving a breach of PACE, it has been applied by OSC inspectors when interpreting private life). See also OSC *Annual Report 2003–2004*, 8.

3.7.2 Audio devices in police cells

Three cases provide guidance about this intrusive surveillance tactic, two of which pre-date RIPA. *R v Bailey and Smith* established the principle that conversations between co-defendants placed in the same cell after charge, which were recorded by police, could be admitted in evidence ([1993] 3 All ER 513). Such admissibility was reconsidered in *R v Roberts (Stephen Paul)*, in which the Appeal Court held that it was for the trial judge to determine admissibility on the merits of each case. The crucial test would be the conduct of the investigators and whether such conduct would result in an unfair trial ([1997] 1 Cr App R 217). In *R v Sutherland* the judge stayed proceedings to prevent abuse of process after police had acted in bad faith when covertly recording conversations between suspects and their lawyers in an exercise yard (unreported, Nottingham Crown Court, 29 January 2002; discussed in *Archbold's Criminal Pleading, Evidence and Practice* (revd edn, Sweet & Maxwell, London, 2005) para 15-532 p 1626; cited in *R v Mason and others* [2002] 2 Cr App R 38 at 643, para 60).

Covert recording of suspects in custody for serious offences was held not to be contrary to PACE in *R v Mason and others* ([2002] 2 Cr App R 38 at 648, para 77), in which Woolf LCJ determined:

The police did no more than arrange a situation which was likely to result in the appellants volunteering confessions. The appellants were not tricked into saying what they did even though they were placed in a position where they were likely to do so. If evidence of a satisfactory nature could be obtained by other means, it is preferable that it is obtained by those means rather than covertly. Here, it was not unreasonably considered by the Chief Constable that the evidence would not be obtained by more conventional means.

3.7.3 **Protection of observation posts**

Recognizing that failure to secure observation posts from which to conduct surveillance could seriously impede legitimate investigations, the Appeal Court applied, in *R v Rankine* [1986] 1 QB 861, the same presumption of protection applied to human sources of information, namely that the identity of locations used should be protected unless doing so would lead to a miscarriage of justice. Minimum evidential standards were applied to this principle in *R v Johnson* [1988] 1 WLR 1377, confirmed by *R v Hewitt and Davis* (1992) 95 Cr App R 81 and *R v Grimes* [1994] Crim LR 213.

....

Case law criteria: *R v Johnson* [1988] 1 WLR 1377

The criteria set out in *R v Johnson* are reproduced in the ACPO *Practice Advice on Core Investigative Doctrine* (2005) 104:

The police officer in charge of observations of a rank not lower than sergeant must be able to testify that beforehand he/she visited all the observation places to be used and ascertained the attitude of the occupiers of the premises:

- As to the use of the premises.
- To the disclosure of the use of the premises.
- To the possible identification of the premises or the occupiers.

The difficulties, if any are encountered, in obtaining observation posts in the area.

In addition, immediately prior to the trial, an officer of a rank not lower than chief inspector must be able to testify that he visited the premises used for observations and ascertained if the occupiers are the same as when the observations were conducted and, whether they are or not, what their attitude is to:

- The possible disclosure of the use made of the premises.
- The disclosure of facts which would lead to the identification of those premises and their occupiers.

This evidence will be given in the absence of the jury when the application to exclude the material evidence is made. The judge should explain to the jury the effect of his or her ruling regarding the disclosure of the premises.

....

Because exposure of unmarked police vehicles would not necessarily involve the same threat of harassment or fear of violence that members of the public who make premises available for observation posts might face (*Blake and Austin v DPP* (1993) 97 Cr App R 169), the same presumption of protection would not, as a matter of policy, be applied to police vehicles from which observations were conducted (*R v Brown and Daley* (1988) 87 Cr App R 52).

3.7.4 Disclosure of surveillance authorizations

The statutory presumption of disclosure is founded in the CPIA 1996. Because surveillance authorities may contain sensitive detail which it would be against the public interest to expose, such authorities will normally be scheduled as sensitive unused material. If the prosecutor recognizes contentious issues regarding the authorization process, a redacted version of the authority should be disclosed and an unedited version supplied to the judge for determination that the defendant is not vulnerable to a miscarriage arising from non-disclosure (*R v Hardy and Hardy* [2002] EWCA Crim 3012).

Further information and reading

- SI 2000/2563
  The Regulation of Investigatory Powers (Notification of Authorizations etc.) Order 2000

- SI 2003/3171
  The Regulation of Investigatory Powers (Directed Surveillance and Covert Human Intelligence Sources) Order 2003

  (Reproduced in Appendix C)

Intrusive surveillance scenario

Intelligence indicates Subject A is involved in the supply of Class A drugs. Subject A is known to meet with an unknown male in a hotel room in which it is believed that drugs are to be exchanged for money.

Considerations:

What is the purpose of the investigation?

If it is to collect more intelligence and gather evidence in order to prevent or detect serious crime and therefore bring a prosecution, consider intrusive surveillance as an appropriate method to gather this information. It is intrusive surveillance because the surveillance will be carried out in a property used wholly or mainly as a dwelling, in this case the bedroom in a hotel, so prior approval by the OSC will also be required.

What details do you need for the authorization?

The authorization is necessary because the information sought cannot be gained by any other means. The collection of intelligence to date has only been able to establish the meeting of Subject A with an unknown male after which Subject A has been in the possession of Class A drugs. In order to establish evidence of supply the investigation needs to establish the details of the meeting with the unknown male.

There is a need to corroborate the intelligence that the commission of the crime is only carried out in that room and intrusive surveillance is now the only way to progress this investigation.

Why this surveillance is proportionate

There is a need to document that the only reliable way of establishing the commission of this serious crime is by evidencing the exchange taking place in that hotel room between Subject A and the unknown male and thereby evidencing the exchange of drugs for money. It is unlikely that a less intrusive means of investigation will provide the information required to achieve the operational directive.

The authorization will also need to contain details of the premises in which the surveillance will take place and, where known, the identities of those subject to the surveillance; details of the type of information the surveillance seeks to obtain (evidence of the exchange of Class A drugs); details of any potential collateral intrusion (the likelihood of any one else being present in the room). If collateral intrusion were likely to occur, the reason why the intrusion is justified must be stated (the person is likely to be involved in the commission that the crime or the only way to establish the Commissioner for crime is still to carry out the surveillance, and it would be focused only on those involved in committing criminal offences).

Intrusive surveillance scenario

A gang involved in the ringing of motor vehicles meet at some railway arches in order to carry out transactions. However, these railway arches are also habitually used by homeless individuals as a place to sleep. Investigators wish to carry out surveillance within the railway arches in order to gain evidence and identify further gang members and those involved in the car ringing group.

As the railway arches are used as a dwelling, prior approval will be required (the permanence of the dwelling is not an issue—it is simply that the place is used as a dwelling). Investigators will also need to ensure that the case for serious crime can be made out as both intrusive surveillance and property interference authorities will be required.

Intrusive surveillance scenario

Adrian Bridge is believed to be a courier for a crime group involved in the trafficking of humans. Investigators wish to carry out surveillance in order to establish the contents of conversations he has with members of the crime group from the cab of his lorry, which he uses in order to transport illegal immigrants from the Continent into the UK.

Even though Adrian Bridge has sleeping accommodation within the cab of his vehicle unless it could be classified as being wholly or mainly used as a dwelling (which is unlikely), then prior approval from authority would not be required. However, an authority for property interference would be required and also an intrusive surveillance authority.

(OSC *Annual Report 2005*, 4.24)

Intrusive surveillance scenario

Robert Miner is a vulnerable pensioner who has been subject to a number of distraction burglaries where offenders have entered his premises purporting to be from the water board. Investigators wish to install surveillance equipment in his home in order to identify the offenders.

A number of issues have to be taken into account in order to ensure that the appropriate authority is obtained. The proposed surveillance is due to take place in a dwelling and is therefore intrusive, although there will be no requirement for property interference to be authorized as the consent of the owner can be sought in this case. However, if the serious crime criterion is not satisfied then intrusive authority can not be granted. If this serious crime criterion is not satisfied then a directed surveillance authority could be sought in the circumstances where Robert Miner is capable of ensuring that any one legitimately on the premises is either not recorded or made aware of the existence of the recording capability. Written documentation of this agreement and understanding should be sought.

If Robert Miner is not capable of explaining the circumstances to visitors, and the crime does not meet the seriousness criteria, then the proposed surveillance could not lawfully be authorized (OSC *Annual Report 2003–2004*, 8). In such circumstances the OSC appears to suggest some flexibility for the surveillance to go ahead without lawful authority (OSC *Annual Report 2005*, 4.35), but at the risk of being challenged at court in any subsequent trial.

Intrusive surveillance scenario

Intelligence identifies three members of a group believed to have been involved in the murder of a former gang member and the subsequent disposal of his body, along with the murder weapon. The senior investigating officer intends to arrest the three named individuals and carry out covert surveillance within the cell block area where three individuals will be held.

Property interference authorities will not be required; however, *intrusive surveillance* authorities will be required as a cell block is regarded as residential premises. *Prior approval* from the OSC will be required. Investigators will also need to consider the types of conversations that will be subject of the surveillance, ensuring that the surveillance is targeted and confined as much as possible to the conversations held by the three members of the group.

Other issues

Unless it can be proved that there are previous and consistent examples where the three individuals have been unwilling to comment in interview, ordinarily investigators should ensure that those arrested have been given the opportunity of a first interview to give an account before beginning the surveillance. In the event of identifying a conversation subject to legal privilege has been recorded, the fact should be noted and the prosecuting authority made aware to ensure any subsequent suggestion that this conversation contains details of an alibi can be confirmed or denied. The matter also has to be brought to the attention of the OSC at the next inspection.

Staff responsible for supplying and deploying should have sight of the authority to ensure that the detailed requirements are understood and the surveillance can remain targeted. There have been instances in which staff deploying equipment received only verbal instructions and in deploying equipment went beyond what had been authorized in writing. Consequently unauthorized surveillance took place, causing prosecutions to fail.

If equipment is to be placed only in communal areas then only a directed surveillance authority may be required. However, consideration will need to be given to the collateral intrusion issues of other persons in custody and whether or not legal privilege material will be acquired which would raise *R v Sutherland* issues (1.8 above; 3.7.2 above).

Intrusive surveillance scenario

Investigators wish to confirm whether a benefit claimant lives at a particular address identified to the social security department. At the address investigators are unable to get an answer to a knock at the door. They consider whether it would be appropriate to push open a window that is slightly ajar at the front of the house in order to look inside.

By opening the window investigators would be engaged in surveillance that is carried out on private premises, i.e. a dwelling house. This would constitute intrusive surveillance and property interference and therefore would not be lawful in these circumstances, unless it was carried out by an investigating authority with such powers in circumstances that met the criteria for conducting intrusive surveillance and property interference.

Checklist of key issues when considering whether or not to deploy covert investigation techniques

- What evidence or intelligence is being sought?

- How is it relevant to the operation under consideration?

- What is the least intrusive means of securing such evidence or information?

- What are the risks to the organization of such tactics? (Chapter 11)

- What are the risks to the organization's staff of such tactics? (Chapter 11)

- What are the risks to the public or specific third parties when such tactics are deployed? (Chapter 11)

- What are the risks to the subject of the investigation? (Chapter 11)

- Will such methods breach Article 8(1)? (1.6.1)

- Is there justification for doing so provided by Article 8(2)? (1.6.4)

- How is the legality test met? (1.6.3)

- How is the legitimacy test met? (1.6.4)

- How is the necessity test met? (1.6.5)

- How is the proportionality test met? (1.6.5)

- Are the arguments justifying the application to use covert investigation based on reliable information/intelligence, or has the applicant adopted a 'tick-the-box' approach to completing the application without giving full consideration to the facts of the case and the issues arising?

- Have the arguments justifying the granting of authorization to use covert investigation been fully articulated, or has the authorizing officer merely paid lip service to the pro forma authorization template via which authority is granted?

  How are the methods by which the evidence/intelligence will be obtained to be protected at trial?

Planning covert investigation actions

Remember to include the PLAN for covert investigation tactics in all investigation policy-book entries relating to covert investigation considerations and decisions.

P PROPORTIONALITY
   Why is it proportionate to obtain the intended product of this surveillance in the manner proposed? (1.6.5)

L LEGITIMACY
   What is the legitimate purpose of the proposed action: the prevention of disorder or crime; the interests of national security; the interests of public safety; the interests of the economic well-being of the country; the protection of health or morals; the protection of the rights and freedoms of others? (1.6.4)

A AUTHORITY TO UNDERTAKE PROPOSED ACTION
   What is the lawful foundation and authority for the proposed action? From whom must authorization be sought? (1.6.3)

N NECESSITY OF PROPOSED ACTION
   Why is the proposed action necessary? (1.6.5)

Flowchart for Authorizing an Intrusive Surveillance Operation

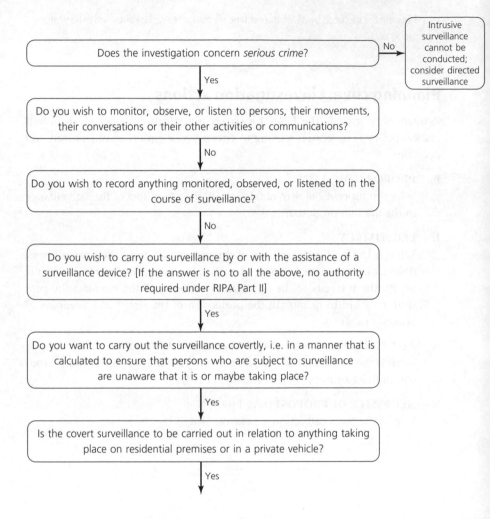

Does the investigation concern *serious crime*? — No → Intrusive surveillance cannot be conducted; consider directed surveillance

Yes ↓

Do you wish to monitor, observe, or listen to persons, their movements, their conversations or their other activities or communications?

No ↓

Do you wish to record anything monitored, observed, or listened to in the course of surveillance?

No ↓

Do you wish to carry out surveillance by or with the assistance of a surveillance device? [If the answer is no to all the above, no authority required under RIPA Part II]

Yes ↓

Do you want to carry out the surveillance covertly, i.e. in a manner that is calculated to ensure that persons who are subject to surveillance are unaware that it is or maybe taking place?

Yes ↓

Is the covert surveillance to be carried out in relation to anything taking place on residential premises or in a private vehicle?

Yes ↓

Flowchart for Authorizing an Intrusive Surveillance Operation *continued*

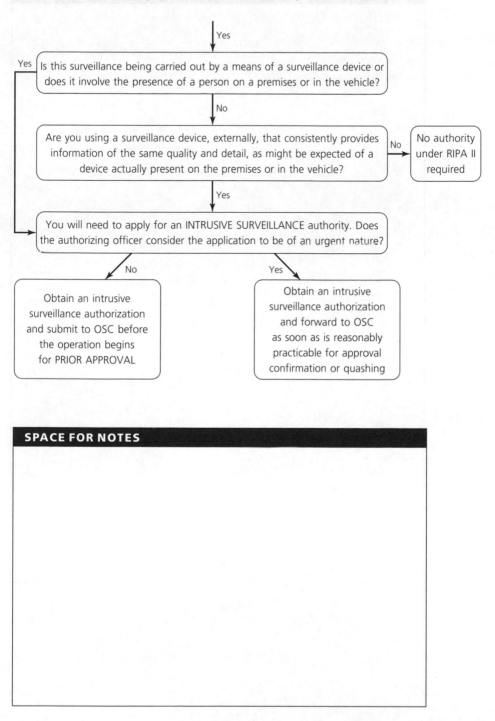

SPACE FOR NOTES

SPACE FOR NOTES

SPACE FOR NOTES

4

Interference with Property or Wireless Telegraphy and Entry onto Land

4.1	Introduction	68
4.2	Which Public Authorities May Interfere with Property or Wireless Telegraphy and Enter onto Land?	68
4.3	What Powers Does the Law Provide in Relation to Interference with Property or Wireless Telegraphy and Entry onto Land?	69
4.4	What Authority Regime Is Required for Interference with Property or Wireless Telegraphy and Entry onto Land?	70
4.5	The Need for Prior Approval from the Office of Surveillance Commissioners	72
4.6	Cancellation of Authorities	72
4.7	What Significant Case Law Has Been Decided in Relation to Property or Wireless Telegraphy Interference and Entry onto Land?	73

4.1 **Introduction**

Certain tactics that facilitate covert investigation involve actions that constitute crimes or torts. The deployment of a listening device at private residential premises, for instance, will certainly involve trespass and could involve criminal damage being caused. Part III PA97 provides the statutory regime under which such actions may be authorized and so rendered lawful within the context of the authorized action. In other circumstances, such as a siege situation, the authorities may regard it as necessary and proportionate to jam or otherwise interfere with radio signals.

Such activity was originally subject to Home Office Guidelines issued in 1984 but guidelines, as discussed in Chapter 1, fail the legality test (in accordance with law) under Article 8(2) ECHR. Concerning property interference, the leading UK case confirming this principle is *Khan*. In filling this particular legislative lacuna, the 1997 Act did not make provision for surveillance itself, hence the need to provide an additional statutory regime for surveillance in the RIPA. Because property interference will often be a prerequisite for intrusive surveillance under RIPA, provision is made for joint authorizations to be made where authority is required for property interference and intrusive surveillance in order to complete a single operation within an investigation.

Further information and reading

R v Khan [1997] AC 558; *Khan v UK* (2001) 31 EHRR 45; see also K Starmer, M Strange, and Q Whitaker, *Criminal Justice, Police Powers and Human Rights* (Blackstone Press, London, 2001), 37.

B Emmerson and D Friedman, *A Guide to the Police Act 1997* (Butterworth, London, 1998), 4.

4.2 **Which Public Authorities May Interfere with Property or Wireless Telegraphy and Enter onto Land?**

The following organizations may carry out these aspects of covert investigation:

- Police forces in England and Wales maintained under s 2 Police Act 1996
- The Metropolitan Police
- The City of London Police
- Police forces maintained under s 1 Police (Scotland) Act 1967
- The Police Service of Northern Ireland
- The National Crime Squad (until SOCA becomes operational)
- The National Criminal Intelligence Service (until SOCA becomes operational)
- HM Customs and Excise (until SOCA becomes operational)

- The Serious Organized Crime Agency (when it becomes operational, likely to be 1 April 2006)
- MI5, MI6, GCHQ.

The organizations are defined by reference to who may authorize such interference and entry (s 93(5) PA97) and, in the case of the intelligence agencies, by virtue of s 5 Intelligence Services Act 1994.

4.3 What Powers Does the Law Provide in Relation to Interference with Property or Wireless Telegraphy and Entry onto Land?

Investigators can take such action, in respect of property or wireless telegraphy in the relevant area, as is specified in the authorization (s 93(1) PA97). Authorizing officers are advised to 'state explicitly what is being authorized' (OSC *Guidance and Procedures*, para 3.4). Thus in relation to the placing of an audio device inside residential premises, for example, every action required to achieve this objective must be specifically authorized, including separate reconnoitring operations to determine feasibility prior to the actual deployment and subsequent operations to retrieve the device.

Certain criteria must be present for the power to be applied.

KEY POINTS FOR AUTHORIZING OFFICERS

Before authorizing such action as may be required the authorizing officer must believe:

(a) that the taking of the action specified is *necessary* for the purpose of preventing or detecting *serious crime*; and

(b) that the taking of such action is *proportionate* to what the action seeks to achieve (s 93(2) PA97).

When considering proportionality, applicants and authorizing officers will have to take into account that increasingly sophisticated surveillance technology may negate the need for property interference: for instance, external monitoring of conversations within a premises rather than internal monitoring.

Definition of serious crime

Conduct will constitute serious crime if:

(a) it involves the use of violence, or it results in substantial financial gain, or it is conducted by a large number of persons in pursuit of a common purpose; or

(b) the offence, or one of the offences, is an offence for which a person who has attained the age of twenty-one and has no previous convictions could reasonably be expected to be sentenced to imprisonment for a term of three years or more (s 93(4) PA97).

4.4 What Authority Regime Is Required for Interference with Property or Wireless Telegraphy and Entry onto Land?

Where the above criteria are met the following may authorize such interference (s 93(5) PA97), in some circumstances (described below 4.5) subject to the prior approval of the OSC:

- Chief Constable (police forces in England, Wales, and Scotland)
- Commissioner or Assistant Commissioner (Metropolitan Police)
- Commissioner (City of London Police)
- Chief Constable and Deputy Chief Constable Police Service of Northern Ireland
- Director General National Crime Squad (until SOCA becomes operational)
- Director General National Criminal Intelligence Service (until SOCA becomes operational)
- A designated authorizing officer within Serious Organized Crime Agency (when it becomes operational, likely to be 1 April 2006)
- Chief Constable British Transport Police
- Chief Constable Ministry of Defence Police
- Provost Marshals in the Army, Royal Navy, and Royal Air Force
- Any customs officer designated by the Commissioners of Customs and Excise for this purpose.

Where it is not reasonably practicable to obtain the authority of the authorizing officer identified above, the Act specifies that designated deputies may make such authorizations (s 94 PA97).

KEY POINTS ON PROPERTY INTERFERENCE AUTHORIZATION TIMESCALES

Property interference authorities are effective from the time of signing, but authorizations are notified to the Commissioner for scrutiny. Property interference authorities requiring prior approval are only effective from the time the authorizing officer receives written approval from the OSC (OSC *Annual Report 2005*, 3.16). Authorizations, renewals, and cancellations should be notified to the OSC within *four working hours* of being given. In the case of *prior approval* authorizations,

---

notifications should be sent to the OSC *at least sixteen working hours* before surveillance is due to start. Decisions on *prior approval* applications from Commissioners should be received within eight working hours.

KEY POINTS ON DRAFTING APPLICATIONS AND AUTHORITIES

- When considering combined authorities (s 33(5) RIPA), first identify whether this will lead to complications as a result of disclosure requirements.
- To ensure precision of applications (and therefore lawful authority), be careful to use words that are not ambiguous (for instance 'monitor' is open to varied interpretation, while 'listen' and 'watch' are more precise; use both if both are required).

KEY POINTS FOR AUTHORIZING OFFICERS

- Do not use the term 'subject' without identifying the person.
- If an authorization is no longer necessary it must be cancelled and notice given to the OSC within four hours of signing the cancellation.
- Rank or position of the authorizing officer must be indicated on the authority and if the authorizing officer is a designated deputy, this must also be indicated on the authority, as must the reason why the deputy has given the authority.
- Designated deputies can only authorize if the authorizing officer is too ill, on annual leave, absent from their office or home and not able to access a secure telephone or fax machine within a reasonable time. The reason for the absence of the authorizing officer must be included in the application.
- The scope of an authority may not be expanded on renewal but it may be reduced. A new authority is required if the scope of the surveillance is to increase.

Authorizing officers must review and renew the authorities they gave.

(OSC *Annual Report 2005*, section 4)

Excepting property warrants issued to the intelligence services by the Secretary of State (s 5 Intelligence Services Act 1994 and Code paras 6.32–6.36), authorizations for such interference or entry onto property must be in writing and will last for three months (s 95 PA97). Authorities issued orally in matters of urgency have effect for seventy-two hours only.

Authorizing officers may only authorize applications made by members of their organization (s 93(3)) and may only authorize activity with the relevant area over which they have jurisdiction (s 93(6)). In each case this includes, where appropriate, the twelve nautical miles of territorial waters adjacent to the relevant area.

Section 96 imposes on authorizing officers the obligation to notify the OSC as soon as reasonably practicable when granting, renewing, or cancelling any authority.

4.5 The Need for Prior Approval from the Office of Surveillance Commissioners

Prior approval must be sought from the OSC before the authorized activity can take place when the property specified in the authority is (s 97(2) PA97):

- wholly or mainly used as a dwelling
- a hotel bedroom
- constitutes office premises

or when the action authorized is likely to result in the acquisition of knowledge about

- matters subject to legal privilege (defined s 98)
- confidential personal information (defined s 99)
- confidential journalistic material (defined s 100).

In such circumstances the authorized action can only commence once the authorizing officer has received written approval from the OSC (Code para 6.30), which will only be given if the Commissioner holds the beliefs specified at s 93(2) (see 'Key points for authorizing officers' box above). Where prior approval is refused, the authorizing officer shall be given a report explaining why. Appeals against a refusal may be made to the Chief Commissioner in the manner prescribed in s 104.

The interference may not take place until the approval has been communicated by the OSC to the authorizing officer.

An authority to interfere with property that is not a dwelling, a hotel bedroom or office premises does not require prior approval.

A combined property interference and intrusive surveillance authority will always require prior approval because of the intrusive element.

4.6 Cancellation of Authorities

'The senior authorising officer who granted or last renewed the authorisation must cancel it, or the person who made the application to the Secretary of State must apply for its cancellation, if he is satisfied that the authorisation no longer meets the criteria upon which it was authorised.' If this individual is no longer available, this statutory duty will fall to the person who has succeeded them in the relevant role (s 95(5) PA97; Code para 6.24; SI 1998/3241).

4.7 What Significant Case Law Has Been Decided in Relation to Property or Wireless Telegraphy Interference and Entry onto Land?

In September 1992 Khan, together with his cousin N, entered the UK at Manchester airport. They were detained by HMCE. N was found to be in possession of heroin with a street value of £100,000 and was prosecuted. In interview Khan made no admissions and, in the absence of other evidence, was not proceeded against.

In January 1993 police deployed a listening device at the house of B in Sheffield who was under separate suspicion of heroin dealing. Deployment of the device involved trespass and minor criminal damage. Unknown to police at the time, B was an associate of Khan. Khan visited B whilst the listening device was deployed and recording. The listening device recorded a casual conversation between B and Khan, in which the latter described his involvement in the heroin shipment the previous September for which N had been convicted. This recording was relied upon in evidence in the prosecution of Khan for importation.

Khan sought exclusion of the recording in a *voir dire* arguing that the Home Office Guidelines (deposited in the library of the House of Commons and available on application from the Home Office) under which the surveillance had been conducted did not constitute law and so breached Article 8(2). The judge admitted the evidence as being relevant regardless of any ECHR breach. The Appeal Court subsequently held he was right to do so (*R v Khan* [1997] AC 558).

The ECtHR subsequently held that the deployment of the device in the absence of a statutory regime constituted a violation of Article 8(2), but the use of the evidence obtained thereby did not constitute a violation of Article 6, nor had the investigators acted in bad faith because they had complied with the prevailing regime even though it subsequently was held to be unlawful (*Khan v UK* (2001) 31 EHRR 45). This decision followed the principles previously asserted in *Govell v UK* (1997) 23 EHRR CD101 and was reasserted in *Lewis v UK* (2004) 39 EHRR 9.

This finding highlighted the need for the statutory regime subsequently established in Part III PA97 and reaffirmed the principle that relevant evidence unlawfully obtained may yet be admitted by the court.

Interference with property scenario

Mr Smith has been arrested and charged with murder. The weapon is still an outstanding. Mr Smith, whilst in custody, has been visited by an associate whom intelligence suggests has been asked to retrieve the weapon and dispose of it. The senior investigating officer seeks authority to track the movements of the vehicle that the associate is believed to use in order to retrieve the weapon.

In order to place the device on vehicles a property interference authority will be required. The authority must cover the full scope of the requirements of the equipment (the deployment, maintenance, replacement, and retrieval). Deployment and replacement must be in the authorizing officer's force area. If maintenance and retrieval is to be undertaken *outside* the force area this must be specified. If equipment fails to work and needs to be replaced this cannot be counted as maintenance, but the installation of new equipment and so new authority is required.

Subsequent surveillance of the tracking device requires a directed surveillance authority.

Hint and tip: If the identity of the vehicle is not known at the time the authorization was given but is subsequently identified, the OSC must be notified in writing as soon as practicable.

Interference with property scenario

Mr Leonard is believed to be a money-launderer from a group involved in people trafficking. His refuse is collected weekly from the front drive of his house. It is desired to examine the contents of the refuse to ascertain details of any bank accounts he may have. In order to do this investigators will need to enter the front drive of Mr Leonard's house and remove the refuse bags.

In order to enter the driveway of the house (a private property), a property interference authority will be required. The refuse bags, although abandoned by the owner, still remain property because they have only been abandoned in favour of the refuse collector. Therefore, investigators will also require an authority to interfere with the refuse bags. This would also be true if the refuse bags were left outside the premises perimeter on the public highway.

(OSC *Annual Report 2005*, 4.7)

Interference with property scenario

Alex Crown is in custody on suspicion of robbery. You wish to covertly obtain impressions of his footwear.

If this is not going to be done by seizing his footwear as evidence under PACE statutory powers, and is to be done without his knowledge, then there is a requirement to obtain a property interference authority for the covert taking of impressions of footwear (as there is a property interference requirement, investigators must ensure a *serious crime* criterion is satisfied).

Interference with property scenario

Delaying travellers' baggage from an entire aircraft at an airport to facilitate the covert search of a suspect passenger's luggage whilst the baggage is held back comprises property interference.

Checklist of key considerations when planning interference with property or wireless telegraphy and entry onto land

- What evidence or intelligence is being sought?
- How is it relevant to the operation under consideration?
- Is property interference or entry onto property absolutely necessary or can external technical devices achieve the same intelligence/evidential product?
- What is the least intrusive means of securing such evidence or information?
- What are the risks to the organization of such tactics? (Chapter 11)
- What are the risks of compromise to technology or techniques remotely deployed? (Chapter 11)
- What are the risks to law enforcement and criminal justice in the event of technology/techniques being compromised? (Chapter 11)
- What are the risks to the organization's staff of such tactics? (Chapter 11)
- What are the risks to the public or specific third parties when such tactics are deployed? (Chapter 11)
- What are the risks to the subject of the investigation? (Chapter 11)
- Will such methods breach Article 8(1)? (1.6.1)

- Is there justification for doing so provided by Article 8(2)? (1.6.4)

- How is the legality test met? (1.6.3)

- How is the legitimacy test met? (1.6.4)

- How is the necessity test met? (1.6.5)

- How is the proportionality test met? (1.6.5)

- Are the arguments justifying the application to use covert investigation based on reliable information/intelligence, or has the applicant adopted a 'tick-the-box' approach to completing the application without giving full consideration to the facts of the case and the issues arising?

- Have the arguments justifying the granting of authorization to use covert investigation been fully articulated, or has the authorizing officer merely paid lip service to the pro forma authorization template via which authority is granted?

- How are the methods by which the evidence/intelligence will be obtained to be protected at trial?

Planning covert investigation actions

Remember to include the PLAN for covert investigation tactics in all investigation policy-book entries relating to covert investigation considerations and decisions.

P PROPORTIONALITY
Why is it proportionate to obtain the intended product of this surveillance in the manner proposed? (1.6.5)

L LEGITIMACY
What is the legitimate purpose of the proposed action: the prevention of disorder or crime; the interests of national security; the interests of public safety; the interests of the economic well-being of the country; the protection of health or morals; the protection of the rights and freedoms of others? (1.6.4)

A AUTHORITY TO UNDERTAKE PROPOSED ACTION
What is the lawful foundation and authority for the proposed action? From whom must authorization be sought? (1.6.3)

N NECESSITY OF PROPOSED ACTION
Why is the proposed action necessary? (1.6.5)

Flowchart for Authorizing Interference with, or Entry onto, Premises or Private Land

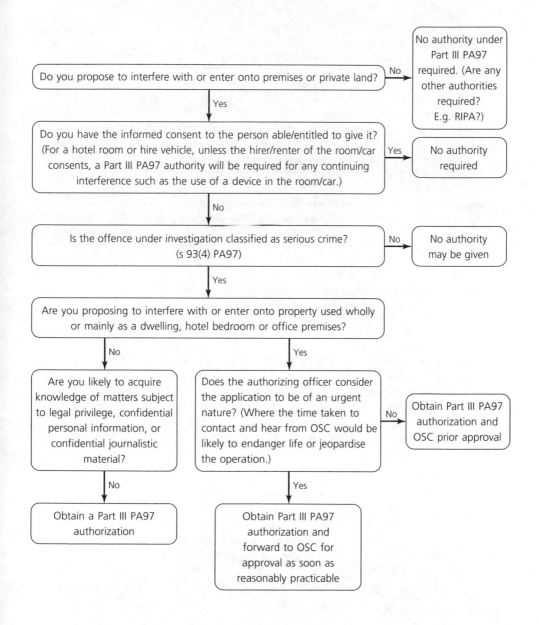

Do you propose to interfere with or enter onto premises or private land? — No → No authority under Part III PA97 required. (Are any other authorities required? E.g. RIPA?)

↓ Yes

Do you have the informed consent to the person able/entitled to give it? (For a hotel room or hire vehicle, unless the hirer/renter of the room/car consents, a Part III PA97 authority will be required for any continuing interference such as the use of a device in the room/car.) — Yes → No authority required

↓ No

Is the offence under investigation classified as serious crime? (s 93(4) PA97) — No → No authority may be given

↓ Yes

Are you proposing to interfere with or enter onto property used wholly or mainly as a dwelling, hotel bedroom or office premises?

No → Are you likely to acquire knowledge of matters subject to legal privilege, confidential personal information, or confidential journalistic material?

Yes → Does the authorizing officer consider the application to be of an urgent nature? (Where the time taken to contact and hear from OSC would be likely to endanger life or jeopardise the operation.)

Does the authorizing officer... — No → Obtain Part III PA97 authorization and OSC prior approval

Are you likely to acquire knowledge... ↓ No → Obtain a Part III PA97 authorization

Does the authorizing officer... ↓ Yes → Obtain Part III PA97 authorization and forward to OSC for approval as soon as reasonably practicable

Flowchart for Authorizing Interference with Property

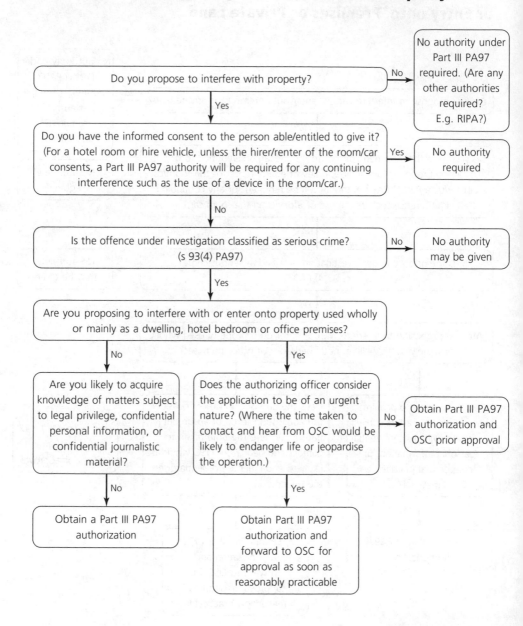

Flowchart for Authorizing Interference with Wireless Telegraphy

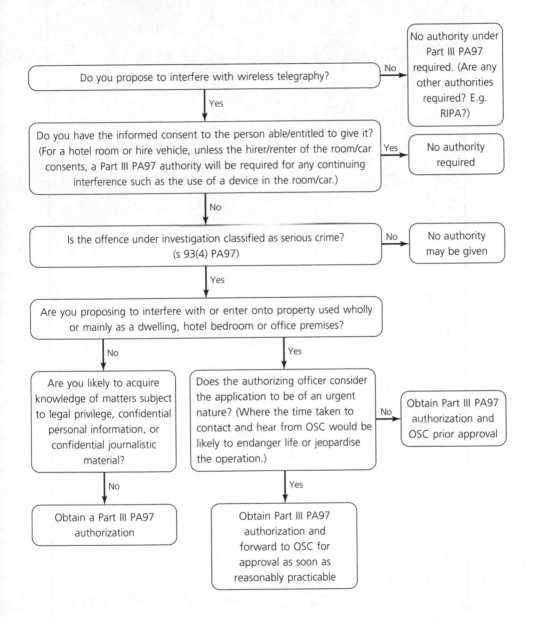

Do you propose to interfere with wireless telegraphy?

No → No authority under Part III PA97 required. (Are any other authorities required? E.g. RIPA?)

Yes ↓

Do you have the informed consent to the person able/entitled to give it? (For a hotel room or hire vehicle, unless the hirer/renter of the room/car consents, a Part III PA97 authority will be required for any continuing interference such as the use of a device in the room/car.)

Yes → No authority required

No ↓

Is the offence under investigation classified as serious crime? (s 93(4) PA97)

No → No authority may be given

Yes ↓

Are you proposing to interfere with or enter onto property used wholly or mainly as a dwelling, hotel bedroom or office premises?

No ↓

Are you likely to acquire knowledge of matters subject to legal privilege, confidential personal information, or confidential journalistic material?

No ↓

Obtain a Part III PA97 authorization

Yes ↓

Does the authorizing officer consider the application to be of an urgent nature? (Where the time taken to contact and hear from OSC would be likely to endanger life or jeopardise the operation.)

No → Obtain Part III PA97 authorization and OSC prior approval

Yes ↓

Obtain Part III PA97 authorization and forward to OSC for approval as soon as reasonably practicable

SPACE FOR NOTES

SPACE FOR NOTES

SPACE FOR NOTES

5

Covert Investigation and Computers

5.1	Introduction	84
5.2	Which Public Authorities Can Investigate Computers Covertly and Which Legal Authorities Are Required?	84
5.3	What Action Requires a Directed Surveillance Authority in Relation to the Investigation of Computers?	87
5.4	What Action Requires an Intrusive Surveillance Authority in Relation to the Investigation of Computers?	88
5.5	What Action Requires a Property Interference Authority in Relation to the Investigation of Computers?	88
5.6	What Action Requires an Interception Authority in Relation to the Investigation of Computers?	89
5.7	What Action Requires a CHIS Authority in Relation to the Investigation of Computers or Using Computers?	89
5.8	What Is the Appropriate Authority for Accessing Data Stored on a Computer?	90
5.9	Good Practice for the Covert Investigation of Computers	90
5.10	Issues for Consideration Regarding the Investigation of Computers	91

5.1 **Introduction**

Computers can be the scene of a crime (victim evidence), the means by which a crime is planned or committed (offender evidence; intelligence), a means of communication when facilitating a conspiracy (offence and offender evidence; intelligence), and a means of (covertly) investigating crime. Once again, precision in the drafting of applications and authorities is important, especially so given the multiple roles of the computer within covert investigation.

This is an area of developing law. It is also an area in which investigators without expertise in hi-tech crime investigation would be well advised to seek up-to-date advice from computer crime investigators when planning covert operations. This chapter should be seen as a general introduction to a rapidly evolving arena.

This is also an area in which particular attention must be made to collateral intrusion since the surveillance can be focused on the use made of a computer rather than direct surveillance of a person. Since in any given household more than one person might use any given computer, the potential for collateral intrusion when monitoring computer use is particularly high and careful consideration to the potential for and management of such intrusion will be required in both applications and authorities. No intrusion can be authorized that is disproportionate to the crime under investigation and the information that is expected to be obtained as a result of this particular investigation tactic.

5.2 **Which Public Authorities Can Investigate Computers Covertly and Which Legal Authorities Are Required?**

Computers are property and so covert investigation of computers will constitute *interference with property* if it is necessary to access, either physically or through the deployment of software, the target computer in order to effect the investigation or surveillance.

Additionally, surveillance of the use of a computer will often take place in circumstances that comprise *intrusive surveillance*. And since live-time email (as opposed to stored emails) is a communication in progress, should that be the subject of investigation, then an *interception* warrant will be required.

The authority regimes for intrusive surveillance, property interference, and interception of communications therefore dictate which public authorities can conduct such covert investigation of computers (see Chapters 2, 3, and 7).

Those agencies empowered to *interfere with property* are:

- Police forces in England and Wales maintained under s 2 Police Act 1996
- Police forces maintained under s 1 Police (Scotland) Act 1967
- The Metropolitan Police

- The City of London Police
- The Police Service of Northern Ireland
- The National Crime Squad (until SOCA becomes operational)
- The National Criminal Intelligence Service (until SOCA becomes operational)
- HM Customs and Excise (until SOCA becomes operational)
- The Serious Organized Crime Agency (when it becomes operational, likely to be 1 April 2006)
- MI5, MI6, and GCHQ (s 5 Intelligence Services Act 1994).

The organizations are defined by reference to who may authorize such inter-ference and entry (s 93(5) PA97 and s 5 Intelligence Services Act 1994).

Those agencies able to conduct *intrusive surveillance* are:

- Any police force maintained under s 2 Police Act 1996
- Any police force maintained under s 1 Police (Scotland) Act 1967
- The Metropolitan Police Service
- The City of London Police
- The Police Service of Northern Ireland
- The Ministry of Defence Police
- The British Transport Police
- The National Criminal Intelligence Service (until SOCA becomes operational)
- The National Crime Squad (until SOCA becomes operational)
- The Serious Organized Crime Agency (when it becomes operational, likely to be 1 April 2006)
- The Army, Navy, Royal Marines, and Air Force
- HM Customs and Excise
- MI5, MI6, and GCHQ (by virtue of s 42 RIPA).

There are circumstances in which computers can be the subject of *directed surveillance*, in which case a greater number of public authorities may lawfully conduct such investigations (see Chapter 2):

- Any police force as defined by s 81(1) RIPA: essentially the 43 police forces of England and Wales, the Scottish police forces, the Police Service of North-ern Ireland, British Transport Police, the Ministry of Defence police, and the military police forces
- The Civil Nuclear Constabulary
- The Force comprising the special constables appointed under s 79 of the Har-bours, Docks and Piers Clauses Act 1847 on the nomination of the Dover Harbour Board
- The force comprising the constables appointed under Article 3 of the Mer-sey Docks and Harbour (Police) Order 1975 on the nomination of the Mersey Docks and Harbour Board
- The Royal Parks Constabulary
- The National Criminal Intelligence Service (until SOCA becomes operational)
- The National Crime Squad (until SOCA becomes operational)

- The Serious Organized Crime Agency (when it becomes operational, likely to be 1 April 2006)
- The Serious Fraud Office
- The Independent Police Complaints Commission
- The Office of the Police Ombudsman of Northern Ireland
- MI5, MI6, and GCHQ
- The Army, Royal Navy, Royal Marines, and Royal Air Force
- The Commissioners of HM Customs and Excise
- The Commissioners of Inland Revenue
- Any local, county, or district council in England, a London borough council, the Common Council of the City of London in its capacity as a local authority, the Council of the Isles of Scilly, and any county council or county borough council in Wales
- Any fire authority within the meaning of the Fire Services Act 1947 (read with para 2 of Schedule 11 to the Local Government Act 1985)
- The Ministry of Defence
- Office of the Deputy Prime Minister
- The Department for Environment, Food and Rural Affairs
- The Department of Health
- The Home Office
- The Northern Ireland Office
- The Department of Trade and Industry
- Department for Work and Pensions
- Department for Transport
- The National Assembly for Wales
- A universal service provider (within the meaning of the Postal Services Act 2000) acting in connection with the provision of a universal postal service (within the meaning of that Act)
- The Postal Services Commission
- The Charity Commission
- The Environment Agency
- The Financial Services Authority
- The Food Standards Agency
- The Gambling Commission
- The Office of Fair Trading
- The Health and Safety Executive
- A Health Authority established under s 8 of the National Health Service Act 1977
- A Special Health Authority established under s 11 of the National Health Service Act 1977
- A National Health Service trust established under s 5 of the National Health Service and Community Care Act 1990
- Local Health Boards in Wales established under s 6 of the National Health Service Reform and Health Care Professions Act 2002

- Her Majesty's Chief Inspector of Schools in England
- The Information Commissioner
- The Royal Pharmaceutical Society of Great Britain
- The Department of Health, Social Services and Public Safety (Northern Ireland)
- The Department of Agriculture and Rural Development (Northern Ireland)
- The Department of Enterprise, Trade and Investment (Northern Ireland)
- The Department of the Environment (Northern Ireland)
- Any district council (within the meaning of s 44 of the Interpretation Act (Northern Ireland) 1954)
- The Department of Regional Development (Northern Ireland)
- The Department of Social Development (Northern Ireland)
- The Department of Culture, Arts and Leisure (Northern Ireland)
- The Foyle, Carlingford and Irish Lights Commission (Northern Ireland)
- The Fisheries Conservancy Board for Northern Ireland (Northern Ireland)
- A Health and Social Services trust established under Article 10 of the Health and Personal Social Services (Northern Ireland) Order 1972
- A Health and Social Services Board established under Article 16 of the Health and Personal Social Services (Northern Ireland) Order 1972
- A Health and Safety Executive for Northern Ireland
- The Northern Ireland Central Services Agency for the Health and Social Services
- The Fire Authority for Northern Ireland
- The Northern Ireland Housing Executive.

Regarding which authorities are required under what circumstances, the simplest approach to answering this question is to distinguish the answers according to investigation technique typology.

5.3 What Action Requires a Directed Surveillance Authority in Relation to the Investigation of Computers?

In circumstances where a kidnapper or blackmailer is communicating with the victim via email, as with the monitoring of phone calls in such circumstances, with the written consent of one of the parties to the communication, the communication may be lawfully monitored under a directed surveillance authority (s 3(2), s 26(2), and s 28 RIPA).

A directed surveillance *may* also be appropriate where the surveillance is to be carried in an internet café, but the exact tactics to be employed and the desired product would dictate the exact authority regime required. For instance, if the investigator's intention was to intercept emails being sent from a terminal in the café, then an interception warrant would be required. A directed surveillance authority would be appropriate in circumstances where the intention was to monitor a suspect's use of the computer by camera or by the deployment of surveillance officers in the café, *but* where the use of a camera meant that both sides of chat-room conversation could be seen and this was the purpose of the surveillance then an interception warrant would be required.

5.4 What Action Requires an Intrusive Surveillance Authority in Relation to the Investigation of Computers?

Where surveillance is to be conducted on use made of a computer in private residential dwellings, hotel rooms, office premises or in a private vehicle, an intrusive surveillance authority with OSC *prior approval* will be required. If the surveillance also requires entry into and trespass onto property, and or interference with the computer that is to be monitored, then a property interference authority will also be required (see Chapters 2, 3, and 4).

For example, the deployment of devices onto a home computer, either by physical attachment or remotely via software, will necessitate interference with property prior to the surveillance being carried out. Because the surveillance is being carried in a dwelling, it will be intrusive. Similarly, remote activation of a home computer will constitute both an interference with property (the remote activation of the computer) and intrusive surveillance (the conduct of surveillance in a private dwelling).

5.5 What Action Requires a Property Interference Authority in Relation to the Investigation of Computers?

Any action that interferes with the hardware of a computer or alters the software profile of a particular computer will require authority under Part III PA97.

This would include, for instance, the covert deployment of a physical device, the loading of software onto a computer without the computer owner's knowledge, or the remote covert activation of a computer. (The latter would additionally require intrusive surveillance authority.)

Where it is proposed to deploy a physical device onto a keyboard or covertly to copy the contents of a hard drive, and the computer is on private premises, then the authorization will have to cover all preparatory acts required to facilitate such a deployment or action, as well as the deployment or action itself. Recovery of equipment will also have to be properly authorized.

Investigators should be aware that certain software remotely deployed will enable alteration of data, an action which might render the computer and any data stored therein unreliable and inadmissible as evidence. The advice of the relevant Computer Crime Unit should be sought.

5.6 What Action Requires an Interception Authority in Relation to the Investigation of Computers?

The interception of communications whilst in the course of their transmission made via computers constitutes interception for which a Secretary of State's warrant is required (see Chapter 7).

Important case law exists in relation to emails. It has been held (and this has not been appealed) that s 1(5) RIPA must be read as providing implicit lawful authority within the context of s 9 PACE, even where the net effect amounts to an interception of email outside the warranted regime provided for under s 5 RIPA (*NTL Group Ltd v Ipswich Crown Court* [2002] EWHC 1585). In this case a service provider had to divert (thus intercept) emails to an alternative server pending judicial consideration of an application for a production order. The production order was granted and investigators were allowed to access the emails that had been stored in this manner. The product from such interception could be used in evidence (s 18(4) and (5) RIPA).

5.7 What Action Requires a CHIS Authority in Relation to the Investigation of Computers or Using Computers?

Where it is proposed to deploy investigators or victims acting on behalf of investigators, to interact with suspects via a computer either by email, webcam or in chat-rooms, a CHIS authority will be required if it is proposed to use, for the purpose of the investigation, any information obtained by the investigator as a result of the on-line relationship in circumstances in which the other party will not be aware of the investigator's true purpose in acquiring such information.

Covert on-line investigation to identify internet offenders creates the potential for 'blue-on-blue' situations to arise: circumstances in which two undercover, on-line investigators interact on-line and begin to investigate each other. Proper procedures through NCIS or the relevant department within SOCA which will replace NCIS are in place to avoid this.

It is good practice to video the interaction of undercover investigators on-line for evidential integrity purposes. The use of webcams should be avoided unless the investigator is an undercover investigator also trained to engage in, and for the purpose of the investigation intending to conduct, face-to-face meetings.

Deployment of a conventional CHIS (formerly known as informants) to obtain information via an on-line interactive relationship also requires a CHIS authority. Where a CHIS coincidentally is requested to obtain information from a database to which he or she has lawful access, if this does *not* involve the CHIS maintaining a relationship that facilitates the accessing or obtaining of the information it would not appear to require an authorization.

5.8 What Is the Appropriate Authority for Accessing Data Stored on a Computer?

Covert investigation of data stored on a computer hard drive constitutes interference with property and so requires the necessary authority under Part III PA97. An alternative, but overt, coercive means of accessing such stored data would be via a PACE warrant or production order.

One of the most frequently asked questions from investigators involves accessing the email account of a suspect when the password to that account has come into the possession of investigators. 'I have X's password: can I access his email account?' Without the informed (and preferably written) consent of the suspect, *no*: such action constitutes a criminal offence under the Computer Misuse Act 1990.

5.9 Good Practice for the Covert Investigation of Computers

It will always be good practice to consult expert advice in relation to computers. Prior to the establishment of computer or hi-tech crime units within the police service, it was not unheard of for colleagues 'who knew a bit about computers' to volunteer to investigate computers and the digital evidence such devices contained. This is no longer advisable. Under the ACPO hi-tech crime strategy all ACPO police forces have both network and digital forensic investigation capability. There is similar expert provision for police in Scotland. Other organizations also have hi-tech investigation units. These experts should be approached for advice and guidance and will probably be the only persons trained to conduct covert computer investigation tactics.

Only trained staff should undertake computer investigation. This applies not only to the deployment of surveillance devices or software, but also to interaction with suspects via computers.

> **Further information and reading**
>
> Covert Internet Investigator training is supplied by the National Specialist Law Enforcement Centre (NSLEC, <http://www.centrex.police.uk/business/law. html>) to provide training for investigators engaged in undercover investigations on the internet, such as the proactive searching for paedophiles in chat-rooms.
>
> ACPO has produced a Good Practice Guide on the Seizure of Digital Data and a Good Practice Guide for Managers of Hi-Tech/Computer Crime Units, which is available as pdf downloads from <http://www.nhtcu.org>.

5.10 Issues for Consideration Regarding the Investigation of Computers

As has been seen, there is much from the armoury of investigation techniques and tactics that can be employed in relation to computers. Nevertheless, there are a number of issues that complicate such investigation and, in some cases, await clarification.

For instance, where it is proposed to access a computer remotely how will investigators ascertain the geographical location of the computer in order to identify the appropriate chief officer to whom to apply for authority under Part III PA97? Designated authorizing officers under Part III PA97 may only authorize activity within their 'force' area (s 93(1)(b) in conjunction with s 93(6)). Preliminary enquiries may be necessary to locate a computer before the appropriate authorizing officer can be identified. If the computer is located abroad, mutual legal assistance procedures will apply to actions that would otherwise constitute interference with property in England and Wales.

Jurisdiction is similarly an issue for the serving of Data Protection Act notices on internet service providers (ISPs). Usually the municipal law of the location of the ISP's servers applies. Web addresses or an email account ending '—.com' may indicate that the address-owner or ISP is US-based, and so application for data will have to be made either via formal mutual legal assistance mechanisms or via other recognized routes such as requests to the FBI legal attaché at the US Embassy, who will be able to issue a notice under US federal law as part of police-to-police informal mutual assistance. A US-based ISP which also runs '—.co.uk' email accounts may, depending on the company, recognize UK Data Protection Act notices in respect of such accounts because they purport to be UK-based, regardless of where the server actually is. At least one US-based ISP with offices in the UK will accept UK Data Protection Act notices served at its UK offices for any of the email accounts it services. Practice will vary from ISP to ISP and computer investigation units will be best placed to advise on such issues.

The legal debate about what constitutes private information on the internet is too vast to consider here in depth. Clearly where an individual has posted information about themselves in a chat-room, or on a website, the privacy of that information has, to some degree, been surrendered depending on the level of public access to the chat-room or website. But if the information has been maliciously or unwittingly posted by a third party, it will clearly remain private information. How is the investigator to know? The best that an investigator can hope to achieve is to act in good faith, recording meticulously every thought process and reasoning as to why a piece of information on the internet is not private, or why it is private and its covert acquisition through surveillance is lawful, necessary, legitimate, and proportionate. It will be for the courts to decide whether to admit or refuse the evidence.

Computer covert investigation scenario

A concerned parent has reported that her thirteen-year-old daughter has struck up a relationship with an individual in a chat-room on the internet using a home-based computer. The individual purports to be a fourteen-year-old male and has suggested to the daughter that they meet. The parent is suspicious because the fourteen-year-old male insists that the daughter keeps the meeting a secret from her parents. After further investigation, information suggests that this is not a fourteen-year-old but a thirty-two-year-old male. Investigators wish to continue communicating in the chat-room with the male using a decoy officer, in order to set up a meeting where the intention is to arrest the male.

Trained specialist *covert computer investigators* or *undercover operatives* must be deployed in order to continue the communication, and therefore a CHIS authority is required. A directed surveillance authority will also be required for the one-sided consensual interception of the communications data.

Checklist of key issues when considering surveillance involving computers

- What evidence or intelligence is being sought?
- How is it relevant to the operation under consideration?
- What is the physical location of the computer that is to be covertly monitored?
- What is the physical location of the data that is to be covertly accessed?
- What is the least intrusive means of securing such evidence or information?
- What are the risks to the organization of such tactics? (Chapter 11)

- Will the surveillance or investigation leave electronic footprints?

- What are the risks to the organization's staff of such tactics? (Chapter 11)

- What are the risks to the public or specific third parties when such tactics are deployed? (Chapter 11)

- What are the risks to the subject of the investigation? (Chapter 11)

- Will such methods breach Article 8(1)? (1.6.1)

- Is there justification for doing so provided by Article 8(2)? (1.6.4)

- How is the legality test met? (1.6.3)

- How is the legitimacy test met? (1.6.4)

- How is the necessity test met? (1.6.5)

- How is the proportionality test met? (1.6.5)

- Are the arguments justifying the application to use covert investigation based on reliable information/intelligence, or has the applicant adopted a 'tick-the-box' approach to completing the application without giving full consideration to the facts of the case and the issues arising?

- Have the arguments justifying the granting of authorization to use covert investigation been fully articulated, or has the authorizing officer merely paid lip service to the pro forma authorization template via which authority is granted?

- How are the methods by which the evidence/intelligence will be obtained to be protected at trial?

Planning covert investigation actions

Remember to include the PLAN for covert investigation tactics in all investigation policy-book entries relating to covert investigation considerations and decisions.

P   PROPORTIONALITY

Why is it proportionate to obtain the intended product of this surveillance in the manner proposed? (1.6.5)

L   LEGITIMACY

What is the legitimate purpose of the proposed action: the prevention of disorder or crime; the interests of national security; the interests of public safety; the interests of the economic well-being of the country; the protection of health or morals; the protection of the rights and freedoms of others? (1.6.4)

A   A AUTHORITY TO UNDERTAKE PROPOSED ACTION
What is the lawful foundation and authority for the proposed action? From whom must authorization be sought? (1.6.3)

N   NECESSITY OF PROPOSED ACTION
Why is the proposed action necessary? (1.6.5)

SPACE FOR NOTES

SPACE FOR NOTES

SPACE FOR NOTES

6

Examining Mobile Phones

6.1 Introduction   98

6.2 Which Public Authorities Can Examine Mobile Phones?   98

6.3 What Powers Does the Law Provide in Relation
to the Examination of Mobile Phones?   99

6.4 What Authority Regime Is Required for the Examination
of Mobile Phones?   99

6.5 What Significant Case Law Has Been Decided in Relation to the
Examination of Mobile Phones?   100

6.1 **Introduction**

Mobile phones, taken here to include any hand-held electronic device capable of voice telecommunication, are potentially a rich source of intelligence and evidence which often come into the possession of investigators. But mere lawful possession or detention of a suspect's mobile phone, for instance when a detained person's property is seized upon taking the individual into custody, does not entitle investigators to access the data contained within the device or accessible via it. Investigators will need the appropriate authorities under RIPA and PA97 to access such data covertly or under PACE if an overt examination with the knowledge of the suspect is proposed.

This is a new and developing area of law and technology and there is as yet almost no case law to provide clarity of interpretation. Here the current 'rules of thumb' are presented as a basis of interpretation subject to confirmation by the courts.

6.2 **Which Public Authorities Can Examine Mobile Phones?**

Public authorities can examine mobile phones to the extent that they have powers to conduct covert investigation under either RIPA or the PA97. Overt examination of mobile phones can be achieved through PACE powers. Not infrequently, those investigators wishing to access covertly data held within or accessible by the mobile phone will require a property interference authority.

Those agencies empowered to *interfere with property* are:

• Police forces in England and Wales maintained under s 2 Police Act 1996
• Police forces maintained under s 1 Police (Scotland) Act 1967
• The Metropolitan Police
• The City of London Police
• The Police Service of Northern Ireland
• The National Crime Squad (until SOCA becomes operational)
• The National Criminal Intelligence Service (until SOCA becomes operational)
• HM Customs and Excise
• The Serious Organized Crime Agency (when it becomes operational, likely to be 1 April 2006)
• MI5, MI6, and GCHQ.

The organizations are defined by reference to who may authorize such interference and entry (s 93(5) PA97 and s 5 Intelligence Services Act 1994).

6.3 **What Powers Does the Law Provide in Relation to the Examination of Mobile Phones?**

Mobile telephony stores data in three different ways. Some data, voicemails for instance, are stored on network servers which can be accessed via the handset. The handset itself contains a SIM card on which data can be stored and also has its own internal memory. The majority of data stored on the handset is likely to be located in the internal memory.

Investigators can use interception powers under Part I RIPA and property interference powers under Part III PA97 to access this data and any communications in the course of transmission.

6.4 **What Authority Regime Is Required for the Examination of Mobile Phones?**

For the latest current advice investigators should always consult the relevant single point of contact (SPOC) within their organization.

The appropriate authority regime depends upon where the data to be examined is held. These different technical solutions dictate different statutory regimes for investigators to use when examining mobile phones. In the absence of case law the prevailing consensus is that accessing data stored on the communication service provider (CSP) network server constitutes interception, subject to this being lawful either through a warrant issued by the Secretary of State or because the circumstances constitute lawful interception within the meaning of the judgment in *NTL Group Ltd v Ipswich Crown Court* [2002] EWHC 1585 (see 6.5). Data stored by either method on the handset is currently considered (subject to any future judgment to the contrary) to be analogous to the data stored on a personal computer hard drive. Therefore a property interference authority combined with a directed surveillance authority will probably be required. (In circumstances where both the PA97 regime and the RIPA regime apply, it is the senior authorizing officer who authorizes the combined authority, which will almost invariably be the authorizing officer designated by PA97.)

Some of the data stored on the handset constitutes communications data (see Chapter 7) in that it records the contact identity of calls made and received. These are data that would normally only be accessible by service of a Part I Chapter II RIPA authorization or notice which would not apply in the case of seized mobile phones. Accessing these data can either be achieved through PACE search powers or, for the purposes of covert investigation, with a Part III PA97 authority to interfere with property in conjunction with a directed surveillance authority to view the data (which will be private information) (OSC *Annual Report 2005*, 4.5).

The location of a mobile phone can also be examined. Again different technologies and different investigation purposes dictate different approaches and the permutations are so varied that they cannot be comprehensively covered in a work of this nature. SPOCs will be able to advise what is feasible with any given CSP and therefore what the appropriate authority regime will be.

6.5 What Significant Case Law Has Been Decided in Relation to the Examination of Mobile Phones?

There is almost no case law yet available specifically in relation to the covert physical investigation of mobile phones. There is, however, relevant case law in relation to interception that would appear to apply to mobile phone emails and voicemail.

In relation to accessing email data intended to be accessed by the recipient via his or her mobile phone and stored on a CSP's network server, case law (not appealed) has held that s 1(5) RIPA must be read as providing implicit lawful authority within the context of s 9 PACE, even where the net effect amounts to an interception of email outside the warranted regime provided for under s 5 RIPA (*NTL Group Ltd v Ipswich Crown Court* [2002] EWHC 1585). In this case a CSP had to divert (thus intercept) emails to an alternative server pending judicial consideration of an application for a production order.

The product from such interception may be used in evidence (s 18(4) and (5) RIPA).

Mobile phone examination scenario

Mrs Thomas has been arrested on suspicion of being concerned in the supply of Class A drugs. She has in her possession a mobile phone and an investigator wishes to examine the mobile phone, in order to establish a list of contacts and phone numbers of those she is believed to supply.

The seizure of the phone is lawful under PACE; however, examination of the phone is for the purpose of acquiring private information which may be used in evidencing the commission of an offence. To obtain the information, interference with the property is required and so authorization should be sought in order to physically examine the phone. In addition, a directed surveillance authority is required to view the information sought.

Mobile phone examination scenario

Alice Dukes has been receiving threatening messages from an ex-partner. The messages are stored as voicemails and can be accessed by dialling 123. Investigators wish to recover this evidence from the voicemail with the intention of prosecuting the ex-partner.

Having obtained the written consent of Alice Dukes, a directed surveillance authority will be required in order to listen to or record the phone calls made.

Checklist of key considerations when planning to examine mobile phones

- What evidence or intelligence is being sought?

- How is it relevant to the operation under consideration?

- What is the least intrusive means of securing such evidence or information?

- Does the power under which the phone has come into the lawful possession of investigators include a power to search its contents? (If not, surveillance authority required.)

- What are the risks to the organization of such tactics? (Chapter 11)

- What are the risks to the organization's staff of such tactics? (Chapter 11)

- What are the risks to the public or specific third parties when such tactics are deployed? (Chapter 11)

- What are the risks to the subject of the investigation? (Chapter 11)

- Will such methods breach Article 8(1)? (1.6.1)

- Is there justification for doing so provided by Article 8(2)? (1.6.4)

- How is the legality test met? (1.6.3)

- How is the legitimacy test met? (1.6.4)

- How is the necessity test met? (1.6.5)

- How is the proportionality test met? (1.6.5)

- Are the arguments justifying the application to use covert investigation based on reliable information/intelligence, or has the applicant adopted a 'tick-the-box' approach to completing the application without giving full consideration to the facts of the case and the issues arising?

- Have the arguments justifying the granting of authorization to use covert investigation been fully articulated, or has the authorizing officer merely paid lip service to the pro forma authorization template via which authority is granted?

- How are the methods by which the evidence/intelligence will be obtained to be protected at trial?

Planning covert investigation actions

Remember to include the PLAN for covert investigation tactics in all investigation policy-book entries relating to covert investigation considerations and decisions.

P   PROPORTIONALITY
Why is it proportionate to obtain the intended product of this surveillance in the manner proposed? (1.6.5)

L   LEGITIMACY
What is the legitimate purpose of the proposed action: the prevention of disorder or crime; the interests of national security; the interests of public safety; the interests of the economic well-being of the country; the protection of health or morals; the protection of the rights and freedoms of others? (1.6.4)

A   AUTHORITY TO UNDERTAKE PROPOSED ACTION
What is the lawful foundation and authority for the proposed action? From whom must authorization be sought? (1.6.3)

N   NECESSITY OF PROPOSED ACTION
Why is the proposed action necessary? (1.6.5)

SPACE FOR NOTES

SPACE FOR NOTES

SPACE FOR NOTES

7

Communications Data

7.1	Introduction	106
7.2	Which Public Authorities Can Investigate Communications Data?	106
7.3	What Powers Does the Law Provide in Relation to Communications Data?	107
7.4	What Authority Regime Is Prescribed for the Acquisition of Communications Data?	109
7.5	What Significant Case Law Has Been Decided in Relation to Communications Data?	111

7.1 **Introduction**

Acquisition of communications data provides intelligence of criminal associations and behaviour patterns that can either inform an application for the deployment of more intrusive surveillance or provide evidence to support a prosecution.

The statutory regime for the acquisition of communications data is prescribed in Chapter II Part I RIPA. Codes of practice are to be issued in respect of this chapter and at the time of writing the early drafts are currently subject to a consultation process.

Communications data acquired pursuant to Chapter II Part I RIPA may be adduced in evidence. Communications data acquired as a coincidental result of the execution of an interception warrant issued under Chapter I Part I RIPA is considered an interception product and so may not be used in evidence by virtue of s 17 RIPA. Investigation managers wishing to use communications data in evidence will have to ensure that it has been acquired using the Chapter II powers (which allow for communications data to be adduced in evidence) and not as a by-product of interception (in which case the data will be subject to the s 17 RIPA prohibition on adducing any references that indicate interception has taken place) (see Chapter 8).

The key role in the acquisition of communications data is that of the *single point of contact* (SPOC) (either an accredited individual or a group of accredited individuals) representing the investigating authority in all data acquisition from communication service providers (CSPs).

No SPOC—no communications data.

7.2 **Which Public Authorities Can Investigate Communications Data?**

Those authorities that may acquire communications data are listed in s 25(1) RIPA:

- A police force
- The National Criminal Intelligence Service (until SOCA becomes operational)
- The National Crime Squad (until SOCA becomes operational)
- The Serious Organized Crime Agency (when it becomes operational, likely to be 1 April 2006)
- The Commissioners of HM Customs and Excise
- The Commissioners of Inland Revenue
- MI5, MI6, and GCHQ.

In addition to these authorities described on the face of the Act, the Home Secretary may by order specify other authorities that may acquire communications data. This has been done in SI 2003/3172 and SI 2005/1083. Amongst the other authorities so specified are various government departments, ambulance services, and fire services. These Statutory Instruments, reproduced in Appendix C, detail which staff may acquire any communications data as defined in s 24(4) RIPA, and which staff may only acquire such data as defined in s 24(4)(b) and (4)(c).

7.3 What Powers Does the Law Provide in Relation to Communications Data?

Section 21 RIPA provides lawful authority without civil liability for any conduct in relation to a postal service or telecommunication system for obtaining or disclosing communications data, other than conduct consisting in the interception of communications during the course of their transmission.

Acquisition of traffic data, service use data, and subscriber information (definition boxes below, this chapter) must be *necessary* for one or more of the purposes detailed in s 22(2) RIPA:

- in the interests of national security;
- for the purpose of preventing or detecting crime (as defined in s 81(5) RIPA) or of preventing disorder;
- in the interests of the economic well-being of the UK (subject to this being directly related to state/national security as defined in Directive 97/66/EC);
- for the purpose, in an emergency, of preventing death or injury or any damage to a person's physical or mental health, or of mitigating any injury or damage to a person's physical or mental health. (Although not explicitly stated, this is unlikely to exclude action taken to identify next-of-kin or the responsible adult in the event of a sudden death, serious injury, or welfare concern for a vulnerable person or child because, although these specific emergency procedures fall outside the scope of covert investigation, they have an obvious social benefit.)

The following necessity criteria are also identified in s 22(2) RIPA, but para 7 SI 2003/3172 restricts the application of these criteria to the acquisition of *subscriber information* only:

- in the interests of public safety;
- for the purpose of protecting public health;
- for the purpose of assessing or collecting any tax, duty, levy, or other imposition, contribution, or charge payable to a government department.

The above criteria do not constitute grounds upon which to acquire traffic data and service data.

Even when legitimacy and necessity criteria are met, data acquisition may only proceed if, and to the extent that, such action is proportionate to what is sought to be achieved by acquiring such data (s 22(5) RIPA).

Communications data may be defined as the *'who'*, *'when'*, *'where'*, and *'how'* of a communication. It does not include any communication content for which the interception provisions apply (see Chapter 8).

There are different types of communications data: *traffic data* (s 21(4)(a), s 21(6) RIPA); *service use information* (s 21(4)(b) RIPA); and *subscriber information* (s 21(4)(c) RIPA).

Investigators sometimes refer to 'billing data'. It is a term that may mean different things to different CSPs and can be interpreted literally. Some telephone service contracts provide free calls within certain networks, or up to a certain usage (after which calls will be charged), or at certain times of the day. For such CSPs billing data is often interpreted as merely those data relating to the incurring of a charge. Therefore an investigator who requests billing data without further qualification may find that he or she receives only data in relation to calls that have been charged and not data in relation to all calls made because some calls may have been free. Itemized call data incorporate all calls made, both charged and free. Here the expertise of the trained and accredited SPOC is vital in avoiding such errors that may seriously impede the investigation.

Any errors made when granting an authority or issuing a notice have to be reported by the investigating authority to the Interception of Communications Commissioner, who, experience has shown, will then require a detailed action plan of how such errors will be avoided in future.

Definition of traffic data

Traffic data means those data, attached to a communication, for the purpose of transmission which identify the addressee and the means of transmission and can include the identity of a computer file or program to which access has been obtained.

Examples include information identifying:

- the origin or destination of a communication
- the location of equipment used to make or receive a communication
- the sender or recipient of the communication
- the equipment through which the communication has passed
- identifying web browsing to the extent that only the host machine, server, or domain is disclosed.

Authority can only be granted or a notice issued by a police superintendent or above. Equivalent ranks from other authorities are detailed in SI 2003/3172 (see Appendix C).

Definition of service use data

Service use data means data identifying the use made by a person of a postal or telecommunication service.

Examples include:

- itemized telephone call records (all numbers called)
- itemized internet connections
- timing and duration of service used
- information about the amount of data uploaded or downloaded
- whether or not forward/redirection services have been used
- records of special services such as recorded deliveries or conference calling.

Authority can only be granted or a notice issued by a police superintendent or above. Equivalent ranks from other authorities are detailed in SI 2003/3172 (see Appendix C).

Definition of subscriber information data

Subscriber information data is that information held by the CSP about the customers to whom communication services have been provided.

Examples include:

- where a suspect's phone bill is in the possession of investigators, the identities of persons whose number the suspect has phoned
- the identity of email account holders
- the identity of persons with posting access to a website
- information about how accounts are paid
- billing and installation addresses
- any demographic data supplied to the CSP by the subscriber when signing up to the communication service.

Authority can only be granted or a notice issued by a police inspector or above. Equivalent ranks from other authorities are detailed in SI 2003/3172 (see Appendix C).

7.4 What Authority Regime Is Prescribed for the Acquisition of Communications Data?

Communications data can be obtained in either of two ways: an *authorization* under s 22(3) RIPA entitling the investigators to gather the data themselves, or a *notice* under s 22(4) RIPA requiring a CSP to supply the data to the investigators. Designated persons (in effect authorizing officers) specified to grant authorities or issue notices are identified in SI 2003/3172 (see Appendix C).

Examples of when it will be appropriate to grant an authorization rather than issue a notice include the following circumstances:

- Where a CSP has no capability to obtain or disclose the required data, but where investigators might have such a capability.

- Where the authorizing officer (designated person) believes an investigation or operation may be compromised if the CSP were to obtain or disclose the data.
- Where an agreement regarding appropriate disclosure mechanisms exists between the investigating authority and a CSP.
- Where there is a need to conduct a telephone subscriber check, but a CSP has yet to be conclusively identified as the holder of the appropriate data.

Definition of a s 22(3) authorization

A *s 22(3) authorization* lasts for one month and may be renewed (s 23(4) and (5)). It:

- must be granted in writing or (if not in writing) in a manner that produces a record of its having been made;
- must describe the conduct (s 21(1)) authorized and the communications data for the acquisition of which authority has been granted;
- must specify the reason the authority is necessary (s 22(2));
- must specify the office, rank, or position held by the person granting the authority.

Definition of a s 22(4) notice

A *s 22(4) notice* lasts for one month and may be renewed (s 23(4) and (5)). It:

- must be granted in writing or (if not in writing) in a manner that produces a record of its having been made;
- must describe the communications data to be obtained or disclosed under the notice;
- must specify the reason the authority is necessary (s 22(2));
- must specify the office, rank, or position held by the person granting the authority;
- must specify the manner in which any disclosure required by the notice is to be made.

When responding to a notice, a CSP may only disclose the required data to the person issuing the notice or the SPOC (s 23(3)).

The relevant ranks or roles for the purposes of granting an authority or issuing notices are listed in SI 2003/3172 Schedule 1. A police inspector or above can issue an authority or notice in relation to *subscriber information* (s 21(4)(c)), whilst a superintendent or above can issue an authorization or notice for *traffic data* and *service use data* (s 21(4)(a) and (b)).

A notice must be cancelled as soon as it is no longer necessary for the CSP to comply with the notice (s 22(4) RIPA). Where a designated person considers that an authorization is no longer required, it will cease to be necessary and proportionate and so must be withdrawn.

7.5 What Significant Case Law Has Been Decided in Relation to Communications Data?

At the time of writing other than in relation to general principles regarding legality, necessity, and proportionality (see Chapter 1), there has been no significant case law decided in relation to communications data, not least because Part I Chapter II RIPA only came into force in January 2004.

Further information and reading

- SI 2003/3172
  The Regulation of Investigatory Powers (Communications Data) Order 2003
- SI 2005/1083
  The Regulation of Investigatory Powers (Communications Data) (Amendment) Order 2005

(Reproduced in Appendix C)

Checklist of key considerations when planning to investigate communications data

- What evidence or intelligence is being sought?

- How is it relevant to the operation under consideration?

- What is the least intrusive means of securing such evidence or information?

- What are the risks to the organization of such tactics? (Chapter 11)

- What are the risks to the organization's staff of such tactics? (Chapter 11)

- What are the risks to the public or specific third parties when such tactics are deployed? (Chapter 11)

- What are the risks to the subject of the investigation? (Chapter 11)

- Will such methods breach Article 8(1)? (1.6.1)

- Is there justification for doing so provided by Article 8(2)? (1.6.4)

- How is the legality test met? (1.6.3)

- How is the legitimacy test met? (1.6.4)

- How is the necessity test met? (1.6.5)

- How is the proportionality test met? (1.6.5)

- Are the arguments justifying the application to use covert investigation based on reliable information/intelligence, or has the applicant adopted a 'tick-the-box' approach to completing the application without giving full consideration to the facts of the case and the issues arising?

- Have the arguments justifying the granting of authorization to use covert investigation been fully articulated, or has the authorizing officer merely paid lip service to the pro forma authorization template via which authority is granted?

- How are the methods by which the evidence/intelligence will be obtained to be protected at trial?

Planning covert investigation actions

Remember to include the PLAN for covert investigation tactics in all investigation policy-book entries relating to covert investigation considerations and decisions.

P PROPORTIONALITY
   Why is it proportionate to obtain the intended product of this surveillance in the manner proposed? (1.6.5)

L LEGITIMACY
   What is the legitimate purpose of the proposed action: the prevention of disorder or crime; the interests of national security; the interests of public safety; the interests of the economic well-being of the country; the protection of health or morals; the protection of the rights and freedoms of others? (1.6.4)

A AUTHORITY TO UNDERTAKE PROPOSED ACTION
   What is the lawful foundation and authority for the proposed action? From whom must authorization be sought? (1.6.3)

N NECESSITY OF PROPOSED ACTION
   Why is the proposed action necessary? (1.6.5)

SPACE FOR NOTES

SPACE FOR NOTES

8

Interception of Communications

8.1	Introduction	116
8.2	Which Public Authorities Can Intercept Communications?	117
8.3	What Powers Does the Law Provide in Relation to Interception of Communications?	118
8.4	What Authority Regime Is Required for Interception of Communications?	118
8.5	What Are the Procedures for Intercepting Legal Privilege Communications?	123
8.6	What Are the Procedures for Intercepting Communications Containing Confidential Personal Information?	123
8.7	What Are the Procedures for Intercepting Communications Containing Confidential Journalistic Material?	124
8.8	What Are the Interception Provisions of s 83 Postal Services Act 2000?	124
8.9	What Are the Procedures for Handling Intercept Products?	124
8.10	How Is Disclosure of an Intercept Product Addressed?	125
8.11	What Is a 'Preston' Briefing?	125
8.12	What Significant Case Law Has Been Decided in Relation to Interception of Communications?	126

8.1 **Introduction**

The interception of communications made between criminal conspirators, particularly telephone calls, is potentially a significant source of intelligence. Conventional and electronic mail can also be intercepted.

The main principle regarding interception of communications in the UK is that the product of such interception cannot be adduced in evidence. In other words, interception is for intelligence purposes only. There are limited exceptions to this general principle, as will be seen below.

Whether all intercept products should be used evidentially has been much debated since the 1950s. The background to the British debate prior to interception being placed on a statutory footing, with the Interception of Communications Act 1985, is summarized in the ECtHR judgment on *Malone v UK* ([1984] 7 EHRR 14; see also D Ormerod and S McKay, 'Telephone intercepts and their admissibility' [2004] Crim LR 15, 18).

More recently the issue has been revisited at length during the Committee stages of RIPA (*Hansard* HL (series 6) vol 614 cols 107–117 (19 June 2000)) and during the Committee and Report stages of the Serious Organized Crime and Police Act 2005 (*Hansard* HC Standing Committee D, cols 205–224 (18 January 2005); *Hansard* HC (series 6) vol 430 cols 1231–1241 (7 February 2005)). Despite finding itself in a position in which it appeared to be arguing that (for terrorist suspects) imprisonment without charge was preferable to allowing intercept evidence at trial, the government remained resolute.

The reasons for not allowing intercept products in evidence are varied. There is a perceived priority to protect the technology by which interception is undertaken. Firstly, there are concerns that the adversarial trial process would expose this technology at court outside the protection of PII. Secondly, there are also concerns that adducing the product in evidence could endanger intelligence sources. Thirdly, given that many criminals talk in code on the telephone precisely in order to frustrate interception efforts, the fact that intercept transcripts would probably have to be translated for the jurors is felt to be an unnecessary additional confusion. On occasions the criminals confuse themselves with their coded language. (For an example of this, see the transcript reproduced in T Barnes, R Elias, and P Walsh, *Cocky: The Rise and Fall of Curtis Warren, Britain's Biggest Drug Baron* (Milo Books, Bury, 2000), 139–141.) Such translation of slang and jargon on behalf of the jurors invites questions about how investigators can be sure they have interpreted the code properly, which again might compromise other intelligence sources. Finally, the government argues, the intelligence derived from interception generates opportunities to gather evidence in more conventional ways so that trials are not seriously impeded through want of interception evidence. For instance, investigators might become aware of a proposed meeting between criminals through interception. That meeting could then be evidenced through other forms of surveillance.

The fact that other jurisdictions are able to rely heavily on intercept evidence at trial does not alter the practical difficulties envisaged concerning such use at trial in the UK. Not only can intercept products not be adduced in evidence at a criminal trial, it is unlawful to ask questions or make any assertion or disclosure which reveals that interception has taken place or which even tends to suggest that a telephone interception has taken place (s 17 RIPA). Disclosure of anything connected with an interception warrant that should have been kept secret is an arrestable offence (s 19 RIPA). This would include unauthorized disclosure to a colleague from the same organization.

Part I RIPA has repealed and updated provisions enacted in the Interception of Communications Act 1985. Pursuant to s 71 RIPA, a Code of Practice for the interception of communications has been issued. It is reproduced in the Appendices below and on-line at <http://www.homeoffice.gov.uk/docs/ioccop. html>. References to 'Code' in this chapter refer to this Code.

Definition of interception and transmission

Interception means (s 2(2) and (4) RIPA) the

- modification of or interference with a telecommunications system;
- monitoring of transmissions made by such a system by means of the system itself or through wireless telegraphy or other apparatus;
- the interception of a postal item

so that some or all of the communication content is made available during the course of transmission to a third party other than the sender or intended recipient.

The interception, interference, modification, or monitoring must take place within the UK. Investigation conduct in relation only to traffic data (the means by which the communication is addressed to its intended recipient) connected with the communication does not constitute interception if none of the contents are made known to the investigator (s 2(5) RIPA).

In the course of transmission includes the time in which a communication is stored in order to enable the intended recipient to collect, download, or otherwise have access to it. This includes a pager message waiting to be collected or an email waiting to be downloaded (s 2(7) RIPA; Code para 2.14).

8.2 **Which Public Authorities Can Intercept Communications?**

Distinction is drawn between private telephone systems and public telephone systems.

Any organization, including public authorities, can intercept telephone calls made on or to its own *private* telephone system for the purposes of business monitoring (s 4(2) RIPA and SI 2000/2699). A person with the right to control the operation or use of a private telephone system may intercept or monitor calls in which users have given express or implied consent for such interception (usually in the form of an employment contract or a notice outlining their terms and conditions of employment; hence it will not, strictly speaking, be covert) (s 1(6) RIPA). The National Offender Management Service (formerly HM Prison Service) can monitor communications of prisoners under existing prison legislation (s 4(4) RIPA).

Only certain organizations can apply for a warrant to intercept *public* postal or telecommunications under s 5 RIPA. These are listed in s 6 RIPA (Code para 2.1):

- MI5
- MI6
- GCHQ
- The Metropolitan Police
- The Police Service of Northern Ireland
- National Criminal Intelligence Service (on behalf of all other police forces in England and Wales until SOCA becomes operational)
- The Serious Organized Crime Agency (when it becomes operational, likely to be 1 April 2006)
- Any Scottish police force
- HM Customs and Excise
- Defence intelligence
- A competent foreign authority seeking mutual legal assistance from the UK concerning the interception of communications.

8.3 What Powers Does the Law Provide in Relation to Interception of Communications?

Types of communication capable of being intercepted are telephone calls, conventional mail, email, voicemail, and answerphone messages. The statutory framework comprises two general offences of unlawful interception, followed by exceptions in which interception will be lawful.

The two general offences are intercepting a public postal or telecommunication without lawful authority (s 1(1) RIPA, a crime) and unauthorized interception on a private telephone system (s 1(2) and (3) RIPA, a tort).

8.4 What Authority Regime Is Required for Interception of Communications?

There are a number of ways in which communications may be intercepted lawfully. These vary according to circumstance.

8.4.1 **Business purposes**

Communications by which business transactions are entered into or communications relating to such a business or conducted during the course of such business may be monitored. This is to ensure a record of such transactions; to facilitate regulatory and self-regulatory practices; to protect the interests of national security; to prevent or detect crime; to investigate or detect unauthorized use of such systems; and to ensure effective system operation (s 4(2) RIPA; SI 2000/2699; Code para 10.6; relevant regulations are at <http://www.dti.gov.uk/cii/regulations.html>).

In connection with the business of providing postal or telecommunication services, providers may lawfully intercept communications pursuant to the provision of their service or to any enforcement, in relation to that service, of any laws regarding the use of such services (s 3(3) RIPA; Code para 10.5). See also s 83 Postal Services Act 2000.

The product from such interception may be used in evidence (s 18(4) and (5) RIPA).

8.4.2 **Two-party consent**

Where both the sender and recipient so consent, a communication may be lawfully intercepted without further authority (s 3(1) RIPA; Code para 10.3).

The product from such interception may be used in evidence (s 18(4) and (5) RIPA).

8.4.3 **One-sided consent**

Where one party (either sender or recipient) to the communication consents *and* there is a surveillance authority under Part II RIPA in respect of the communication and either the recipient or sender, then the communication may be lawfully intercepted without further authority (s 3(2) RIPA; Code para 10.4).

This makes it lawful to monitor the communications of undercover officers with persons subject of investigation, or to monitor communications between kidnappers or blackmailers and the persons of whom they are making their demands. Such actions should be specifically authorized in the text of the CHIS or surveillance authority.

The product from such interception may be used in evidence (s 18(4) and (5) RIPA). However, where police used this technique to acquire evidence by asking a rape victim to phone her attacker (who had denied the offence in interview) and instigate discussion of the offence, this was held to constitute entrapment and the evidence was excluded as unfair under s 78 PACE (*R v H* [1987] Crim LR 47).

8.4.4 **In connection with wireless telegraphy**

With the authority of a person designated under s 5 Wireless Telegraphy Act 1949 (WTA), interception will be lawful for purposes connected with the issuing of WTA licences; with the prevention and detection of interference with wireless telegraphy (s 3(4) and (5) RIPA).

The product from such interception may be used in evidence (s 18(4) and (5) RIPA).

8.4.5 **Existing statutory power to acquire stored communications**

Search warrants or production orders issued pursuant to s 9 PACE, together with Schedule 1 PACE, provide statutory authority in prescribed circumstances to access stored communications (*Archbold's Criminal Pleading, Evidence and Practice* (revd edn, Sweet & Maxwell, London, 2005 paras 15-74 to 15-89a, together with 25-368 to 25-385; see also Code para 2.15). An example would be where investigators come into possession of a pager and wish to access messages stored on it. The same procedure could be used to access messages stored on the SIM card or internal memory of a mobile phone, although this is slightly more ambiguous as there is a school of thought that argues such messages are still in the course of transmission. The issue has yet to be determined by case law.

Case law (not appealed) has held that s 1(5) RIPA must be read as providing implicit lawful authority within the context of s 9 PACE, even where the net effect amounts to an interception of email outside the warranted regime provided for under s 5 RIPA (*NTL Group Ltd v Ipswich Crown Court* [2002] EWHC 1585). In this case a service provider had to divert (thus intercept) emails to an alternative server pending judicial consideration of an application for a production order.

The product from such interception may be used in evidence (s 18(4) and (5) RIPA).

8.4.6 **Interception by warrant**

The final lawful means of interception provides products that *cannot* be used in evidence: interception of public telecommunications and postal systems under the authority of a Secretary of State's warrant (s 5 RIPA) upon application by those public authorities are listed in s 6 RIPA.

The Secretary of State shall not issue a warrant permitting interception, unless he believes that it is necessary for the grounds laid out in s 5(3) RIPA (which include national security and *serious* crime) and that such conduct is proportionate to what is sought to be achieved (s 5(2) RIPA; Code para 2.4). There are two types of interception warrant: s 8(1) warrants refer to interception as defined in s 2(1) RIPA (Code para 4.1), whilst s 8(4) warrants permit the interception of external communications defined as communications sent or received from outside the British Islands (Code para 5.1).

Definition of serious crime

Serious crime is defined in s 81(3) RIPA as:

- an offence for which a person aged twenty-one or over with no previous convictions could reasonably expect to be sentenced to three years imprisonment or more; or
- an offence where violence is involved; or
- in which there is substantial financial gain; or
- in which a large number of persons are in pursuit of a common purpose.

By excluding reference to serious financial loss, RIPA departs from the formula for a serious arrestable offence prescribed in PACE, which it otherwise follows.

The National Criminal Intelligence Service will advise on the application process and the proper content of an application. Guidance will also be found in paras 4.2 and 5.2 of the Code. In the absence of information to the contrary, and in light of the Serious Organized Crime and Police Act 2005, it is assumed here that such functions will pass to SOCA.

Arranging and executing interception is not a quick process and whilst there are urgency provisions even these take time (Code paras 4.6 and 5.7). There is also a limited capacity. Investigators should not therefore regard interception as the immediate and primary option for investigation.

The warrant is issued in respect of a specific person or premises, together with a schedule that lists the communications to be intercepted (s 8 RIPA). This affords some flexibility for investigators where the subject of an investigation uses multiple phones. Amending the schedule of phone numbers is a simpler process than applying for the warrant (s 10 RIPA). The Secretary of State must certify the material he considers it necessary and proportionate to examine. No other material may be examined notwithstanding that it has been intercepted under warrant.

Thus two elements constitute lawful interception of public systems:

(a) the interception must be warranted (s 5 RIPA), and
(b) in the case of external communications, the examination must be certified (s 8(4) and (5) RIPA).

Warrants have a duration of three months and may be renewed. Warrants issued under the urgency procedure last for five days (s 9 RIPA).

The heavy strictures imposed by s 17(1) RIPA dictate careful handling of intercept products. The product must be destroyed once it has been examined. The procedure for doing this is outlined in section 8.9 below.

8.4.7 **Interception in prisons**

Section 4(4) RIPA provides that prisoner's communications can be intercepted under Prison Rules. The Prison Rules 1999 rules 35A to 35D, inserted by the Prison (Amendment) (No. 2) Rules 2000, apply. Similar provisions exist for Young Offender Institutions. A protocol between NCIS and the National Offender Management Service (NOMS) details the regime within which prison governors will afford assistance in this matter. Investigators are advised to contact their Prison Liaison Officer who will assess the feasibility of any planned operation. Written application must be made via the Police Advisors Section at NOMS HQ. Upon approval, investigators will be given access to intercept products obtained under Prison Rules.

KEY POINTS REGARDING INTERCEPTION IN PRISONS

- Any intercept product will usually be for intelligence purposes only.
- The subject of the interception *must* be the principal subject of the investigation, the 'pivotal player'. Police cannot use Prison Rules as a means of by-passing RIPA to intercept communications where the subject of interest is outside the prison communicating with an inmate.
- The Police Advisors Section will quality assure applications for interception to ensure that they comply both with RIPA and with the Protocol.

The action must be proportionate to what is sought to be achieved by the interception and it must be:

(a) in the interests of national security;
(b) for the prevention, detection, investigation, or prosecution of serious crime (as defined in s 81(3) RIPA);
(c) in the interests of public safety;
(d) for securing or maintaining prison security or good order and discipline in prison.

If investigators wish to intercept the communications of a prisoner who is not the principal subject of the investigation, it will be necessary to seek a warrant for interception under s 5 RIPA as with a subject who was not in prison.

Nothing prevents a prison governor from disclosing on an ad hoc basis information that has come to the attention of prison staff. This is not a means of circumventing prison rules or s 5 RIPA.

Where telephone calls previously made by a prisoner are stored in a prison (e.g. in a high-security prison), investigators can apply for production orders under PACE for the stored communications to be produced. This mechanism is available only where interception is not feasible and is not a means of avoiding a warrant under s 5 RIPA.

Subject always to the authority of the prison governor, given that material intercepted under Prison Rules is normally provided on an intelligence-only basis, such a product would be admissible as evidence at trial under s 18(4) RIPA because interception in prisons is lawful under s 4(4) RIPA.

8.5 What Are the Procedures for Intercepting Legal Privilege Communications?

Matters subject to legal privilege are defined in s 98 PA97 and Article 12 Police and Criminal Evidence (Northern Ireland) Order 1989. Legal privilege is attached to the provision of professional legal advice by persons or organizations qualified to do so. Communications made with the intent of furthering a criminal purpose are not protected by privilege.

RIPA does not prohibit the interception of communications likely to contain legally privileged material, but it does provide additional criteria to be met when applying for a warrant to intercept such communications. Paragraph 3.6 of the Code outlines the procedures to be adopted in such circumstances (the Code is reproduced in Appendix F).

8.6 What Are the Procedures for Intercepting Communications Containing Confidential Personal Information?

Confidential personal information is defined in s 99 PA97. It comprises personal information (from which an individual can be identified and which concerns his physical or mental health or spiritual counselling and guidance afforded to the individual concerned) acquired or created in the course of any trade, business, profession, or other occupation or for the purposes of any paid or unpaid office, which is held in confidence.

RIPA does not prohibit the interception of communications likely to contain confidential personal information, but it does provide additional criteria to be met when applying for a warrant to intercept such communications. Paragraph 3.9 of the Code outlines the procedures to be adopted in such circumstances (the Code is reproduced in Appendix F).

8.7 What Are the Procedures for Intercepting Communications Containing Confidential Journalistic Material?

Confidential journalistic material is defined in s 100 PA97. It is essentially material acquired for or created for the purposes of journalism which is held in confidence.

RIPA does not prohibit the interception of communications likely to contain confidential journalistic material, but it does provide additional criteria to be met when applying for a warrant to intercept such communications. Again, para 3.9 of the Code outlines the procedures to be adopted in such circumstances (the Code is reproduced in Appendix F).

8.8 What Are the Interception Provisions of s 83 Postal Services Act 2000?

Postal items are considered Crown property. There are only certain circumstances in which they can be interfered with during the course of posting and delivery:

- when a lawful interception warrant is in existence;
- at points of entry and exit to the UK for the purposes of HM Revenue and Customs;
- where the mailed item is likely to cause injury to postal staff;
- where an item is likely to obtain obscene material.

Investigators cannot seek a PACE warrant to search an item whilst it is in the course of delivery (transmission).

8.9 What Are the Procedures for Handling Intercept Products?

The Home Secretary has statutory obligations under s 15 and 16 RIPA to ensure safeguards for the handling of intercept products. These are dealt with in detail in s 6 of the Code.

As soon as it is no longer required for the purpose of preventing or detecting crime (which for RIPA Part I specifically excludes gathering evidence for legal proceedings: s 81(5)), or for any of the other purposes for which an interception may be issued under s 5(3) or listed at s 15(4) (Code para 6.2), intercept material (including copies, extracts, or summaries which can be identified as the product of interception) *must be destroyed* (s 15(3) RIPA; Code para 6.8).

'Intercepted material must not be disclosed to any person unless that person's duties, which must relate to one of the authorised purposes (s 15(4)), are such that he needs to know about the material to carry out those duties' (Code para 6.4). Dissemination of an intercept product is limited to the minimum number of persons necessary to execute any of the functions listed at s 15(4).

8.10 How Is Disclosure of an Intercept Product Addressed?

Given that s 17 RIPA prohibits any reference to interception in criminal proceedings, and that s 15(3) requires the prompt destruction of an intercept product, the general principle of disclosure is set aside in respect of an intercept product. Sections 3(7), 8(6), 9(9), and 23(6) CPIA 1996 (as amended by RIPA) confirms this by prescribing that material must not be disclosed if it has been intercepted under s 5 RIPA or its disclosure is prohibited under s 17.

Nevertheless there is, under s 18(7), provision for limited disclosure by investigators to either the prosecutor or a judge of any material that has not yet been destroyed pursuant to s 15(3), because it has been retained for an authorized purpose under s 15(4). This is so that the prosecutor can satisfy the continuing duty under CPIA in the interests of fairness to review the obligation to disclose up to the moment of determination in a trial. Under exceptional circumstances, which are not defined, a judge can order disclosure to himself if he is satisfied that the exceptional circumstances demand this in the interests of justice.

The prosecutor cannot use material of which he is aware under s 18(7) other than to determine what needs to be done to ensure a fair trial. As the defendant will not know of the interception, none of its product must be used against him in evidence. However, where material still exists, the prosecutor must determine whether it constitutes information that will be of benefit to the defence.

Intercept material can never be disclosed to the defence (Code para 7.14).

8.11 What Is a 'Preston' Briefing?

Section 18(7) follows pre-RIPA case law in which the contradictory obligations of secrecy and disclosure were considered (*R v Preston* [1994] 2 AC 130, 166–168). Where the intercept product has been destroyed and so no longer exists to be disclosed to the prosecutor under s 18(7), and where a person relevant to a trial has been arrested as a result of intelligence derived from warranted interception, this must be disclosed to the prosecutor together with the declarations that all the material has been destroyed in accordance with s 15(3); that no one has an accurate recollection of exactly what was said in the intercepted conversations; and that a copy of the warrant is available at NCIS to prove the lawfulness of the interception.

125

8.12 **What Significant Case Law Has Been Decided in Relation to Interception of Communications?**

Malone v UK was the catalyst for the IOCA 1985 (*Malone v UK* (1984) 7 EHRR 14). *Halford v UK* ensured that RIPA would extend provision for lawful interception to private telephone systems (*Halford v UK* (1997) 24 EHRR 523).

In an era of mobile communications it is probable that covert listening devices deployed in premises or vehicles will record persons within operational range of the device talking on mobile phones. This will not amount to an interception (s 2(2) RIPA) if the speech of the other party to such a communication is not recorded. In other words, it is not an interception if only one end of the conversation is monitored in such circumstances (*R v E* [2004] EWCA Crim 1243).

Because the restrictions under s 17 RIPA apply only to interception conducted in the UK, communications lawfully intercepted by foreign authorities in their own jurisdictions may be adduced in evidence in the UK assuming they are relevant (*R v Aujla* [1998] 2 Cr App R 16; approved in *R v P (Telephone Intercepts: Admissibility of Evidence)* [2001] 2 WLR 463). Where the prosecution proposes to do this, all of the material must be considered with a view to disclosure.

R v Preston is the key case in determining how the prosecution should discharge its duties of disclosure within the context of interception secrecy ([1994] 2 AC 130, 166–168). The practical implications of *Preston* have already been considered above (8.11).

Further information and reading

- SI 2000/2699
  The Telecommunications (Lawful Business Practice) (Interception of Communications) Order 2000

- SI 2004/157
  The Regulation of Investigatory Powers (Conditions for Lawful Interception of Persons outside the United Kingdom) Regulations 2004

  (Reproduced in Appendix C)

Checklist of key considerations when planning to apply for an interception warrant

Before an application for interception can be made to the Home Office, investigators will have to identify the following for inclusion in their application:

- The specific phones (or correspondence) being used by the subject(s)

- How the phones (or correspondence) are being used for a criminal purpose (sequential event analysis using phone billing data could demonstrate this, for instance)

- Why interception is relevant, necessary, and proportionate within the context of the specific investigation and what other investigation methods have been considered, deployed, or rejected

- How compliance with the statutory safeguards is to be achieved

- What collateral intrusion will occur

- The likelihood of legally privileged material, confidential personal information, or confidential journalistic material being intercepted

- The feasibility of undertaking this interception.

Besides these specific criteria that will form part of the application for interception, the general considerations include:

- Is the interception necessary under s 5(3) RIPA?

- Is the criminality involved serious as defined in s 81(3) RIPA?

- What evidence or intelligence is being sought?

- Whose communications are to be intercepted? (Are they in prison?)

- What communications are to be intercepted?

- Which are the relevant communication service providers?

- How is it relevant to the operation under consideration?

- Is interception proportionate to what is sought to be achieved?

- What will be the extent of collateral intrusion arising from this interception?

- What are the risks to the organization of such tactics? (Chapter 11)

- What are the risks to the organization's staff of such tactics? (Chapter 11)

- What are the risks to the public or specific third parties when such tactics are deployed? (Chapter 11)

- What are the risks to the subject of the investigation? (Chapter 11)

- Will such methods breach Article 8(1)? (1.6.1)

- Is there justification for doing so provided by Article 8(2)? (1.6.4)

- How is the legality test met? (1.6.3)

- How is the legitimacy test met? (1.6.4)

necessity test met? (1.6.5)

roportionality test met? (1.6.5)

utory safeguards in place concerning the handling of the intercept material?

- Who needs to know that the application is being sought? Why?

- Who will have access to the product, an extract, or a summary of it? Why?

Planning covert investigation actions

Remember to include the PLAN for covert investigation tactics in all investigation policy-book entries relating to covert investigation considerations and decisions.

P PROPORTIONALITY
Why is it proportionate to obtain the intended product of this surveillance in the manner proposed? (1.6.5)

L LEGITIMACY
What is the legitimate purpose of the proposed action: the prevention of disorder or crime; the interests of national security; the interests of public safety; the interests of the economic well-being of the country; the protection of health or morals; the protection of the rights and freedoms of others? (1.6.4)

A AUTHORITY TO UNDERTAKE PROPOSED ACTION
What is the lawful foundation and authority for the proposed action? From whom must authorization be sought? (1.6.3)

N NECESSITY OF PROPOSED ACTION
Why is the proposed action necessary? (1.6.5)

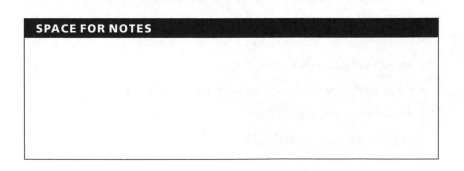

SPACE FOR NOTES

SPACE FOR NOTES

SPACE FOR NOTES

9

Covert Human Intelligence Sources

9.1	Introduction	132
9.2	Which Public Authorities May Deploy CHISs?	132
9.3	What Is a CHIS?	133
9.4	What Is a 'Confidential Source' or 'Confidential Contact'?	134
9.5	What Powers Does the Law Provide in Relation to CHISs?	134
9.6	What Authority Regime Is Required for a CHIS?	135
9.7	Juveniles and Vulnerable Persons as CHISs	136
9.8	Acquisition of Confidential Information by a CHIS	136
9.9	What Management Regime Is Required for a CHIS?	137
9.10	What Significant Case Law Applies to CHISs?	137
9.11	Good Practice in Light of the Above Case Law	142

9.1 **Introduction**

Informants, paid or unpaid, and staff working undercover or as test purchase operatives are all covert human intelligence sources (CHIS), as defined in s 26(8) RIPA. Their use and deployment requires authorization. The manner in which they should be managed is also prescribed and specified individuals have statutory obligations in respect of source management.

A Code of Practice has been issued in respect of CHISs. It is reproduced in the Appendices and is available on-line at <http://www.homeoffice.gov.uk/docs3/chiscodeofpractice.doc>. In this chapter references to the Code refer to this Code.

This is an area in which there has been a considerable amount of relevant case law, which is summarized below. This chapter represents an introduction and general guide to an area of law enforcement that could easily occupy an entire book.

9.2 **Which Public Authorities May Deploy CHISs?**

Public authorities empowered to deploy CHISs are defined in Schedule 1 to the RIPA. They are:

- Any police force as defined by s 81(1) RIPA: essentially the forty-three police forces of England and Wales, the Scottish police forces, the Police Service of Northern Ireland, British Transport Police, the Ministry of Defence police, and the military police forces
- The Civil Nuclear Constabulary
- The force comprising the special constables appointed under s 79 of the Harbours, Docks and Piers Clauses Act 1847 on the nomination of the Dover Harbour Board
- The force comprising the constables appointed under Article 3 of the Mersey Docks and Harbour (Police) Order 1975 on the nomination of the Mersey Docks and Harbour Board
- The National Criminal Intelligence Service (until SOCA becomes operational)
- The National Crime Squad (until SOCA becomes operational)
- The Serious Organized Crime Agency (when it becomes operational, likely to be 1 April 2006)
- The Serious Fraud Office
- The Independent Police Complaints Commission
- MI5, MI6, and GCHQ
- The Army, Royal Navy, Royal Marines, and Royal Air Force
- The Commissioners of HM Customs and Excise
- The Commissioners of Inland Revenue
- Any local, county, or district council in England, a London borough council, the Common Council of the City of London in its capacity as a local

authority, the Council of the Isles of Scilly, and any county council or county borough council in Wales

- Any fire authority within the meaning of the Fire Services Act 1947 (read with para 2 of Schedule 11 to the Local Government Act 1985)
- The Ministry of Defence
- Office of the Deputy Prime Minister
- The Department for Environment, Food and Rural Affairs
- The Department of Health
- The Home Office
- The Northern Ireland Office
- Department for Work and Pensions
- Department for Transport
- The National Assembly for Wales
- The Charity Commission
- The Financial Services Authority
- The Food Standards Agency
- The Gambling Commission
- The Office of Fair Trading
- The Office of the Police Ombudsman of Northern Ireland
- The Postal Services Commission
- A universal service provider (within the meaning of the Postal Services Act 2000) acting in connection with the provision of a universal postal service (within the meaning of that Act)
- The Department of Agriculture and Rural Development (Northern Ireland)
- The Department of Enterprise, Trade and Investment (Northern Ireland)
- The Department of the Environment (Northern Ireland)
- Any district council (within the meaning of s 44 of the Interpretation Act (Northern Ireland) 1954).

9.3 **What Is a CHIS?**

The following are sequential tests derived from the statutory definition at s 26(8).

Definition of a CHIS

---

(1) Does the potential source establish or maintain a relationship (personal or otherwise)?
(2) Is the relationship conducted in a manner calculated to ensure that one party is unaware of its real purpose? (See s 28(9) RIPA for a definition of covert purpose.)

If the answer to these preliminary tests is *yes*, three further tests are applied:

(3) Is the purpose of the relationship to facilitate the obtaining of information?

133

(4) Is the purpose of the relationship to facilitate access to information?

(5) Is the purpose of the relationship to facilitate the disclosure of information obtained during (or as a consequence of) the relationship without the knowledge of one of the parties?

If the answer to any one of these three tests is *yes*, then taken in conjunction with tests 1 and 2, the source is a CHIS whose conduct must be properly authorized and managed.

9.4 What Is a 'Confidential Source' or 'Confidential Contact'?

There has been considerable confusion in a number of organizations over what have been termed 'confidential sources', 'confidential contacts', and 'confidential source (or contact) register'. These terms appear to have come into use well before the enacting of RIPA as a means of managing informants from a variety of backgrounds whose true identity had to be protected. They are not terms that have any statutory basis under RIPA.

Any person providing information to investigating authorities under circumstances outlined in the definition box above will be a CHIS and must be managed according to the statutory provisions of RIPA and the relevant Code.

Where organizations have categories of confidential sources or contacts and a register of such, these should be reviewed to ascertain whether or not they should be registered as CHISs.

9.5 What Powers Does the Law Provide in Relation to CHISs?

Three general types of conduct may be authorized for a CHIS (s 29(4) RIPA; Code para 4.6).

- Any such activities involving conduct by a CHIS or the use of a CHIS as are specified in the authorization. This gives considerable latitude to authorizing officers and is very flexible. By the same token, if a particular conduct is not mentioned on the authority, it will not be authorized. This reaffirms the importance of precision when drafting applications and authorizations.
- Conduct by or in relation to a specified subject to whose actions the CHIS authorization relates.
- Conduct carried out for the purposes of or in connection with a specific investigation or operation, as described in the authorization.

In terms of participation, either by an informant or by an undercover operative, RIPA is silent, leaving much room for interpretation.

One interpretation holds that, since RIPA does not specifically permit infiltration and participation (in other words there is no specific statutory provision for participation), no CHIS may be authorized to engage in such conduct. This would severely inhibit the use of CHISs, particularly when investigating serious organized crime, and such an interpretation is inconsistent with a case law tradition that unambiguously authorizes such conduct within strict parameters.

Parliament's intentions about how far infiltration should go were further outlined in debate about one of the many statutory instruments:

> It was always the intention that the Act would not provide immunity from prosecution. The intention was that it would provide ECHR cover for the use of a CHIS. However, we have since reconsidered, taken further advice and concluded that, in a very limited range of circumstances, it may be possible that participation in a criminal offence might be rendered lawful by virtue of a *correctly authorised CHIS authorisation*. Ultimately, it still remains a matter for the prosecution authorities and the courts to decide whether an authorisation would render conduct that would usually be considered unlawful as lawful. (Bob Ainsworth MP, *Hansard* Fifth Standing Committee on Delegated Legislation, col 004 (3 July 2002); emphasis added.)

9.6 **What Authority Regime Is Required for a CHIS?**

Before authorizing the deployment of a CHIS, the authorizing officer must believe (s 29(2) and (3)) that

(1) It is *necessary* to so deploy for one of the following reasons:
   - in the interests of national security;
   - for the purpose of preventing or detecting any crime or preventing disorder;
   - in the interests of the economic well-being of the UK;
   - in the interests of public safety;
   - for the purpose of protecting public health;
   - for the purpose of assessing or collecting any tax, duty, levy, or other imposition, contribution, or charge payable to a government department; or
   - for other purposes which may be specified by order of the Secretary of State.
(2) The authorized conduct is *proportionate* to what is sought to be achieved by the conduct or use.
(3) That arrangements are in place for the management of the CHIS that meet the criteria prescribed in s 29(5) RIPA.

Persons who can act as authorizing officers are prescribed in SI 2000/2417 reproduced in the Appendices. They include, amongst others: a police superintendent; Royal Navy Provost Marshal or Commander; RAF Wing Commander;

an Army Lieutenant Colonel; an Assistant Director of the SFO; a Senior Executive Officer in the Child Support Agency; an individual on integrated pay band
3 in the Department of Health.

Where a combined authorization is sought for the deployment of a CHIS and
from the Secretary of State for the carrying out of intrusive surveillance, the Secretary of State is the authorizing officer.

Written authorities last for twelve months and may be renewed. An authorization issued under the urgency provisions (Code paras 4.10 and 4.11) lasts for
seventy-two hours. Authorizations must be cancelled by the authorizing officer
as soon as there is no further need for the registered individual to act as a CHIS.
There is no need to wait until the end of the twelve-month period to cancel an
authorization.

9.7 Juveniles and Vulnerable Persons as CHISs

Special safeguards apply when investigators contemplate the deployment of a
CHIS who is under the age of eighteen years. A more senior authorizing officer is
required than for an adult CHIS: in the case of the police service the authorizing
officer must be at least an assistant chief constable. The relevant customs officer
will be band 11 or above and in other organizations the designated individual
is often the chief executive or director. The relevant ranks and positions and
special conditions are defined in SI 2000/2793 (see Appendix C).

The authorization of a juvenile CHIS lasts for one month instead of the
twelve-month authorization for adult CHISs. No CHIS under sixteen can be
authorized to provide information about any person with parental responsibility for the juvenile (Code para 3.14).

Code para 3.13 describes a vulnerable individual as a 'person who is or may
be in need of community care services by reason of mental or other disability,
age or illness and who is or may be unable to take care of himself, or unable to
protect himself against specific harm or exploitation'. Such individuals should
only be deployed as CHISs in the most exceptional circumstances and, as with
juveniles, a higher level of authorizing officer is specified in Annex A of the Code
(Code para 3.13).

9.8 Acquisition of Confidential Information by a CHIS

Where a CHIS is likely to acquire communications subject to legal privilege,
confidential personal information of confidential journalistic material, special
rules for authorizations are outlined in Section 3 and Annexe A of the Code
(see Appendix E). These include the fact that a more senior authorizing officer is
required to authorize such operations than is required for normal deployment
of a CHIS. Legally privileged material obtained by a source is unlikely ever to

be admissible at trial and deployment of a source in circumstances in which such material is likely to be acquired can only be authorized in exceptional and compelling circumstances (Code paras 3.5 and 3.6).

Where any confidential information is acquired, the OSC Commissioner or Inspector must be informed at the next inspection of that organization.

9.9 **What Management Regime Is Required for a CHIS?**

The management regime is defined in s 29(5) RIPA. It is essentially a statutory requirement for CHIS risk management.

It includes specific arrangements to ensure that the source is independently managed and supervised via a three-tier hierarchy of supervision, that records are kept of the use made of the source, and that the source's identity is protected from those who do not need to know it. (The Secretary of State can amend these arrangements by order.) The responsibility for the management and supervision of a source falls to specified individuals within the organization benefiting from the use of the source. As there may be cases where a source carries out activities for more than one organization, it is provided that only one organization will be identified as having responsibility for each requirement in relation to such arrangements and record-keeping.

There must be a person within the organization using the CHIS who is responsible for day-to-day dealings with the CHIS (usually called the handler). Handlers will be supervised by controllers who must have general oversight of the use of the source.

The highest tier comprises an individual of suitable rank whose function it is to maintain records of how CHISs are used. These records are scrutinized annually by the OSC.

Risk assessment (see Chapter 10) is a vital ingredient of successful CHIS management whether the CHIS be an informant or an undercover investigator. It is an ongoing dynamic process which should be documented as thoroughly as possible.

9.10 **What Significant Case Law Applies to CHISs?**

In the absence of precise statute prior to RIPA, the lawful parameters around informants, infiltration, and the use of test purchase as an evidence-gathering mechanism were determined by case law. RIPA is largely silent on CHISs other than to provide the framework for authorization and the risk management regime.

General endorsement for deployment of informants and undercover investigators was approved in *R v Birtles*: 'whilst the police are entitled to make use of information concerning an offence already laid on and while . . . it may be proper for the police to encourage the informer to take part in the offence . . . the police must never use an informer to encourage another to commit an offence which he would not otherwise commit' ([1969] 1 WLR 1047; and confirmed in *R v Horseferry Road Magistrates Court ex p Bennett (No. 1)* (1994) 98 Cr App R 114).

In *R v Clarke* the court accepted that motive was irrelevant to the liability of an accessory to the fact, but held that it was 'quite another thing to conclude . . . that conduct which is overall calculated and intended not to further but to frustrate the ultimate result of the crime is always immaterial and irrelevant' ((1984) 80 Cr App R 344). In essence this provides a mechanism outside RIPA for rendering lawful behaviour that would otherwise be unlawful, which should be viewed within the context of para 2.10 of the Code.

It is helpful to consider the numerous key cases thematically. They draw some very fine lines between what is acceptable and what is not.

9.10.1 Agents provocateurs

It is a fundamental principle that CHISs, be they (participating) informants or undercover investigators, should never incite the commission of a crime. Participating informants, as seen in the general authority of *R v Birtles*, may only participate in offences which are already laid on, i.e. are already planned. Their role should only be minor.

An *agent provocateur* is defined in *R v Mealey and Sheridan* [1974] 60 Cr App R 59 at 61, quoting the 1928 Royal Commission on Police Powers (Cmd 3297): 'a person who entices another to commit an express breach of the law which he would not otherwise have committed and then proceeds or informs against him in respect of such offence'. This sets the boundary of unacceptable behaviour.

But in also defining what was acceptable, the same judgment held that a person infiltrating a criminal organization, either as an undercover investigator or as a participating informant, must show a 'certain amount of interest and enthusiasm' for the proposed criminality in order to maintain their cover and render the infiltration tactic effective.

Teixeira de Castro v Portugal (1999) 28 EHRR 101 provides a clear example of investigators who went too far. Two undercover investigators posed as drug addicts and asked Teixeira to supply them with heroin. He had no heroin in his house, being a dealer in cannabis, but the investigators took him to another house and persuaded him to buy heroin there in order to sell it to the investigators. The Strasbourg court held that the investigators had incited the commission of an offence that would not otherwise have been committed.

The investigators in *R v Edwards* [1991] Crim LR 45 adopted a more passive role, making a test purchase which, far from being the isolated instigation argued by the defence, was demonstrably within the context of a wider pattern of drug dealing by the suspect.

Behaviour that similarly fell short of constituting incitement was confirmed in *R v Pattemore* [1994] Crim LR 836, in which the defendant had acquiesced with the requests of an informer. The court held there had been no pressure applied to the defendant and that fairness to the defence had to be balanced in this case by fairness to the public.

Specifically in relation to test purchase operations, *DPP v Marshall and Downes* [1988] Crim LR 750 established that the tactic itself was not deception just because investigators did not reveal their true identities. The tactic itself was reaffirmed as legitimate in *Borough of Ealing v Woolworths Plc* [1998] Crim LR 58, which also held that deploying an eleven-year-old boy to try to purchase products restricted to persons over eighteen years old was legitimate where the test purchaser had passively sought a purchase rather than actively tried to persuade the retailer.

Code para 4.29 makes it clear that where the individual undertaking a test purchase is not required to establish or maintain a relationship for that purpose, then the operation does not require RIPA authorization. An example might be a trading standards investigator purchasing retail items misleadingly labelled to prove that they were offered for sale. Where a test purchase operation is intended to demonstrate a pattern of drug dealing, invariably the undercover investigators will have to establish a relationship with the dealer in order to maintain their cover as a regular drugs user. Therefore such operations require the investigators to be authorized as CHISs.

....

Case law criteria establishing whether an informant has acted as an *agent provocateur*

(1) Was a crime of the same kind as that charged already afoot at the time of the intervention of the CHIS?
(2) Had the defendant committed an offence of a class which he would not have committed but for the encouragement of the CHIS?
(3) Had the defendants a propensity to engage in the crime charged?
(4) Did the CHIS play a major part in the criminal activity?
(5) Is the Court certain, in retrospect, of the CHIS's reliability?
(6) Was the CHIS's participation approved in accordance with the statutory regime?
(7) Is the offence so grave that the public interest could justify the use of such tactics?

Based on *R v Ameer and Lucas* [1977] Crim LR 104. The judgment in *R v Ameer and Lucas* was disapproved by *R v Sang* [1980] AC 402, at 430, but this seven-part test applied in the case still has relevance.

....

9.10.2 Entrapment

Closely connected to the problem of investigators acting as *agents provocateurs* is the issue of entrapment: investigators creating situations in which suspects commit offences that they would not otherwise have committed.

It is well established in English law that entrapment is no defence (*R v Sang* [1980] AC 402; *R v Smurthwaite and Gill* [1994] 1 All ER 898), but that does not release investigators from the obligation to act lawfully. If offenders take advantage of an opportunity to commit a crime and in doing so play a trick on themselves, then this is considered a lawful means of securing evidence. Hence *R v Christou and another* [1992] 4 All ER 559, in which the defendants sold stolen property to undercover police officers masquerading as second-hand property dealers in a shop. Police had established the shop for the very purpose of recovering stolen property from those willing to sell it. Another example is *Williams and another v DPP* [1993] 3 All ER 365, in which an insecure lorry containing dummy packets of cigarettes was parked unattended in a street, thus constituting a tethered-goat-type lure. Once again, those who took the opportunity to steal from the lorry were held to have played a trick on themselves.

In *Nottingham City Council v Amin* [2000] Crim LR 174, a taxi driver had agreed to take two special constables on duty in plain clothes to a specified area in the city for which they paid a fare. The taxi driver had no licence to ply for hire in that area. It was held that the police had a duty to enforce the law and that it was not offensive to provide an individual with an opportunity to commit a crime which had then been taken up. The defendant did not have to take advantage of the opportunity.

These should be viewed within the context of *R v Loosley* [2002] Crim LR 301, which reaffirmed that where the involvement of an accused was a direct result of incitement by an investigator, then the evidence should rightfully be excluded under s 78 PACE. But where the investigator had done no more than provide an opportunity for the accused to commit a crime, in exactly the same circumstances as another person might have provided such an opportunity (i.e. a test purchase investigator purporting to be a drug addict when trying to secure evidence of the accused's dealing), there was no reason why the evidence should be excluded, particularly if it was part of a properly authorized operation in which every effort had been made to secure corroboration through tape-recording.

9.10.3 Securing evidence

The extent to which undercover investigators can secure evidence by questioning those with whom they interact is constrained by the PACE Codes of Practice in relation to interviews. The Codes have been held to apply to interviews outside a police station or other custody centre (*R v Christou and another* [1992] 4 All ER 559).

In *R v Bryce* [1992] 4 All ER 567, investigators asked questions that were essentially evidential in nature and so constituted an unlawful interview. In *R v Christou and another* [1992] 4 All ER 559, the undercover officers had asked only such questions as were necessary to maintain their cover as second-hand property dealers.

In *Bryce* the conversations had not been tape-recorded, whereas in *Christou* they had been. Tape-recording such interactions ensures that there is an accurate and unassailable record of conversations between CHISs and suspects. Tape-recordings will demonstrate, for instance, that a conversation is an offence in the commission rather than a conversation about past events that constitutes an admission. The value of this was established in *R v Smurthwaite and Gill* [1994] 1 All ER 898, which also identified good-practice criteria for such recordings, reaffirmed in *R v Mann and Dixon* [1995] Crim LR 647, and in *R v Horseferry Road Magistrates Court ex p Bennett (No. 1)* (1994) 98 Cr App R 114.

....

Case law criteria for assessing fairness at trial where it is sought to exclude evidence from undercover operations

The Court will consider:

(1) Whether the CHIS acted as an *agent provocateur*
(2) The nature of any entrapment
(3) Whether the recorded evidence constitutes an offence in progress or an admission of an historical offence
(4) Whether the investigator's role in securing the evidence was active or passive
(5) Whether there is an unassailable record or robust corroboration of what occurred
(6) Whether the CHIS abused his role to ask questions that should have been put only under the PACE Codes.

Based on *R v Smurthwaite and Gill* [1994] 1 All ER 898.

....

9.10.4 **Protecting informants**

Case law going back as far as 1794 has established the principle that it is in the public interest to protect the identities of CHISs, unless to do so would deny a defendant the chance to establish innocence and thus lead to a miscarriage. As was seen in 2.6.2, the same principle was extended to the protection of observation points.

Further information and reading

The protection of informants. The historical precedent for the protection of the identity of police informants is to be found in: *Hardy's case* (1794) 24 St Tr 199; *AG v Bryant* (1846) 15 M&W 169; *Marks v Beyfus* [1890] 25 QBD 494; *D v NSPCC* [1978] AC 171; *R v Hennessy* (1979) 68 Cr App R 419; *R v Hallett and others* [1986] Crim LR 462; *R v Turner (Paul)* [1995] 2 Cr App R 94; *R v Pattemore* [1994] Crim LR 836.

Swinney and another v Chief Constable of Northumbria [1996] 3 All ER 449 affirmed that there was a general duty of care to take reasonable steps to avoid public disclosure of information provided by a CHIS.

Exceptional circumstances have proved this rule notwithstanding specific decisions. Hence *R v Agar* [1990] 2 All ER 442 established that where there were *specific, detailed* allegations of a set-up, the defence could ask investigators about their sources. This did not establish a disclosure precedent nor did it provide a vehicle for defence fishing-trips.

Savage v Chief Constable of Hampshire [1997] 2 All ER 631 held that an informant who chose to disclose his role could not be prevented from doing so on public policy grounds.

In relation to protecting CHISs through a Public Interest Immunity application, *R v H and C* [2004] 2 AC 134 confirms that neutral material or material damaging to the defendant need not be disclosed and should not, therefore, be brought to the attention of the court. Where a CHIS testifies at court (as envisaged in the Code para 1.9), it is legitimate for the defence to seek to ascertain the circumstances in which the CHIS was recruited, details of the assistance provided and the rewards made, and the motivation of the CHIS.

9.11 Good Practice in Light of the Above Case Law

The importance of precise and detailed documentation in relation to CHIS conduct cannot be overemphasized, particularly given the absence of specific statutory reference concerning infiltration and participation.

Where it is necessary to conduct directed surveillance of an individual to evaluate the potential benefit and risks involved in their deployment as a CHIS, this should be fully authorized.

The lawfulness of a CHIS's conduct will be contingent upon the extent to which the CHIS complies with the authorization. It follows that the authority itself must be precise and detailed with reasons given for each decision and direction. Conduct not specified in the authorization will not be lawful. The briefing of CHISs should be fully documented so as to demonstrate not only that the individual has been properly briefed but that the terms of reference are fully understood, particularly where infiltration or participation are being authorized.

Corroboration of information provided by a CHIS is crucial. For undercover or test purchase investigators this can be achieved through technical means (where it is safe for the investigator to wear a tape-recorder) or through other surveillance as appropriate. In relation to informants reporting on their encounters with criminal associates there will rarely be the opportunity to corroborate conversations during such interaction, and so their intelligence must be assessed accordingly and actions arising therefrom suitably risk-managed.

Similarly the debriefing of CHISs should be fully documented and adjustments made to their risk assessment or conduct authorization as required.

KEY POINTS FOR TEST PURCHASE OPERATIVES

(1) A test purchase investigator must not act as an *agent provocateur*. This means they must not incite or procure a person, or through that person anybody else, to commit an offence or an offence of a more serious character, which that person would not otherwise have committed.

(2) However, a test purchase officer is entitled to join a conspiracy which is already in being or an offence which is already laid on or, for example, where a person has made an offer to supply goods, including drugs, which involves the commission of a criminal offence.

(3) If, during the course of an investigation into an offence or series of offences, a person involved suggests the commission of, or offers to commit, a further similar offence, a test purchase officer is entitled to participate in the proposed offence. The investigator must not incite such an offence.

(4) It is proper for the test purchase investigator to show interest in, and enthusiasm for, proposals made even though they are unlawful, but in doing so they must try to tread the difficult line between showing the necessary interest and enthusiasm to keep their cover (and pursue their investigation) and actually becoming an *agent provocateur*. Invariably this means the investigator will enter a criminal conspiracy or become part of a pre-arranged criminal offence.

(5) Test purchase investigators must obtain confirmation that the information they are acting on is accurate and reliable before becoming involved in operations.

(6) Test purchase investigators must bear in mind that, by virtue of s 78 PACE, a judge may take into account the circumstances in which evidence was obtained in considering its adverse effect on the fairness of proceedings in court.

(7) Police officers must be fully conversant with Article 6 ECHR (right to fair trial) and Article 8 (right to respect for private and family life).

CHIS scenario

Mr Daniel, a local resident, has attended the police station in order to speak to his local community beat officer. Mr Daniel has identified what he believes is suspicious activity taking place in an address opposite where he lives. He has noted down a number of vehicle descriptions and registration numbers, along with descriptions of the vehicle occupants who have been visiting the house at various times of the day and night.

There is no need to register Mr Daniel as a CHIS. He is a resident in the street where he is passively collecting the information and no relationship is established or maintained with either the neighbour or road-users in order for him to do this (9.3).

If Mr Daniel were to go beyond the present actions and establish a relationship with the neighbour under suspicion, then he would have to be registered as a CHIS.

CHIS scenario

Investigators are carrying out a test purchase operation where conversations will be recorded in order to secure evidence of the criminal activity taking place.

Test purchase operations must be authorized as CHIS activity and the authority must cover not only the actions of the test purchase operatives as undercover officers but also directed surveillance (in the form of recorded conversations).

CHIS scenario

A registered CHIS has been tasked to obtain more detailed information of the activities of an individual identified by the CHIS as the person responsible for a spate of burglaries.

As long as any existing authority for *conduct* is appropriate for this tasking, then only a record of the tasking need be completed. However, if the authority does not include this type of activity, then a new *use* authority must be completed.

CHIS scenario

Alex Moore is currently in custody and has been identified to investigators as an individual who may be usefully recruited as a CHIS. For reasons of security it has been decided that the officers will follow Mr Moore once he is released from custody in order to approach him for the purposes of recruitment.

Surveillance to determine the suitability of an individual to be approached with a view to recruiting them as a CHIS is accepted as necessary in para 2.12 of the CHIS Code of Practice. A directed surveillance authority will be required in these circumstances.

CHIS scenario

Investigators wish to use a professional witness to pose as a tenant in order to gain evidence against alleged nuisance neighbours.

As the intention is to maintain a relationship in order to obtain information to be used as evidence, then a CHIS authority will be required. A directed surveillance authority will also be required for any recording of the evidence gathered.

CHIS scenario

Information suggests that a local shop owner is running their business in an unlawful manner. Investigators wish to deploy test purchase officers with recording equipment in order to collect evidence of the offences.

A CHIS authority would be required for the deployment of the test purchase officers. A directed surveillance authority is required for deployment of the recording of the test purchase.

If there was no requirement to establish a relationship and record conversations, and the test purchaser was doing no more than purchasing suspect goods displayed in the shop, then there would be no requirement to authorize this passive purchase as CHIS activity.

Further information and reading

- SI 2000/2725
  The Regulation of Investigatory Powers (Source Records) Regulations 2000
- SI 2000/2793
  The Regulation of Investigatory Powers (Juveniles) Order 2000
- SI 2005/1084
  The Regulation of Investigatory Powers (Directed Surveillance and Covert Human Intelligence Sources) (Amendment) Order 2005

(Reproduced in Appendix C)

Checklist of key issues when considering whether or not to deploy a CHIS

- What evidence or intelligence is being sought?

- How is it relevant to the operation under consideration?

- What is the least intrusive means of securing such evidence or information?

- What are the risks to the organization of such tactics? (Chapter 11)

- What are the risks to the organization's staff, especially the CHIS, of such tactics? (Chapter 11)

- What are the risks of the CHIS being compromised by another person? (Chapter 11)

- What are the risks of the CHIS compromising themselves? (Chapter 11)

- If the CHIS has compromised themselves, how are the additional risks going to be managed? (Chapter 11)

- What are the risks to the public or specific third parties, including the family and friends of the CHIS, when such tactics are deployed? (Chapter 11)

- What are the risks to the subject of the investigation? (Chapter 11)

- Will such methods breach Article 8(1)? (1.6.1)

- Is there justification for doing so provided by Article 8(2)? (1.6.4)

- How is the legality test met? (1.6.3)

- How is the legitimacy test met? (1.6.4)

- How is the necessity test met? (1.6.5)

- How is the proportionality test met? (1.6.5)

- Has the CHIS been properly trained as an undercover investigator?

- Has the CHIS been properly assessed, evaluated, briefed, and debriefed as a paid informant?

- Is the CHIS prepared to enter into the witness protection scheme if necessary?

- Is the organization prepared to provide the resources necessary to place the CHIS on the witness protection scheme?

- Are the arguments justifying the application to use covert investigation based on reliable information/intelligence, or has the applicant adopted a 'tick-the-box' approach to completing the application without giving full consideration to the facts of the case and the issues arising?

- Have the arguments justifying the granting of authorization to use covert investigation been fully articulated, or has the authorizing officer merely paid lip service to the pro forma authorization template via which authority is granted?

- How are the methods by which the evidence/intelligence will be obtained to be protected at trial?

Planning covert investigation actions

Remember to include the PLAN for covert investigation tactics in all investigation policy-book entries relating to covert investigation considerations and decisions.

P   PROPORTIONALITY
    Why is it proportionate to obtain the intended product of this surveillance in the manner proposed? (1.6.5)

L   LEGITIMACY
    What is the legitimate purpose of the proposed action: the prevention of disorder or crime; the interests of national security; the interests of public safety; the interests of the economic well-being of the country; the protection of health or morals; the protection of the rights and freedoms of others? (1.6.4)

A   AUTHORITY TO UNDERTAKE PROPOSED ACTION
    What is the lawful foundation and authority for the proposed action? From whom must authorization be sought? (1.6.3)

N   NECESSITY OF PROPOSED ACTION
    Why is the proposed action necessary? (1.6.5)

Flowchart for Authorizing CHIS Operations

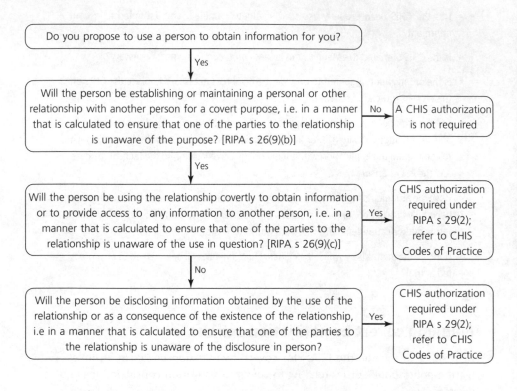

Do you propose to use a person to obtain information for you?

Yes

Will the person be establishing or maintaining a personal or other relationship with another person for a covert purpose, i.e. in a manner that is calculated to ensure that one of the parties to the relationship is unaware of the purpose? [RIPA s 26(9)(b)]

No → A CHIS authorization is not required

Yes

Will the person be using the relationship covertly to obtain information or to provide access to any information to another person, i.e. in a manner that is calculated to ensure that one of the parties to the relationship is unaware of the use in question? [RIPA s 26(9)(c)]

Yes → CHIS authorization required under RIPA s 29(2); refer to CHIS Codes of Practice

No

Will the person be disclosing information obtained by the use of the relationship or as a consequence of the existence of the relationship, i.e in a manner that is calculated to ensure that one of the parties to the relationship is unaware of the disclosure in person?

Yes → CHIS authorization required under RIPA s 29(2); refer to CHIS Codes of Practice

SPACE FOR NOTES

SPACE FOR NOTES

SPACE FOR NOTES

10

Covert Investigation
Abroad

10.1	Introduction	152
10.2	Which Public Authorities May Conduct Covert Investigation Abroad?	153
10.3	What Powers Does the Law Provide in Relation to Covert Investigation Abroad?	153
10.4	What Authority Regime Is Required for Covert Investigation Abroad?	156
10.5	What Significant Case Law Has Been Decided in Relation to Covert Investigation Abroad?	157
10.6	Sources of Advice	159

10.1 **Introduction**

Criminals have always utilized jurisdiction borders as a means of evading pro-secution or disrupting investigation. In the final quarter of the twentieth cen-tury, as global communications and transport networks became accessible to ever more people, it became easier to escape from a jurisdiction and easier to commit crime on a transnational scale, for instance the trafficking of illicit commodities from source countries to criminal markets overseas. To counter transnational criminality a corpus of instruments and conventions has been created to facilitate mutual legal assistance and international law enforcement co-operation: these are the means by which domestic investigators can secure help as required in their own investigations where evidence or the suspect is located outside their own jurisdiction.

Further information and reading

This is an area of increasing activity for investigators and lawyers alike. For legal commentary (together with the reproduction of some key legal instruments) see D McClean, *International Judicial Assistance* (Clarendon Press, Oxford, 1992); C Murray and L Harris, *Mutual Assistance in Criminal Matters* (Sweet & Maxwell, London, 2000); A Jones and A Doobay, *Jones and Doobay on Extradition and Mutual Assistance* (Sweet & Maxwell, London, 2005), 362–377. For a collection of key legal instruments, C Van den Wyngaert (ed), *International Criminal Law: A Collection of International and European Instruments* (3rd revd edn, Martinus Nijhoff, Leiden, 2005).

The term *transnational* (cross-border) is preferred here to *international* (be-tween states) because the latter term is used to qualify specific behaviours, instruments, and institutions in relation to international law that do not apply to the cross-border investigation of crimes proscribed in domestic jurisdictions. The International Criminal Court has permissive jurisdiction only over geno-cide, crimes against humanity, war crimes, and international aggression, not domestic crimes committed on a transnational scale (Statute of the Internation-al Court, Article 5 (Rome, 17 July 1998, UN Doc A/CONF 183/9) *International Legal Materials* 1998, 999; alternatively, Van den Wyngaert, *International Crim-inal Law*, 139, 140).

In the absence of an international or supranational criminal code, differ-ent domestic jurisdictions have to be able to work alongside each other in co-operation when criminality crosses their mutual border. This is the *raison d'être* of mutual legal assistance treaty law and the premise underpinning the new philosophy of mutual recognition now being promoted within the EU by the UK (*Hansard* HL (series 6) vol 411 col 973 (2 December 2003)).

10.2 **Which Public Authorities May Conduct Covert Investigation Abroad?**

Section 27(3) RIPA prescribes that surveillance authorized under s 26 can include 'conduct outside the United Kingdom'. In respect of directed or intrusive surveillance and the deployment of CHISs, those authorities empowered to conduct such investigations within the UK can also conduct such authorized activity abroad without offending UK law.

Part III PA97 limits the area of lawful authorization in relation to property interference to the relevant area overseen by the authorizing officer and, as appropriate, adjacent UK territorial waters (s 93).

Therefore relevant empowered investigators are as described in Chapters 2 and 8.

10.3 **What Powers Does the Law Provide in Relation to Covert Investigation Abroad?**

Section 27(3) RIPA prescribes that surveillance authorized under s 26 can include 'conduct outside the United Kingdom'. In respect of directed or intrusive surveillance and the deployment of CHISs, conduct that can be authorized within the UK can also be authorized to take place in a foreign jurisdiction without offending UK law. However, such activity may breach the domestic law of the foreign jurisdiction in which it is proposed to conduct surveillance.

Part III PA97 limits the area of lawful authorization in relation to property interference to the relevant area overseen by the authorizing officer and, as appropriate, adjacent UK territorial waters (s 93).

Therefore relevant investigation powers are as described in Chapters 2 and 8, taking into account the provisions of the foreign jurisdiction in which it is proposed to conduct the covert investigation.

Two international instruments make provision for international law enforcement covert investigation co-operation within the EU: the Schengen Convention 1990 (International Legal Materials 1991, 84) and the EU Convention on Mutual Assistance in Criminal Matters 2000, done 29 May 2000 Brussels, OJ 2000/C 197/1. The latter supplements the 1959 Convention on Mutual Assistance in Criminal Matters, which is open to Member States of the Council of Europe and not just EU members but which contains no specific provisions for covert investigation (European Treaty Series 30, done Strasbourg 20 April 1959).

Article 40 of the Schengen Convention provides for 'cross-border surveillance', where a person under surveillance and presumed to have taken part in a criminal offence to which extradition may apply (Article 40(7)) crosses the mutual border of two contracting parties to the Convention. If investigators in the requesting state have prior authorization to do so from the requested state which the suspect enters during the course of the surveillance, Article 40(1) permits the original investigators to continue their surveillance in the territory of the requested state, subject to any request to the requested state to assume responsibility for the surveillance. In spontaneous circumstances where it was not possible to seek prior authorization, surveillance may be continued for up to five hours in the territory of the requested state whilst authorization to continue the surveillance is sought from the requested state. Article 40(3)(f) expressly prohibits the domestic surveillance team operating in a foreign territory pursuant to this article from challenging or arresting the subject under surveillance whilst in the jurisdiction of another state. The UK entered into this Article of the Schengen Convention on 22 December 2004 (*Mutual Legal Assistance Newsletter 19*, UK Central Authority, February 2005), the obligations being given domestic effect in s 83 Crime (International Co-Operation) Act 2003 which creates new s 76A RIPA.

Article 40 can only be applied by police and customs investigators engaged on a criminal investigation. Although the government has repeatedly asserted that SOCA is not a police force (*Hansard* HC Standing Committee D, cols 9 and 34 (11 January 2005); see also cols 32, 33, 35, 38 and 43), SOCA will be designated as such to enable its staff to utilize Article 40. (Authorities designated for the purposes of Article 40 are listed in the *Schengen Handbook on Cross-Border Police Co-Operation*, OJL 239, 408, 22 September 2000.)

This provision is not to be confused with 'hot pursuit' permitted by Article 41 Schengen Convention, which is restricted to uniformed officers (or plainclothes officers clearly displaying visible insignia identifying them as police officers) pursuing a suspect fleeing the scene of a crime or escaping from custody across a land border. As the UK and Eire have not entered into this part of the Schengen Convention, hot pursuit is not permitted across the UK's only EU land border. Contracting parties and the law enforcement agencies permitted to use Articles 40 and 41 are listed in the Schengen Handbook.

Other covert investigation tactics may be permitted under Article 14 of the EU Mutual Legal Assistance Convention subject to the agreement of the requesting and requested states. Under this provision it is for the requested state to decide whether or not to implement the request for covert investigation put to it, having 'due regard to its national law and procedures'. The domestic law of the state in which the covert investigation takes place shall apply to the activities undertaken.

Article 13 EU Mutual Legal Assistance Convention makes provision for the establishment of multi-national joint investigation teams (JITs), members of which could apply for any such domestic covert or coercive measures within their own jurisdictions without recourse to mutual legal assistance procedures. Diplomatic negotiation is required to establish a JIT and advice should be sought from the Home Office Judicial Co-Operation Unit (Home Office Circulars 53/2002 and 26/2004 refer).

Further information and reading

Joint investigation teams are given a liability framework by ss 103 and 104 Police Reform Act 2002 and a statutory powers framework by ss 26(2)(b), 26(4)(b), 18(2), and 27(1) Crime (International Co-Operation) Act 2003. See also the EU Council Framework Decision of 13 June 2002 on Joint Investigation Teams (2002/465/JHA) OJ 2002/L 162/1 and the EU Commission Recommendation for a Model Agreement for setting up Joint Investigation Teams, 7 April 2003, CRIMORG 17, 7061/0. For UK government guidance on JITs, see Home Office Circulars 53/2002 and 26/2004.

In relation to non-EU states, the capability to request covert investigation assistance abroad will depend upon the nature of any mutual legal assistance treaty in force between the UK and the other state in question. On existing mutual legal assistance treaties and their provisions, advice should be sought from the UK Central Authority.

Further information and reading

The UK Central Authority is the single point of contact in England and Wales by which international letters of request (also known as *Commissions Rogatoires*) are transmitted and received. Information about the UK Central Authority and mutual legal assistance is contained on <http://www.homeoffice.gov.uk/crimpol/oic/mutuallegal/index.html>. In the event that this site does not contain an answer to the query raised, contact the UK Central Authority on +44 (0)20 7035 1280.

UK accession to the EU Mutual Legal Assistance Convention meant that provision had to be made for providing assistance in respect of communication interception notwithstanding the general prohibition on the use of intercepted communications as evidence in UK criminal trials (s 17 RIPA).

Section 1(4) RIPA permits UK investigators to request foreign interception of communications when three conditions are met: (1) where the UK is party to a designated international agreement which has come into force; (2) where the interception is being carried out for the purposes of a criminal investigation; and (3) where the investigation is being carried out in the territory of a state party to the designated agreement. The EU Mutual Legal Assistance Convention is the only such designated agreement at time of writing. (See Regulation of Investigatory Powers (Conditions for the Lawful Interception of Persons outside the UK) Regulations 2004, SI 2004/157; Regulation of Investigatory Powers (Designation of an International Agreement) Order 2004, SI 2004/158.)

Such requested intercepted communications could not be used in evidence in the UK by virtue of the prohibition in s 17 RIPA.

The reciprocal arrangement is provided under s 5(1)(c). The Secretary of State is able to stipulate that any communications intercepted in the UK and provided to foreign authorities should not be used in evidence abroad.

Further information and reading

It is useful to read the official record of parliamentary debates on these issues to understand the Government's position. See Caroline Flint, Parliamentary Under-Secretary of State for the Home Department (*Hansard* HC, Standing Committee D col 219 (18 January 2005)). The whole issue of interception evidence was debated during consideration of the Serious Organized Crime Bill (*Hansard* HC, Standing Committee D cols 205–224 (18 January 2005)). It was previously debated at length during the RIP Bill debates (*Hansard* HL (series 5) vol 613 cols 1407–1444 (12 June 2000)).

10.4 What Authority Regime Is Required for Covert Investigation Abroad?

The authority provided by s 27(3) RIPA is constrained by mutual legal assistance treaty law. An investigator cannot simply operate abroad on the basis of this RIPA sub-section alone.

Thus *in addition* to the authority regimes for directed and intrusive surveillance and the deployment of CHISs described in Chapters 2 and 8, *permission must be sought* from the foreign authorities in whose jurisdiction the surveillance is going to take place.

With the exception of circumstances provided for by Article 40 Schengen Convention, covert investigation abroad will normally be conducted on behalf of English investigators by the authorities in the requested state. This fact does not negate the need for a RIPA authority to be in place authorizing the covert investigation to take place.

Where the evidence required and to be obtained by covert investigation overseas is to be relied upon by the prosecution, in any cases of doubt about the need for a surveillance authority it is good practice to have a surveillance authority in place (OSC *Procedures and Guidance* 2005, para 4.39). Evidence derived from unauthorized covert investigation is vulnerable to exclusion from trial under s 78 PACE (arguments for which could be based on Articles 6 or 8 ECHR, as well as English case law).

Where a vehicle-tracking device is deployed and it is anticipated that the vehicle will travel through multiple national jurisdictions, a single authorization naming the different jurisdictions will suffice rather than a different authorization for each jurisdiction (OSC *Procedures and Guidance* 2005, para 3.33).

Where the work of a JIT will lead to trial in the UK and reliance therein on evidence from covert investigations undertaken by the JIT, the appropriate surveillance authority for the covert investigation will be required no matter where it took place. The establishment of a JIT does not negate the necessity of obtaining the appropriate surveillance authorities.

Where the subject of the covert investigation is neither a UK national nor likely to be the subject of criminal proceedings in the UK, and the conduct under investigation would neither affect a UK national nor give rise to material likely to be used in evidence before a UK court, it would appear in these specific circumstances (which might arise from a JIT investigation) that a RIPA authority would not be required (OSC *Procedures and Guidance* 2005, para 3.9).

In respect of interception of communications, the powers and authority regime (Secretary of State's warrant) are stipulated in s 1(4) RIPA.

10.5 What Significant Case Law Has Been Decided in Relation to Covert Investigation Abroad?

Further information and reading

For illuminating discussions of the various issues that can arise from gathering evidence abroad, including by means of covert investigation, see C Gane and M Mackarel 'The admissibility of evidence obtained from abroad into criminal proceedings: the interpretation of mutual legal assistance treaties and use of evidence irregularly obtained' 4 *European Journal of Crime, Criminal Law and Criminal Justice* (1996) 98–119.

Although it pre-dates RIPA, it nevertheless contains much pertinent consideration and comparative study of covert investigation principles within the context of mutual legal assistance.

The fact that evidence for use in an English trial has been obtained from abroad with the aid of a mutual legal assistance treaty does not guarantee its admissibility nor preclude any procedural challenge by the defence. The evidence may be subject to restrictions placed on its use by the requested state and cannot be used for any other purpose than was specified in the original request for assistance (s 9 Crime (International Co-Operation) Act 2003). Where evidence is relied upon both to secure a conviction and subsequently confiscate assets, both purposes should be articulated in the international letter of request (*R v Gooch (No. 1)* [1999] 1 Cr App R (S) 283).

Investigators must also beware of how evidence is perceived and used abroad when supplying covert investigation material gathered within the UK to requesting foreign jurisdictions. Criminal intelligence material supplied to foreign jurisdictions on an 'intelligence only' basis has, nevertheless and within the context of foreign evidential laws, legitimately been disclosed to the defendant (and in some cases also the press) before trial. Hence, for instance, 'evidence is unlimited in French law, when acts discovered by foreign judicial or police authorities are used in a French case, they are considered as information and are therefore subject to discussion during the arguments in the trial as to the facts of the case' (*Kamal Jain*, Appeal Court of Aix en Provence 4 May 1992, confirmed by the Cour de Cassation, Paris, 7 October 1993, case no. M92-83.707 D). Information that might normally and successfully be protected from disclosure at trial through PII applications in the UK may not be so protected abroad. In some jurisdictions, if it exists, it must be used at trial.

Further information and reading

For comparative studies on criminal procedure, including rules of evidence, in Belgium, England, France, Germany and Italy, see M Delmas-Marty and J Spencer (eds), *European Criminal Procedures* (Cambridge, Cambridge University Press, 2002).

Whether or not the contents of an international letter of request are disclosable is debatable. Confidentiality cannot be relied upon in mutual legal assistance. See Jones and Doobay, *Jones and Doobay on Extradition and Mutual Assistance*, 402. See also Murray and Harris, *Mutual Assistance in Criminal Matters*, 47.

Similarly CPIA disclosure issues can be complicated further when evidence from foreign jurisdiction is relied upon. With careful investigation planning and prior consultation with the appropriate prosecutor, such issues need not be prohibitively problematic.

Other case law guidance suggests that the discretion permitted the court under s 78 PACE extends to evidence sought to be adduced from abroad. Indeed, some authorities argue such discretion affords investigators the opportunity to engage in 'forum shopping' or 'process laundering'. Certainly the courts have held that violation of Article 8 ECHR will not automatically result in exclusion of the evidence obtained as a result, but investigators and the prosecution cannot rely upon that discretion as a means of by-passing prescribed procedure (*R v Governor of Pentonville Prison, ex p Chinoy* [1992] 1 All ER 317, following *R v Sang* [1979] 2 All ER 1222; *Khan v UK* (2001) 31 EHRR 45 supporting *R v Khan* [1997] AC 558). 'Fishing expeditions' have been criticized by courts and requests for covert investigation should be specific and closely founded upon the chain of evidence, although it is accepted that not all evidence obtained through mutual legal assistance will necessarily be relied on in court (*R v Secretary of State ex p Finninvest SpA* [1997] 1 WLR 743).

R v Aujla [1998] 2 Cr App R 16 highlights an anomaly in respect of intercepted communications evidence and mutual legal assistance. It was held that intercept products by a foreign jurisdiction that had already been adduced at trial in the Netherlands was admissible in an English trial because the prohibition on the use of intercept products as evidence in the UK (at the time prohibited under s 9 Interception of Communications Act 1985; a restriction subsequently preserved under s 17 RIPA) applied only to intercept products obtained in the UK. The prohibition on evidential use thus does not apply to intercept products obtained abroad by foreign authorities for their own purposes. This reasoning was affirmed by the House of Lords in *R v P (Telephone intercepts: Admissibility of Evidence)* [2001] 2 WLR 463.

10.6 Sources of Advice

Once it is clear that an investigation is likely to necessitate evidence or intelligence-gathering abroad and that such needs are likely to require the use of covert investigation methods, investigators will need to engage with a number of different agencies in order to achieve a successful outcome.

Failure to follow protocols in transnational investigation can lead to any or all of the following consequences: loss of or inability to access evidence; abandonment of investigation or prosecution; or, where investigators have operated unilaterally and without permission overseas, the arrest, conviction, and imprisonment abroad of the investigators concerned.

The numerous sources of specialist advice are listed in Table 10.1.

Further information and reading

The UK Central Authority is the single point of contact in England and Wales by which international letters of request (also known as *Commissions Rogatoires*) are transmitted and received. There is limited scope for direct transmission of requests with the EU. The latest list of states allowing direct transmission is held by the UK Central Authority. See <http://www.homeoffice.gov.uk/crimpol/oic/mutuallegal/index.html>.

The UK National Central Bureau of Interpol is currently hosted, at time of writing in 2005, by the National Criminal Intelligence Service, +44 (0)20 7238 8000, where it is co-located with the UK Europol Bureau. It is not yet certain where these bureaux will be located after the abolition of the NCIS on 31 March 2006, but it is likely to be within the new Serious Organized Crime Agency.

The first source of advice should be the prosecutor: is covert investigation abroad vital in achieving a successful conviction? The question is as much practical as legal.

For instance, some foreign jurisdictions do not permit their surveillance personnel to testify in court. Their evidence is adduced in the inquisitorial trial system by way of third-party report, a method prohibited by the hearsay rules in the adversarial court process. How foreign surveillance evidence might be adduced in an English court must inform the operational planning of the surveillance as such practicalities may limit the surveillance options available, although with UK adoption of Article 40 Schengen Convention this has become

**Table 10.1 Sources of guidance for investigators planning (covert)
investigations abroad**

Mutual legal assistance law	A Jones and A Doobay, *Jones and Doobay on Extradition and Mutual Assistance* (Sweet & Maxwell, London, 2005), ch 20
	Crown Prosecution Service (or equivalent prosecution authority)
	UK Central Authority, Home Office
Non-evidential foreign assistance	Europol (EU only)
	Interpol
Planning an international request	Crown Prosecution Service
	Eurojust
	European Judicial Network
	UK Central Authority
Drafting an international request	Crown Prosecution Service
	Eurojust
	UK Central Authority
Request transmission procedures	Crown Prosecution Service
	UK Central Authority
Joint investigation teams	Judicial Co-Operation Unit, Home Office
	Eurojust

less of a problem for English investigators within the EU. Prosecutors (supported by Eurojust) will be able to resolve such practicalities.

There are other factors for consideration. Is there a realistic prospect of conviction without the foreign evidence? Would a conviction for a different charge (which did not require foreign surveillance evidence) achieve the same reduction in harm? As the person whose role it is to present the evidence and case at court, the prosecutor is often as well positioned as an investigator, if not better positioned, to make such a determination.

Once the decision has been made in conjunction with a prosecutor to proceed with a request for covert surveillance to be conducted abroad, the advice of the other authorities listed in Table 10.1 should be sought. Because the prosecutor is pivotal in the management of investigations in many foreign jurisdictions, British investigators may find that foreign authorities will expect to deal with a British prosecutor rather than a British investigator.

Checklist of key considerations when planning covert investigation abroad

- What evidence or intelligence is being sought?

- How is it relevant to the operation under consideration?

- Is it absolutely necessary, in order to secure a conviction, to conduct covert investigation abroad?

- Would an alternative charge, not dependent upon foreign evidence, secure the same reduction in harm upon conviction (e.g. the same length of prison sentence as a conviction that relied upon the foreign evidence)?

- What is the advice of the prosecutor?

- What is the advice, if applicable, of Eurojust?

- What is the advice of Europol or Interpol?

- What is the least intrusive means of securing such evidence or information?

- What are the risks to the organization of such tactics? (Chapter 11)

- What are the risks to the organization's staff of such tactics? (Chapter 11)

- What are the risks to the British public, the foreign public, or specific third parties when such tactics are deployed? (Chapter 11)

- What are the political/diplomatic risks arising from this operation? (Chapter 11)

- What are the risks to the subject of the investigation? (Chapter 11)

- Will such methods breach Article 8(1)? (1.6.1)

- Is there justification for doing so provided by Article 8(2)? (1.6.4)

- How is the legality test met? (1.6.3)

- How is the legitimacy test met? (1.6.4)

- How is the necessity test met? (1.6.5)

- How is the proportionality test met? (1.6.5)

- Are the arguments justifying the application to use covert investigation based on reliable information/intelligence, or has the applicant adopted a 'tick-the-box' approach to completing the application without giving full consideration to the facts of the case and the issues arising?

- Have the arguments justifying the granting of authorization to use covert investigation been fully articulated, or has the authorizing officer merely paid lip service to the pro forma authorization template via which authority is granted?

- How are the methods by which the evidence/intelligence will be obtained to be protected at trial in the UK?

- If covert investigation product from the UK is to be used in a trial abroad how are the methods by which the evidence/intelligence will be obtained to be protected at trial overseas?

- What are the consequences of foreign authorities disclosing confidential intelligence or unused material supplied by British authorities?

- What risk management plan is in place to address these consequences?

Planning covert investigation actions

Remember to include the PLAN for covert investigation tactics in all investigation policy-book entries relating to covert investigation considerations and decisions.

P   PROPORTIONALITY
Why is it proportionate to obtain the intended product of this surveillance in the manner proposed? (1.6.5)

L   LEGITIMACY
What is the legitimate purpose of the proposed action: the prevention of disorder or crime; the interests of national security; the interests of public safety; the interests of the economic well-being of the country; the protection of health or morals; the protection of the rights and freedoms of others? (1.6.4)

A   AUTHORITY TO UNDERTAKE PROPOSED ACTION
What is the lawful foundation and authority for the proposed action? From whom must authorization be sought? (1.6.3)

N   NECESSITY OF PROPOSED ACTION
Why is the proposed action necessary? (1.6.5)

SPACE FOR NOTES

SPACE FOR NOTES

11

Risk Management

11.1	Introduction	166
11.2	What Positive Obligations Are Imposed on Investigators?	166
11.3	The Benefits of Good Risk Assessment	167
11.4	Identifying Risks and How to Manage Them: The Model Approach	168
11.5	The PPPLEM Model	169
11.6	Vulnerability and RARA	169
11.7	Conclusion	172

11.1 **Introduction**

Society today tends to be risk averse. The fear of compensation litigation looms large. But risks are everywhere and cannot be avoided. They exist on parallel continuums from low probability/high impact to high probability/low impact. They are inherent in every covert investigation and are multi-faceted. There is a growing literature on risk and policing risk, particularly in relation to the dangerousness of serious or serial offenders released on completion of sentence. Managing risk is a complex and developing subject and it is one that investigators and their managers conducting and supervising covert investigations have to consider when planning and executing such operations. It is helpful to have a framework withi which to make such considerations, and with which to identify appropriate risk control measures and so determine a risk management strategy. This chapter presents some models to use as such a framework.

11.2 **What Positive Obligations Are Imposed on Investigators?**

The failure to consider risks and apply an appropriate strategy constitutes negligence. In certain circumstances such omission goes beyond mere negligence. Court interpretations of Article 2 ECHR place upon public authorities the positive obligation to protect life. *Osman v UK* [1999] 1 FLR 193 illustrates this point (see also K Starmer, *European Human Rights Law* (Legal Action Group, London, 1999) 89–90, 199–200 for general discussion). A positive obligation was held to exist where 'the authorities knew or ought to have known at the time of the existence of a real and immediate risk to the life of an identified individual or individuals from the criminal acts of a third party and that they failed to take measures within the scope of their powers which, judged reasonably, might have been expected to avoid that risk' (*Osman v UK* [1999] 1 FLR 193, note 19 at para 116).

This general principle can be held to apply elsewhere even where positive obligations under ECHR do not apply: investigators and investigation managers should take reasonable measures to manage foreseeable risks. Application forms for covert investigation authority, both in paper form and in the various software versions commercially available, usually include pages or boxes that have to be completed to demonstrate that the applicant has identified the risks involved with the application and determined an appropriate risk management strategy. The risks anticipated and how they are managed might have a bearing on the necessity and proportionality arguments supporting the application. Experience has shown that risk assessments for covert investigation applications are not infrequently omitted altogether on initial submission. Those that are submitted are often inadequate. And even where a risk assessment is included on first submission, for subsequent reviews and renewals the assessment is almost never revised and is very often dispensed with a perfunctory 'no change'.

Surveillance conducted for covert investigation may not produce the intelligence anticipated nor the evidence sought, but the one guaranteed product of covert surveillance will be vital information with which to review the risk assessment.

At initial application risk assessments will be estimations. Investigators will identify what they think the risks of the operation might be and how these anticipated risks should be managed. Managers and authorizing officers will review such assessments from their own perspectives, considering any additional risks posed by the operation to the organization as a whole. Once a period of surveillance has been conducted information about risks will have been updated by default in one or more of three ways: new risks may have been identified; previously anticipated risks may now be discounted; or previously anticipated risks will have been confirmed. It is important that this information is captured and included in subsequent risk assessments on submission of investigation authority reviews and renewal applications.

Where initial surveillance has demonstrated that there are no additional risks to take into consideration, and none that can now be dismissed, and where there has been no compromise of staff or equipment, then this should be incorporated in the risk assessment attached to the review consideration or renewal application. It is not simply a case of stating 'no change'. What was previously an initial estimation is now supported by hard information. An initial estimation has become an informed evaluation. At the very least such a revised risk assessment should say: 'Following x hours/days of surveillance, no new risks associated with this operation have been identified. None of the previously identified risks can be discounted. There is no intelligence to indicate that staff or surveillance techniques deployed in this operation have been compromised. Therefore the current risk management plan remains valid.'

Risk management or reduction is as dynamic a process as is the manifestation of the risks themselves. It must be held under constant review. In some operations it will be so dynamic that the commanding officer will have undertaken several revised risk assessments during the course of any given phase of the operation, possibly within a very short space of time and with little or no opportunity to record the rationale at the time, in which case documenting the variation as soon as practicable after the event must suffice.

11.3 The Benefits of Good Risk Assessment

Some definitions at this stage will be helpful. *Risk* can be defined as the likelihood of an adverse harm occurring. This is not to be confused with a *threat*, which is the source of that harm. *Vulnerability* is the measurement of probability against impact. A *risk assessment* is the means by which the risks involved in an operation can be balanced against the benefits.

The relevance to covert investigation is to be found at a number of levels. Some operations involve physical danger to staff. All covert investigations run the risk of investigators acting unlawfully in the absence of effective management or in cases where enthusiasm exceeds knowledge and competence. Depending on particular community sensitivities, a clumsily managed operation might result in public disorder.

Particularly where an operation engages Article 8 rights, risk assessment helps validate the thinking of applicant and authorizing officer alike, producing the following benefits:

- professional, credible risk management/reduction processes
- reviews of working assumptions, taking into account changing risk circumstances
- a process for real-time decision-making amenable to subsequent review (either in an operational debrief or a subsequent public enquiry)
- reduction in the number of perverse decisions
- reduction in corporate/personal liability.

Lives have been lost, investigations irretrievably compromised, and careers irrevocably damaged through inadequate risk assessment.

11.4 Identifying Risks and How to Manage Them: The Model Approach

Structuring thinking around established conceptual models aids precise consideration of risk issues. From the police service, created by Deputy Assistant Commissioner John Grieve whilst serving with the Metropolitan Police Service, comes a useful model that helps an investigator and the manager to begin to identify risks associated with any given operation, often referred to as the '3 Ps L E M' model because of its acronym (PPPLEM) (see 11.5 below).

It is helpful to apply the PPPLEM model to all the different facets of risk, otherwise regarded as the different 'at risk' groups: risk to the organization, risk to staff and other resources engaged in the operation (including for this purpose technical equipment, remotely deployed CHISs and members of the public who allow their premises to be used as observation points), risk to the subject of the operation, and risk to third parties such as members of the public unconnected with the investigation but likely to be present in the surveillance arena.

Once risks have been identified, a determination has to be made on how to manage them. For this there is the RARA model (see 11.6 below), which can be used in conjunction with the vulnerability assessment.

The culmination of this consideration should be a structured risk management plan or risk reduction strategy for those risks, amongst the many identified, which are likely to cause the most harm. The use of models aids thinking for both applicants and authorizing officers and should thus facilitate a more succinct written assessment, ensuring that it does not become a bureaucratic nightmare that actually adds nothing of value to the investigation or its management.

Overarching the risk management plan or reduction strategy must be the assessment of how the identified risk control measures themselves might engage the ECHR rights of staff, investigation subject, and general public.

Although the investigator and manager have primary responsibility for risk assessment and management, on occasions they will need to draw upon expert advice when encountering specialist fields and techniques. For instance, experts from computer crime units will be best placed to advise on what sort of electronic footprints will be created when computers are used to conduct e-surveillance. Non-experts will not necessarily appreciate that there may be risks to be managed in specialist arenas.

11.5 The PPPLEM Model

The acronym translates as shown in Table 11.1.

The PPPLEM model, applied to the four risk groups, will help identify the risks inherent in any given operation. A matrix is a useful aid to complete the assessment, with the 'at risk' groups placed on the vertical axis and the PPPLEM elements placed along the horizontal axis (Table 11.2).

It may well be the case that not all the elements of the model apply to all the 'at risk' groups. Indeed, if there was something significant to say in each of the matrix boxes the proposed operation should probably be considered too risky! The advantage of using this model lies not only in helping structured consideration: it demonstrates and records the thought processes of investigators and managers alike and in this way saves the trouble involved in composing lengthy prose to make the same point. More detailed discussion can thus be saved for those risks identified through the vulnerability and RARA models as requiring particular management (see 11.6 below).

11.6 Vulnerability and RARA

Vulnerability, *probability versus impact*, can be measured as two scales of 1 to 10, one for each of probability and impact. Alternatively it can more simply be expressed in terms of 'high', 'medium', or 'low' set in a matrix, with one axis representing probability and the other impact (Table 11.3).

Table 11.1 The PPPLEM model for risk assessment

P—Police and community risks	Alternatively, public and organizational risks. In general terms: what are the risks to the organization within the community of engaging in this operation? Is there any general risk to/from the community at large? Adverse publicity? Public disorder possible? What are the risks to the organization from the investigation subject/staff/public at large? What are the risks to the community from the organization engaging in this operation? What are the risks to the community from the investigation subject? What are the risks to the community from the organization staff? What are the risks of not doing anything?
P—Physical risks	What are the physical risks to staff/subject/third parties? Organization premises or premises borrowed for the purpose?
P—Psychological risks	What are the psychological risks to staff/subject/third parties?
L—Legal risks	What are the legal risks to the organization? Its staff? The subject? Third parties?
E—Economic risks	What are the economic risks to the organization? Its staff? The subject? Third parties? The community? Cost of operation? Possible litigation claims?
M—Moral risks	What are the moral risks to the organization? Its staff? The subject? Third parties? Can the operation be justified morally as well as legally? Is there a danger that the very essence of the ECHR will be breached as well as the Article 8 rights in question? What are the risks of not doing anything?

Table 11.2 PPPLEM matrix

PPPLEM matrix	Police/ community	Physical	Psychological	Legal	Economic	Moral
Organization						
Staff						
Subject						
Third parties						

Table 11.3 Impact/probability matrix

High impact			
Medium impact			
Low impact			
Impact/probability matrix	Low probability	Medium probability	High probability

Greatest vulnerability, and therefore risk, will be inherent where the probability and impact are both high or where one is high and the other medium. These are the risks that require management or a reduction strategy (shaded areas in Table 11.3).

Risks that are both low in impact and low in probability need not concern the investigator, investigation manager, or authorizing officer too greatly.

Once the vulnerability factor has been identified risk management and reduction prioritization can be undertaken. For this the RARA model can be applied.

There are four strategies that can be adopted in relation to any given risk: *remove* it, *avoid* it, *reduce* it, *accept* it—hence RARA. This is a sliding scale of strategies. Preferably operations should be planned so as to remove all risks. This ideal world is rarely achievable, however. Changing tactics to achieve the same objective may afford a means of avoiding a risk. If the risk cannot be removed or avoided, then there may be measures that can be put in place to reduce the risk. There will be a number of risks that investigators will wish simply to accept. This might be because the risks have a low vulnerability factor: low probability/low impact.

Potential control measures aimed at reducing the likelihood or adverse consequences of any given risk may themselves have risks attached. It may not be possible, for instance, to deploy a full surveillance team to provide protective cover for the deployment of an undercover operative because the surveillance team itself would show out in the deployment arena. In such a case alternative means of providing protection and rescue for such operatives must be devised, or else the desired evidence or intelligence must be acquired by other means—a way of avoiding identified risks.

As with the PPPLEM model, the application of the RARA model in determining a risk management strategy and appropriate control measures illustrates and records the thought processes of the decision-takers based on available information at the time, and herein lies its value to investigators, managers, and authorizing officers.

11.7 **Conclusion**

Risk assessment depends upon having information that is as accurate as possible and as up-to-date as possible. Such information is to be found, in part, as a by-product of surveillance. If such information has not been recorded and assessments reviewed consequently reviewed, then individuals and organizations are vulnerable not only to the risks inherent in the investigation, but to the risk of being negligent.

There is always scope for the unforeseen to occur. Use of these models to aid risk management will not alter that truism. These models cannot accurately predict the future. They will help identify those risks that can reasonably be foreseen. They will help prioritize a risk management strategy according to whether any given risk can be removed, avoided, reduced, or accepted. The models must be utilized in conjunction with the latest available information and intelligence. In the event of something unforeseen occurring that leads to particularly adverse consequences, the documented use of these models may well determine whether the investigators and the organizations concerned had done everything that was reasonable in the circumstances or whether they are vulnerable to a civil claim based on negligence.

SPACE FOR NOTES

SPACE FOR NOTES

SPACE FOR NOTES

Appendix A
Relevant Extracts of Part III Police Act 1997 as Amended

Footnotes indicate where the Serious Organised Crime and Police Act 2005 will amend RIPA to accommodate the creation of SOCA and the abolition of the NCS and NCIS. Essentially, SOCA and its staff will assume the powers and functions of the NCS and NCIS and their staff. The text of this Act as originally enacted can be found at <http://www.opsi.gov.uk/acts/acts2005/20050015.htm>. Minor amendments are also prospectively made by the Constitutional Reform Act 2005 <http://www.opsi. gov.uk/acts/acts2005/20050004.htm> and by the Criminal Justice and Court Services Act <http://www.opsi.gov.uk/acts/acts2000/20000043.htm>.

The Commissioners

The Commissioners

91.—(1) The Prime Minister, after consultation with the Scottish Ministers, shall appoint for the purposes of this Part—
  (a) a Chief Commissioner, and
  (b) such number of other Commissioners as the Prime Minister thinks fit.
(2) The persons appointed under subsection (1) shall be persons who hold or have held high judicial office within the meaning of Part 3 of the Constitutional Reform Act 2005 or are or have been members of the Judicial Committee of the Privy Council.[1]
(3) Subject to subsections (4) to (7), each Commissioner shall hold and vacate office in accordance with the terms of his appointment.
(4) Each Commissioner shall be appointed for a term of three years.
(5) A person who ceases to be a Commissioner (otherwise than under subsection (7)) may be reappointed under this section.
(6) Subject to subsection (7), a Commissioner shall not be removed from office before the end of the term for which he is appointed unless—
  (a) a resolution approving his removal has been passed by each House of Parliament; and
  (b) a resolution approving his removal has been passed by the Scottish Parliament.
(7) A Commissioner may be removed from office by the Prime Minister if after his appointment—
  (a) a bankruptcy order is made against him or his estate is sequestrated or he makes a composition or arrangement with, or grants a trust deed for, his creditors;

---

[1] Prospectively amended by the Constitutional Reform Act 2005 Sch 17 Pt 2 para 27.

(b) a disqualification order under the Company Directors Disqualification Act 1986 or Part II of the Companies (Northern Ireland) Order 1989, or an order under section 429(2)(b) of the Insolvency Act 1986 (failure to pay under county court administration order), is made against him or his disqualification undertaking is accepted under section 7 or 8 of the Company Directors Disqualification Act 1986; or

(c) he is convicted in the United Kingdom, the Channel Islands or the Isle of Man of an offence and has passed on him a sentence of imprisonment (whether suspended or not).

(8) The Secretary of State shall pay to each Commissioner, other than a Commissioner carrying out functions as mentioned in subsection 8A, such allowances as the Secretary of State considers appropriate.

(8A) The Scottish Ministers shall pay to any Commissioner who carries out his functions under this Part wholly or mainly in Scotland such allowances as the Scottish Ministers consider appropriate.

(9) The Secretary of State shall, after consultation with the Chief Commissioner, and subject to the approval of the Treasury as to numbers, provide the Commissioners and any Assistant Surveillance Commissioners holding office under section 63 of the Regulation of Investigatory Powers Act 2000, other than any Commissioner carrying out functions as mentioned in subsection (9A), with such staff as the Secretary of State considers necessary for the discharge of their functions.

(9A) The Scottish Ministers shall, after consultation with the Chief Commissioner, provide any Commissioner who carries out his function wholly or mainly in Scotland with such staff as the Scottish Ministers consider necessary for the discharge of his functions.

(10) The decisions of the Chief Commissioner or, subject to sections 104 and 106, any other Commissioner (including decisions as to his jurisdiction) shall not be subject to appeal or liable to be questioned in any court.

Authorisations

Effect of authorisation under Part III

92. No entry on or interference with property or with wireless telegraphy shall be unlawful if it is authorised by an authorisation having effect under this Part.

Authorisations to interfere with property etc.

93.—(1) Where subsection (2) applies, an authorising officer may authorise—

(a) the taking of such action, in respect of such property in the relevant area, as he may specify, or

(ab) the taking of such action, falling within subsection (7A), in respect of property outside the relevant area, as he may specify, or

(b) the taking of such action in the relevant area as he may specify, in respect of wireless telegraphy.

(1A) The action falling within this subsection is action for maintaining or retrieving any equipment, apparatus or device, the placing or use of which in the relevant area has been authorised under this Part or Part II of the Regulation of Investigatory Powers Act 2000 or under any enactment contained in or made under an

Act of the Scottish Parliament which makes provision equivalent to that made by Part II of that Act of 2000.

(1B) Subsection (1) applies where the authorising officer is a customs officer with the omission of—

(a) the words 'in the relevant area', in each place where they occur; and

(b) paragraph (ab).[2]

(2) This subsection applies where the authorising officer believes—

(a) that it is necessary for the action specified to be taken on the ground that it is likely to be of substantial value in the prevention or detection of serious crime, and

(b) that the taking of the action is proportionate to what the action seeks to achieve.

(2A) Subsection 2 applies where the authorising officer is the Chief Constable or Deputy Chief Constable of the Police Service of Northern Ireland as if the reference in subsection (2)(a) to preventing or detecting serious crime included a reference to the interests of national security.

(2AA) Where the authorising officer is the chairman of the Office of Fair Trading, the only purpose falling within subsection (2)(a) is the purpose of preventing or detecting an offence under section 188 of the Enterprise Act 2002.

(2B) The matters to be taken into account in considering whether the requirements of subsection (2) are satisfied in the case of any authorisations shall include whether what it is thought necessary to achieve by the authorised action could reasonably be achieved by other means.

(3) An authorising officer shall not give an authorisation under this section except on an application made—

(a) if the authorising officer is within subsection (5)(a) to (ea) or (ee), by a member of his police force,

(aa) if the authorising officer is within subsection (5)(eb) to (ed), by a member, as the case may be, of the Royal Navy Regulating Branch, the Royal Military Police or the Royal Air Force Police,

(ab) if the authorising officer is within subsection (5)(ef), by a member of staff of the Independent Police Complaints Commission who has been designated under paragraph 19(2) of Schedule 3 to the Police Reform Act 2002,

(b) if the authorising officer is within subsection (5)(f), by a member of the National Criminal Intelligence Service,[3]

(c) if the authorising officer is within subsection (5)(g), by a member of the National Crime Squad,[4] or

(d) if the authorising officer is within subsection (5)(h), by a customs officer, or

(e) if the authorising officer is within subsection (5)(i), by an officer of the Office of Fair Trading.

(4) For the purposes of subsection (2), conduct which constitutes one or more offences shall be regarded as serious crime if, and only if,—

(a) it involves the use of violence, results in substantial financial gain or is conducted by a large number of persons in pursuit of a common purpose, or

---

[2] Prospectively amended by SOCAPA 2005 Sch 4 para 97(2).

[3] Prospectively amended by SOCAPA 2005 Sch 4 para 97(3).

[4] ibid.

(b) the offence or one of the offences is an offence for which a person who has attained the age of twenty-one and has no previous convictions could reasonably be expected to be sentenced to imprisonment for a term of three years or more,[5]

and, where the authorising officer is within subsection (5)(h), it relates to an assigned matter within the meaning of section 1(1) of the Customs and Excise Management Act 1979.

(5) In this section 'authorising officer' means—

(a) the chief constable of a police force maintained under section 2 of the Police Act 1996 (maintenance of police forces for areas in England and Wales except London);

(b) the Commissioner, or an Assistant Commissioner, of Police of the Metropolis;

(c) the Commissioner of Police for the City of London;

(d) the chief constable of a police force maintained under or by virtue of section 1 of the Police (Scotland) Act 1967 (maintenance of police forces for areas in Scotland);

(e) the Chief Constable or a Deputy Chief Constable of the Police Service of Northern Ireland;

(ea) the Chief Constable of the Ministry of Defence Police;

(eb) the Provost Marshal of the Royal Navy Regulating Branch;

(ec) the Provost Marshal of the Royal Military Police;

(ed) the Provost Marshal of the Royal Air Force Police;

(ee) the Chief Constable of the British Transport Police;

(ef) the Chairman of the Independent Police Complaints Commission;

(f) the Director General of the National Criminal Intelligence Service;[6]

(g) the Director General of the National Crime Squad; or any person holding the rank of assistant chief constable in that Squad who is designated for the purposes of this paragraph by that Director General; or[7]

(h) any customs officer designated by the Commissioners of Customs and Excise for the purposes of this paragraph; or

(i) the chairman of the Office of Fair Trading.

(6) In this section 'relevant area'—

(a) in relation to a person within paragraph (a), (b) or (c) of subsection (5), means the area in England and Wales for which his police force is maintained;

(b) in relation to a person within paragraph (d) of that subsection means the area in Scotland for which his police force is maintained;

(c) in relation to a person within paragraph (e) of that subsection, means Northern Ireland;

(ca) in relation to a person within paragraph (ea), means any place where, under section 2 of the Ministry of Defence Police Act 1987, the members of the Ministry of Defence Police have the powers and privileges of a constable;

(cb) in relation to a person within paragraph (ee), means the United Kingdom;

---

[5] Prospectively amended by the Criminal Justice and Court Services Act 2000 Sch 7 Pt II para 149.

[6] Prospectively amended by SOCAPA 2005 Sch 4 para 97(4).

[7] ibid.

(d) in relation to the Director General of the National Criminal Intelligence Service, means the United Kingdom;[8]

(e) in relation to the chairman of the Independent Police Complaints Commission or the Director General of the National Crime Squad, means England and Wales;[9]

and in each case includes the adjacent United Kingdom waters.

(6A) For the purposes of any authorisation by a person within paragraph (eb), (ec) or (ed) of subsection (5) property is in the relevant area or action in respect of wireless telegraphy is taken in the relevant area it, as the case may be—

(a) the property is owned, occupied, in the possession of or being used by a person subject to service discipline; or

(b) the action is taken in relation to the use of wireless telegraphy by such a person.

(6B) For the purposes of this section a person is subject to service discipline—

(a) in relation to the Royal Navy Regulating Branch, if he is subject to the Naval Discipline Act 1957 or is a civilian to whom Parts I and II of that Act for the time being apply by virtue of section 118 of that Act;

(b) in relation to the Royal Military Police, if he is subject to military law or is a civilian to whom Part II of the Army Act 1955 for the time being applies by virtue of section 209 of that Act; and

(c) in relation to the Royal Air Force Police, if he is subject to air force law or is a civilian to whom Parts I and II of the Air Force Act 1955 for the time being applies by virtue of section 209 of that Act.

(7) The powers conferred by, or by virtue of, this section are additional to any other powers which a person has as a constable either at common law or under or by virtue of any other enactment and are not to be taken to affect any of those other powers.

Authorisations given in absence of authorising officer

94.—(1) Subsection (2) applies where it is not reasonably practicable for an authorising officer to consider an application for an authorisation under section 93 and—

(a) if the authorising officer is within paragraph (b) or (e) of section 93(5), it is also not reasonably practicable for the application to be considered by any of the other persons within the paragraph concerned;[10]

(b) if the authorising officer is within paragraph (a), (c), (d), or (f) of section 93(5), it is also not reasonably practicable for the application to be considered by his designated deputy; or[11]

(c) if the authorising officer is within paragraph (g) of section 93(5), it is also not reasonably practicable for the application to be considered either—

(i) by any other person designated for the purposes of that paragraph; or

(ii) by the designated deputy of the Director General of the National Crime Squad.[12]

---

[8] Prospectively repealed by SOCAPA 2005 Sch 4 para 97(5) and Sch 17 Part II.

[9] ibid.

[10] Prospectively amended by SOCAPA 2005 Sch 4 para 98(2).

[11] ibid.

[12] Prospectively repealed by SOCAPA 2005 Sch 4 para 98(2) and Sch 17 Pt II.

(2) Where this subsection applies, the powers conferred on the authorising officer by section 93 may, in an urgent case, be exercised—

(a) where the authorising officer is within paragraph (a) or (d) of subsection (5) of that section, by a person holding the rank of assistant chief constable in his force;

(b) where the authorising officer is within paragraph (b) of that subsection, by a person holding the rank of commander in the metropolitan police force;

(c) where the authorising officer is within paragraph (c) of that subsection, by a person holding the rank of commander in the City of London police force;

(d) where the authorising officer is within paragraph (e) of that subsection, by a person holding the rank of assistant chief constable in the Police Service of Northern Ireland;

(da) where the authorising officer is within paragraph (ea) of that subsection, by a person holding the rank of deputy or assistant chief constable in the Ministry of Defence Police;

(db) where the authorising officer is within paragraph (eb) of that subsection, by a person holding the rank of assistant Provost Marshall of the Royal Navy Regulating Branch;

(dc) where the authorising officer is within paragraph (ec) or (ed) of that subsection, by a person holding the rank of deputy Provost Marshall in the Royal Military Police or, as the case may be, in the Royal Air Force Police;

(dd) where the authorising officer is within paragraph (ee) of that subsection, by a person holding the rank of deputy or assistant chief constable in the British Transport Police;

(de) where the authorising person is within paragraph (ef) of that subsection, by any other member of the Independent Police Complaints Commission;

(e) where the authorising officer is within paragraph (f) of that subsection by a person designated for the purposes of this section by the Director General of the National Criminal Intelligence Service or, as the case may be, of the National Crime Squad;[13]

(ea) where the authorising officer is within paragraph (g) of that subsection, by a person designated for the purposes of this paragraph by the Director General of the National Crime Squad as a person entitled to act in an urgent case;[14]

(f) where the authorising officer is within paragraph (h) of that subsection, by a customs officer designated by the Commissioners of Customs and Excise for the purposes of this section;

(g) where the authorising officer is within paragraph (i) of that subsection, by an officer of the Office of Fair Trading designated by it for the purposes of this section.

(3) A police member of the National Criminal Intelligence Service or the National Crime Squad appointed under section 9(1)(b) or 55(1)(b) may not be designated under subsection (2)(e) or 2(ea) unless he holds the rank of assistant chief constable in that Service or Squad.[15]

(4) In subsection (1), 'designated deputy'—

---

[13] Prospectively amended by SOCAPA 2005 Sch 4 para 98(3).

[14] ibid.

[15] Prospectively repealed by SOCAPA 2005 Sch 4 para 98(4) and Sch 17 Pt II.

(a) in the case of an authorising officer within paragraph (a) or (d) of section 93(5), means the person holding the rank of assistant chief constable designated to act in his absence under section 12(4) of the Police Act 1996 or, as the case may be, section 5(4) of the Police (Scotland) Act 1967;

(b) in the case of an authorising officer within paragraph (c) of section 93(5), means the person authorised to act in his absence under section 25 of the City of London Police Act 1839;

(c) in the case of an authorising officer within paragraph (f) or (g) of section 93(5), means the person designated to act under section 8 or 54;[16]

(d) in the case of an authorising officer within paragraph (ef) of section 93(5), means a person appointed as deputy chairman of the Independent Police Complaints Commission under paragraph 3(1) of Schedule 2 to the Police Reform Act 2002.

Authorisations: form and duration etc.

95.—(1) An authorisation shall be in writing, except that in an urgent case an authorisation (other than one given by virtue of section 94) may be given orally.

(2) An authorisation shall, unless renewed under subsection (3), cease to have effect—

(a) if given orally or by virtue of section 94, at the end of the period of 72 hours beginning with the time when it took effect;

(b) in any other case, at the end of the period of three months beginning with the day on which it took effect.

(3) If at any time before an authorisation would cease to have effect the authorising officer who gave the authorisation, or in whose absence it was given, considers it necessary for the authorisation to continue to have effect for the purpose for which it was issued, he may, in writing, renew it for a period of three months beginning with the day on which it would cease to have effect.

(4) A person shall cancel an authorisation given by him if satisfied that the authorisation is one in relation to which the requirements of paragraphs (a) and (b) of section 93(2) are no longer satisfied.

(5) An authorising officer shall cancel an authorisation given in his absence if satisfied that the authorisation is one in relation to which the requirements of paragraphs (a) and (b) of section 93(2) are no longer satisfied.

(6) If the authorising officer who gave the authorisation is within paragraph (b), (e) or (g) of section 93(5), the power conferred on that person by subsections (3) and (4) above shall also be exercisable by each of the other persons within the paragraph concerned.[17]

(7) Nothing in this section shall prevent a designated deputy from exercising the powers conferred on an authorising officer within paragraph (a), (c), (d), (ef), (f) or (g) of section 93(5) by subsections (3), (4) and (5) above.[18]

Notification of authorisations etc.

96.—(1) Where a person gives, renews or cancels an authorisation, he shall, as soon as is reasonably practicable and in accordance with arrangements made by the

---

[16] ibid.

[17] Prospectively amended by SOCAPA 2005 Sch 4 para 99.

[18] ibid.

Chief Commissioner, give notice in writing that he has done so to a Commissioner appointed under section 91(1)(b).

(2) Subject to subsection (3), a notice under this section shall specify such matters as the Secretary of State may by order prescribe.

(3) A notice under this section of the giving or renewal of an authorisation shall specify—

(a) whether section 97 applies to the authorisation or renewal, and

(b) where that section does not apply by virtue of subsection (3) of that section, the grounds on which the case is believed to be one of urgency.

(4) Where a notice is given to a Commissioner under this section, he shall, as soon as is reasonably practicable, scrutinise the notice.

(5) An order under subsection (2) shall be made by statutory instrument.

(6) A statutory instrument which contains an order under subsection (2) shall not be made unless a draft has been laid before, and approved by a resolution of, each House of Parliament.

Authorisations requiring approval

Authorisations requiring approval

97.—(1) An authorisation to which this section applies shall not take effect until—

(a) it has been approved in accordance with this section by a Commissioner appointed under section 91(1)(b), and

(b) the person who gave the authorisation has been notified under subsection (4).

(2) Subject to subsection (3), this section applies to an authorisation if, at the time it is given, the person who gives it believes—

(a) that any of the property specified in the authorisation—

(i) is used wholly or mainly as a dwelling or as a bedroom in a hotel, or

(ii) constitutes office premises, or

(b) that the action authorised by it is likely to result in any person acquiring knowledge of—

(i) matters subject to legal privilege,

(ii) confidential personal information, or

(iii) confidential journalistic material.

(3) This section does not apply to an authorisation where the person who gives it believes that the case is one of urgency.

(4) Where a Commissioner receives a notice under section 96 which specifies that this section applies to the authorisation, he shall as soon as is reasonably practicable—

(a) decide whether to approve the authorisation or refuse approval, and

(b) give written notice of his decision to the person who gave the authorisation.

(5) A Commissioner shall approve an authorisation if, and only if, he is satisfied that there are reasonable grounds for believing the matters specified in section 93(2).

(6) Where a Commissioner refuses to approve an authorisation, he shall, as soon as is reasonably practicable, make a report of his findings to the authorising officer who gave it or in whose absence it was given.

(6A) The reference in subsection (6) to the authorising officer who gave the authorisation or in whose absence it was given shall be construed, in the case of an authorisation given by or in the absence of a person within paragraph (b), (e) or (g) of section 93(5), as a reference to the Commissioner of Police, Chief Constable or, as the case may be, Director General mentioned in the paragraph concerned.[19]

(7) This section shall apply in relation to a renewal of an authorisation as it applies in relation to an authorisation (the references in subsection (2)(a) and (b) to the authorisation being construed as references to the authorisation renewed).

(8) In this section—

'office premises' has the meaning given in section 1(2) of the Offices, Shops and Railway Premises Act 1963;

'hotel' means premises used for the reception of guests who desire to sleep in the premises.

Matters subject to legal privilege

98.—(1) Subject to subsection (5) below, in section 97 'matters subject to legal privilege' means matters to which subsection (2), (3) or (4) below applies.

(2) This subsection applies to communications between a professional legal adviser and—

(a) his client, or

(b) any person representing his client,

which are made in connection with the giving of legal advice to the client.

(3) This subsection applies to communications—

(a) between a professional legal adviser and his client or any person representing his client, or

(b) between a professional legal adviser or his client or any such representative and any other person,

which are made in connection with or in contemplation of legal proceedings and for the purposes of such proceedings.

(4) This subsection applies to items enclosed with or referred to in communications of the kind mentioned in subsection (2) or (3) and made—

(a) in connection with the giving of legal advice, or

(b) in connection with or in contemplation of legal proceedings and for the purposes of such proceedings.

(5) For the purposes of section 97—

(a) communications and items are not matters subject to legal privilege when they are in the possession of a person who is not entitled to possession of them, and

(b) communications and items held, or oral communications made, with the intention of furthering a criminal purpose are not matters subject to legal privilege.

Confidential personal information

99.—(1) In section 97 'confidential personal information' means—

(a) personal information which a person has acquired or created in the course of any trade, business, profession or other occupation or for the purposes of any paid or unpaid office, and which he holds in confidence, and

---

[19] Prospectively amended and new (6B) inserted by SOCAPA 2005 Sch 4 para 100.

(b) communications as a result of which personal information—

    (i)   is acquired or created as mentioned in paragraph (a), and

    (ii) is held in confidence.

(2) For the purposes of this section 'personal information' means information concerning an individual (whether living or dead) who can be identified from it and relating—

  (a) to his physical or mental health, or

  (b) to spiritual counselling or assistance given or to be given to him.

(3) A person holds information in confidence for the purposes of this section if he holds it subject—

  (a) to an express or implied undertaking to hold it in confidence, or

  (b) to a restriction on disclosure or an obligation of secrecy contained in any enactment (including an enactment contained in an Act passed after this Act).

Confidential journalistic material

100.—(1) In section 97 'confidential journalistic material' means—

  (a) material acquired or created for the purposes of journalism which—

    (i)   is in the possession of persons who acquired or created it for those purposes,

    (ii) is held subject to an undertaking, restriction or obligation of the kind mentioned in section 99(3), and

    (iii) has been continuously held (by one or more persons) subject to such an undertaking, restriction or obligation since it was first acquired or created for the purposes of journalism, and

  (b) communications as a result of which information is acquired for the purposes of journalism and held as mentioned in paragraph (a)(ii).

(2) For the purposes of subsection (1), a person who receives material, or acquires information, from someone who intends that the recipient shall use it for the purposes of journalism is to be taken to have acquired it for those purposes.

Code of Practice

Code of practice

101.—[repealed]

Complaints etc.

Complaints

102.—[repealed]

Quashing of authorisations etc.

103.—(1) Where, at any time, a Commissioner appointed under section 91(1)(b) is satisfied that, at the time an authorisation was given or renewed, there were no reasonable grounds for believing the matters specified in section 93(2), he may quash the authorisation or, as the case may be, renewal.

(2) Where, in the case of an authorisation or renewal to which section 97 does not apply, a Commissioner appointed under section 91(1)(b) is at any time satisfied that, at the time the authorisation was given or, as the case may be, renewed,—

   (a) there were reasonable grounds for believing any of the matters specified in subsection (2) of section 97, and

   (b) there were no reasonable grounds for believing the case to be one of urgency for the purposes of subsection (3) of that section,

he may quash the authorisation or, as the case may be, renewal.

(3) Where a Commissioner quashes an authorisation or renewal under subsection (1) or (2), he may order the destruction of any records relating to information obtained by virtue of the authorisation (or, in the case of a renewal, relating wholly or partly to information so obtained after the renewal) other than records required for pending criminal or civil proceedings.

(4) If a Commissioner appointed under section 91(1)(b) is satisfied that, at any time after an authorisation was given or, in the case of an authorisation renewed under section 95, after it was renewed, there were no reasonable grounds for believing the matters specified in section 93(2), he may cancel the authorisation.

(5) Where—

   (a) an authorisation has ceased to have effect (otherwise than by virtue of subsection (1) or (2)), and

   (b) a Commissioner appointed under section 91(1)(b) is satisfied that, at any time during the period of the authorisation, there were no reasonable grounds for believing the matters specified in section 93(2),

he may order the destruction of any records relating, wholly or partly, to information which was obtained by virtue of the authorisation after that time (other than records required for pending criminal or civil proceedings).

(6) Where a Commissioner exercises his powers under subsection (1), (2) or (4), he shall, if he is satisfied that there are reasonable grounds for doing so, order that the authorisation shall be effective, for such period as he shall specify, so far as it authorises the taking of action to retrieve anything left on property in accordance with the authorisation.

(7) Where a Commissioner exercises a power conferred by this section, he shall, as soon as is reasonably practicable, make a report of his findings—

   (a) to the authorising officer who gave the authorisation or in whose absence it was given, and

   (b) to the Chief Commissioner;

and subsection (6A) of section 97 shall apply for the purposes of this subsection as it applies for the purposes of subsection (6) of that section.

(8) Where—

   (a) a decision is made under subsection (1) or (2) and an order for the destruction of records is made under subsection (3), or

   (b) a decision to order the destruction of records is made under subsection (5),

the order shall not become operative until the period for appealing against the decision has expired and, where an appeal is made, a decision dismissing it has been made by the Chief Commissioner.

(9) A Commissioner may exercise any of the powers conferred by this section notwithstanding any approval given under section 97.

Appeals

Appeals by authorising officers

104.—(1) An authorising officer who gives an authorisation, or in whose absence it is given, may, within the prescribed period, appeal to the Chief Commissioner against—

(a) any refusal to approve the authorisation or any renewal of it under section 97;

(b) any decision to quash the authorisation, or any renewal of it, under subsection (1) of section 103;

(c) any decision to quash the authorisation, or any renewal of it, under subsection (2) of that section;

(d) any decision to cancel the authorisation under subsection (4) of that section;

(e) any decision to order the destruction of records under subsection (5) of that section;

(f) any refusal to make an order under subsection (6) of that section.

(2) In subsection (1), 'the prescribed period' means the period of seven days beginning with the day on which the refusal, decision or, as the case may be, determination appealed against is reported to the authorising officer.

(3) In determining an appeal within subsection (1)(a), the Chief Commissioner shall, if he is satisfied that there are reasonable grounds for believing the matters specified in section 93(2), allow the appeal and direct the Commissioner to approve the authorisation or renewal under that section.

(4) In determining—

(a) an appeal within subsection (1)(b),

the Chief Commissioner shall allow the appeal unless he is satisfied that, at the time the authorisation was given or, as the case may be, renewed there were no reasonable grounds for believing the matters specified in section 93(2).

(5) In determining—

(a) an appeal within subsection (1)(c),

the Chief Commissioner shall allow the appeal unless he is satisfied as mentioned in section 103(2).

(6) In determining—

(a) an appeal within subsection (1)(d) or (e),

the Chief Commissioner shall allow the appeal unless he is satisfied that at the time to which the decision relates there were no reasonable grounds for believing the matters specified in section 93(2).

(7) In determining an appeal within subsection (1)(f), the Chief Commissioner shall allow the appeal and order that the authorisation shall be effective to the extent mentioned in section 103(6), for such period as he shall specify, if he is satisfied that there are reasonable grounds for making such an order.

(8) Where an appeal is allowed under this section, the Chief Commissioner shall—

(a) in the case of an appeal within subsection (1)(b) or (c), also quash any order made by the Commissioner to destroy records relating to information obtained by virtue of the authorisation concerned.

Appeals by authorising officers: supplementary

105.—(1) Where the Chief Commissioner determines an appeal under section 104—

(a) he shall give notice of his determination—

    (i)   to the authorising officer concerned, and

    (ii) to the Commissioner against whose refusal, decision or determination the appeal was made,

(b) if he dismisses the appeal, he shall make a report of his findings—

    (i)   to the authorising officer concerned,

    (ii) to the Commissioner against whose refusal, decision or determination the appeal was made, and

    (iii) under section 107(2), to the Prime Minister, and the Scottish Ministers.

(2) Subject to subsection (1)(b), the Chief Commissioner shall not give any reasons for a determination under section 104.

(3) Nothing in section 104 shall prevent a designated deputy from exercising the powers conferred by subsection (1) of that section on an authorising officer within paragraph (a), (c), (d), (ef), (f) or (g) of section 93(5).[20]

Appeals by complainants

106.—[repealed]

General

Supplementary provisions relating to Commissioners

107.—(1) The Chief Commissioner shall keep under review the performance of functions under this Part.

(2) The Chief Commissioner shall make an annual report on the matters with which he is concerned to the Prime Minister and to the Scottish Ministers and may at any time report to him or them (as the case may require) on anything relating to any of those matters.

(3) The Prime Minister shall lay before each House of Parliament a copy of each annual report made by the Chief Commissioner under subsection (2), together with a statement as to whether any matter has been excluded from that copy in pursuance of subsection (4) below.

(3A) The Scottish Ministers shall lay before the Scottish Parliament a copy of each annual report made by the Chief Commissioner under subsection (2), together with a statement as to whether any matter has been excluded from that copy in pursuance of subsection (4) below.

(4) The Prime Minister may exclude a matter from the copy of a report as laid before each House of Parliament, if it appears to him, after consultation with the Chief Commissioner and the Scottish Ministers, that the publication of that matter in the report would be prejudicial to any of the purposes for which authorisations may be given or granted under this Part of this Act or Part II of the Regulation of Investigatory Powers Act 2000 or under any enactment contained in or made under an Act of the Scottish Parliament which makes provision equivalent to that made by Part II of that Act of 2000 to the discharge of—

(a) the functions of any police authority,

---

[20] Prospectively amended by SOCAPA 2005 Sch 4 para 101.

(aa) the functions of the Independent Police Complaints Commission;

(b) the functions of the Service Authority for the National Criminal Intelligence Service or the Service Authority for the National Crime Squad, or[21]

(c) the duties of the Commissioners of Customs and Excise.

(5) Any person having functions under this Part, and any person taking action in relation to which an authorisation was given, shall comply with any request of a Commissioner for documents or information required by him for the purpose of enabling him to discharge his functions.

(5A) It shall be the duty of—

(a) every person by whom, or on whose application, there has been given or granted any authorisation the function of giving or granting which is subject to review by the Chief Commissioner,

(b) every person who has engaged in conduct with the authority of such an authorisation,

(c) every person who holds or has held any office, rank or position with the same public authority as a person falling within paragraph (a),

(d) every person who holds or has held any office, rank or position with any public authority for whose benefit (within the meaning of Part II of the Regulation of Investigatory Powers Act 2000) activities which are or may be carried out, and

(e) every person to whom a notice under section 49 of the Regulation of Investigatory Powers Act 2000 (notices imposing a disclosure requirement in respect of information protected by a key) has been given in relation to any information obtained by conduct to which such an authorisation relates,

to disclose or provide to the Chief Commissioner all such documents and information as he may require for the purpose of enabling him to carry out his functions.

(5B) It shall be the duty of every Commissioner to give the tribunal established under section 65 of the Regulation of Investigatory Powers Act 2000 all such assistance (including his opinion as to any issue falling to be determined by that tribunal) as that tribunal may require—

(a) in connection with the investigation of any matter by that tribunal; or

(b) otherwise for the purposes of that tribunal's consideration or determination of any matter.

(5C) In this section 'public authority' means any public authority within the meaning of section 6 of the Human Rights Act 1998 (acts of public authorities) other than a court or tribunal.

Interpretation of Part III

108.—(1) In this Part—

'Assistant Commissioner of Police of the Metropolis' includes the Deputy Commissioner of Police of the Metropolis;

'authorisation' means an authorisation under section 93;

'authorising officer' has the meaning given by section 93(5);

'criminal proceedings' includes—

---

[21] Prospectively amended by SOCAPA 2005 Sch 4 para 102.

(a) proceedings in the United Kingdom or elsewhere before a court-martial constituted under the Army Act 1955, the Air Force Act 1955 or the Naval Discipline Act 1957,

(b) proceedings before the Courts-Martial Appeal Court, and

(c) proceedings before a Standing Civilian Court;

'customs officer' means an officer commissioned by the Commissioners of Customs and Excise under section 6(3) of the Customs and Excise Management Act 1979;

'designated deputy' has the meaning given in section 94(4);

'United Kingdom waters' has the meaning given in section 30(5) of the Police Act 1996; and

'wireless telegraphy' has the same meaning as in the Wireless Telegraphy Act 1949 and, in relation to wireless telegraphy, 'interfere' has the same meaning as in that Act.

(2) Where, under this Part, notice of any matter is required to be given in writing, the notice may be transmitted by electronic means.

(3) For the purposes of this Part, an authorisation (or renewal) given—

(a) by the designated deputy of an authorising officer, or

(b) by a person on whom an authorising officer's powers are conferred by section 94,

shall be treated as an authorisation (or renewal) given in the absence of the authorising officer concerned; and references to the authorising officer in whose absence an authorisation (or renewal) was given shall be construed accordingly.

Appendix B
Extracts from the Regulation of Investigatory Powers Act 2000 as Amended

Footnotes indicate where the Serious Organised Crime and Police Act 2005 will amend RIPA to accommodate the creation of SOCA and the abolition of the NCS and NCIS. Essentially, SOCA and its staff will assume the powers and functions of the NCS and NCIS and their staff. The text of this Act as originally enacted can be found at <http://www.opsi.gov.uk/acts/acts2005/20050015.htm>.

PART I

COMMUNICATIONS

CHAPTER I

INTERCEPTION

Unlawful and authorised interception

Unlawful interception

1.—(1) It shall be an offence for a person intentionally and without lawful authority to intercept, at any place in the United Kingdom, any communication in the course of its transmission by means of–

(a) a public postal service; or

(b) a public telecommunication system.

(2) It shall be an offence for a person–

(a) intentionally and without lawful authority, and

(b) otherwise than in circumstances in which his conduct is excluded by sub-section (6) from criminal liability under this subsection,

to intercept, at any place in the United Kingdom, any communication in the course of its transmission by means of a private telecommunication system.

(3) Any interception of a communication which is carried out at any place in the United Kingdom by, or with the express or implied consent of, a person having the right to control the operation or the use of a private telecommunication system shall be actionable at the suit or instance of the sender or recipient, or intended recipient, of the communication if it is without lawful authority and is either–

(a) an interception of that communication in the course of its transmission by means of that private system; or

(b) an interception of that communication in the course of its transmission, by means of a public telecommunication system, to or from apparatus comprised in that private telecommunication system.

(4) Where the United Kingdom is a party to an international agreement which–
    (a) relates to the provision of mutual assistance in connection with, or in the form of, the interception of communications,
    (b) requires the issue of a warrant, order or equivalent instrument in cases in which assistance is given, and
    (c) is designated for the purposes of this subsection by an order made by the Secretary of State,
it shall be the duty of the Secretary of State to secure that no request for assistance in accordance with the agreement is made on behalf of a person in the United Kingdom to the competent authorities of a country or territory outside the United Kingdom except with lawful authority.

(5) Conduct has lawful authority for the purposes of this section if, and only if,–
    (a) it is authorised by or under section 3 or 4;
    (b) it takes place in accordance with a warrant under section 5 ('an interception warrant'); or
    (c) it is in exercise, in relation to any stored communication, of any statutory power that is exercised (apart from this section) for the purpose of obtaining information or of taking possession of any document or other property;
and conduct (whether or not prohibited by this section) which has lawful authority for the purposes of this section by virtue of paragraph (a) or (b) shall also be taken to be lawful for all other purposes.

(6) The circumstances in which a person makes an interception of a communication in the course of its transmission by means of a private telecommunication system are such that his conduct is excluded from criminal liability under subsection (2) if–
    (a) he is a person with a right to control the operation or the use of the system; or
    (b) he has the express or implied consent of such a person to make the interception.

(7) A person who is guilty of an offence under subsection (1) or (2) shall be liable–
    (a) on conviction on indictment, to imprisonment for a term not exceeding two years or to a fine, or to both;
    (b) on summary conviction, to a fine not exceeding the statutory maximum.

(8) No proceedings for any offence which is an offence by virtue of this section shall be instituted–
    (a) in England and Wales, except by or with the consent of the Director of Public Prosecutions;
    (b) in Northern Ireland, except by or with the consent of the Director of Public Prosecutions for Northern Ireland.

Meaning and location of 'interception' etc.

2.—(1) In this Act–
    'postal service' means any service which–
    (a) consists in the following, or in any one or more of them, namely, the collection, sorting, conveyance, distribution and delivery (whether in the United Kingdom or elsewhere) of postal items; and
    (b) is offered or provided as a service the main purpose of which, or one of the main purposes of which, is to make available, or to facilitate, a means

of transmission from place to place of postal items containing communications;

'private telecommunication system' means any telecommunication system which, without itself being a public telecommunication system, is a system in relation to which the following conditions are satisfied–

(a) it is attached, directly or indirectly and whether or not for the purposes of the communication in question, to a public telecommunication system; and

(b) there is apparatus comprised in the system which is both located in the United Kingdom and used (with or without other apparatus) for making the attachment to the public telecommunication system;

'public postal service' means any postal service which is offered or provided to, or to a substantial section of, the public in any one or more parts of the United Kingdom;

'public telecommunications service' means any telecommunications service which is offered or provided to, or to a substantial section of, the public in any one or more parts of the United Kingdom;

'public telecommunication system' means any such parts of a telecommunication system by means of which any public telecommunications service is provided as are located in the United Kingdom;

'telecommunications service' means any service that consists in the provision of access to, and of facilities for making use of, any telecommunication system (whether or not one provided by the person providing the service); and

'telecommunication system' means any system (including the apparatus comprised in it) which exists (whether wholly or partly in the United Kingdom or elsewhere) for the purpose of facilitating the transmission of communications by any means involving the use of electrical or electro-magnetic energy.

(2) For the purposes of this Act, but subject to the following provisions of this section, a person intercepts a communication in the course of its transmission by means of a telecommunication system if, and only if, he–

(a) so modifies or interferes with the system, or its operation,

(b) so monitors transmissions made by means of the system, or

(c) so monitors transmissions made by wireless telegraphy to or from apparatus comprised in the system,

as to make some or all of the contents of the communication available, while being transmitted, to a person other than the sender or intended recipient of the communication.

(3) References in this Act to the interception of a communication do not include references to the interception of any communication broadcast for general reception.

(4) For the purposes of this Act the interception of a communication takes place in the United Kingdom if, and only if, the modification, interference or monitoring or, in the case of a postal item, the interception is effected by conduct within the United Kingdom and the communication is either–

(a) intercepted in the course of its transmission by means of a public postal service or public telecommunication system; or

    (b) intercepted in the course of its transmission by means of a private telecommunication system in a case in which the sender or intended recipient of the communication is in the United Kingdom.

(5) References in this Act to the interception of a communication in the course of its transmission by means of a postal service or telecommunication system do not include references to–

    (a) any conduct that takes place in relation only to so much of the communication as consists in any traffic data comprised in or attached to a communication (whether by the sender or otherwise) for the purposes of any postal service or telecommunication system by means of which it is being or may be transmitted; or

    (b) any such conduct, in connection with conduct falling within paragraph (a), as gives a person who is neither the sender nor the intended recipient only so much access to a communication as is necessary for the purpose of identifying traffic data so comprised or attached.

(6) For the purposes of this section references to the modification of a telecommunication system include references to the attachment of any apparatus to, or other modification of or interference with–

    (a) any part of the system; or

    (b) any wireless telegraphy apparatus used for making transmissions to or from apparatus comprised in the system.

(7) For the purposes of this section the times while a communication is being transmitted by means of a telecommunication system shall be taken to include any time when the system by means of which the communication is being, or has been, transmitted is used for storing it in a manner that enables the intended recipient to collect it or otherwise to have access to it.

(8) For the purposes of this section the cases in which any contents of a communication are to be taken to be made available to a person while being transmitted shall include any case in which any of the contents of the communication, while being transmitted, are diverted or recorded so as to be available to a person subsequently.

(9) In this section 'traffic data', in relation to any communication, means–

    (a) any data identifying, or purporting to identify, any person, apparatus or location to or from which the communication is or may be transmitted,

    (b) any data identifying or selecting, or purporting to identify or select, apparatus through which, or by means of which, the communication is or may be transmitted,

    (c) any data comprising signals for the actuation of apparatus used for the purposes of a telecommunication system for effecting (in whole or in part) the transmission of any communication, and

    (d) any data identifying the data or other data as data comprised in or attached to a particular communication,

but that expression includes data identifying a computer file or computer program access to which is obtained, or which is run, by means of the communication to the extent only that the file or program is identified by reference to the apparatus in which it is stored.

(10) In this section–

    (a) references, in relation to traffic data comprising signals for the actuation of apparatus, to a telecommunication system by means of which a communication is being or may be transmitted include references to any telecommunication system in which that apparatus is comprised; and

    (b) references to traffic data being attached to a communication include references to the data and the communication being logically associated with each other;

and in this section 'data', in relation to a postal item, means anything written on the outside of the item.

(11) In this section 'postal item' means any letter, postcard or other such thing in writing as may be used by the sender for imparting information to the recipient, or any packet or parcel.

Lawful interception without an interception warrant

3.—(1) Conduct by any person consisting in the interception of a communication is authorised by this section if the communication is one which, or which that person has reasonable grounds for believing, is both

    (a) a communication sent by a person who has consented to the interception; and

    (b) a communication the intended recipient of which has so consented.

(2) Conduct by any person consisting in the interception of a communication is authorised by this section if–

    (a) the communication is one sent by, or intended for, a person who has consented to the interception; and

    (b) surveillance by means of that interception has been authorised under Part II.

(3) Conduct consisting in the interception of a communication is authorised by this section if–

    (a) it is conduct by or on behalf of a person who provides a postal service or a telecommunications service; and

    (b) it takes place for purposes connected with the provision or operation of that service or with the enforcement, in relation to that service, of any enactment relating to the use of postal services or telecommunications services.

(4) Conduct by any person consisting in the interception of a communication in the course of its transmission by means of wireless telegraphy is authorised by this section if it takes place–

    (a) with the authority of a designated person under section 5 of the Wireless Telegraphy Act 1949 (misleading messages and interception and disclosure of wireless telegraphy messages); and

    (b) for purposes connected with anything falling within subsection (5).

(5) Each of the following falls within this subsection–

    (a) the issue of licences under the Wireless Telegraphy Act 1949;

    (b) the prevention or detection of anything which constitutes interference with wireless telegraphy; and

    (c) the enforcement of any enactment contained in that Act or of any enactment not so contained that relates to such interference.

Power to provide for lawful interception

4.—(1) Conduct by any person ('the interceptor') consisting in the interception of a communication in the course of its transmission by means of a telecommunication system is authorised by this section if–

(a) the interception is carried out for the purpose of obtaining information about the communications of a person who, or who the interceptor has reasonable grounds for believing, is in a country or territory outside the United Kingdom;

(b) the interception relates to the use of a telecommunications service provided to persons in that country or territory which is either–

   (i) a public telecommunications service; or

   (ii) a telecommunications service that would be a public telecommunications service if the persons to whom it is offered or provided were members of the public in a part of the United Kingdom;

(c) the person who provides that service (whether the interceptor or another person) is required by the law of that country or territory to carry out, secure or facilitate the interception in question;

(d) the situation is one in relation to which such further conditions as may be prescribed by regulations made by the Secretary of State are required to be satisfied before conduct may be treated as authorised by virtue of this subsection; and

(e) the conditions so prescribed are satisfied in relation to that situation.

(2) Subject to subsection (3), the Secretary of State may by regulations authorise any such conduct described in the regulations as appears to him to constitute a legitimate practice reasonably required for the purpose, in connection with the carrying on of any business, of monitoring or keeping a record of–

(a) communications by means of which transactions are entered into in the course of that business; or

(b) other communications relating to that business or taking place in the course of its being carried on.

(3) Nothing in any regulations under subsection (2) shall authorise the interception of any communication except in the course of its transmission using apparatus or services provided by or to the person carrying on the business for use wholly or partly in connection with that business.

(4) Conduct taking place in a prison is authorised by this section if it is conduct in exercise of any power conferred by or under any rules made under section 47 of the Prison Act 1952, section 39 of the Prisons (Scotland) Act 1989 or section 13 of the Prison Act (Northern Ireland) 1953 (prison rules).

(5) Conduct taking place in any hospital premises where high security psychiatric services are provided is authorised by this section if it is conduct in pursuance of, and in accordance with, any direction given under section 17 of the National Health Service Act 1977 (directions as to the carrying out of their functions by health bodies) to the body providing those services at those premises.

(6) Conduct taking place in a state hospital is authorised by this section if it is conduct in pursuance of, and in accordance with, any direction given to the State Hospitals Board for Scotland under section 2(5) of the National Health Service

(Scotland) Act 1978 (regulations and directions as to the exercise of their functions by health boards) as applied by Article 5(1) of and the Schedule to The State Hospitals Board for Scotland Order 1995 (which applies certain provisions of that Act of 1978 to the State Hospitals Board).

(7) In this section references to a business include references to any activities of a government department, of any public authority or of any person or office holder on whom functions are conferred by or under any enactment.

(8) In this section—

'government department' includes any part of the Scottish Administration, a Northern Ireland department and the National Assembly for Wales;

'high security psychiatric services' has the same meaning as in the National Health Service Act 1977;

'hospital premises' has the same meaning as in section 4(3) of that Act; and

'state hospital' has the same meaning as in the National Health Service (Scotland) Act 1978.

(9) In this section 'prison' means—

(a) any prison, young offender institution, young offenders centre or remand centre which is under the general superintendence of, or is provided by, the Secretary of State under the Prison Act 1952 or the Prison Act (Northern Ireland) 1953, or

(b) any prison, young offenders institution or remand centre which is under the general superintendence of the Scottish Ministers under the Prisons (Scotland) Act 1989,

and includes any contracted out prison, within the meaning of Part IV of the Criminal Justice Act 1991 or section 106(4) of the Criminal Justice and Public Order Act 1994, and any legalised police cells within the meaning of section 14 of the Prisons (Scotland) Act 1989.

Interception with a warrant

5.—(1) Subject to the following provisions of this Chapter, the Secretary of State may issue a warrant authorising or requiring the person to whom it is addressed, by any such conduct as may be described in the warrant, to secure any one or more of the following—

(a) the interception in the course of their transmission by means of a postal service or telecommunication system of the communications described in the warrant;

(b) the making, in accordance with an international mutual assistance agreement, of a request for the provision of such assistance in connection with, or in the form of, an interception of communications as may be so described;

(c) the provision, in accordance with an international mutual assistance agreement, to the competent authorities of a country or territory outside the United Kingdom of any such assistance in connection with, or in the form of, an interception of communications as may be so described;

(d) the disclosure, in such manner as may be so described, of intercepted material obtained by any interception authorised or required by the warrant, and of related communications data.

(2) The Secretary of State shall not issue an interception warrant unless he believes—

(a) that the warrant is necessary on grounds falling within subsection (3); and

    (b) that the conduct authorised by the warrant is proportionate to what is sought to be achieved by that conduct.

(3) Subject to the following provisions of this section, a warrant is necessary on grounds falling within this subsection if it is necessary–

    (a) in the interests of national security;

    (b) for the purpose of preventing or detecting serious crime;

    (c) for the purpose of safeguarding the economic well-being of the United Kingdom; or

    (d) for the purpose, in circumstances appearing to the Secretary of State to be equivalent to those in which he would issue a warrant by virtue of paragraph (b), of giving effect to the provisions of any international mutual assistance agreement.

(4) The matters to be taken into account in considering whether the requirements of subsection (2) are satisfied in the case of any warrant shall include whether the information which it is thought necessary to obtain under the warrant could reasonably be obtained by other means.

(5) A warrant shall not be considered necessary on the ground falling within subsection (3)(c) unless the information which it is thought necessary to obtain is information relating to the acts or intentions of persons outside the British Islands.

(6) The conduct authorised by an interception warrant shall be taken to include–

    (a) all such conduct (including the interception of communications not identified by the warrant) as it is necessary to undertake in order to do what is expressly authorised or required by the warrant;

    (b) conduct for obtaining related communications data; and

    (c) conduct by any person which is conduct in pursuance of a requirement imposed by or on behalf of the person to whom the warrant is addressed to be provided with assistance with giving effect to the warrant.

Interception warrants

Application for issue of an interception warrant

6.—(1) An interception warrant shall not be issued except on an application made by or on behalf of a person specified in subsection (2).

(2) Those persons are–

    (a) the Director General of the Security Service;

    (b) the Chief of the Secret Intelligence Service;

    (c) the Director of GCHQ;

    (d) the Director General of the National Criminal Intelligence Service;[1]

    (e) the Commissioner of Police of the Metropolis;

    (f) the Chief Constable of the Police Service of Northern Ireland;

    (g) the chief constable of any police force maintained under or by virtue of section 1 of the Police (Scotland) Act 1967;

    (h) the Commissioners of Customs and Excise;

    (i) the Chief of Defence Intelligence;

---

[1] Prospectively amended by SOCAPA 2005 Sch 4 para 132.

(j) a person who, for the purposes of any international mutual assistance agreement, is the competent authority of a country or territory outside the United Kingdom.

(3) An application for the issue of an interception warrant shall not be made on behalf of a person specified in subsection (2) except by a person holding office under the Crown.[2]

Issue of warrants

7.—(1) An interception warrant shall not be issued except–

(a) under the hand of the Secretary of State or, in the case of a warrant issued by the Scottish Ministers (by virtue of provision made under section 63 of the Scotland Act 1998), a member of the Scottish Executive; or

(b) in a case falling within subsection (2), under the hand of a senior official; or

(c) in a case falling within subsection (2) (aa), under the hand of a member of the staff of the Scottish Administration who is a member of the Senior Civil Service and who is designated by the Scottish Ministers as a person under whose hand a warrant may be issued in such a case.

(2) Those cases are–

(a) an urgent case in which the Secretary of State has himself expressly authorised the issue of the warrant in that case; and

(aa) an urgent case in which the Scottish Ministers have themselves (by virtue of provision made under section 63 of the Scotland Act 1998) expressly authorised the use of the warrant in that case and a statement of that fact is endorsed on the warrant; and

(b) a case in which the warrant is for the purposes of a request for assistance made under an international mutual assistance agreement by the competent authorities of a country or territory outside the United Kingdom and either–

(i) it appears that the interception subject is outside the United Kingdom; or

(ii) the interception to which the warrant relates is to take place in relation only to premises outside the United Kingdom.

(3) An interception warrant–

(a) must be addressed to the person falling within section 6(2) by whom, or on whose behalf, the application for the warrant was made; and

(b) in the case of a warrant issued under the hand of a senior official, must contain, according to whatever is applicable–

(i) one of the statements set out in subsection (4); and

(ii) if it contains the statement set out in subsection (4)(b), one of the statements set out in subsection (5).

(4) The statements referred to in subsection (3)(b)(i) are–

(a) a statement that the case is an urgent case in which the Secretary of State has himself expressly authorised the issue of the warrant;

(b) a statement that the warrant is issued for the purposes of a request for assistance made under an international mutual assistance agreement by the competent authorities of a country or territory outside the United Kingdom.

(5) The statements referred to in subsection (3)(b)(ii) are–

---

[2] ibid.

(a) a statement that the interception subject appears to be outside the United Kingdom;

(b) a statement that the interception to which the warrant relates is to take place in relation only to premises outside the United Kingdom.

Contents of warrants

8.—(1) An interception warrant must name or describe either–

(a) one person as the interception subject; or

(b) a single set of premises as the premises in relation to which the interception to which the warrant relates is to take place.

(2) The provisions of an interception warrant describing communications the interception of which is authorised or required by the warrant must comprise one or more schedules setting out the addresses, numbers, apparatus or other factors, or combination of factors, that are to be used for identifying the communications that may be or are to be intercepted.

(3) Any factor or combination of factors set out in accordance with subsection (2) must be one that identifies communications which are likely to be or to include–

(a) communications from, or intended for, the person named or described in the warrant in accordance with subsection (1); or

(b) communications originating on, or intended for transmission to, the premises so named or described.

(4) Subsections (1) and (2) shall not apply to an interception warrant if–

(a) the description of communications to which the warrant relates confines the conduct authorised or required by the warrant to conduct falling within subsection (5); and

(b) at the time of the issue of the warrant, a certificate applicable to the warrant has been issued by the Secretary of State certifying–

(i) the descriptions of intercepted material the examination of which he considers necessary; and

(ii) that he considers the examination of material of those descriptions necessary as mentioned in section 5(3)(a), (b) or (c).

(5) Conduct falls within this subsection if it consists in–

(a) the interception of external communications in the course of their transmission by means of a telecommunication system; and

(b) any conduct authorised in relation to any such interception by section 5(6).

(6) A certificate for the purposes of subsection (4) shall not be issued except under the hand of the Secretary of State.

Duration, cancellation and renewal of warrants

9.—(1) An interception warrant–

(a) shall cease to have effect at the end of the relevant period; but

(b) may be renewed, at any time before the end of that period, by an instrument under the hand of the Secretary of State or, in the case of a warrant issued by the Scottish Ministers (by virtue of provision made under section 63 of the Scotland Act 1998), a member of the Scottish Executive or, in a case falling within section 7(2)(b), under the hand of a senior official.

(2) An interception warrant shall not be renewed under subsection (1) unless the Secretary of State believes that the warrant continues to be necessary on grounds falling within section 5(3).

(3) The Secretary of State shall cancel an interception warrant if he is satisfied that the warrant is no longer necessary on grounds falling within section 5(3).

(4) The Secretary of State shall cancel an interception warrant if, at any time before the end of the relevant period, he is satisfied in a case in which–

    (a) the warrant is one which was issued containing the statement set out in section 7(5)(a) or has been renewed by an instrument containing the statement set out in subsection (5)(b)(i) of this section, and

    (b) the latest renewal (if any) of the warrant is not a renewal by an instrument under the hand of the Secretary of State,

that the person named or described in the warrant as the interception subject is in the United Kingdom.

(5) An instrument under the hand of a senior official that renews an interception warrant must contain–

    (a) a statement that the renewal is for the purposes of a request for assistance made under an international mutual assistance agreement by the competent authorities of a country or territory outside the United Kingdom; and

    (b) whichever of the following statements is applicable–

        (i) a statement that the interception subject appears to be outside the United Kingdom;

        (ii) a statement that the interception to which the warrant relates is to take place in relation only to premises outside the United Kingdom.

(6) In this section 'the relevant period'–

    (a) in relation to an unrenewed warrant issued in a case falling within section 7(2)(a) under the hand of a senior official, means the period ending with the fifth working day following the day of the warrant's issue;

    (b) in relation to a renewed warrant the latest renewal of which was by an instrument endorsed under the hand of the Secretary of State with a statement that the renewal is believed to be necessary on grounds falling within section 5(3)(a) or (c), means the period of six months beginning with the day of the warrant's renewal; and

    (c) in all other cases, means the period of three months beginning with the day of the warrant's issue or, in the case of a warrant that has been renewed, of its latest renewal.

Modification of warrants and certificates

10.—(1) The Secretary of State may at any time–

    (a) modify the provisions of an interception warrant; or

    (b) modify a section 8(4) certificate so as to include in the certified material any material the examination of which he considers to be necessary as mentioned in section 5(3)(a), (b) or (c).

(2) If at any time the Secretary of State considers that any factor set out in a schedule to an interception warrant is no longer relevant for identifying communications which, in the case of that warrant, are likely to be or to include communications falling within section 8(3)(a) or (b), it shall be his duty to modify the warrant by the deletion of that factor.

(3) If at any time the Secretary of State considers that the material certified by a section 8(4) certificate includes any material the examination of which is no longer necessary as mentioned in any of paragraphs (a) to (c) of section 5(3), he shall modify the certificate so as to exclude that material from the certified material.

(4) Subject to subsections (5) to (8), a warrant or certificate shall not be modified under this section except by an instrument under the hand of the Secretary of State or of a senior official.

(4A) Subject to subsections (5A), (6) and (8), a warrant issued by the Scottish Ministers (by virtue of provision made under section 63 of the Scotland Act 1998) shall not be modified under this section except by an instrument under the hand of a member of the Scottish Executive or a member of the staff of the Scottish Administration who is a member of the Senior Civil Service and is designated by the Scottish Ministers as a person under whose hand an instrument may be issued in such a case (in this section referred to as 'a designated official').

(5) Unscheduled parts of an interception warrant shall not be modified under the hand of a senior official except in an urgent case in which–
(a) the Secretary of State has himself expressly authorised the modification; and
(b) a statement of that fact is endorsed on the modifying instrument.

(5A) Unscheduled parts of an interception warrant issued by the Scottish Ministers shall not be modified under the hand of a designated official except in an urgent case in which–
(a) they have themselves (by virtue of provision made under section 63 of the Scotland Act 1998) expressly authorised the modification; and
(b) a statement of that fact is endorsed on the modifying instrument.

(6) Subsection (4) shall not authorise the making under the hand of either–
(a) the person to whom the warrant is addressed, or
(b) any person holding a position subordinate to that person,
of any modification of any scheduled parts of an interception warrant.

(7) A section 8(4) certificate shall not be modified under the hand of a senior official except in an urgent case in which–
(a) the official in question holds a position in respect of which he is expressly authorised by provisions contained in the certificate to modify the certificate on the Secretary of State's behalf; or
(b) the Secretary of State has himself expressly authorised the modification and a statement of that fact is endorsed on the modifying instrument.

(8) Where modifications in accordance with this subsection are expressly authorised by provision contained in the warrant, the scheduled parts of an interception warrant may, in an urgent case, be modified by an instrument under the hand of–
(a) the person to whom the warrant is addressed; or
(b) a person holding any such position subordinate to that person as may be identified in the provisions of the warrant.

(9) Where–
(a) a warrant or certificate is modified by an instrument under the hand of a person other than the Secretary of State, and

(b) a statement for the purposes of subsection (5)(b) or (7)(b) is endorsed on the instrument, or the modification is made under subsection (8),

that modification shall cease to have effect at the end of the fifth working day following the day of the instrument's issue.

(10) For the purposes of this section—

(a) the scheduled parts of an interception warrant are any provisions of the warrant that are contained in a schedule of identifying factors comprised in the warrant for the purposes of section 8(2); and

(b) the modifications that are modifications of the scheduled parts of an interception warrant include the insertion of an additional such schedule in the warrant;

and references in this section to unscheduled parts of an interception warrant, and to their modification, shall be construed accordingly.

Implementation of warrants

11.—(1) Effect may be given to an interception warrant either—

(a) by the person to whom it is addressed; or

(b) by that person acting through, or together with, such other persons as he may require (whether under subsection (2) or otherwise) to provide him with assistance with giving effect to the warrant.

(2) For the purpose of requiring any person to provide assistance in relation to an interception warrant the person to whom it is addressed may—

(a) serve a copy of the warrant on such persons as he considers may be able to provide such assistance; or

(b) make arrangements under which a copy of it is to be or may be so served.

(3) The copy of an interception warrant that is served on any person under subsection (2) may, to the extent authorised—

(a) by the person to whom the warrant is addressed, or

(b) by the arrangements made by him for the purposes of that subsection,

omit any one or more of the schedules to the warrant.

(4) Where a copy of an interception warrant has been served by or on behalf of the person to whom it is addressed on—

(a) a person who provides a postal service,

(b) a person who provides a public telecommunications service, or

(c) a person not falling within paragraph (b) who has control of the whole or any part of a telecommunication system located wholly or partly in the United Kingdom,

it shall (subject to subsection (5)) be the duty of that person to take all such steps for giving effect to the warrant as are notified to him by or on behalf of the person to whom the warrant is addressed.

(5) A person who is under a duty by virtue of subsection (4) to take steps for giving effect to a warrant shall not be required to take any steps which it is not reasonably practicable for him to take.

(6) For the purposes of subsection (5) the steps which it is reasonably practicable for a person to take in a case in which obligations have been imposed on him by or under section 12 shall include every step which it would have been reasonably practicable for him to take had he complied with all the obligations so imposed on him.

(7) A person who knowingly fails to comply with his duty under subsection (4) shall be guilty of an offence and liable–

    (a) on conviction on indictment, to imprisonment for a term not exceeding two years or to a fine, or to both;

    (b) on summary conviction, to imprisonment for a term not exceeding six months or to a fine not exceeding the statutory maximum, or to both.

(8) A person's duty under subsection (4) to take steps for giving effect to a warrant shall be enforceable by civil proceedings by the Secretary of State for an injunction, or for specific performance of a statutory duty under section 45 of the Court of Session Act 1988, or for any other appropriate relief.

(9) For the purposes of this Act the provision of assistance with giving effect to an interception warrant includes any disclosure to the person to whom the warrant is addressed, or to persons acting on his behalf, of intercepted material obtained by any interception authorised or required by the warrant, and of any related communications data.

Interception capability and costs

Maintenance of interception capability

12.—(1) The Secretary of State may by order provide for the imposition by him on persons who–

    (a) are providing public postal services or public telecommunications services, or

    (b) are proposing to do so,

of such obligations as it appears to him reasonable to impose for the purpose of securing that it is and remains practicable for requirements to provide assistance in relation to interception warrants to be imposed and complied with.

(2) The Secretary of State's power to impose the obligations provided for by an order under this section shall be exercisable by the giving, in accordance with the order, of a notice requiring the person who is to be subject to the obligations to take all such steps as may be specified or described in the notice.

(3) Subject to subsection (11), the only steps that may be specified or described in a notice given to a person under subsection (2) are steps appearing to the Secretary of State to be necessary for securing that that person has the practical capability of providing any assistance which he may be required to provide in relation to relevant interception warrants.

(4) A person shall not be liable to have an obligation imposed on him in accordance with an order under this section by reason only that he provides, or is proposing to provide, to members of the public a telecommunications service the provision of which is or, as the case may be, will be no more than–

    (a) the means by which he provides a service which is not a telecommunications service; or

    (b) necessarily incidental to the provision by him of a service which is not a telecommunications service.

(5) Where a notice is given to any person under subsection (2) and otherwise than by virtue of subsection (6)(c), that person may, before the end of such period as may be specified in an order under this section, refer the notice to the Technical Advisory Board.

(6) Where a notice given to any person under subsection (2) is referred to the Technical Advisory Board under subsection (5)–

(a) there shall be no requirement for that person to comply, except in pursuance of a notice under paragraph (c)(ii), with any obligations imposed by the notice;

(b) the Board shall consider the technical requirements and the financial consequences, for the person making the reference, of the notice referred to them and shall report their conclusions on those matters to that person and to the Secretary of State; and

(c) the Secretary of State, after considering any report of the Board relating to the notice, may either–

(i) withdraw the notice; or

(ii) give a further notice under subsection (2) confirming its effect, with or without modifications.

(7) It shall be the duty of a person to whom a notice is given under subsection (2) to comply with the notice; and that duty shall be enforceable by civil proceedings by the Secretary of State for an injunction, or for specific performance of a statutory duty under section 45 of the Court of Session Act 1988, or for any other appropriate relief.

(8) A notice for the purposes of subsection (2) must specify such period as appears to the Secretary of State to be reasonable as the period within which the steps specified or described in the notice are to be taken.

(9) Before making an order under this section the Secretary of State shall consult with–

(a) such persons appearing to him to be likely to be subject to the obligations for which it provides,

(b) the Technical Advisory Board,

(c) such persons representing persons falling within paragraph (a), and

(d) such persons with statutory functions in relation to persons falling within that paragraph, as he considers appropriate.

(10) The Secretary of State shall not make an order under this section unless a draft of the order has been laid before Parliament and approved by a resolution of each House.

(11) For the purposes of this section the question whether a person has the practical capability of providing assistance in relation to relevant interception warrants shall include the question whether all such arrangements have been made as the Secretary of State considers necessary–

(a) with respect to the disclosure of intercepted material;

(b) for the purpose of ensuring that security and confidentiality are maintained in relation to, and to matters connected with, the provision of any such assistance; and

(c) for the purpose of facilitating the carrying out of any functions in relation to this Chapter of the Interception of Communications Commissioner;

but before determining for the purposes of the making of any order, or the imposition of any obligation, under this section what arrangements he considers necessary for the purpose mentioned in paragraph (c) the Secretary of State shall consult that Commissioner.

(12) In this section 'relevant interception warrant'–
  (a) in relation to a person providing a public postal service, means an interception warrant relating to the interception of communications in the course of their transmission by means of that service; and
  (b) in relation to a person providing a public telecommunications service, means an interception warrant relating to the interception of communications in the course of their transmission by means of a telecommunication system used for the purposes of that service.

Technical Advisory Board

13.—(1) There shall be a Technical Advisory Board consisting of such number of persons appointed by the Secretary of State as he may by order provide.

(2) The order providing for the membership of the Technical Advisory Board must also make provision which is calculated to ensure—
  (a) that the membership of the Technical Advisory Board includes persons likely effectively to represent the interests of the persons on whom obligations may be imposed under section 12;
  (b) that the membership of the Board includes persons likely effectively to represent the interests of the persons by or on whose behalf applications for interception warrants may be made;
  (c) that such other persons (if any) as the Secretary of State thinks fit may be appointed to be members of the Board; and
  (d) that the Board is so constituted as to produce a balance between the representation of the interests mentioned in paragraph (a) and the representation of those mentioned in paragraph (b).

(3) The Secretary of State shall not make an order under this section unless a draft of the order has been laid before Parliament and approved by a resolution of each House.

Grants for interception costs

14.—(1) It shall be the duty of the Secretary of State to ensure that such arrangements are in force as are necessary for securing that a person who provides–
  (a) a postal service, or
  (b) a telecommunications service,
receives such contribution as is, in the circumstances of that person's case, a fair contribution towards the costs incurred, or likely to be incurred, by that person in consequence of the matters mentioned in subsection (2).

(2) Those matters are–
  (a) in relation to a person providing a postal service, the issue of interception warrants relating to communications transmitted by means of that postal service;
  (b) in relation to a person providing a telecommunications service, the issue of interception warrants relating to communications transmitted by means of a telecommunication system used for the purposes of that service;
  (c) in relation to each description of person, the imposition on that person of obligations provided for by an order under section 12.

(3) For the purpose of complying with his duty under this section, the Secretary of State may make arrangements for payments to be made out of money provided by Parliament.

Restrictions on use of intercepted material etc.

General safeguards

15.—(1) Subject to subsection (6), it shall be the duty of the Secretary of State to ensure, in relation to all interception warrants, that such arrangements are in force as he considers necessary for securing–

    (a) that the requirements of subsections (2) and (3) are satisfied in relation to the intercepted material and any related communications data; and

    (b) in the case of warrants in relation to which there are section 8(4) certificates, that the requirements of section 16 are also satisfied.

(2) The requirements of this subsection are satisfied in relation to the intercepted material and any related communications data if each of the following–

    (a) the number of persons to whom any of the material or data is disclosed or otherwise made available,

    (b) the extent to which any of the material or data is disclosed or otherwise made available,

    (c) the extent to which any of the material or data is copied, and

    (d) the number of copies that are made,

is limited to the minimum that is necessary for the authorised purposes.

(3) The requirements of this subsection are satisfied in relation to the intercepted material and any related communications data if each copy made of any of the material or data (if not destroyed earlier) is destroyed as soon as there are no longer any grounds for retaining it as necessary for any of the authorised purposes.

(4) For the purposes of this section something is necessary for the authorised purposes if, and only if,–

    (a) it continues to be, or is likely to become, necessary as mentioned in section 5(3);

    (b) it is necessary for facilitating the carrying out of any of the functions under this Chapter of the Secretary of State;

    (c) it is necessary for facilitating the carrying out of any functions in relation to this Part of the Interception of Communications Commissioner or of the Tribunal;

    (d) it is necessary to ensure that a person conducting a criminal prosecution has the information he needs to determine what is required of him by his duty to secure the fairness of the prosecution; or

    (e) it is necessary for the performance of any duty imposed on any person by the Public Records Act 1958 or the Public Records Act (Northern Ireland) 1923.

(5) The arrangements for the time being in force under this section for securing that the requirements of subsection (2) are satisfied in relation to the intercepted material or any related communications data must include such arrangements as the Secretary of State considers necessary for securing that every copy of the material or data that is made is stored, for so long as it is retained, in a secure manner.

(6) Arrangements in relation to interception warrants which are made for the purposes of subsection (1)–

    (a) shall not be required to secure that the requirements of subsections (2) and (3) are satisfied in so far as they relate to any of the intercepted material or related communications data, or any copy of any such material or data, possession of which has been surrendered to any authorities of a country or territory outside the United Kingdom; but

    (b) shall be required to secure, in the case of every such warrant, that possession of the intercepted material and data and of copies of the material or data is surrendered to authorities of a country or territory outside the United Kingdom only if the requirements of subsection (7) are satisfied.

(7) The requirements of this subsection are satisfied in the case of a warrant if it appears to the Secretary of State–

    (a) that requirements corresponding to those of subsections (2) and (3) will apply, to such extent (if any) as the Secretary of State thinks fit, in relation to any of the intercepted material or related communications data possession of which, or of any copy of which, is surrendered to the authorities in question; and

    (b) that restrictions are in force which would prevent, to such extent (if any) as the Secretary of State thinks fit, the doing of anything in, for the purposes of or in connection with any proceedings outside the United Kingdom which would result in such a disclosure as, by virtue of section 17, could not be made in the United Kingdom.

(8) In this section 'copy', in relation to intercepted material or related communications data, means any of the following (whether or not in documentary form)–

    (a) any copy, extract or summary of the material or data which identifies itself as the product of an interception, and

    (b) any record referring to an interception which is a record of the identities of the persons to or by whom the intercepted material was sent, or to whom the communications data relates,

and 'copied' shall be construed accordingly.

Extra safeguards in the case of certificated warrants

16.—(1) For the purposes of section 15 the requirements of this section, in the case of a warrant in relation to which there is a section 8(4) certificate, are that the intercepted material is read, looked at or listened to by the persons to whom it becomes available by virtue of the warrant to the extent only that it–

    (a) has been certified as material the examination of which is necessary as mentioned in section 5(3)(a), (b) or (c); and

    (b) falls within subsection (2).

(2) Subject to subsections (3) and (4), intercepted material falls within this subsection so far only as it is selected to be read, looked at or listened to otherwise than according to a factor which–

    (a) is referable to an individual who is known to be for the time being in the British Islands; and

    (b) has as its purpose, or one of its purposes, the identification of material contained in communications sent by him, or intended for him.

(3) Intercepted material falls within subsection (2), notwithstanding that it is selected by reference to any such factor as is mentioned in paragraph (a) and (b) of that subsection, if–

  (a) it is certified by the Secretary of State for the purposes of section 8(4) that the examination of material selected according to factors referable to the individual in question is necessary as mentioned in subsection 5(3)(a), (b) or (c); and

  (b) the material relates only to communications sent during a period of not more than three months specified in the certificate.

(4) Intercepted material also falls within subsection (2), notwithstanding that it is selected by reference to any such factor as is mentioned in paragraph (a) and (b) of that subsection, if–

  (a) the person to whom the warrant is addressed believes, on reasonable grounds, that the circumstances are such that the material would fall within that subsection; or

  (b) the conditions set out in subsection (5) below are satisfied in relation to the selection of the material.

(5) Those conditions are satisfied in relation to the selection of intercepted material if–

  (a) it has appeared to the person to whom the warrant is addressed that there has been such a relevant change of circumstances as, but for subsection (4)(b), would prevent the intercepted material from falling within subsection (2);

  (b) since it first so appeared, a written authorisation to read, look at or listen to the material has been given by a senior official; and

  (c) the selection is made before the end of the first working day after the day on which it first so appeared to that person.

(6) References in this section to its appearing that there has been a relevant change of circumstances are references to its appearing either–

  (a) that the individual in question has entered the British Islands; or

  (b) that a belief by the person to whom the warrant is addressed in the individual's presence outside the British Islands was in fact mistaken.

Exclusion of matters from legal proceedings

17.—(1) Subject to section 18, no evidence shall be adduced, question asked, assertion or disclosure made or other thing done in, for the purposes of or in connection with any legal proceedings or Inquiries Act proceedings which (in any manner)–

  (a) discloses, in circumstances from which its origin in anything falling within subsection (2) may be inferred, any of the contents of an intercepted communication or any related communications data; or

  (b) tends (apart from any such disclosure) to suggest that anything falling within subsection (2) has or may have occurred or be going to occur.

(2) The following fall within this subsection–

  (a) conduct by a person falling within subsection (3) that was or would be an offence under section 1(1) or (2) of this Act or under section 1 of the Interception of Communications Act 1985;

  (b) a breach by the Secretary of State of his duty under section 1(4) of this Act;

(c) the issue of an interception warrant or of a warrant under the Interception of Communications Act 1985;

(d) the making of an application by any person for an interception warrant, or for a warrant under that Act;

(e) the imposition of any requirement on any person to provide assistance with giving effect to an interception warrant.

(3) The persons referred to in subsection (2)(a) are–

(a) any person to whom a warrant under this Chapter may be addressed;

(b) any person holding office under the Crown;

(c) any member of the National Criminal Intelligence Service;[3]

(d) any member of the National Crime Squad;[4]

(e) any person employed by or for the purposes of a police force;

(f) any person providing a postal service or employed for the purposes of any business of providing such a service; and

(g) any person providing a public telecommunications service or employed for the purposes of any business of providing such a service.

(4) In this section–

'Inquiries Act proceedings' means proceedings of an inquiry under the Inquiries Act 2005;

'intercepted communications' means any communication intercepted in the course of its transmission by means of a postal service or telecommunication system.

Exceptions to section 17

18.—(1) Section 17(1) shall not apply in relation to–

(a) any proceedings for a relevant offence;

(b) any civil proceedings under section 11(8);

(c) any proceedings before the Tribunal;

(d) any proceedings on an appeal or review for which provision is made by an order under section 67(8);

(da) any control order proceedings (within the meaning of the Prevention of Terrorism Act 2005) or any proceedings arising out of such proceedings;

(e) any proceedings before the Special Immigration Appeals Commission or any proceedings arising out of proceedings before that Commission; or

(f) any proceedings before the Proscribed Organisations Appeal Commission or any proceedings arising out of proceedings before that Commission.

(2) Subsection (1) shall not, by virtue of paragraphs (da) to (f), authorise the disclosure of anything–

(za) in the case of any proceedings falling within paragraph (da) to–

(i) a person who, within the meaning of the Schedule to the Prevention of Terrorism Act 2005, is or was a relevant party to the control order proceedings; or

(ii) any person who for the purposes of any proceedings so falling (but otherwise than by virtue of an appointment under paragraph 7 of that Schedule) represents a person falling within sub-paragraph (i);

---

[3] Prospectively amended by SOCAPA 2005 Sch 4 para 133.
[4] ibid.

    (a) in the case of any proceedings falling within paragraph (e), to–

        (i)   the appellant to the Special Immigration Appeals Commission; or

        (ii) any person who for the purposes of any proceedings so falling (but otherwise than by virtue of an appointment under section 6 of the Special Immigration Appeals Commission Act 1997) represents that appellant; or

    (b) in the case of proceedings falling within paragraph (f), to–

        (i)   the applicant to the Proscribed Organisations Appeal Commission;

        (ii) the organisation concerned (if different);

        (iii) any person designated under paragraph 6 of Schedule 3 to the Terrorism Act 2000 to conduct proceedings so falling on behalf of that organisation; or

        (iv) any person who for the purposes of any proceedings so falling (but otherwise than by virtue of an appointment under paragraph 7 of that Schedule) represents that applicant or that organisation.

(3) Section 17(1) shall not prohibit anything done in, for the purposes of, or in connection with, so much of any legal proceedings as relates to the fairness or unfairness of a dismissal on the grounds of any conduct constituting an offence under section 1(1) or (2), 11(7) or 19 of this Act, or section 1 of the Interception of Communications Act 1985.

(4) Section 17(1)(a) shall not prohibit the disclosure of any of the contents of a communication if the interception of that communication was lawful by virtue of section 1(5)(c), 3 or 4.

(5) Where any disclosure is proposed to be or has been made on the grounds that it is authorised by subsection (4), section 17(1) shall not prohibit the doing of anything in, or for the purposes of, so much of any proceedings as relates to the question whether that disclosure is or was so authorised.

(6) Section 17(1)(b) shall not prohibit the doing of anything that discloses any conduct of a person for which he has been convicted of an offence under section 1(1) or (2), 11(7) or 19 of this Act, or section 1 of the Interception of Communications Act 1985.

(7) Nothing in section 17(1) shall prohibit any such disclosure of any information that continues to be available for disclosure as is confined to–

    (a) a disclosure to a person conducting a criminal prosecution for the purpose only of enabling that person to determine what is required of him by his duty to secure the fairness of the prosecution; or

    (b) a disclosure to a relevant judge in a case in which that judge has ordered the disclosure to be made to him alone; or

    (c) a disclosure to the panel of an inquiry held under the Inquiries Act 2005 in the course of which the panel has ordered the disclosure to be made to the panel alone.

(8) A relevant judge shall not order a disclosure under subsection (7)(b) except where he is satisfied that the exceptional circumstances of the case make the disclosure essential in the interests of justice.

(8A) The panel of an inquiry shall not order a disclosure under subsection (7)(c) except where it is satisfied that the exceptional circumstances of the case make the disclosure essential to enable the inquiry to fulfil its terms of reference.

(9) Subject to subsection (10), where in any criminal proceedings–
   (a) a relevant judge does order a disclosure under subsection (7)(b), and
   (b) in consequence of that disclosure he is of the opinion that there are excep-
       tional circumstances requiring him to do so,
   he may direct the person conducting the prosecution to make for the purposes
   of the proceedings any such admission of fact as that judge thinks essential in
   the interests of justice.

(10) Nothing in any direction under subsection (9) shall authorise or require any-
    thing to be done in contravention of section 17(1).

(11) In this section 'a relevant judge' means–
   (a) any judge of the High Court or of the Crown Court or any Circuit judge;
   (b) any judge of the High Court of Justiciary or any sheriff;
   (c) in relation to a court-martial, the judge advocate appointed in relation to
       that court-martial under section 84B of the Army Act 1955, section 84B of
       the Air Force Act 1955 or section 53B of the Naval Discipline Act 1957; or
   (d) any person holding any such judicial office as entitles him to exercise the
       jurisdiction of a judge falling within paragraph (a) or (b).

(12) In this section 'relevant offence' means–
   (a) an offence under any provision of this Act;
   (b) an offence under section 1 of the Interception of Communications Act 1985;
   (c) an offence under section 5 of the Wireless Telegraphy Act 1949;
   (d) an offence under section 83 or 84 of the Postal Services Act 2000;
   (e) [repealed];
   (f) an offence under section 4 of the Official Secrets Act 1989 relating to any
       such information, document or article as is mentioned in subsection (3)(a)
       of that section;
   (g) an offence under section 1 or 2 of the Official Secrets Act 1911 relating to any
       sketch, plan, model, article, note, document or information which incor-
       porates or relates to the contents of any intercepted communication or any
       related communications data or tends to suggest as mentioned in section
       17(1)(b) of this Act;
   (h) perjury committed in the course of any proceedings mentioned in subsec-
       tion (1) or (3) of this section;
   (i) attempting or conspiring to commit, or aiding, abetting, counselling or pro-
       curing the commission of, an offence falling within any of the preceding
       paragraphs; and
   (j) contempt of court committed in the course of, or in relation to, any pro-
       ceedings mentioned in subsection (1) or (3) of this section.

(13) In subsection (12) 'intercepted communication' has the same meaning as in
    section 17.

Offence for unauthorised disclosures

19.—(1) Where an interception warrant has been issued or renewed, it shall be the
    duty of every person falling within subsection (2) to keep secret all the matters
    mentioned in subsection (3).

(2) The persons falling within this subsection are–
   (a) the persons specified in section 6(2);
   (b) every person holding office under the Crown;

(c) every member of the National Criminal Intelligence Service;[5]

(d) every member of the National Crime Squad;[6]

(e) every person employed by or for the purposes of a police force;

(f) persons providing postal services or employed for the purposes of any business of providing such a service;

(g) persons providing public telecommunications services or employed for the purposes of any business of providing such a service;

(h) persons having control of the whole or any part of a telecommunication system located wholly or partly in the United Kingdom.

(3) Those matters are–

(a) the existence and contents of the warrant and of any section 8(4) certificate in relation to the warrant;

(b) the details of the issue of the warrant and of any renewal or modification of the warrant or of any such certificate;

(c) the existence and contents of any requirement to provide assistance with giving effect to the warrant;

(d) the steps taken in pursuance of the warrant or of any such requirement; and

(e) everything in the intercepted material, together with any related communications data.

(4) A person who makes a disclosure to another of anything that he is required to keep secret under this section shall be guilty of an offence and liable–

(a) on conviction on indictment, to imprisonment for a term not exceeding five years or to a fine, or to both;

(b) on summary conviction, to imprisonment for a term not exceeding six months or to a fine not exceeding the statutory maximum, or to both.

(5) In proceedings against any person for an offence under this section in respect of any disclosure, it shall be a defence for that person to show that he could not reasonably have been expected, after first becoming aware of the matter disclosed, to take steps to prevent the disclosure.

(6) In proceedings against any person for an offence under this section in respect of any disclosure, it shall be a defence for that person to show that–

(a) the disclosure was made by or to a professional legal adviser in connection with the giving, by the adviser to any client of his, of advice about the effect of provisions of this Chapter; and

(b) the person to whom or, as the case may be, by whom it was made was the client or a representative of the client.

(7) In proceedings against any person for an offence under this section in respect of any disclosure, it shall be a defence for that person to show that the disclosure was made by a legal adviser–

(a) in contemplation of, or in connection with, any legal proceedings; and

(b) for the purposes of those proceedings.

(8) Neither subsection (6) nor subsection (7) applies in the case of a disclosure made with a view to furthering any criminal purpose.

---

[5] Prospectively amended by SOCAPA 2005 Sch 4 para 134.

[6] ibid.

(9) In proceedings against any person for an offence under this section in respect of any disclosure, it shall be a defence for that person to show that the disclosure was confined to a disclosure made to the Interception of Communications Commissioner or authorised–

(a) by that Commissioner;

(b) by the warrant or the person to whom the warrant is or was addressed;

(c) by the terms of the requirement to provide assistance; or

(d) by section 11(9).

Interpretation of Chapter I

Interpretation of Chapter I

20. In this Chapter–

'certified', in relation to a section 8(4) certificate, means of a description certified by the certificate as a description of material the examination of which the Secretary of State considers necessary;

'external communication' means a communication sent or received outside the British Islands;

'intercepted material', in relation to an interception warrant, means the contents of any communications intercepted by an interception to which the warrant relates;

'the interception subject', in relation to an interception warrant, means the person about whose communications information is sought by the interception to which the warrant relates;

'international mutual assistance agreement' means an international agreement designated for the purposes of section 1(4);

'related communications data', in relation to a communication intercepted in the course of its transmission by means of a postal service or telecommunication system, means so much of any communications data (within the meaning of Chapter II of this Part) as–

(a) is obtained by, or in connection with, the interception; and

(b) relates to the communication or to the sender or recipient, or intended recipient, of the communication;

'section 8(4) certificate' means any certificate issued for the purposes of section 8(4).

PART I, CHAPTER II
ACQUISITION AND DISCLOSURE OF COMMUNICATIONS DATA

Lawful acquisition and disclosure of communications data

21.—(1) This Chapter applies to–

(a) any conduct in relation to a postal service or telecommunication system for obtaining communications data, other than conduct consisting in the interception of communications in the course of their transmission by means of such a service or system; and

(b) the disclosure to any person of communications data.

(2) Conduct to which this Chapter applies shall be lawful for all purposes if–
  (a) it is conduct in which any person is authorised or required to engage by an authorisation or notice granted or given under this Chapter; and
  (b) the conduct is in accordance with, or in pursuance of, the authorisation or requirement.

(3) A person shall not be subject to any civil liability in respect of any conduct of his which–
  (a) is incidental to any conduct that is lawful by virtue of subsection (2); and
  (b) is not itself conduct an authorisation or warrant for which is capable of being granted under a relevant enactment and might reasonably have been expected to have been sought in the case in question.

(4) In this Chapter 'communications data' means any of the following–
  (a) any traffic data comprised in or attached to a communication (whether by the sender or otherwise) for the purposes of any postal service or telecommunication system by means of which it is being or may be transmitted;
  (b) any information which includes none of the contents of a communication (apart from any information falling within paragraph (a)) and is about the use made by any person–
    (i) of any postal service or telecommunications service; or
    (ii) in connection with the provision to or use by any person of any telecommunications service, of any part of a telecommunication system;
  (c) any information not falling within paragraph (a) or (b) that is held or obtained, in relation to persons to whom he provides the service, by a person providing a postal service or telecommunications service.

(5) In this section 'relevant enactment' means–
  (a) an enactment contained in this Act;
  (b) section 5 of the Intelligence Services Act 1994 (warrants for the intelligence services); or
  (c) an enactment contained in Part III of the Police Act 1997 (powers of the police and of customs officers).

(6) In this section 'traffic data', in relation to any communication, means–
  (a) any data identifying, or purporting to identify, any person, apparatus or location to or from which the communication is or may be transmitted;
  (b) any data identifying or selecting, or purporting to identify or select, apparatus through which, or by means of which, the communication is or may be transmitted;
  (c) any data comprising signals for the actuation of apparatus used for the purposes of a telecommunication system for effecting (in whole or in part) the transmission of any communication; and
  (d) any data identifying the data or other data as data comprised in or attached to a particular communication,
but that expression includes data identifying a computer file or computer program access to which is obtained, or which is run, by means of the communication to the extent only that the file or program is identified by reference to the apparatus in which it is stored.

(7) In this section–

    (a) references, in relation to traffic data comprising signals for the actuation of apparatus, to a telecommunication system by means of which a communication is being or may be transmitted include references to any telecommunication system in which that apparatus is comprised; and

    (b) references to traffic data being attached to a communication include references to the data and the communication being logically associated with each other;

and in this section 'data', in relation to a postal item, means anything written on the outside of the item.

Obtaining and disclosing communications data

22.—(1) This section applies where a person designated for the purposes of this Chapter believes that it is necessary on grounds falling within subsection (2) to obtain any communications data.

(2) It is necessary on grounds falling within this subsection to obtain communications data if it is necessary–

    (a) in the interests of national security;

    (b) for the purpose of preventing or detecting crime or of preventing disorder;

    (c) in the interests of the economic well-being of the United Kingdom;

    (d) in the interests of public safety;

    (e) for the purpose of protecting public health;

    (f) for the purpose of assessing or collecting any tax, duty, levy or other imposition, contribution or charge payable to a government department;

    (g) for the purpose, in an emergency, of preventing death or injury or any damage to a person's physical or mental health, or of mitigating any injury or damage to a person's physical or mental health; or

    (h) for any purpose (not falling within paragraphs (a) to (g)) which is specified for the purposes of this subsection by an order made by the Secretary of State.

(3) Subject to subsection (5), the designated person may grant an authorisation for persons holding offices, ranks or positions with the same relevant public authority as the designated person to engage in any conduct to which this Chapter applies.

(4) Subject to subsection (5), where it appears to the designated person that a postal or telecommunications operator is or may be in possession of, or be capable of obtaining, any communications data, the designated person may, by notice to the postal or telecommunications operator, require the operator–

    (a) if the operator is not already in possession of the data, to obtain the data; and

    (b) in any case, to disclose all of the data in his possession or subsequently obtained by him.

(5) The designated person shall not grant an authorisation under subsection (3), or give a notice under subsection (4), unless he believes that obtaining the data in question by the conduct authorised or required by the authorisation or notice is proportionate to what is sought to be achieved by so obtaining the data.

(6) It shall be the duty of the postal or telecommunications operator to comply with the requirements of any notice given to him under subsection (4).

(7) A person who is under a duty by virtue of subsection (6) shall not be required to do anything in pursuance of that duty which it is not reasonably practicable for him to do.

(8) The duty imposed by subsection (6) shall be enforceable by civil proceedings by the Secretary of State for an injunction, or for specific performance of a statutory duty under section 45 of the Court of Session Act 1988, or for any other appropriate relief.

(9) The Secretary of State shall not make an order under subsection (2)(h) unless a draft of the order has been laid before Parliament and approved by a resolution of each House.

Form and duration of authorisations and notices

23.—(1) An authorisation under section 22(3)–

  (a) must be granted in writing or (if not in writing) in a manner that produces a record of its having been granted;

  (b) must describe the conduct to which this Chapter applies that is authorised and the communications data in relation to which it is authorised;

  (c) must specify the matters falling within section 22(2) by reference to which it is granted; and

  (d) must specify the office, rank or position held by the person granting the authorisation.

(2) A notice under section 22(4) requiring communications data to be disclosed or to be obtained and disclosed–

  (a) must be given in writing or (if not in writing) must be given in a manner that produces a record of its having been given;

  (b) must describe the communications data to be obtained or disclosed under the notice;

  (c) must specify the matters falling within section 22(2) by reference to which the notice is given;

  (d) must specify the office, rank or position held by the person giving it; and

  (e) must specify the manner in which any disclosure required by the notice is to be made.

(3) A notice under section 22(4) shall not require the disclosure of data to any person other than–

  (a) the person giving the notice; or

  (b) such other person as may be specified in or otherwise identified by, or in accordance with, the provisions of the notice;

  but the provisions of the notice shall not specify or otherwise identify a person for the purposes of paragraph (b) unless he holds an office, rank or position with the same relevant public authority as the person giving the notice.

(4) An authorisation under section 22(3) or notice under section 22(4)–

  (a) shall not authorise or require any data to be obtained after the end of the period of one month beginning with the date on which the authorisation is granted or the notice given; and

  (b) in the case of a notice, shall not authorise or require any disclosure after the end of that period of any data not in the possession of, or obtained by, the postal or telecommunications operator at a time during that period.

(5) An authorisation under section 22(3) or notice under section 22(4) may be renewed at any time before the end of the period of one month applying (in accordance with subsection (4) or subsection (7)) to that authorisation or notice.

(6) A renewal of an authorisation under section 22(3) or of a notice under section 22(4) shall be by the grant or giving, in accordance with this section, of a further authorisation or notice.

(7) Subsection (4) shall have effect in relation to a renewed authorisation or renewal notice as if the period of one month mentioned in that subsection did not begin until the end of the period of one month applicable to the authorisation or notice that is current at the time of the renewal.

(8) Where a person who has given a notice under subsection (4) of section 22 is satisfied–

   (a) that it is no longer necessary on grounds falling within subsection (2) of that section for the requirements of the notice to be complied with, or

   (b) that the conduct required by the notice is no longer proportionate to what is sought to be achieved by obtaining communications data to which the notice relates,

   he shall cancel the notice.

(9) The Secretary of State may by regulations provide for the person by whom any duty imposed by subsection (8) is to be performed in a case in which it would otherwise fall on a person who is no longer available to perform it; and regulations under this subsection may provide for the person on whom the duty is to fall to be a person appointed in accordance with the regulations.

Arrangements for payments

24.—(1) It shall be the duty of the Secretary of State to ensure that such arrangements are in force as he thinks appropriate for requiring or authorising, in such cases as he thinks fit, the making to postal and telecommunications operators of appropriate contributions towards the costs incurred by them in complying with notices under section 22(4).

(2) For the purpose of complying with his duty under this section, the Secretary of State may make arrangements for payments to be made out of money provided by Parliament.

Interpretation of Chapter II

25.—(1) In this Chapter–

   'communications data' has the meaning given by section 21(4);

   'designated' shall be construed in accordance with subsection (2);

   'postal or telecommunications operator' means a person who provides a postal service or telecommunications service;

   'relevant public authority' means (subject to subsection (4)) any of the following–

   (a) a police force;

   (b) the National Criminal Intelligence Service;[7]

   (c) the National Crime Squad;[8]

---

[7] Prospectively amended by SOCAPA 2005 Sch 4 para 135.
[8] ibid.

(d) the Commissioners of Customs and Excise;

(e) the Commissioners of Inland Revenue;

(f) any of the intelligence services;

(g) any such public authority not falling within paragraphs (a) to (f) as may be specified for the purposes of this subsection by an order made by the Secretary of State.

(2) Subject to subsection (3), the persons designated for the purposes of this Chapter are the individuals holding such offices, ranks or positions with relevant public authorities as are prescribed for the purposes of this subsection by an order made by the Secretary of State.

(3) The Secretary of State may by order impose restrictions–

(a) on the authorisations and notices under this Chapter that may be granted or given by any individual holding an office, rank or position with a specified public authority; and

(b) on the circumstances in which, or the purposes for which, such authorisations may be granted or notices given by any such individual.[9]

(4) The Secretary of State may by order remove any person from the list of persons who are for the time being relevant public authorities for the purposes of this Chapter.[10]

(5) The Secretary of State shall not make an order under this section that adds any person to the list of persons who are for the time being relevant public authorities for the purposes of this Chapter unless a draft of the order has been laid before Parliament and approved by a resolution of each House.[11]

PART II
SURVEILLANCE AND COVERT HUMAN INTELLIGENCE SOURCES

Introductory

Conduct to which Part II applies

26.—(1) This Part applies to the following conduct–

(a) directed surveillance;

(b) intrusive surveillance; and

(c) the conduct and use of covert human intelligence sources.

(2) Subject to subsection (6), surveillance is directed for the purposes of this Part if it is covert but not intrusive and is undertaken–

(a) for the purposes of a specific investigation or a specific operation;

(b) in such a manner as is likely to result in the obtaining of private information about a person (whether or not one specifically identified for the purposes of the investigation or operation); and

(c) otherwise than by way of an immediate response to events or circumstances the nature of which is such that it would not be reasonably practicable for an authorisation under this Part to be sought for the carrying out of the surveillance.

---

[9] New subsection (3A) prospectively inserted by SOCAPA 2005 Sch 4 para 135.

[10] Prospectively amended by SOCAPA 2005 Sch 4 para 135.

[11] ibid.

(3) Subject to subsections (4) to (6), surveillance is intrusive for the purposes of this Part if, and only if, it is covert surveillance that–

    (a) is carried out in relation to anything taking place on any residential premises or in any private vehicle; and

    (b) involves the presence of an individual on the premises or in the vehicle or is carried out by means of a surveillance device.

(4) For the purposes of this Part surveillance is not intrusive to the extent that–

    (a) it is carried out by means only of a surveillance device designed or adapted principally for the purpose of providing information about the location of a vehicle; or

    (b) it is surveillance consisting in any such interception of a communication as falls within section 48(4).

(5) For the purposes of this Part surveillance which–

    (a) is carried out by means of a surveillance device in relation to anything taking place on any residential premises or in any private vehicle, but

    (b) is carried out without that device being present on the premises or in the vehicle,

is not intrusive unless the device is such that it consistently provides information of the same quality and detail as might be expected to be obtained from a device actually present on the premises or in the vehicle.

(6) For the purposes of this Part surveillance which–

    (a) is carried out by means of apparatus designed or adapted for the purpose of detecting the installation or use in any residential or other premises of a television receiver (within the meaning of Part 4 of the Communications Act 2003), and

    (b) is carried out from outside those premises exclusively for that purpose,

is neither directed nor intrusive.

(7) In this Part–

    (a) references to the conduct of a covert human intelligence source are references to any conduct of such a source which falls within any of paragraphs (a) to (c) of subsection (8), or is incidental to anything falling within any of those paragraphs; and

    (b) references to the use of a covert human intelligence source are references to inducing, asking or assisting a person to engage in the conduct of such a source, or to obtain information by means of the conduct of such a source.

(8) For the purposes of this Part a person is a covert human intelligence source if–

    (a) he establishes or maintains a personal or other relationship with a person for the covert purpose of facilitating the doing of anything falling within paragraph (b) or (c);

    (b) he covertly uses such a relationship to obtain information or to provide access to any information to another person; or

    (c) he covertly discloses information obtained by the use of such a relationship, or as a consequence of the existence of such a relationship.

(9) For the purposes of this section–
  (a) surveillance is covert if, and only if, it is carried out in a manner that is calcu-lated to ensure that persons who are subject to the surveillance are unaware that it is or may be taking place;
  (b) a purpose is covert, in relation to the establishment or maintenance of a per-sonal or other relationship, if and only if the relationship is conducted in a manner that is calculated to ensure that one of the parties to the relationship is unaware of the purpose; and
  (c) a relationship is used covertly, and information obtained as mentioned in subsection (8)(c) is disclosed covertly, if and only if it is used or, as the case may be, disclosed in a manner that is calculated to ensure that one of the parties to the relationship is unaware of the use or disclosure in question.
(10) In this section 'private information', in relation to a person, includes any information relating to his private or family life.
(11) References in this section, in relation to a vehicle, to the presence of a surveil-lance device in the vehicle include references to its being located on or under the vehicle and also include references to its being attached to it.

Authorisation of surveillance and human intelligence sources

Lawful surveillance etc.

27.—(1) Conduct to which this Part applies shall be lawful for all purposes if–
  (a) an authorisation under this Part confers an entitlement to engage in that conduct on the person whose conduct it is; and
  (b) his conduct is in accordance with the authorisation.
(2) A person shall not be subject to any civil liability in respect of any conduct of his which–
  (a) is incidental to any conduct that is lawful by virtue of subsection (1); and
  (b) is not itself conduct an authorisation or warrant for which is capable of being granted under a relevant enactment and might reasonably have been expec-ted to have been sought in the case in question.
(3) The conduct that may be authorised under this Part includes conduct outside the United Kingdom.
(4) In this section 'relevant enactment' means–
  (a) an enactment contained in this Act;
  (b) section 5 of the Intelligence Services Act 1994 (warrants for the intelligence services); or
  (c) an enactment contained in Part III of the Police Act 1997 (powers of the police and of customs officers).
[See SI 2001/1057 in Appendix C for amendments having the effect of creating new section (27A) for the purposes of surveillance conducted by TV licensing investigators.]

Authorisation of directed surveillance

28.—(1) Subject to the following provisions of this Part, the persons designated for the purposes of this section shall each have power to grant authorisations for the carrying out of directed surveillance.

(2) A person shall not grant an authorisation for the carrying out of directed surveil-lance unless he believes–

(a) that the authorisation is necessary on grounds falling within subsection (3); and

(b) that the authorised surveillance is proportionate to what is sought to be achieved by carrying it out.

(3) An authorisation is necessary on grounds falling within this subsection if it is necessary–

(a) in the interests of national security;

(b) for the purpose of preventing or detecting crime or of preventing disorder;

(c) in the interests of the economic well-being of the United Kingdom;

(d) in the interests of public safety;

(e) for the purpose of protecting public health;

(f) for the purpose of assessing or collecting any tax, duty, levy or other impos-ition, contribution or charge payable to a government department; or

(g) for any purpose (not falling within paragraphs (a) to (f)) which is specified for the purposes of this subsection by an order made by the Secretary of State.

(4) The conduct that is authorised by an authorisation for the carrying out of direc-ted surveillance is any conduct that–

(a) consists in the carrying out of directed surveillance of any such description as is specified in the authorisation; and

(b) is carried out in the circumstances described in the authorisation and for the purposes of the investigation or operation specified or described in the authorisation.

(5) The Secretary of State shall not make an order under subsection (3)(g) unless a draft of the order has been laid before Parliament and approved by a resolution of each House.

Authorisation of covert human intelligence sources

29.—(1) Subject to the following provisions of this Part, the persons designated for the purposes of this section shall each have power to grant authorisations for the conduct or the use of a covert human intelligence source.

(2) A person shall not grant an authorisation for the conduct or the use of a covert human intelligence source unless he believes–

(a) that the authorisation is necessary on grounds falling within subsection (3);

(b) that the authorised conduct or use is proportionate to what is sought to be achieved by that conduct or use; and

(c) that arrangements exist for the source's case that satisfy the requirements of subsection (5) and such other requirements as may be imposed by order made by the Secretary of State.

(3) An authorisation is necessary on grounds falling within this subsection if it is necessary–

(a) in the interests of national security;

(b) for the purpose of preventing or detecting crime or of preventing disorder;

(c) in the interests of the economic well-being of the United Kingdom;

(d) in the interests of public safety;

(e) for the purpose of protecting public health;

    (f) for the purpose of assessing or collecting any tax, duty, levy or other imposition, contribution or charge payable to a government department; or

    (g) for any purpose (not falling within paragraphs (a) to (f)) which is specified for the purposes of this subsection by an order made by the Secretary of State.

(4) The conduct that is authorised by an authorisation for the conduct or the use of a covert human intelligence source is any conduct that–

    (a) is comprised in any such activities involving conduct of a covert human intelligence source, or the use of a covert human intelligence source, as are specified or described in the authorisation;

    (b) consists in conduct by or in relation to the person who is so specified or described as the person to whose actions as a covert human intelligence source the authorisation relates; and

    (c) is carried out for the purposes of, or in connection with, the investigation or operation so specified or described.

(5) For the purposes of this Part there are arrangements for the source's case that satisfy the requirements of this subsection if such arrangements are in force as are necessary for ensuring–

    (a) that there will at all times be a person holding an office, rank or position with the relevant investigating authority who will have day-to-day responsibility for dealing with the source on behalf of that authority, and for the source's security and welfare;

    (b) that there will at all times be another person holding an office, rank or position with the relevant investigating authority who will have general oversight of the use made of the source;

    (c) that there will at all times be a person holding an office, rank or position with the relevant investigating authority who will have responsibility for maintaining a record of the use made of the source;

    (d) that the records relating to the source that are maintained by the relevant investigating authority will always contain particulars of all such matters (if any) as may be specified for the purposes of this paragraph in regulations made by the Secretary of State; and

    (e) that records maintained by the relevant investigating authority that disclose the identity of the source will not be available to persons except to the extent that there is a need for access to them to be made available to those persons.

(6) The Secretary of State shall not make an order under subsection (3)(g) unless a draft of the order has been laid before Parliament and approved by a resolution of each House.

(7) The Secretary of State may by order–

    (a) prohibit the authorisation under this section of any such conduct or uses of covert human intelligence sources as may be described in the order; and

    (b) impose requirements, in addition to those provided for by subsection (2), that must be satisfied before an authorisation is granted under this section for any such conduct or uses of covert human intelligence sources as may be so described.

(8) In this section 'relevant investigating authority', in relation to an authorisation for the conduct or the use of an individual as a covert human intelligence source,

means (subject to subsection (9)) the public authority for whose benefit the activities of that individual as such a source are to take place.

(9) In the case of any authorisation for the conduct or the use of a covert human intelligence source whose activities are to be for the benefit of more than one public authority, the references in subsection (5) to the relevant investigating authority are references to one of them (whether or not the same one in the case of each reference).

Persons entitled to grant authorisations under ss. 28 and 29

30.—(1) Subject to subsection (3), the persons designated for the purposes of sections 28 and 29 are the individuals holding such offices, ranks or positions with relevant public authorities as are prescribed for the purposes of this subsection by an order under this section.

(2) For the purposes of the grant of an authorisation that combines—
  (a) an authorisation under section 28 or 29, and
  (b) an authorisation by the Secretary of State for the carrying out of intrusive surveillance,
  the Secretary of State himself shall be a person designated for the purposes of that section.

(3) An order under this section may impose restrictions—
  (a) on the authorisations under sections 28 and 29 that may be granted by any individual holding an office, rank or position with a specified public authority; and
  (b) on the circumstances in which, or the purposes for which, such authorisations may be granted by any such individual.

(4) A public authority is a relevant public authority for the purposes of this section—
  (a) in relation to section 28 if it is specified in Part I or II of Schedule 1; and
  (b) in relation to section 29 if it is specified in Part I of that Schedule.

(5) An order under this section may amend Schedule 1 by—
  (a) adding a public authority to Part I or II of that Schedule;
  (b) removing a public authority from that Schedule;
  (c) moving a public authority from one Part of that Schedule to the other;
  (d) making any change consequential on any change in the name of a public authority specified in that Schedule.

(6) Without prejudice to section 31, the power to make an order under this section shall be exercisable by the Secretary of State.

(7) The Secretary of State shall not make an order under subsection (5) containing any provision for—
  (a) adding any public authority to Part I or II of that Schedule, or
  (b) moving any public authority from Part II to Part I of that Schedule,
  unless a draft of the order has been laid before Parliament and approved by a resolution of each House.

Orders under s. 30 for Northern Ireland

31.—(1) Subject to subsections (2) and (3), the power to make an order under section 30 for the purposes of the grant of authorisations for conduct in Northern Ireland shall be exercisable by the Office of the First Minister and deputy

First Minister in Northern Ireland (concurrently with being exercisable by the Secretary of State).

(2) The power of the Office of the First Minister and deputy First Minister to make an order under section 30 by virtue of subsection (1) or (3) of that section shall not be exercisable in relation to any public authority other than–
   (a) the Food Standards Agency;
   (b) [repealed]
   (c) an authority added to Schedule 1 by an order made by that Office;
   (d) an authority added to that Schedule by an order made by the Secretary of State which it would (apart from that order) have been within the powers of that Office to add to that Schedule for the purposes mentioned in subsection (1) of this section.

(3) The power of the Office of the First Minister and deputy First Minister to make an order under section 30–
   (a) shall not include power to make any provision dealing with an excepted matter;
   (b) shall not include power, except with the consent of the Secretary of State, to make any provision dealing with a reserved matter.

(4) The power of the Office of the First Minister and deputy First Minister to make an order under section 30 shall be exercisable by statutory rule for the purposes of the Statutory Rules (Northern Ireland) Order 1979.

(5) A statutory rule containing an order under section 30 which makes provision by virtue of subsection (5) of that section for–
   (a) adding any public authority to Part I or II of Schedule 1, or
   (b) moving any public authority from Part II to Part I of that Schedule,
   shall be subject to affirmative resolution (within the meaning of section 41(4) of the Interpretation Act (Northern Ireland) 1954).

(6) A statutory rule containing an order under section 30 (other than one to which subsection (5) of this section applies) shall be subject to negative resolution (within the meaning of section 41(6) of the Interpretation Act (Northern Ireland) 1954).

(7) An order under section 30 made by the Office of the First Minister and deputy First Minister may–
   (a) make different provision for different cases;
   (b) contain such incidental, supplemental, consequential and transitional provision as that Office thinks fit.

(8) The reference in subsection (2) to an addition to Schedule 1 being within the powers of the Office of the First Minister and deputy First Minister includes a reference to its being within the powers exercisable by that Office with the consent for the purposes of subsection (3)(b) of the Secretary of State.

(9) In this section 'excepted matter' and 'reserved matter' have the same meanings as in the Northern Ireland Act 1998; and, in relation to those matters, section 98(2) of that Act (meaning of 'deals with') applies for the purposes of this section as it applies for the purposes of that Act.

Authorisation of intrusive surveillance

32.—(1) Subject to the following provisions of this Part, the Secretary of State and each of the senior authorising officers shall have power to grant authorisations for the carrying out of intrusive surveillance.

(2) Neither the Secretary of State nor any senior authorising officer shall grant an authorisation for the carrying out of intrusive surveillance unless he believes–

(a) that the authorisation is necessary on grounds falling within subsection (3); and

(b) that the authorised surveillance is proportionate to what is sought to be achieved by carrying it out.

(3) Subject to the following provisions of this section, an authorisation is necessary on grounds falling within this subsection if it is necessary–

(a) in the interests of national security;

(b) for the purpose of preventing or detecting serious crime; or

(c) in the interests of the economic well-being of the United Kingdom.

(3A) In the case of an authorisation granted by the chairman of the OFT, the authorisation is necessary on grounds falling within subsection (3) only if it is necessary for the purpose of preventing or detecting an offence under section 188 of the Enterprise Act 2002 (cartel offence).

(4) The matters to be taken into account in considering whether the requirements of subsection (2) are satisfied in the case of any authorisation shall include whether the information which it is thought necessary to obtain by the authorised conduct could reasonably be obtained by other means.

(5) The conduct that is authorised by an authorisation for the carrying out of intrusive surveillance is any conduct that–

(a) consists in the carrying out of intrusive surveillance of any such description as is specified in the authorisation;

(b) is carried out in relation to the residential premises specified or described in the authorisation or in relation to the private vehicle so specified or described; and

(c) is carried out for the purposes of, or in connection with, the investigation or operation so specified or described.

(6) For the purposes of this section the senior authorising officers are–

(a) the chief constable of every police force maintained under section 2 of the Police Act 1996 (police forces in England and Wales outside London);

(b) the Commissioner of Police of the Metropolis and every Assistant Commissioner of Police of the Metropolis;

(c) the Commissioner of Police for the City of London;

(d) the chief constable of every police force maintained under or by virtue of section 1 of the Police (Scotland) Act 1967 (police forces for areas in Scotland);

(e) the Chief Constable of the Police Service of Northern Ireland and the Deputy Chief Constable of the Police Service of Northern Ireland;

(f) the Chief Constable of the Ministry of Defence Police;

(g) the Provost Marshal of the Royal Navy Regulating Branch;

(h) the Provost Marshal of the Royal Military Police;

(i) the Provost Marshal of the Royal Air Force Police;

(j) the Chief Constable of the British Transport Police;

(ja) the chairman of the Independent Police Complaints Commission;

(k) the Director General of the National Criminal Intelligence Service;[12]

(l) the Director General of the National Crime Squad and any person holding the rank of assistant chief constable in that Squad who is designated for the purposes of this paragraph by that Director General;[13]

(m) any customs officer designated for the purposes of this paragraph by the Commissioners of Customs and Excise; and

(n) the chairman of the OFT.

Police and customs authorisations

Rules for grant of authorisations

33.—(1) A person who is a designated person for the purposes of section 28 or 29 by reference to his office, rank or position with a police force, the National Criminal Intelligence Service or the National Crime Squad shall not grant an authorisation under that section except on an application made by a member of the same force, Service or Squad.[14]

(2) A person who is designated for the purposes of section 28 or 29 by reference to his office, rank or position with the Commissioners of Customs and Excise shall not grant an authorisation under that section except on an application made by a customs officer.

(3) A person who is a senior authorising officer by reference to a police force, the National Criminal Intelligence Service or the National Crime Squad shall not grant an authorisation for the carrying out of intrusive surveillance except–

(a) on an application made by a member of the same force, Service or Squad; and

(b) in the case of an authorisation for the carrying out of intrusive surveillance in relation to any residential premises, where those premises are in the area of operation of that force, Service or Squad.[15]

(4) A person who is a senior authorising officer by virtue of a designation by the Commissioners of Customs and Excise shall not grant an authorisation for the carrying out of intrusive surveillance except on an application made by a customs officer.

(4A) The chairman of the OFT shall not grant an authorisation for the carrying out of intrusive surveillance except on an application made by an officer of the OFT.

(5) A single authorisation may combine both–

(a) an authorisation granted under this Part by, or on the application of, an individual who is a member of a police force, the National Criminal Intelligence Service or the National Crime Squad, or who is a customs officer, or the chairman or an officer of the OFT, and[16]

---

[12] Prospectively amended by SOCAPA 2005 Sch 4 para 136.

[13] ibid.

[14] Prospectively amended by SOCAPA 2005 Sch 4 para 137 and Sch 17 Pt II, and new subsection (1A) prospectively inserted.

[15] Prospectively amended by SOCAPA 2005 Sch 4 para 137 and Sch 17 Pt II, and new subsection (3A) prospectively inserted.

[16] Prospectively amended by SOCAPA 2005 Sch 4 para 137.

(b) an authorisation given by, or on the application of, that individual under Part III of the Police Act 1997;

but the provisions of this Act or that Act that are applicable in the case of each of the authorisations shall apply separately in relation to the part of the combined authorisation to which they are applicable.

(6) For the purposes of this section–

    (a) the area of operation of a police force maintained under section 2 of the Police Act 1996, of the metropolitan police force, of the City of London police force or of a police force maintained under or by virtue of section 1 of the Police (Scotland) Act 1967 is the area for which that force is maintained;

    (b) the area of operation of the Police Service of Northern Ireland is Northern Ireland;

    (c) residential premises are in the area of operation of the Ministry of Defence Police if they are premises where the members of that police force, under section 2 of the Ministry of Defence Police Act 1987, have the powers and privileges of a constable;

    (d) residential premises are in the area of operation of the Royal Navy Regulating Branch, the Royal Military Police or the Royal Air Force Police if they are premises owned or occupied by, or used for residential purposes by, a person subject to service discipline;

    (e) the area of operation of the British Transport Police and also of the National Criminal Intelligence Service is the United Kingdom;[17]

    (f) the area of operation of the National Crime Squad is England and Wales;[18]

and references in this section to the United Kingdom or to any part or area of the United Kingdom include any adjacent waters within the seaward limits of the territorial waters of the United Kingdom.

(7) For the purposes of this section a person is subject to service discipline–

    (a) in relation to the Royal Navy Regulating Branch, if he is subject to the Naval Discipline Act 1957 or is a civilian to whom Parts I and II of that Act for the time being apply by virtue of section 118 of that Act;

    (b) in relation to the Royal Military Police, if he is subject to military law or is a civilian to whom Part II of the Army Act 1955 for the time being applies by virtue of section 209 of that Act; and

    (c) in relation to the Royal Air Force Police, if he is subject to air-force law or is a civilian to whom Part II of the Air Force Act 1955 for the time being applies by virtue of section 209 of that Act.

Grant of authorisations in the senior officer's absence

34.—(1) This section applies in the case of an application for an authorisation for the carrying out of intrusive surveillance where–

    (a) the application is one made by a member of a police force, of the National Criminal Intelligence Service or of the National Crime Squad or by a member of staff of the Independent Police Complaints Commission or by an officer of the OFT or a customs officer; and[19]

---

[17] Prospectively amended by SOCAPA 2005 Sch 4 para 137 and Sch 17 Pt II.

[18] Prospectively repealed ibid.

[19] Prospectively amended by SOCAPA 2005 Sch 4 para 138.

(b) the case is urgent.

(2) If–

    (a) it is not reasonably practicable, having regard to the urgency of the case, for the application to be considered by any person who is a senior authorising officer by reference to the force, Service or Squad in question or the Independent Police Complaints Commission or, as the case may be, as chairman of the OFT or by virtue of a designation by the Commissioners of Customs and Excise, and[20]

    (b) it also not reasonably practicable, having regard to the urgency of the case, for the application to be considered by a person (if there is one) who is entitled, as a designated deputy of a senior authorising officer, to exercise the functions in relation to that application of such an officer,

the application may be made to and considered by any person who is entitled under subsection (4) to act for any senior authorising officer who would have been entitled to consider the application.

(3) A person who considers an application under subsection (1) shall have the same power to grant an authorisation as the person for whom he is entitled to act.

(4) For the purposes of this section–

    (a) a person is entitled to act for the chief constable of a police force maintained under section 2 of the Police Act 1996 if he holds the rank of assistant chief constable in that force;

    (b) a person is entitled to act for the Commissioner of Police of the Metropolis, or for an Assistant Commissioner of Police of the Metropolis, if he holds the rank of commander in the metropolitan police force;

    (c) a person is entitled to act for the Commissioner of Police for the City of London if he holds the rank of commander in the City of London police force;

    (d) a person is entitled to act for the chief constable of a police force maintained under or by virtue of section 1 of the Police (Scotland) Act 1967 if he holds the rank of assistant chief constable in that force;

    (e) a person is entitled to act for the Chief Constable of the Police Service of Northern Ireland, or for the Deputy Chief Constable of the Police Service of Northern Ireland, if he holds the rank of assistant chief constable in the Police Service of Northern Ireland;

    (f) a person is entitled to act for the Chief Constable of the Ministry of Defence Police if he holds the rank of deputy or assistant chief constable in that force;

    (g) a person is entitled to act for the Provost Marshal of the Royal Navy Regulating Branch if he holds the position of assistant Provost Marshal in that Branch;

    (h) a person is entitled to act for the Provost Marshal of the Royal Military Police or the Provost Marshal of the Royal Air Force Police if he holds the position of deputy Provost Marshal in the police force in question;

    (i) a person is entitled to act for the Chief Constable of the British Transport Police if he holds the rank of deputy or assistant chief constable in that force;

---

[20] Prospectively amended by SOCAPA 2005 Sch 4 para 138.

(j) a person is entitled to act for the Director General of the National Criminal Intelligence Service if he is a person designated for the purposes of this paragraph by that Director General;[21]

(k) a person is entitled to act for the Director General of the National Crime Squad if he is designated for the purposes of this paragraph by that Director General as a person entitled so to act in an urgent case;[22]

(l) a person is entitled to act for a person who is a senior authorising officer by virtue of a designation by the Commissioners of Customs and Excise, if he is designated for the purposes of this paragraph by those Commissioners as a person entitled so to act in an urgent case;

(m) a person is entitled to act for the chairman of the OFT if he is an officer of the OFT designated by it for the purposes of this paragraph as a person entitled so to act in an urgent case;

(n) person is entitled to act for the chairman of the Independent Police Complaints Commission if he is any other member of the Independent Police Complaints Commission.

(5) A police member of the National Criminal Intelligence Service or the National Crime Squad appointed under section 9(1)(b) or 55(1)(b) of the Police Act 1997 (police members) may not be designated under subsection (4)(j) or (k) unless he holds the rank of assistant chief constable in that Service or Squad.[23]

(6) In this section 'designated deputy'–

(a) in relation to a chief constable, means a person holding the rank of assistant chief constable who is designated to act under section 12(4) of the Police Act 1996 or section 5(4) of the Police (Scotland) Act 1967;

(b) in relation to the Commissioner of Police for the City of London, means a person authorised to act under section 25 of the City of London Police Act 1839;

(c) in relation to the Director General of the National Criminal Intelligence Service or the Director General of the National Crime Squad, means a person designated to act under section 8 or, as the case may be, section 54 of the Police Act 1997;[24]

(d) in relation to the Chairman of the Independent Police Complaints Commission, means a person appointed as deputy chairman of the Independent Police Complaints Commission under paragraph 3(1) of Schedule 2 to the Police Reform Act 2002.

Notification of authorisations for intrusive surveillance

35.—(1) Where a person grants or cancels a police, customs or OFT authorisation for the carrying out of intrusive surveillance, he shall give notice that he has done so to an ordinary Surveillance Commissioner.[25]

(2) A notice given for the purposes of subsection (1)–

(a) must be given in writing as soon as reasonably practicable after the grant or, as the case may be, cancellation of the authorisation to which it relates;

---

[21] Prospectively amended by SOCAPA 2005 Sch 4 para 138.

[22] ibid.

[23] Prospectively repealed by SOCAPA 2005 Sch 4 para 138 and Sch 17 Pt II.

[24] ibid.

[25] Prospectively amended by SOCAPA 2005 Sch 4 para 139.

    (b) must be given in accordance with any such arrangements made for the purposes of this paragraph by the Chief Surveillance Commissioner as are for the time being in force; and

    (c) must specify such matters as the Secretary of State may by order prescribe.

(3) A notice under this section of the grant of an authorisation shall, as the case may be, either–

    (a) state that the approval of a Surveillance Commissioner is required by section 36 before the grant of the authorisation will take effect; or

    (b) state that the case is one of urgency and set out the grounds on which the case is believed to be one of urgency.

(4) Where a notice for the purposes of subsection (1) of the grant of an authorisation has been received by an ordinary Surveillance Commissioner, he shall, as soon as practicable–

    (a) scrutinise the authorisation; and

    (b) in a case where notice has been given in accordance with subsection (3)(a), decide whether or not to approve the authorisation.

(5) Subject to subsection (6), the Secretary of State shall not make an order under subsection (2)(c) unless a draft of the order has been laid before Parliament and approved by a resolution of each House.

(6) Subsection (5) does not apply in the case of the order made on the first occasion on which the Secretary of State exercises his power to make an order under subsection (2)(c).

(7) The order made on that occasion shall cease to have effect at the end of the period of forty days beginning with the day on which it was made unless, before the end of that period, it has been approved by a resolution of each House of Parliament.

(8) For the purposes of subsection (7)–

    (a) the order's ceasing to have effect shall be without prejudice to anything previously done or to the making of a new order; and

    (b) in reckoning the period of forty days no account shall be taken of any period during which Parliament is dissolved or prorogued or during which both Houses are adjourned for more than four days.

(9) Any notice that is required by any provision of this section to be given in writing may be given, instead, by being transmitted by electronic means.

(10) In this section references to a police, customs or OFT authorisation are references to an authorisation granted by–

    (a) a person who is a senior authorising officer by reference to a police force, the Independent Police Complaints Commission, the National Criminal Intelligence Service or the National Crime Squad;[26]

    (b) a person who is a senior authorising officer by virtue of a designation by the Commissioners of Customs and Excise;

    (ba) the chairman of the OFT; or

    (c) a person who for the purposes of section 34 is entitled to act for a person falling within paragraph (a) or for a person falling within paragraph (b) or for a person falling within paragraph (ba).

---

[26] ibid.

Approval required for authorisations to take effect

36.—(1) This section applies where an authorisation for the carrying out of intrusive surveillance has been granted on the application of–

(a) a member of a police force;

(aa) a member of staff of the Independent Police Complaints Commission who has been designated under paragraph 19(2) of Schedule 3 to the Police Reform Act 2002;

(b) a member of the National Criminal Intelligence Service;[27]

(c) a member of the National Crime Squad;[28]

(d) a customs officer; or

(e) an officer of the OFT.

(2) Subject to subsection (3), the authorisation shall not take effect until such time (if any) as–

(a) the grant of the authorisation has been approved by an ordinary Surveillance Commissioner; and

(b) written notice of the Commissioner's decision to approve the grant of the authorisation has been given, in accordance with subsection (4), to the person who granted the authorisation.

(3) Where the person who grants the authorisation–

(a) believes that the case is one of urgency, and

(b) gives notice in accordance with section 35(3)(b),

subsection (2) shall not apply to the authorisation, and the authorisation shall have effect from the time of its grant.

(4) Where subsection (2) applies to the authorisation–

(a) a Surveillance Commissioner shall give his approval under this section to the authorisation if, and only if, he is satisfied that there are reasonable grounds for believing that the requirements of section 32(2)(a) and (b) are satisfied in the case of the authorisation; and

(b) a Surveillance Commissioner who makes a decision as to whether or not the authorisation should be approved shall, as soon as reasonably practicable after making that decision, give written notice of his decision to the person who granted the authorisation.

(5) If an ordinary Surveillance Commissioner decides not to approve an authorisation to which subsection (2) applies, he shall make a report of his findings to the most senior relevant person.

(6) In this section 'the most senior relevant person' means–

(a) where the authorisation was granted by the senior authorising officer with any police force who is not someone's deputy, that senior authorising officer;

(b) where the authorisation was granted by the Director General of the National Criminal Intelligence Service or the Director General of the National Crime Squad, that Director General;[29]

(ba) where the authorisation was granted by the Chairman of the Independent Police Complaints Commission, by the designated deputy of the Chairman of the Independent Police Complaints Commission or by another member

---

[27] Prospectively amended by SOCAPA 2005 Sch 4 para 140.

[28] ibid.

[29] ibid.

of that Commission entitled to act for that Chairman by virtue of section 34(4)(m), that Chairman;

(c) where the authorisation was granted by a senior authorising officer with a police force who is someone's deputy, the senior authorising officer whose deputy granted the authorisation;

(d) where the authorisation was granted by the designated deputy of the Director General of the National Criminal Intelligence Service or a person entitled to act for him by virtue of section 34(4)(j), that Director General;[30]

(e) where the authorisation was granted by the designated deputy of the Director General of the National Crime Squad or by a person designated by that Director General for the purposes of section 32(6)(l) or 34(4)(k), that Director General;[31]

(f) where the authorisation was granted by a person entitled to act for a senior authorising officer under section 34(4)(a) to (i), the senior authorising officer in the force in question who is not someone's deputy;

(g) where the authorisation was granted by a customs officer, the customs officer for the time being designated for the purposes of this paragraph by a written notice given to the Chief Surveillance Commissioner by the Commissioners of Customs and Excise; and

(h) where the authorisation was granted by the chairman of the OFT or a person entitled to act for him by virtue of 34(4)(m), that chairman.

(7) The references in subsection (6) to a person's deputy are references to the following–

(a) in relation to–

(i) a chief constable of a police force maintained under section 2 of the Police Act 1996,

(ii) the Commissioner of Police for the City of London, or

(iii) a chief constable of a police force maintained under or by virtue of section 1 of the Police (Scotland) Act 1967,

to his designated deputy;

(b) in relation to the Commissioner of Police of the Metropolis, to an Assistant Commissioner of Police of the Metropolis; and

(c) in relation to the Chief Constable of the Police Service of Northern Ireland, to the Deputy Chief Constable of the Police Service of Northern Ireland;

and in this subsection and that subsection 'designated deputy' has the same meaning as in section 34.

(8) Any notice that is required by any provision of this section to be given in writing may be given, instead, by being transmitted by electronic means.

Quashing of police and customs authorisations etc.

37.—(1) This section applies where an authorisation for the carrying out of intrusive surveillance has been granted on the application of–

(a) a member of a police force;

---

[30] ibid.
[31] ibid.

      (aa) a member of staff of the Independent Police Complaints Commission who has been designated under paragraph 19(2) of Schedule 3 to the Police Reform Act 2002;

      (b) a member of the National Criminal Intelligence Service;[32]

      (c) a member of the National Crime Squad;[33]

      (d) a customs officer; or

      (e) an officer of the OFT.

(2) Where an ordinary Surveillance Commissioner is at any time satisfied that, at the time when the authorisation was granted or at any time when it was renewed, there were no reasonable grounds for believing that the requirements of section 32(2)(a) and (b) were satisfied, he may quash the authorisation with effect, as he thinks fit, from the time of the grant of the authorisation or from the time of any renewal of the authorisation.

(3) If an ordinary Surveillance Commissioner is satisfied at any time while the authorisation is in force that there are no longer any reasonable grounds for believing that the requirements of section 32(2)(a) and (b) are satisfied in relation to the authorisation, he may cancel the authorisation with effect from such time as appears to him to be the time from which those requirements ceased to be so satisfied.

(4) Where, in the case of any authorisation of which notice has been given in accordance with section 35(3)(b), an ordinary Surveillance Commissioner is at any time satisfied that, at the time of the grant or renewal of the authorisation to which that notice related, there were no reasonable grounds for believing that the case was one of urgency, he may quash the authorisation with effect, as he thinks fit, from the time of the grant of the authorisation or from the time of any renewal of the authorisation.

(5) Subject to subsection (7), where an ordinary Surveillance Commissioner quashes an authorisation under this section, he may order the destruction of any records relating wholly or partly to information obtained by the authorised conduct after the time from which his decision takes effect.

(6) Subject to subsection (7), where–

      (a) an authorisation has ceased to have effect (otherwise than by virtue of subsection (2) or (4)), and

      (b) an ordinary Surveillance Commissioner is satisfied that there was a time while the authorisation was in force when there were no reasonable grounds for believing that the requirements of section 32(2)(a) and (b) continued to be satisfied in relation to the authorisation,

    he may order the destruction of any records relating, wholly or partly, to information obtained at such a time by the authorised conduct.

(7) No order shall be made under this section for the destruction of any records required for pending criminal or civil proceedings.

(8) Where an ordinary Surveillance Commissioner exercises a power conferred by this section, he shall, as soon as reasonably practicable, make a report of his exercise of that power, and of his reasons for doing so–

      (a) to the most senior relevant person (within the meaning of section 36); and

---

[32] Prospectively amended by SOCAPA 2005 Sch 4 para 141.

[33] ibid.

(b) to the Chief Surveillance Commissioner.

(9) Where an order for the destruction of records is made under this section, the order shall not become operative until such time (if any) as–

    (a) the period for appealing against the decision to make the order has expired; and

    (b) any appeal brought within that period has been dismissed by the Chief Surveillance Commissioner.

(10) No notice shall be required to be given under section 35(1) in the case of a cancellation under subsection (3) of this section.

Appeals against decisions by Surveillance Commissioners

38.—(1) Any senior authorising officer may appeal to the Chief Surveillance Commissioner against any of the following–

    (a) any refusal of an ordinary Surveillance Commissioner to approve an authorisation for the carrying out of intrusive surveillance;

    (b) any decision of such a Commissioner to quash or cancel such an authorisation;

    (c) any decision of such a Commissioner to make an order under section 37 for the destruction of records.

(2) In the case of an authorisation granted by the designated deputy of a senior authorising office or by a person who for the purposes of section 34 is entitled to act for a senior authorising officer, that designated deputy or person shall also be entitled to appeal under this section.

(3) An appeal under this section must be brought within the period of seven days beginning with the day on which the refusal or decision appealed against is reported to the appellant.

(4) Subject to subsection (5), the Chief Surveillance Commissioner, on an appeal under this section, shall allow the appeal if–

    (a) he is satisfied that there were reasonable grounds for believing that the requirements of section 32(2)(a) and (b) were satisfied in relation to the authorisation at the time in question; and

    (b) he is not satisfied that the authorisation is one of which notice was given in accordance with section 35(3)(b) without there being any reasonable grounds for believing that the case was one of urgency.

(5) If, on an appeal falling within subsection (1)(b), the Chief Surveillance Commissioner–

    (a) is satisfied that grounds exist which justify the quashing or cancellation under section 37 of the authorisation in question, but

    (b) considers that the authorisation should have been quashed or cancelled from a different time from that from which it was quashed or cancelled by the ordinary Surveillance Commissioner against whose decision the appeal is brought,

he may modify that Commissioner's decision to quash or cancel the authorisation, and any related decision for the destruction of records, so as to give effect to the decision under section 37 that he considers should have been made.

(6) Where, on an appeal under this section against a decision to quash or cancel an authorisation, the Chief Surveillance Commissioner allows the appeal he shall

also quash any related order for the destruction of records relating to information obtained by the authorised conduct.

(7) In this section 'designated deputy' has the same meaning as in section 34.

Appeals to the Chief Surveillance Commissioner: supplementary

39.—(1) Where the Chief Surveillance Commissioner has determined an appeal under section 38, he shall give notice of his determination to both–

(a) the person by whom the appeal was brought; and

(b) the ordinary Surveillance Commissioner whose decision was appealed against.

(2) Where the determination of the Chief Surveillance Commissioner on an appeal under section 38 is a determination to dismiss the appeal, the Chief Surveillance Commissioner shall make a report of his findings–

(a) to the persons mentioned in subsection (1); and

(b) to the Prime Minister.

(3) Subsections (3) and (4) of section 107 of the Police Act 1997 (reports to be laid before Parliament and exclusion of matters from the report) apply in relation to any report to the Prime Minister under subsection (2) of this section as they apply in relation to any report under subsection (2) of that section.

(4) Subject to subsection (2) of this section, the Chief Surveillance Commissioner shall not give any reasons for any determination of his on an appeal under section 38.

Information to be provided to Surveillance Commissioners

40. It shall be the duty of–

(a) every member of a police force,

(aa) every member and every employee of the Independent Police Complaints Commission;

(b) every member of the National Criminal Intelligence Service,[34]

(c) every member of the National Crime Squad,[35]

(d) every customs officer, and

(e) an officer of the OFT,

to comply with any request of a Surveillance Commissioner for documents or information required by that Commissioner for the purpose of enabling him to carry out the functions of such a Commissioner under sections 35 to 39.

Other authorisations

Secretary of State authorisations

41.—(1) The Secretary of State shall not grant an authorisation for the carrying out of intrusive surveillance except on an application made by–

(a) a member of any of the intelligence services;

(b) an official of the Ministry of Defence;

(c) a member of Her Majesty's forces;

---

[34] Prospectively amended by SOCAPA 2005 Sch 4 para 142.

[35] ibid.

(d) an individual holding an office, rank or position with any such public authority as may be designated for the purposes of this section as an authority whose activities may require the carrying out of intrusive surveillance.

(2) Section 32 shall have effect in relation to the grant of an authorisation by the Secretary of State on the application of an official of the Ministry of Defence, or of a member of Her Majesty's forces, as if the only matters mentioned in subsection (3) of that section were–

   (a) the interests of national security; and

   (b) the purpose of preventing or detecting serious crime.

(3) The designation of any public authority for the purposes of this section shall be by order made by the Secretary of State.

(4) The Secretary of State may by order provide, in relation to any public authority, that an application for an authorisation for the carrying out of intrusive surveillance may be made by an individual holding an office, rank or position with that authority only where his office, rank or position is one prescribed by the order.

(5) The Secretary of State may by order impose restrictions–

   (a) on the authorisations for the carrying out of intrusive surveillance that may be granted on the application of an individual holding an office, rank or position with any public authority designated for the purposes of this section; and

   (b) on the circumstances in which, or the purposes for which, such authorisations may be granted on such an application.

(6) The Secretary of State shall not make a designation under subsection (3) unless a draft of the order containing the designation has been laid before Parliament and approved by a resolution of each House.

(7) References in this section to a member of Her Majesty's forces do not include references to any member of Her Majesty's forces who is a member of a police force by virtue of his service with the Royal Navy Regulating Branch, the Royal Military Police or the Royal Air Force Police.

Intelligence services authorisations

42.—(1) The grant by the Secretary of State or the Scottish Ministers (by virtue of provision under section 63 of the Scotland Act 1998) on the application of a member of one of the intelligence services of any authorisation under this Part must be made by the issue of a warrant.

(2) A single warrant issued by the Secretary of State or the Scottish Ministers (by virtue of provision under section 63 of the Scotland Act 1998) may combine both–

   (a) an authorisation under this Part; and

   (b) an intelligence services warrant;

   but the provisions of this Act or the Intelligence Services Act 1994 that are applicable in the case of the authorisation under this Part or the intelligence services warrant shall apply separately in relation to the part of the combined warrant to which they are applicable.

(3) Intrusive surveillance in relation to any premises or vehicle in the British Islands shall be capable of being authorised by a warrant issued under this Part on the application of a member of the Secret Intelligence Service or GCHQ only if the authorisation contained in the warrant is one satisfying the requirements of

section 32(2)(a) otherwise than in connection with any functions of that intelligence service in support of the prevention or detection of serious crime.

(4) Subject to subsection (5), the functions of the Security Service shall include acting on behalf of the Secret Intelligence Service or GCHQ in relation to–.

    (a) the application for and grant of any authorisation under this Part in connection with any matter within the functions of the Secret Intelligence Service or GCHQ; and

    (b) the carrying out, in connection with any such matter, of any conduct authorised by such an authorisation.

(5) Nothing in subsection (4) shall authorise the doing of anything by one intelligence service on behalf of another unless–

    (a) it is something which either the other service or a member of the other service has power to do; and

    (b) it is done otherwise than in connection with functions of the other service in support of the prevention or detection of serious crime.

(6) In this section 'intelligence services warrant' means a warrant under section 5 of the Intelligence Services Act 1994.

Grant, renewal and duration of authorisations

General rules about grant, renewal and duration

43.—(1) An authorisation under this Part–

    (a) may be granted or renewed orally in any urgent case in which the entitlement to act of the person granting or renewing it is not confined to urgent cases; and

    (b) in any other case, must be in writing.

(2) A single authorisation may combine two or more different authorisations under this Part; but the provisions of this Act that are applicable in the case of each of the authorisations shall apply separately in relation to the part of the combined authorisation to which they are applicable.

(3) Subject to subsections (4) and (8), an authorisation under this Part shall cease to have effect at the end of the following period–

    (a) in the case of an authorisation which–

        (i) has not been renewed and was granted either orally or by a person whose entitlement to act is confined to urgent cases, or

        (ii) was last renewed either orally or by such a person,

    the period of seventy-two hours beginning with the time when the grant of the authorisation or, as the case may be, its latest renewal takes effect;

    (b) in a case not falling within paragraph (a) in which the authorisation is for the conduct or the use of a covert human intelligence source, the period of twelve months beginning with the day on which the grant of the authorisation or, as the case may be, its latest renewal takes effect; and

    (c) in any case not falling within paragraph (a) or (b), the period of three months beginning with the day on which the grant of the authorisation or, as the case may be, its latest renewal takes effect.

(4) Subject to subsection (6), an authorisation under this Part may be renewed, at any time before the time at which it ceases to have effect, by any person who would be entitled to grant a new authorisation in the same terms.

(5) Sections 28 to 41 shall have effect in relation to the renewal of an authorisation under this Part as if references to the grant of an authorisation included references to its renewal.

(6) A person shall not renew an authorisation for the conduct or the use of a covert human intelligence source, unless he–

    (a) is satisfied that a review has been carried out of the matters mentioned in subsection (7); and

    (b) has, for the purpose of deciding whether he should renew the authorisation, considered the results of that review.

(7) The matters mentioned in subsection (6) are–

    (a) the use made of the source in the period since the grant or, as the case may be, latest renewal of the authorisation; and

    (b) the tasks given to the source during that period and the information obtained from the conduct or the use of the source.

(8) The Secretary of State may by order provide in relation to authorisations of such descriptions as may be specified in the order that subsection (3) is to have effect as if the period at the end of which an authorisation of a description so specified is to cease to have effect were such period shorter than that provided for by that subsection as may be fixed by or determined in accordance with that order.

(9) References in this section to the time at which, or the day on which, the grant or renewal of an authorisation takes effect are references–

    (a) in the case of the grant of an authorisation to which paragraph (c) does not apply, to the time at which or, as the case may be, day on which the authorisation is granted;

    (b) in the case of the renewal of an authorisation to which paragraph (c) does not apply, to the time at which or, as the case may be, day on which the authorisation would have ceased to have effect but for the renewal; and

    (c) in the case of any grant or renewal that takes effect under subsection (2) of section 36 at a time or on a day later than that given by paragraph (a) or (b), to the time at which or, as the case may be, day on which the grant or renewal takes effect in accordance with that subsection.

(10) In relation to any authorisation granted by a member of any of the intelligence services, and in relation to any authorisation contained in a warrant issued by the Secretary of State on the application of a member of any of the intelligence services, this section has effect subject to the provisions of section 44.

[See SI 2001/1057 in Appendix C for modifications to section 43 for the purposes of surveillance conducted by TV licensing investigators.]

Special rules for intelligence services authorisations

44.—(1) Subject to subsection (2), a warrant containing an authorisation for the carrying out of intrusive surveillance–

    (a) shall not be issued on the application of a member of any of the intelligence services, and

    (b) if so issued shall not be renewed,

except under the hand of the Secretary of State or, in the case of a warrant issued by the Scottish Ministers (by virtue of provision made under section 63 of the Scotland Act 1998), a member of the Scottish Executive.

(2) In an urgent case in which–

    (a) an application for a warrant containing an authorisation for the carrying out of intrusive surveillance has been made by a member of any of the intelligence services, and

    (b) the Secretary of State has himself or the Scottish Ministers (by virtue of provision under section 63 of the Scotland Act 1998) have themselves expressly authorised the issue of the warrant in that case or, as the case may be, a member of the staff of the Scottish Administration who is a member of the Senior Civil Service and is designated by the Scottish Ministers as a person under whose hand a warrant may be issued in such a case (in this section referred to as 'a designated official'), expressly authorised the issue of the warrant in that case,

the warrant may be issued (but not renewed) under the hand of a senior official.

(3) Subject to subsection (6), a warrant containing an authorisation for the carrying out of intrusive surveillance which–

    (a) was issued, on the application of a member of any of the intelligence services, under the hand of a senior official, and

    (b) has not been renewed under the hand of the Secretary of State,

shall cease to have effect at the end of the second working day following the day of the issue of the warrant, instead of at the time provided for by section 43(3).

(4) Subject to subsections (3) and (6), where any warrant for the carrying out of intrusive surveillance which is issued or was last renewed on the application of a member of any of the intelligence services, the warrant (unless renewed or, as the case may be, renewed again) shall cease to have effect at the following time, instead of at the time provided for by section 43(3), namely–

    (a) in the case of a warrant that has not been renewed, at the end of the period of six months beginning with the day on which it was issued; and

    (b) in any other case, at the end of the period of six months beginning with the day on which it would have ceased to have effect if not renewed again.

(5) Subject to subsection (6), where–

    (a) an authorisation for the carrying out of directed surveillance is granted by a member of any of the intelligence services, and

    (b) the authorisation is renewed by an instrument endorsed under the hand of the person renewing the authorisation with a statement that the renewal is believed to be necessary on grounds falling within section 32(3)(a) or (c),

the authorisation (unless renewed again) shall cease to have effect at the end of the period of six months beginning with the day on which it would have ceased to have effect but for the renewal, instead of at the time provided for by section 43(3).

(6) The Secretary of State may by order provide in relation to authorisations of such descriptions as may be specified in the order that subsection (3), (4) or (5) is to have effect as if the period at the end of which an authorisation of a description so specified is to cease to have effect were such period shorter than that provided for by that subsection as may be fixed by or determined in accordance with that order.

(7) Notwithstanding anything in section 43(2), in a case in which there is a combined warrant containing both–

    (a) an authorisation for the carrying out of intrusive surveillance, and

(b) an authorisation for the carrying out of directed surveillance,

the reference in subsection (4) of this section to a warrant for the carrying out of intrusive surveillance is a reference to the warrant so far as it confers both authorisations.

Cancellation of authorisations

45.—(1) The person who granted or, as the case may be, last renewed an authorisation under this Part shall cancel it if–

(a) he is satisfied that the authorisation is one in relation to which the requirements of section 28(2)(a) and (b), 29(2)(a) and (b) or, as the case may be, 32(2)(a) and (b) are no longer satisfied; or

(b) in the case of an authorisation under section 29, he is satisfied that arrangements for the source's case that satisfy the requirements mentioned in subsection (2)(c) of that section no longer exist.

[See SI 2001/1057 for the effect of this section on TV licensing investigators.]

(2) Where an authorisation under this Part was granted or, as the case may be, last renewed–

(a) by a person entitled to act for any other person, or

(b) by the deputy of any other person,

that other person shall cancel the authorisation if he is satisfied as to either of the matters mentioned in subsection (1).

(3) Where an authorisation under this Part was granted or, as the case may be, last renewed by a person whose deputy had power to grant it, that deputy shall cancel the authorisation if he is satisfied as to either of the matters mentioned in subsection (1).

(4) The Secretary of State may by regulations provide for the person by whom any duty imposed by this section is to be performed in a case in which it would otherwise fall on a person who is no longer available to perform it.

(5) Regulations under subsection (4) may provide for the person on whom the duty is to fall to be a person appointed in accordance with the regulations.

(6) The references in this section to a person's deputy are references to the following–

(a) in relation to–

  (i) a chief constable of a police force maintained under section 2 of the Police Act 1996,

  (ii) the Commissioner of Police for the City of London, or

  (iii) a chief constable of a police force maintained under or by virtue of section 1 of the Police (Scotland) Act 1967,

  to his designated deputy;

(b) in relation to the Commissioner of Police of the Metropolis, to an Assistant Commissioner of Police of the Metropolis;

(c) in relation to the Chief Constable of the Police Service of Northern Ireland, to the Deputy Chief Constable of the Police Service of Northern Ireland;

(d) in relation to the Director General of the National Criminal Intelligence Service, to his designated deputy; and[36]

---

[36] Prospectively repealed by SOCAPA 2005 Sch 4 para 143 and Sch 17 Pt II.

(e) in relation to the Director General of the National Crime Squad, to any person designated by him for the purposes of section 32(6)(l) or to his designated deputy.[37]

(7) In this section 'designated deputy' has the same meaning as in section 34.

[See SI 2001/1057 in Appendix C for modifications to section 45(1) for the purposes of surveillance conducted by TV licensing investigators.]

Scotland

Restrictions on authorisations extending to Scotland

46.—(1) No person shall grant or renew an authorisation under this Part for the carrying out of any conduct if it appears to him—

    (a) that the authorisation is not one for which this Part is the relevant statutory provision for all parts of the United Kingdom; and

    (b) that all the conduct authorised by the grant or, as the case may be, renewal of the authorisation is likely to take place in Scotland.

(2) In relation to any authorisation, this Part is the relevant statutory provision for all parts of the United Kingdom in so far as it—

    (a) is granted or renewed on the grounds that it is necessary in the interests of national security or in the interests of the economic well-being of the United Kingdom;

    (b) is granted or renewed by or on the application of a person holding any office, rank or position with any of the public authorities specified in subsection (3);

    (c) authorises conduct of a person holding an office, rank or position with any of the public authorities so specified;

    (d) authorises conduct of an individual acting as a covert human intelligence source for the benefit of any of the public authorities so specified; or

    (e) authorises conduct that is surveillance by virtue of section 48(4).

(3) The public authorities mentioned in subsection (2) are—

    (a) each of the intelligence services;

    (b) Her Majesty's forces;

    (c) the Ministry of Defence;

    (d) the Ministry of Defence Police;

    (dza) the Civil Nuclear Constabulary;

    (da) the OFT;[38]

    (e) the Commissioners of Customs and Excise; and

    (f) the British Transport Police.

(4) For the purposes of so much of this Part as has effect in relation to any other public authority by virtue of—

    (a) the fact that it is a public authority for the time being specified in Schedule 1, or

    (b) an order under subsection (1)(d) of section 41 designating that authority for the purposes of that section,

---

[37] Prospectively repealed by SOCAPA 2005 Sch 4 para 143 and Sch 17 Pt II.

[38] New subparagraph (db) prospectively inserted by SOCAPA 2005 Sch 4 para 144.

the authorities specified in subsection (3) of this section shall be treated as including that authority to the extent that the Secretary of State by order directs that the authority is a relevant public authority or, as the case may be, is a designated authority for all parts of the United Kingdom.

Supplemental provision for Part II

Power to extend or modify authorisation provisions

47.—(1) The Secretary of State may by order do one or both of the following–
  (a) apply this Part, with such modifications as he thinks fit, to any such surveillance that is neither directed nor intrusive as may be described in the order;
  (b) provide for any description of directed surveillance to be treated for the purposes of this Part as intrusive surveillance.
(2) No order shall be made under this section unless a draft of it has been laid before Parliament and approved by a resolution of each House.

Interpretation of Part II

48.—(1) In this Part–
  'covert human intelligence source' shall be construed in accordance with section 26(8);
  'directed' and 'intrusive', in relation to surveillance, shall be construed in accordance with section 26(2) to (6);
  'OFT' means the Office of Fair Trading;
  'private vehicle' means (subject to subsection (7)(a)) any vehicle which is used primarily for the private purposes of the person who owns it or of a person otherwise having the right to use it;
  'residential premises' means (subject to subsection (7)(b)) so much of any premises as is for the time being occupied or used by any person, however temporarily, for residential purposes or otherwise as living accommodation (including hotel or prison accommodation that is so occupied or used);
  'senior authorising officer' means a person who by virtue of subsection (6) of section 32 is a senior authorising officer for the purposes of that section;
  'surveillance' shall be construed in accordance with subsections (2) to (4);
  'surveillance device' means any apparatus designed or adapted for use in surveillance.
(2) Subject to subsection (3), in this Part 'surveillance' includes–
  (a) monitoring, observing or listening to persons, their movements, their conversations or their other activities or communications;
  (b) recording anything monitored, observed or listened to in the course of surveillance; and
  (c) surveillance by or with the assistance of a surveillance device.
(3) References in this Part to surveillance do not include references to–
  (a) any conduct of a covert human intelligence source for obtaining or recording (whether or not using a surveillance device) any information which is disclosed in the presence of the source;
  (b) the use of a covert human intelligence source for so obtaining or recording information; or

(c) any such entry on or interference with property or with wireless telegraphy as would be unlawful unless authorised under–

    (i) section 5 of the Intelligence Services Act 1994 (warrants for the intelligence services); or

    (ii) Part III of the Police Act 1997 (powers of the police and of customs officers).

(4) References in this Part to surveillance include references to the interception of a communication in the course of its transmission by means of a postal service or telecommunication system if, and only if–

(a) the communication is one sent by or intended for a person who has consented to the interception of communications sent by or to him; and

(b) there is no interception warrant authorising the interception.

(5) References in this Part to an individual holding an office or position with a public authority include references to any member, official or employee of that authority.

(6) For the purposes of this Part the activities of a covert human intelligence source which are to be taken as activities for the benefit of a particular public authority include any conduct of his as such a source which is in response to inducements or requests made by or on behalf of that authority.

(7) In subsection (1)–

(a) the reference to a person having the right to use a vehicle does not, in relation to a motor vehicle, include a reference to a person whose right to use the vehicle derives only from his having paid, or undertaken to pay, for the use of the vehicle and its driver for a particular journey; and

(b) the reference to premises occupied or used by any person for residential purposes or otherwise as living accommodation does not include a reference to so much of any premises as constitutes any common area to which he has or is allowed access in connection with his use or occupation of any accommodation.

(8) In this section–

'premises' includes any vehicle or moveable structure and any other place whatever, whether or not occupied as land;

'vehicle' includes any vessel, aircraft or hovercraft.

SCHEDULE 1 AS AMENDED
RELEVANT PUBLIC AUTHORITIES

PART I
RELEVANT AUTHORITIES FOR THE PURPOSES OF SS. 28 AND 29

Police forces etc.

1.   Any police force.

1A. The Civil Nuclear Constabulary.

2.   The National Criminal Intelligence Service.[39]

3.   The National Crime Squad.[40]

---

[39] Prospectively amended by SOCAPA 2005 Sch 4 para 155.

[40] ibid.

4.   The Serious Fraud Office.

4A. The Independent Police Complaints Commission.

4B. The force comprising the special constables appointed under section 79 of the Harbours, Docks and Piers Clauses Act 1847 on the nomination of the Dover Harbour Board.

4C. The force comprising the constables appointed under article 3 of the Mersey Docks and Harbour (Police) Order 1975 on the nomination of the Mersey Docks and Harbour Board.

The intelligence services

5.   Any of the intelligence services.

The armed forces

6.   Any of Her Majesty's forces.

The revenue departments

7.   The Commissioners of Customs and Excise.

8.   The Commissioners of Inland Revenue.

Government departments

9.   [repealed]

10. The Ministry of Defence.

10i. The Department for Environment, Food and Rural Affairs.

11. [repealed]

12. The Department of Health.

13. The Home Office.

13A. The Northern Ireland Office.

14. The Department for Transport.

15. The Department of Trade and Industry.

15i. The Office of the Deputy Prime Minister.

15ii. Department for Work & Pensions.

The National Assembly for Wales

16. The National Assembly for Wales.

Local authorities

17. Any local, county or district council in England, a London borough council, the Common Council of the City of London in its capacity as a local authority, the Council of the Isles of Scilly, and any county council or county borough council in Wales.

17A. Any fire authority within the meaning of the Fire Services Act 1947 (read with paragraph 2 of Schedule 11 to the Local Government Act 1985).

Other bodies

17B. The Charity Commission.

18. The Environment Agency.

19. The Financial Services Authority.

20. The Food Standards Agency.

20A. The Gaming Board for Great Britain.

20B. The Office of Fair Trading.

20C. The Office of the Police Ombudsman of Northern Ireland.

20D. The Postal Services Commission.

21. [repealed]

22. [repealed]

Northern Ireland Authorities

23. A universal service provider (within the meaning of the Postal Services Act 2000) acting in connection with the provision of a universal postal service (within the meaning of that Act).

23A. The Department of Agriculture and Rural Development.

23B. The Department of Enterprise, Trade and Investment.

23C. The Department of the Environment.

23D. Any district council (within the meaning of s 44 of the Interpretation Act (Northern Ireland) 1954).[41]

PART II
RELEVANT AUTHORITIES FOR THE PURPOSES ONLY OF S. 28

The Health and Safety Executive

24. The Health and Safety Executive.

NHS bodies in England and Wales

25. A Health Authority established under section 8 of the National Health Service Act 1977.

26. A Special Health Authority established under section 11 of the National Health Service Act 1977.

27. A National Heath Service trust established under section 5 of the National Health Service and Community Care Act 1990.

27A. Local Health Boards in Wales established under section 6 of the National Health Service reform and Health Care Professions Act 2002.

Her Majesty's Chief Inspector of Schools in England

27B. Her Majesty's Chief Inspector of Schools in England.

The Information Commissioner

27C. The Information Commissioner.

The Royal Parks Constabulary

27D. The Royal Parks Constabulary.

The Royal Pharmaceutical Society of Great Britain

28. The Royal Pharmaceutical Society of Great Britain.

Northern Ireland Authorities

29. The Department of Health, Social Services and Public Safety.

30. The Department of Regional Development.

---

[41] Prospectively repealed by SOCAPA 2005 Sch 17 Pt II.

31. The Department of Social Development.
32. The Department of Culture, Arts and Leisure.
33. The Foyle, Carlingford and Irish Lights Commission.
34. The Fisheries Conservancy Board for Northern Ireland.
35. A Health and Social Services trust established under Article 10 of the Health and Personal Social Services (Northern Ireland) Order 1972.
36. A Health and Social Services Board established under Article 16 of the Health and Personal Social Services (Northern Ireland) Order 1972.
37. A Health and Safety Executive for Northern Ireland.
38. The Northern Ireland Central Services Agency for the Health and Social Services.
39. The Fire Authority for Northern Ireland.
40. The Northern Ireland Housing Executive.

Appendix C
Extracts from Statutory Instruments Issued Pursuant to RIPA 2000

Numerous Statutory Instruments (secondary legislation) have been issued supplementing or amending RIPA. Some introduce amendments to the legislation that have been incorporated into Appendix B. Those reproduced here have been selected because they provide supplementary material such as ranks, roles, and positions specified for the various authorizing functions demanded by RIPA. They have been arranged by relevance to the chapters in this book. Those not reproduced here are accessible on-line at <http://www.opsi.gov.uk/stat.htm>.

		Pages			Pages
Chapters 2 and 3	SI 2000/2563	249	Chapter 8	SI 2000/2699	269
	SI 2003/3171	251	Chapter 9	SI 2004/157	273
	SI 2005/1084	260		SI 2000/2725	274
Chapter 7	SI 2003/3172	262		SI 2000/2793	276
	SI 2005/1083	267		SI 2001/1057	278

Statutory Instruments Relevant to Chapters 2 and 3

2000 No. 2563
Investigatory Powers

The Regulation of Investigatory Powers (Notification of Authorisations etc.) Order 2000

Approved by both Houses of Parliament

Made 20th September 2000
Laid before Parliament 22nd September 2000
Coming into force 25th September 2000

Whereas the Secretary of State may make an order under section 35(2)(c) of the Regulation of Investigatory Powers Act 2000;

And whereas subsections (6) and (7) of section 35 provide that the order made on the first occasion on which the power is exercised does not need to be approved by Parliament before being made, but must be approved after being made in accordance with subsection (7);

And whereas this is the first occasion on which the Secretary of State exercises the power;

Now, therefore, the Secretary of State, in exercise of the power conferred on him by section 35(2)(c) of the Regulation of Investigatory Powers Act 2000, hereby makes the following Order:

Citation and commencement

1. This Order may be cited as the Regulation of Investigatory Powers (Notification of Authorisations etc.) Order 2000 and shall come into force on 25th September 2000.

Interpretation

2. In this Order—

    'the 2000 Act' means the Regulation of Investigatory Powers Act 2000;

    'authorisation' means a police or customs authorisation for the carrying out of intrusive surveillance;

    'Commissioner' means an ordinary Surveillance Commissioner; and

    'notice to a Commissioner' means the notice required to be given under section 35(1) of the 2000 Act.

Notice of authorisation

3. Where a person grants an authorisation, the notice to a Commissioner shall, in addition to the statement required by section 35(3) of the 2000 Act, specify the following matters:

    (a) the grounds on which he believes the matters specified in section 32(2)(a) and (b) of the 2000 Act;

    (b) the nature of the authorised conduct including the residential premises or private vehicle in relation to which the conduct is authorised and the identity, where known, of persons to be the subject of the authorised conduct; and

    (c) whether the conduct to be authorised is likely to lead to intrusion on the privacy of persons other than any person who is to be the subject of that conduct.

Notice of renewal of authorisation

4. Where a person renews an authorisation, the notice to a Commissioner shall, in addition to the statement required by section 35(3) of the 2000 Act, specify the following matters:

    (a) whether the authorisation is being renewed for the first time, or, where it has been previously renewed, each occasion on which it has been renewed;

    (b) the matters required by article 3, as they apply at the time of notice of renewal;

    (c) every respect in which the information provided in the previous notice has changed;

    (d) the reason why it is considered to be necessary to renew the authorisation;

    (e) the content, and value to the investigation, of the information obtained to date by the conduct authorised;

    (f) the results of any reviews of the authorisation; and

    (g) the period for which the authorisation is considered likely to continue to be necessary.

Notice of cancellation of authorisation

5. Where a person cancels an authorisation, the notice to a Commissioner shall specify the following matters:
   (a) the date and time when he gave the instructions to cease the conduct authorised;
   (b) the reasons for cancelling the authorisation;
   (c) the outcome of the investigation to which the authorisation related, and details of any criminal proceedings instituted or intended to be instituted; and
   (d) what arrangements have been made for the storage of material obtained as a result of the conduct authorised, for its review and its destruction when its retention is no longer required, and for the immediate destruction of any material unrelated to the purposes for which the conduct was authorised.

Charles Clarke
Minister of State

Home Office
20th September 2000

Explanatory Note
(This note is not part of the Order)

This Order specifies the matters which must be notified to an ordinary Surveillance Commissioner when a person grants, renews or cancels a police or customs authorisation for the carrying out of intrusive surveillance under Part II of the Regulation of Investigatory Powers Act 2000.

2003 No. 3171
Investigatory Powers

The Regulation of Investigatory Powers (Directed Surveillance and Covert Human Intelligence Sources) Order 2003

[See SI 2005/1084, reproduced below, for subsequent amendments to this SI]
Made 5th December 2003
Coming into force 5th January 2004

Whereas a draft of this Order has been approved by a resolution of each House of Parliament;

Now, therefore, the Secretary of State, in exercise of the powers conferred on him by sections 30(1), (3), (5) and (6) and 78(5) of the Regulation of Investigatory Powers Act 2000, hereby makes the following Order:

Citation, commencement and interpretation

1.—(1) This Order may be cited as the Regulation of Investigatory Powers (Directed Surveillance and Covert Human Intelligence Sources) Order 2003 and shall come into force one month after the day on which it is made.
   (2) In this Order 'the 2000 Act' means the Regulation of Investigatory Powers Act 2000.

Amendments to Schedule 1 to the 2000 Act

2.—(1) Part I of Schedule 1 to the 2000 Act shall be amended as follows.

(2) After paragraph 1 add the words–

'**1A.** The United Kingdom Atomic Energy Authority Constabulary.'.

(3) After paragraph 13 add the words–

'**13A.** The Northern Ireland Office.'.

(4) For paragraph 17 substitute–

'**17.** Any county council or district council in England, a London borough council, the Common Council of the City of London in its capacity as a local authority, the Council of the Isles of Scilly, and any county council or county borough council in Wales.'.

(5) After paragraph 17 add the words–

'**17A.** Any fire authority within the meaning of the Fire Services Act 1947 (read with paragraph 2 of Schedule 11 to the Local Government Act 1985).'.

(6) After the heading '*Other bodies*' add the words–

'**17B.** The Charity Commission.'.

(7) After paragraph 20 add the words–

'**20A.** The Gaming Board for Great Britain.

20B. The Office of Fair Trading.

20C. The Office of the Police Ombudsman for Northern Ireland.

20D. The Postal Services Commission.'.

3.—(1) Part II of Schedule 1 to the 2000 Act shall be amended as follows.

(2) After paragraph 27 add the words–

'**27A.** Local Health Boards in Wales established under section 6 of the National Health Service Reform and Health Care Professions Act 2002.

Her Majesty's Chief Inspector of Schools in England

27B. Her Majesty's Chief Inspector of Schools in England.

The Information Commissioner

27C. The Information Commissioner.

The Royal Parks Constabulary

27D. The Royal Parks Constabulary.'.

Prescribed offices, ranks and positions

4.—(1) The offices, ranks and positions listed in column 2 of Part I of the Schedule to this Order (being offices, ranks or positions with the relevant public authorities listed in column 1 of Part I of that Schedule which are relevant public authorities for the purposes of sections 28 and 29 of the 2000 Act) are hereby prescribed for the purpose of section 30(1) of the 2000 Act, subject to the restrictions in articles 7, 8 and 9.

(2) The offices, ranks and positions listed in column 2 of Part II of the Schedule to this Order (being offices, ranks or positions with the relevant public authorities listed in column 1 of Part II of that Schedule which are relevant public authorities for the purposes only of section 28 of the 2000 Act) are hereby prescribed for the purpose of section 30(1) of the 2000 Act, subject to the restrictions in articles 7, 8 and 9.

More senior offices, ranks and positions

5.—(1) Where an office, rank or position with a relevant public authority is prescribed by virtue of article 4, all more senior offices, ranks or positions with that authority are also prescribed for the purpose of section 30(1) of the 2000 Act, subject to article 10.

(2) Where an office, rank or position with a relevant public authority is described in column 2 of the Schedule to this Order by reference to an agency, unit, branch, division or other part of that authority, the reference in paragraph (1) to all more senior offices, ranks or positions with that authority is a reference to all more senior offices, ranks or positions with that agency, unit, branch, division or part.

Additional offices, ranks and positions prescribed for urgent cases

6.—(1) The additional offices, ranks and positions listed in column 3 of the Schedule to this Order (being offices, ranks or positions with the relevant public authorities listed in column 1) are hereby prescribed for the purposes of section 30(1) of the 2000 Act, subject to the restrictions in articles 7, 8 and 9 in the circumstances described in paragraph (2).

(2) An individual holding an office, rank or position which is listed in column 3 of the Schedule to this Order may only grant an authorisation where it is not reasonably practicable, having regard to the urgency of the case, for the application to be considered by an individual with the same authority holding an office, rank or position listed in column 2 of the Schedule to this Order.

(3) Where an office, rank or position with a relevant public authority is described in column 3 of the Schedule to this Order by reference to an agency, unit, branch, division or other part of that authority, the reference in paragraph (2) to an individual with the same authority is a reference to an individual with that agency, unit, branch, division or part.

Restrictions on the granting of authorisations

7. The restriction in this article is that an individual holding an office, rank or position which is listed in column 2 or 3 of the Schedule to this Order may not grant an authorisation unless he believes it is necessary on the grounds set out in one or more of the paragraphs of sections 28(3) and 29(3) of the 2000 Act listed in the corresponding entry in column 4 of that Schedule.

8. The restriction in this article is that where any entry in column 2 or 3 of Part I of the Schedule to this Order is headed by a reference to an authorisation under section 28 or section 29 of the 2000 Act, an individual holding an office, rank or position which is listed in that entry may only grant an authorisation under the section of the 2000 Act with which that entry is headed.

9. The restriction in this article is that an individual holding an office, rank or position with the Food Standards Agency or the Rural Payments Agency may not grant an authorisation for conduct in Northern Ireland.

10. The restrictions on the granting of authorisations under section 28 and 29 of the 2000 Act that apply to an individual holding an office, rank or position with a relevant public authority listed in column 2 of the Schedule to this Order shall also apply to individuals holding all more senior offices, ranks or positions with that authority that are prescribed by article 5.

Revocation

11. The Regulation of Investigatory Powers (Prescription of Offices, Ranks and Positions) Order 2000 is hereby revoked.

Caroline Flint
Parliamentary Under-Secretary of State

Home Office
5th December 2003

SCHEDULE

Article 4

Part I (Prescriptions for public authorities in Part I of Schedule 1 to the 2000 Act that are relevant public authorities for the purposes of sections 28 and 29 of the 2000 Act)

(1) Relevant public authorities in Part I of Schedule 1 to the 2000 Act	(2) Prescribed offices etc.	(3) Urgent cases	(4) Grounds set out in the paragraphs of sections 28(3) and 29(3) of the 2000 Act for which an authorisation can be given
A police force maintained under section 2 of the Police Act 1996 (police forces in England and Wales outside London)	Superintendent	Inspector	(a)(b)(c)(d)(e)
A police force maintained under or by virtue of section 1 of the Police (Scotland) Act 1967	Superintendent	Inspector	(a)(b)(c)(d)(e)
The metropolitan police force	Superintendent	Inspector	(a)(b)(c)(d)(e)
The City of London police force	Superintendent	Inspector	(a)(b)(c)(d)(e)
The Police Service of Northern Ireland	Superintendent	Inspector	(a)(b)(c)(d)(e)
The Ministry of Defence Police	Superintendent	Inspector	(a)(b)(c)
The Royal Navy Regulating Branch	Provost Marshal		(a)(b)(c)
The Royal Military Police	Lieutenant Colonel	Major	(a)(b)(c)
The Royal Air Force Police	Wing Commander	Squadron Leader	(a)(b)(c)
The British Transport Police	Superintendent	Inspector	(a)(b)(c)(d)(e)
The United Kingdom Atomic Energy Authority Constabulary	Superintendent	Inspector	(a)(b)

The National Criminal Intelligence Service	Superintendent, Level 2 or any individual on secondment to the National Criminal Intelligence Service who holds any office, rank or position in any other relevant public authority listed in column 2 of Part I of the Schedule to this Order	Inspector, Level 4 or any individual on secondment to the National Criminal Intelligence Service who holds any office, rank or position in any other relevant public authority listed in column 3 of Part I of the Schedule to this Order	(a)(b)(c)(d)(e)
The National Crime Squad	Superintendent	Inspector	(a)(b)(c)(d)(e)
The Serious Fraud Office	Assistant Director		(b)
Government Communications Headquarters	GC8		(a)(b)(c)
The Security Service	General Duties 3 or any other Officer at Level 3		(a)(b)(c)
The Secret Intelligence Service	Grade 6 or equivalent		(a)(b)(c)
The Royal Navy	Commander	Lieutenant Commander	(a)(b)(c)(d)(e)
The Army	Lieutenant Colonel	Major	(a)(b)(c)(d)(e)
The Royal Air Force	Wing Commander	Squadron Leader	(a)(b)(c)(d)(e)
The Commissioners of Customs and Excise	Band 9	Band 7 or 8	(a)(b)(c)(d)(e)(f)
The Commissioners of Inland Revenue	Band C1	Band C2	(b)(c)(f)
Ministry of Defence	Band C1	Band C2	(b)
Department for Environment, Food and Rural Affairs	Senior Investigation Officer in DEFRA Investigation Branch		(b)
	Senior Counter Fraud Officer in the Counter Fraud and Compliance Unit of the Rural Payments Agency		(b)
	Senior Investigation Officer in Centre for Environment, Fisheries and Aquaculture Science		(b)
	Section 28 authorisation Regional Horticultural Marketing Inspector in Horticultural Marketing Inspectorate		(b)
	Section 28 authorisation Senior Plant Health and Seed Inspector in Plant Health and Seed Inspectorate		(b)

	Section 28 authorisation Chief Egg Marketing Inspector in Egg Marketing Inspectorate		(b)
	Section 28 authorisation District Inspector in Sea Fisheries Inspectorate		(b)
The Department of Health	Integrated Payband 3 (Standard 2) in Medicines and Healthcare Products Regulatory Agency		(b)(d)(e)
The Home Office	Section 28 authorisation Area Manager in HM Prison Service		(a)(b)(d)
	Section 29 authorisation Prison Source System Manager in HM Prison Service	Section 29 authorisation A Governor, Duty Governor or Deputy Controller in HM Prison Service	(a)(b)(d)
	Immigration Inspector in the Immigration Service	Chief Immigration Officer in the Immigration Service	(b)(c)
	Section 28 authorisation The Head of the Unit responsible for Security and Anti Corruption within the Immigration and Nationality Directorate	Section 28 authorisation Senior Executive Officer within the Unit responsible for Security and Anti Corruption within the Immigration and Nationality Directorate	(b)
The Northern Ireland Office	Deputy Principal or Governor 3 in the Northern Ireland Prison Service	Staff Officer or Governor 4 in the Northern Ireland Prison Service	(b)(d)
The Department of Trade and Industry	Deputy Inspector of Companies in Companies Investigation Branch		(b)
	Chief Investigation Officer in the Investigation Officers Section of Legal Services Directorate D or a member of the Senior Civil Service in Legal Services Directorate D		(b)
	Section 28 authorisation Radio Specialist 5 or Range 9 Officer in Radiocommunications Agency	Section 28 authorisation Radio Specialist 4 or Range 8 Officer in Radiocommunications Agency	(b)

	Section 29 authorisation Member of Senior Civil Service in Radiocommunications Agency		(b)
	Section 28 authorisation Member of Senior Civil Service in British Trade International		(b)
	Section 28 authorisation Range 10 Officer in Coal Health Claims Unit	**Section 28 authorisation** Range 9 Officer in Coal Health Claims Unit	(b)
The Department for Transport	Head of Maritime Section		(b)(d)
	Assistant Director Transport Security		(b)(d)
	Head of Operational Support		(b)(d)
	Head of Land Transport Security		(b)(d)
	Head of Aviation Security Compliance		(b)(d)
	Head of Aviation Security Domestic Policy		(b)(d)
	Head of Aviation Security International Policy		(b)(d)
	Senior Transport Security Inspector		(b)(d)
	Section 28 authorisation Area Manager or National Intelligence Co-ordinator in the Vehicle and Operator Services Agency	**Section 28 authorisation** Senior Vehicle Examiner or Senior Traffic Examiner or Intelligence Officer in the Vehicle and Operator Services Agency	(b)(d)
	Section 29 authorisation Enforcement Manager in the Vehicle and Operator Services Agency	**Section 29 authorisation** Area Manager in the Vehicle and Operator Services Agency	(b)(d)(b)(d)
	Principal Enforcement Officer in the Maritime and Coastguard Agency	Enforcement Officer in the Maritime and Coastguard Agency	(b)(d)
The Department for Work and Pensions	Senior Executive Officer or equivalent grades in Jobcentre Plus	Higher Executive Officer or equivalent grades in Jobcentre Plus	(b)
	Senior Executive Officer or equivalent grades in DWP Internal Assurance Services		(b)

	Senior Executive Officer or equivalent grades in Child Support Agency	Higher Executive Officer or equivalent grades in Child Support Agency	(b)
National Assembly for Wales	Head of NHS Directorate	Member of NHS Directorate at a level equivalent to Grade 7	(b)(d)(e)
	Head of NHS Finance Division	Member of NHS Finance Division at a level equivalent to Grade 7	(b)(d)(e)
	Head of Common Agricultural Policy Management Division	Member of Common Agricultural Policy Management Division at a level equivalent to Grade 7	(b)(e)
	Regional Director in the Care Standards Inspectorate for Wales	Senior Inspector in the Care Standards Inspectorate for Wales	(b)(d)(e)
Any county council or district council in England, a London Borough Council, the Common Council of the City of London in its capacity as a local authority, the Council of the Isles of Scilly, and any county council or county borough council in Wales	Assistant Chief Officer, Assistant Head of Service, Service Manager or equivalent		(b)
Any fire authority within the meaning of the Fire Services Act 1947 (read with paragraph 2 of Schedule 11 to the Local Government Act 1985)	Divisional Officer 2	Divisional Officer 3	(b)(d)
The Charity Commission	Senior Investigations Manager	Investigations Manager	(b)
The Environment Agency	**Section 28 authorisation** Area Management Team Member	**Section 28 authorisation** Area Team Leader	(b)(d)(e)
	Section 29 authorisation Area Manager	**Section 29 authorisation** Area Management Team Member	(b)(d)(e)
The Financial Services Authority	Head of Department in Enforcement Division	Manager in Enforcement Division	(b)
The Food Standards Agency	**Section 28 authorisation** Head of Division or equivalent grade		(b)(d)(e)
	Section 29 authorisation Deputy Director of Legal Services or any Director		(b)(d)(e)

The Gaming Board for Great Britain	Chief Inspector	Deputy Chief Inspector	(b)
The Office of Fair Trading	Director of Cartel Investigations	Principal Investigation Officer in the Cartel Investigation Branch	(b)(c)
The Office of the Police Ombudsman for Northern Ireland	Senior Investigating Officer	Deputy Senior Investigating Officer	(b)
The Postal Services Commission	**Section 28 authorisation** Legal Adviser	**Section 28 authorisation** Deputy Director	(b)
	Section 29 authorisation Chief Legal Adviser		(b)
A Universal Service Provider within the meaning of the Postal Services Act 2000	Senior Investigation Manager in Royal Mail Group plc		(b)

Explanatory Note

(This note is not part of the Order)

Articles 2 and 3 of this Order amend Schedule 1 to the Regulation of Investigatory Powers Act 2000 ('the 2000 Act') by adding to it a number of new public authorities. Designated individuals in the public authorities listed in Part I of Schedule 1 are entitled to authorise directed surveillance and the use and conduct of covert human intelligence sources under sections 28 and 29 of the 2000 Act, respectively. Designated individuals in the public authorities listed in Part II of Schedule 1 are only entitled to authorise directed surveillance under section 28 of the 2000 Act. Article 4 of this Order prescribes offices, ranks and positions for the purposes of section 30(1) of the 2000 Act for both the public authorities already in Schedule 1 and those added to it by this Order. Individuals holding these prescribed offices, ranks or positions are designated under sections 28 and 29 of the 2000 Act as able to authorise directed surveillance and the use and conduct of covert human intelligence sources. An earlier Order that prescribed offices, ranks and positions in the public authorities that were in Schedule 1 when the 2000 Act was passed is revoked by article 10 of this Order.

Column 1 of the Schedule to this Order lists the public authorities. Column 2 specifies the individuals within each public authority that can authorise directed surveillance and the use and conduct of covert human intelligence sources. An individual holding an office, rank or position listed in column 2 of Part I of the Schedule may grant an authorisation under either section 28 or section 29 of the 2000 Act, other than where the Schedule indicates to the contrary. An individual holding an office, rank or position listed in column 2 of Part II of the Schedule may only grant an authorisation under section 28 of the 2000 Act. Individuals holding more senior offices, ranks or positions to those listed in column 2 may also authorise in the same circumstances as those to whom they are senior. Column 3 sets out certain less senior officials who can authorise in urgent cases. Column 4 sets out the grounds on which an authorisation can be given by reference to the grounds set out in the different paragraphs of sections 28(3) and 29(3) of the 2000 Act. For example, ground (b) is for the purpose of preventing or detecting crime or of preventing disorder.

2005 No. 1084
Investigatory Powers

The Regulation of Investigatory Powers (Directed Surveillance and Covert Human Intelligence Sources) (Amendment) Order 2005

Made 4th April 2005
Coming into force in accordance with article 1(2) and (3)

The Secretary of State, in exercise of the powers conferred upon him by sections 30(1), (3), (5)(a) and (b), and (6) and 78(5) of the **Regulation** of **Investigatory Powers Act 2000** hereby makes the following Order (a draft of which has been approved by resolution of each House of Parliament):

Citation, commencement and interpretation

1.—(1) This Order may be cited as the **Regulation** of **Investigatory Powers** (Directed Surveillance and Covert Human Intelligence Sources) (Amendment) Order 2005.

(2) Subject to paragraph (3), this Order shall come into force one month after the day on which it is made.

(3) Article 3(3) of this Order shall come into force on the day on which either–
   (a) the other provisions of this Order come into force, or
   (b) paragraph 8 of Schedule 14 to the Energy **Act** 2004 comes into force, whichever is the later.

(4) In this Order 'the **Act**' means the **Regulation** of **Investigatory Powers Act 2000**.

Amendment of Schedule 1 to the Act

2.—(1) After paragraph 4 of Part 1 of Schedule 1 to the **Act**, add the words–
   '**4A.** The force comprising the special constables appointed under section 79 of the Harbours, Docks and Piers Clauses **Act** 1847 on the nomination of the Dover Harbour Board.
   4B. The force comprising the constables appointed under article 3 of the Mersey Docks and Harbour (Police) Order 1975 on the nomination of the Mersey Docks and Harbour Company.'.

(2) Paragraph 25 of Part 2 of Schedule 1 to the **Act** is omitted.

Amendment of the Regulation of Investigatory Powers (Directed Surveillance and Covert Human Intelligence Sources) Order 2003

3.—(1) Part 1 of the Schedule (prescriptions for public authorities in Part 1 of Schedule 1 to the **Act** that are relevant authorities for the purposes of sections 28 and 29 of the **Act**) to the **Regulation** of **Investigatory Powers** (Directed Surveillance and Covert Human Intelligence Sources) Order 2003 is amended as follows.

(2) After the entry for the British Transport Police, insert–

The force comprising the special constables appointed under section 79 of the Harbours, Docks and Piers Clauses Act 1847 on the nomination of the Dover Harbour Board	Superintendent	Inspector	(a)(b)(d)(e)
The force comprising the constables appointed under article 3 of the Mersey Docks and Harbour (Police) Order 1975 on the nomination of the Mersey Docks and Harbour Company	Superintendent	Inspector	(a)(b)(d)(e)

(3) For the entry for the United Kingdom Atomic Energy Authority Constabulary, substitute–

The Civil Nuclear Constabulary	Superintendent	Inspector	(a)(b)

(4) In the entry for the Department of Trade and Industry, omit all references to individuals holding office, rank or position in the Radiocommunications Agency.

(5) In the entry for the Department for Transport, omit the first eight references in columns 2 and 4 (Head of Maritime Section to and including the Senior Transport Security Inspector).

(6) At the end, insert–

The Office of Communications	**Section 28 authorisation** Manager of Spectrum Operations or Head of Enforcement and Interference Policy	**Section 28 authorisation** Area Manager or Senior Enforcement Policy Manager	(b)
	Section 29 authorisation Head of Field Operations		(b)

Caroline Flint
Parliamentary Under-Secretary of State

Home Office
4th April 2005

Explanatory Note

(This note is not part of the Order)

Article 2 of this Order amends Schedule 1 to the **Regulation** of **Investigatory Powers Act 2000** ('the Act') by inserting new paragraphs 4A and 4B and omitting paragraph 25 of that Schedule. The effect of the addition is that the Port of Dover Police and the Port of Liverpool Police are now relevant public authorities for the purposes of section 28 and 29 of the **Act**, and thereby have the power to authorise directed sur-veillance and the use and conduct of covert human intelligence sources. The effect of omitting paragraph 25 is that a Health Authority established under section 8 of the National Health Service **Act** 1977 (c. 49) is no longer a relevant public author-ity for the purposes of section 28 of the **Act**, and thus no longer has the power to authorise directed surveillance.

Article 3 of this Order amends Part 1 of the Schedule to the **Regulation** of **Investig-atory Powers** (Directed Surveillance and Covert Human Intelligence Sources) Order 2003 ('the 2003 Order'). Article 3(2) and (6) add new entries relating to the Port of Dover Police and the Port of Liverpool Police and the Office of Communications. Article 3(4) omits the entries relating to the Radiocommunications Agency, as this Agency no longer exists. Article 3(5) omits many of the prescribed offices etc. within the entry for the Department for Transport, on the basis that there is no longer any need for these powers by those parts of the department.

The Energy **Act** 2004 reforms the governance arrangements of the United King-dom Atomic Energy Authority Constabulary and provides for the transfer of its mem-bers to the Civil Nuclear Constabulary, to be established under that **Act**. Paragraph 8(2) of Schedule 14 to the Energy **Act** 2004 amends Schedule 1 of the **Regulation** of **Investigatory Act 2000** to reflect this change in relation to relevant authorities for the purposes of sections 28 and 29 of the **Act**. Article 3(3) of this Order makes a corresponding amendment to the Schedule to the 2003 Order. Article 3(3) will come into force on the day that paragraph 8 of Schedule 14 to the Energy **Act** 2004 (which amends the **2000 Act** to substitute references to the Civil Nuclear Constabu-lary for references to the United Kingdom Atomic Energy Authority Constabulary) is commenced.

Statutory Instruments Relevant to Chapter 7

2003 No. 3172
Investigatory Powers

The Regulation of Investigatory Powers
(Communications Data)
Order 2003

Made 5th December 2003
Coming into force 5th January 2004

Whereas a draft of this Order has been approved by resolution of each House of Parliament;

Now, therefore, the Secretary of State, in exercise of the powers conferred on him by paragraph (g) of the definition of 'relevant public authority' in section 25(1) of the Regulation of Investigatory Powers Act 2000 and by sections 25(2) and (3) and 78(5) of that Act, hereby makes the following Order:

Citation, commencement and interpretation

1.—(1) This Order may be cited as the Regulation of Investigatory Powers (Communications Data) Order 2003 and shall come into force one month after the day on which it is made.

(2) In this Order–

'the 2000 Act' means the Regulation of Investigatory Powers Act 2000;

'authorisation' means an authorisation under section 22(3) of the 2000 Act; and

'notice' means a notice under section 22(4) of the 2000 Act.

Prescribed offices, ranks and positions

2. The offices, ranks and positions listed in columns 2 and 3 of Schedule 1 (being offices, ranks and positions with the relevant public authorities in column 1 of that Schedule) are hereby prescribed for the purposes of section 25(2) of the 2000 Act, subject to the restrictions in articles 6, 7 and 10.

Additional public authorities

3. The public authorities set out in column 1 of Parts I, III and IV of Schedule 2 are hereby specified as relevant public authorities for the purposes of section 25(1) of the 2000 Act.

Prescribed offices, ranks and positions in the additional public authorities

4. The offices, ranks and positions listed in columns 2 and 3 of Parts I, II, III and IV of Schedule 2 (being offices, ranks and positions with the relevant public authorities in column 1 of that Schedule) are hereby prescribed for the purposes of section 25(2) of the 2000 Act, subject to the restrictions in articles 6, 7, 8 and 9.

More senior offices, ranks and positions

5.—(1) Where an office, rank or position with a relevant public authority listed in column 2 of Schedule 1 or column 2 of Schedule 2 is prescribed by virtue of article 2 or 4, all more senior offices, ranks or positions with that authority are also prescribed for the purposes of section 25(2) of the 2000 Act, subject to article 11.

(2) Where an office, rank or position with a relevant public authority is described in column 2 of Schedule 1 or column 2 of Schedule 2 by reference to an agency, unit, branch, division or other part of that authority, the reference in paragraph (1) to all more senior offices, ranks or positions with that authority is a reference to all more senior offices, ranks or positions with that agency, unit, branch, division or part.

Restrictions on the granting of authorisations or the giving of notices

6. The restriction in this article is that an individual holding an office, rank or position which is listed in column 2 or 3 of Schedule 1 or column 2 or 3 of Schedule 2 may not grant an authorisation or give a notice unless he believes it is necessary on the grounds set out in one or more of the paragraphs of section 22(2) of the 2000 Act listed in the corresponding entry in column 4 of those Schedules.

7.—(1) The restriction in this paragraph is that an individual holding an office, rank or position which is listed in column 2 of Schedule 1 or column 2 of Schedule 2 may only grant an authorisation or give a notice that he believes is necessary on grounds other than those set out in paragraphs (a), (b), (c) and (g) of section 22(2) of the 2000 Act where that authorisation or notice satisfies the condition in paragraph (3).

(2) The restriction in this paragraph is that an individual holding an office, rank or position which is listed in column 3 of Schedule 1 or column 3 of Schedule 2 may only grant an authorisation or give a notice which satisfies the condition set out in paragraph (3).

(3) The condition referred to in paragraphs (1) and (2) is that the only communications data authorised to be obtained by the authorisation, or required to be obtained or disclosed by the notice, is communications data falling within section 21(4)(c) of the 2000 Act.

8.—(1) The restriction in this article is that an individual holding an office, rank or position which is listed in column 2 of Part II or Part III of Schedule 2 may only grant an authorisation or give a notice which satisfies the condition set out in paragraph (2).

(2) The condition referred to in paragraph (1) is that the only communications data authorised to be obtained by the authorisation, or required to be obtained or disclosed by the notice, is communications data falling within section 21(4)(b) or (c) of the 2000 Act.

9.—(1) The restriction in this article is that an individual holding an office, rank or position which is listed in column 2 of Part IV of Schedule 2 may only grant an authorisation or give a notice which satisfies the condition set out in paragraph (2).

(2) The condition referred to in paragraph (1) is that the only communications data authorised to be obtained by the authorisation, or required to be obtained or disclosed by the notice, is communications data relating to a postal service.

10.—(1) The restriction in this article is that an individual holding an office, rank or position with the Commissioners of Inland Revenue (being a relevant public authority listed in Schedule 1) may only grant an authorisation or give a notice which satisfies the condition set out in paragraph (2).

(2) The condition referred to in paragraph (1) is that the only communications data falling with section 21(4)(a) of the 2000 Act authorised to be obtained by the authorisation, or required to be obtained or disclosed by the notice, is communications data relating to a postal service.

11. The restrictions on the granting of authorisations and the giving of notices that apply to an individual holding an office, rank or position with a relevant public authority listed in column 2 of Schedule 1 or column 2 of Schedule 2 shall also apply to all individuals holding all more senior offices, ranks or positions with that authority that are prescribed by article 5.

Caroline Flint
Parliamentary Under-Secretary of State

Home Office
5th December 2003

SCHEDULE 1

Article 2

INDIVIDUALS IN PUBLIC AUTHORITIES WITHIN SECTION 25(1) OF THE 2000 ACT

(1)	(2)	(3)	(4)
Relevant public authorities	Prescribed offices etc (All authorisations/notices)	Additional prescribed offices etc (Authorisations/notices relating solely to communications data falling within section 21(4)(c))	Purposes within section 22(2) for which an authorisation may be granted or a notice given
Police Forces			
A police force maintained under section 2 of the Police Act 1996 (police forces in England and Wales outside London)	Superintendent	Inspector	(a)(b)(c)(d)(e)(g)
A police force maintained under or by virtue of section 1 of the Police (Scotland) Act 1967	Superintendent	Inspector	(a)(b)(c)(d)(e)(g)
The metropolitan police force	Superintendent	Inspector	(a)(b)(c)(d)(e)(g)
The City of London police force	Superintendent	Inspector	(a)(b)(c)(d)(e)(g)
The Police Service of Northern Ireland	Superintendent	Inspector	(a)(b)(c)(d)(e)(g)
The Ministry of Defence Police	Superintendent	Inspector	(a)(b)(c)(g)
The Royal Navy Regulating Branch	Provost Marshal	—	(a)(b)(c)(g)
The Royal Military Police	Lieutenant Colonel	Major	(a)(b)(c)(g)
The Royal Air Force Police	Wing Commander	Squadron Leader	(a)(b)(c)(g)
The British Transport Police	Superintendent	Inspector	(a)(b)(c)(d)(e)(g)
The National Criminal Intelligence Service	Superintendent, Level 2 or any individual on secondment to the National Criminal Intelligence Service who holds any other office, rank or position in any relevant public authority listed in column 2 of Schedule 1	Inspector, Level 4 or any individual on secondment to the National Criminal Intelligence Service who holds any other office, rank or position in any relevant public authority listed in column 3 of Schedule 1	(a)(b)(c)(d)(e)(g)

The National Crime Squad	Superintendent, Band I or any individual on secondment to the National Crime Squad who holds any other office, rank or position in any relevant public authority listed in column 2 of Schedule 1	Inspector, Band F or any individual on secondment to the National Crime Squad who holds any other office, rank or position in any relevant public authority listed in column 3 of Schedule 1	(a)(b)(c)(d)(e)(g)
The Commissioners of Customs and Excise	Band 9	Band 7 or 8	(b)(f)
The Commissioners of Inland Revenue	Band C1	Band C2	(b)(f)
The Intelligence Services			
Government Communications Headquarters	GC8	—	(a)(b)(c)
The Security Service	General Duties 3 or any other Officer at Level 3	General Duties 4	(a)(b)(c)
The Secret Intelligence Service	Grade 6 or equivalent	—	(a)(b)(c)

Explanatory Note

(This note is not part of the Order)

This Order specifies additional public authorities for the purposes of section 25(1) of the Regulation of Investigatory Powers Act 2000 ('the 2000 Act'). Public authorities specified for the purposes of section 25 are entitled to acquire communications data under the provisions in Chapter II of Part I of the 2000 Act. The Order specifies which individuals within those public authorities, and the public authorities already listed in the 2000 Act, are entitled to acquire communications data. It also places restrictions on the grounds on which they may acquire communications data and the types of communications data they way acquire.

Column 1 of the two Schedules to the Order lists the public authorities. Column 1 of Schedule 1 contains the public authorities already listed within section 25(1) of the 2000 Act. The public authorities listed in Parts I, III and IV of column 1 of Schedule 2 are specified by article 3 as additional public authorities under the 2000 Act.

By virtue of articles 2 and 4 column 2 of the Schedules lists the individuals holding an office, rank or position within each public authority who may acquire communications data. Article 5 provides that more senior individuals with those public authorities may also acquire communications data in the same circumstances to those to whom they are senior. Certain less senior officials listed in column 3 of the Schedules can acquire communications data defined in section 21(4)(c) of the 2000 Act. This type of data is known as subscriber data.

An individual holding a particular office, rank or position can only acquire communications data on the particular grounds, set out in the different paragraphs of section 22(2) of the 2000 Act, found in the entry in column 4 of the Schedules corresponding to the entry for that individual in column 2 or 3. Where the grounds on which communications data is to be obtained is not national security, the prevention or detection of crime or the prevention of disorder, the economic well being of the UK, or in an emergency to prevent death or injury, then only subscriber data may be acquired.

Subject to these restrictions individuals holding offices, ranks or positions listed in Schedule 1 or Part I of Schedule 2 are entitled to acquire all types of communications data. Individuals holding offices, ranks or positions listed in Parts II and III of Schedule 2 are not entitled to acquire traffic data as defined in section 21(4)(a) (read with sections 21(6) and (7)) of the 2000 Act. Individuals within the Postal Services Commission can only acquire communications data about postal services. Individuals in the Inland Revenue can acquire all communications data other than traffic data that does not relate to a postal service.

2005 No. 1083
Investigatory Powers

The Regulation of Investigatory Powers (Communications Data) (Amendment) Order 2005

Made 4th April 2005
Coming into force in accordance with article 1(2) and (3)

The Secretary of State, in exercise of the powers conferred upon him by paragraph (g) of the definition of 'relevant public authority' in section 25(1) of the Regulation of Investigatory Powers Act 2000 and by sections 25(2), (3) and (4) and 78(5) of that Act, hereby makes the following Order (a draft of which has been approved by resolution of each House of Parliament):

Citation and commencement

1.—(1) This Order may be cited as the Regulation of Investigatory Powers (Communications Data) (Amendment) Order 2005.
(2) Subject to paragraph (3), this Order shall come into force one month after the day on which it is made.
(3) Article 2(3) of this Order shall come into force on the day on which either–
   (a) the other provisions of this Order come into force, or
   (b) paragraph 8 of Schedule 14 to the Energy Act 2004 comes into force, whichever is the later.

Amendment of the Regulation of Investigatory Powers (Communications Data) Order 2003

2.—(1) Part 1 of Schedule 2 (individuals in additional public authorities that may acquire all types of communications data within section 21(4) of the Regulation of Investigatory Powers Act 2000) to the Regulation of Investigatory Powers (Communications Data) Order 2003 is amended as follows.
(2) For the entry for the Scottish Crime Squad, substitute–

The Scottish Drug Enforcement Agency, meaning the organisation known by that name and established under section 36(1)(a)(ii) of the Police (Scotland) Act 1967	Superintendent, Grade PO7 or any individual on secondment to the Scottish Drug Enforcement Agency who holds the rank of Superintendent or Grade PO7 with the police force from which that person is seconded	Inspector or any individual on secondment to the Scottish Drug Enforcement Agency who holds the rank of Inspector with the police force from which that person is seconded	(b)(d)(g)

(3) For the entry for the United Kingdom Atomic Energy Authority Constabulary, substitute—

The Civil Nuclear Constabulary	Superintendent	Inspector	(a)(b)

(4) Delete the entry for the Department of Trade and Industry.

(5) After the entry for the Office of the Police Ombudsman for Northern Ireland, add the following entries—

The Independent Police Complaints Commission	Commissioner, Regional Director, Director of Investigations or Deputy Director of Investigations	—	(b)
The Office of Communications	Senior Enforcement Policy Manager	—	(b)
The force comprising the special constables appointed under section 79 of the Harbours, Docks and Piers Clauses Act 1847 on the nomination of the Dover Harbour Board	Superintendent	Inspector	(a)(b)(d)(e)
The force comprising the constables appointed under article 3 of the Mersey Docks and Harbour (Police) Order 1975 on the nomination of the Mersey Docks and Harbour Company	Superintendent	Inspector	(a)(b)(d)(e)

Caroline Flint
Parliamentary Under-Secretary of State

Home Office
4th April 2005

Explanatory Note

(This note is not part of the Order)

This Order amends Part 1 of Schedule 2 to the Regulation of Investigatory Powers (Communications Data) Order 2003 ('the 2003 Order').

This Order adds four new entries to the 2003 Order. Column 1 of the table inserted by article 2(5) of this Order into the 2003 Order specifies the Independent Police Complaints Commission, the Office of Communications, the Port of Dover Police and the Port of Liverpool Police as relevant public authorities for the purpose of section 25(1) of the Regulation of Investigatory Powers Act 2000 ('the Act'). Column 2 of the table designates which persons within those authorities may authorise or require the acquisition of communications data under the provisions of Chapter 2 of Part 1 of the 2000 Act (persons senior to those designated are also entitled to authorise or require the acquisition of communications data). Column 3 of the table designates which persons may authorise or require the acquisition only of communications data falling within section 21(4)(c) of the Act. By virtue of column 4 of the table, those entitled to authorise or require the acquisition of communications data within the newly specified public authorities are only so entitled if it is necessary to obtain the data on the particular grounds specified.

Article 2(2) of this Order adds further prescribed offices etc. in relation to the Scottish Drug Enforcement Agency (which has replaced the Scottish Crime Squad in relation to investigatory powers), including some civilian grades and certain persons on secondment.

The Energy Act 2004 reforms the governance arrangements of the United Kingdom Atomic Energy Authority Constabulary and provides for the transfer of its members to the Civil Nuclear Constabulary, to be established under that Act. Article 2(3) of this Order makes a corresponding change to the Schedule to the 2003 Order, and this provision will come into force on the day that paragraph 8 of Schedule 14 to the Energy Act 2004 (which amends the 2000 Act to substitute references to the Civil Nuclear Constabulary for references to the United Kingdom Atomic Energy Authority Constabulary) is commenced.

Finally, article 2(4) of this Order deletes the entry in Part 1 of Schedule 2 to the 2003 Order relating to the Department of Trade and Industry, as the Radiocommunications Agency no longer exists.

Statutory Instruments Relevant to Chapter 8

2000 No. 2699
Investigatory Powers

The Telecommunications (Lawful Business Practice) (Interception of Communications) Regulations 2000

Made 2nd October 2000
Laid before Parliament 3rd October 2000
Coming into force 24th October 2000

The Secretary of State, in exercise of the powers conferred on him by sections 4(2) and 78(5) of the Regulation of Investigatory Powers Act 2000 ('the Act'), hereby makes the following Regulations:–

Citation and commencement

1. These Regulations may be cited as the Telecommunications (Lawful Business Practice) (Interception of Communications) Regulations 2000 and shall come into force on 24th October 2000.

Interpretation

2. In these Regulations–
    (a) references to a business include references to activities of a government department, of any public authority or of any person or office holder on whom functions are conferred by or under any enactment;
    (b) a reference to a communication as relevant to a business is a reference to–
        (i) a communication–
            (aa) by means of which a transaction is entered into in the course of that business, or
            (bb) which otherwise relates to that business, or
        (ii) a communication which otherwise takes place in the course of the carrying on of that business;
    (c) 'regulatory or self-regulatory practices or procedures' means practices or procedures–
        (i) compliance with which is required or recommended by, under or by virtue of–
            (aa) any provision of the law of a member state or other state within the European Economic Area, or
            (bb) any standard or code of practice published by or on behalf of a body established in a member state or other state within the European Economic Area which includes amongst its objectives the publication of standards or codes of practice for the conduct of business, or
        (ii) which are otherwise applied for the purpose of ensuring compliance with anything so required or recommended;
    (d) 'system controller' means, in relation to a particular telecommunication system, a person with a right to control its operation or use.

Lawful interception of a communication

3.—(1) For the purpose of section 1(5)(a) of the Act, conduct is authorised, subject to paragraphs (2) and (3) below, if it consists of interception of a communication, in the course of its transmission by means of a telecommunication system, which is effected by or with the express or implied consent of the system controller for the purpose of–
    (a) monitoring or keeping a record of communications–
        (i) in order to–
            (aa) establish the existence of facts, or

        (bb) ascertain compliance with regulatory or self-regulatory practices or procedures which are–

           applicable to the system controller in the carrying on of his business or

           applicable to another person in the carrying on of his business where that person is supervised by the system controller in respect of those practices or procedures, or

        (cc) ascertain or demonstrate the standards which are achieved or ought to be achieved by persons using the system in the course of their duties, or

    (ii) in the interests of national security, or

    (iii) for the purpose of preventing or detecting crime, or

    (iv) for the purpose of investigating or detecting the unauthorised use of that or any other telecommunication system, or

    (v) where that is undertaken–

        (aa) in order to secure, or

        (bb) as an inherent part of,

the effective operation of the system (including any monitoring or keeping of a record which would be authorised by section 3(3) of the Act if the conditions in paragraphs (a) and (b) thereof were satisfied); or

(b) monitoring communications for the purpose of determining whether they are communications relevant to the system controller's business which fall within regulation 2(b)(i) above; or

(c) monitoring communications made to a confidential voice-telephony counselling or support service which is free of charge (other than the cost, if any, of making a telephone call) and operated in such a way that users may remain anonymous if they so choose.

(2) Conduct is authorised by paragraph (1) of this regulation only if–

  (a) the interception in question is effected solely for the purpose of monitoring or (where appropriate) keeping a record of communications relevant to the system controller's business;

  (b) the telecommunication system in question is provided for use wholly or partly in connection with that business;

  (c) the system controller has made all reasonable efforts to inform every person who may use the telecommunication system in question that communications transmitted by means thereof may be intercepted; and

  (d) in a case falling within–

    (i) paragraph (1)(a)(ii) above, the person by or on whose behalf the interception is effected is a person specified in section 6(2)(a) to (i) of the Act;

    (ii) paragraph (1)(b) above, the communication is one which is intended to be received (whether or not it has been actually received) by a person using the telecommunication system in question.

(3) Conduct falling within paragraph (1)(a)(i) above is authorised only to the extent that Article 5 of Directive 97/66/EC of the European Parliament and of the Council of 15 December 1997 concerning the processing of personal data and the protection of privacy in the telecommunications sector [2] so permits.

Patricia Hewitt
Minister for Small Business and E-Commerce, Department of Trade and Industry
2nd October 2000

Explanatory Note

(This note is not part of the Regulations)

These Regulations authorise certain interceptions of telecommunication communications which would otherwise be prohibited by section 1 of the Regulation of Investigatory Powers Act 2000. To the extent that the interceptions are also prohibited by Article 5.1 of Directive 97/66/EC, the authorisation does not exceed that permitted by Articles 5.2 and 14.1 of the Directive.

The interception has to be by or with the consent of a person carrying on a business (which includes the activities of government departments, public authorities and others exercising statutory functions) for purposes relevant to that person's business and using that business's own telecommunication system.

Interceptions are authorised for–
  monitoring or recording communications–
    to establish the existence of facts, to ascertain compliance with regulatory or self-regulatory practices or procedures or to ascertain or demonstrate standards which are or ought to be achieved (quality control and training),
    in the interests of national security (in which case only certain specified public officials may make the interception),
    to prevent or detect crime,
    to investigate or detect unauthorised use of telecommunication systems or,
    to secure, or as an inherent part of, effective system operation;
  monitoring received communications to determine whether they are business or personal communications;
  monitoring communications made to anonymous telephone helplines.

Interceptions are authorised only if the controller of the telecommunications system on which they are effected has made all reasonable efforts to inform potential users that interceptions may be made.

The Regulations do not authorise interceptions to which the persons making and receiving the communications have consented: they are not prohibited by the Act.

A regulatory impact assessment is available and can be obtained from Communications and Information Industries Directorate, Department of Trade and Industry, 151 Buckingham Palace Road, London SW1W 9SS. Copies have been placed in the libraries of both Houses of Parliament.

2004 No. 157
Investigatory Powers

The Regulation of Investigatory Powers (Conditions for the Lawful Interception of Persons outside the United Kingdom) Regulations 2004

Made 27th January 2004
Laid before Parliament 3rd February 2004
Coming into force in accordance with regulation 2

The Secretary of State, in exercise of the powers conferred on him by section 4(1)(d) of the Regulation of Investigatory Powers Act 2000(a), hereby makes the following Regulations:

Citation

1. These Regulations may be cited as the Regulation of Investigatory Powers (Conditions for the Lawful Interception of Persons outside the United Kingdom) Regulations 2004.

Commencement

2.—(1) These Regulations shall come into force–
   (a) if the United Kingdom is one of the first eight Member States of the European Union to ratify the Convention on Mutual Assistance in Criminal Matters established by Council Act of 29th May 2000 (2000/C197/01) ('the Convention'), 90 days after the day on which the eighth Member State ratifies; or
   (b) otherwise, 90 days after the day on which the United Kingdom ratifies the Convention.

(2) For the purposes of paragraph (1)–
   (a) a Member State ratifies the Convention when it notifies the Secretary-General of the Council of the European Union of the completion of its constitutional procedures for the adoption of the Convention, in accordance with Article 27(2) of the Convention;
   (b) the reference to a 'Member State' is only to a state that was a Member State on 29th May 2000.

Conditions for the lawful interception of persons outside the United Kingdom

3. For the purposes of section 4(1)(d) of the Regulation of Investigatory Powers Act 2000, the following conditions are prescribed–
   (a) the interception is carried out for the purposes of a criminal investigation;
   (b) the criminal investigation is being carried out in a country or territory that is party to an international agreement designated for the purposes of section 1(4) of that Act.

Caroline Flint
Parliamentary Under-Secretary of State

Home Office
27th January 2004

Explanatory Note

(This note is not part of the Regulations)

Part 1 of the Regulation of Investigatory Powers Act 2000 contains provisions about the interception of communications. Section 4(1) provides that the interception of a communication is authorised (and therefore lawful) if it is carried out for the purpose of obtaining information about the communications of a person who is, or is reasonably believed to be, in a country or territory outside the United Kingdom, it relates to the use of a public telecommunications service provided to persons in that country or territory and the person who provides that service is required by the law of that country or territory to carry out, secure or facilitate the interception in question.

Under section 4(1)(d) the Secretary of State may impose additional conditions that must be met before this type of interception will be authorised. These Regulations set out those conditions.

Regulation 2 ensures that these Regulations will come into force at the same time as the Convention on Mutual Assistance in Criminal Matters established by Council Act of 29th May 2000 (2000/C197/01) comes into force in the United Kingdom.

Statutory Instruments Relevant to Chapter 9

2000 No. 2725
Investigatory Powers

The Regulation of Investigatory Powers (Source Records) Regulations 2000

Made 4th October 2000
Laid before Parliament 10th October 2000
Coming into force 1st November 2000

The Secretary of State, in exercise of the powers conferred on him by section 29(5)(d) of the Regulation of Investigatory Powers Act 2000, hereby makes the following Regulations:

Citation and commencement

1. These Regulations may be cited as the Regulation of Investigatory Powers (Source Records) Regulations 2000 and shall come into force on 1st November 2000.

Interpretation

2. In these Regulations–
    'the 2000 Act' means the Regulation of Investigatory Powers Act 2000;
    'relevant investigating authority' has the meaning given by section 29(8) of the 2000 Act, but the qualification in section 29(9) does not apply;
    'source' means a covert human intelligence source; and
    'undercover operative' means a source who holds an office, rank or position with a relevant investigating authority.

Particulars to be contained in records

3. The following matters are specified for the purposes of paragraph (d) of section 29(5) of the 2000 Act (as being matters particulars of which must be included in the records relating to each source):

    (a) the identity of the source;

    (b) the identity, where known, used by the source;

    (c) any relevant investigating authority other than the authority maintaining the records;

    (d) the means by which the source is referred to within each relevant investigating authority;

    (e) any other significant information connected with the security and welfare of the source;

    (f) any confirmation made by a person granting or renewing an authorisation for the conduct or use of a source that the information in paragraph (d) has been considered and that any identified risks to the security and welfare of the source have where appropriate been properly explained to and understood by the source;

    (g) the date when, and the circumstances in which, the source was recruited;

    (h) the identities of the persons who, in relation to the source, are discharging or have discharged the functions mentioned in section 29(5)(a) to (c) of the 2000 Act or in any order made by the Secretary of State under section 29(2)(c);

    (i) the periods during which those persons have discharged those responsibilities;

    (j) the tasks given to the source and the demands made of him in relation to his activities as a source;

    (k) all contacts or communications between the source and a person acting on behalf of any relevant investigating authority;

    (l) the information obtained by each relevant investigating authority by the conduct or use of the source;

    (m) any dissemination by that authority of information obtained in that way; and

    (n) in the case of a source who is not an undercover operative, every payment, benefit or reward and every offer of a payment, benefit or reward that is made or provided by or on behalf of any relevant investigating authority in respect of the source's activities for the benefit of that or any other relevant investigating authority.

Charles Clarke
Minister of State

Home Office
4th October 2000

Explanatory Note

(This note is not part of the Regulations)

Under section 29(2)(c) of the Regulation of Investigatory Powers Act 2000 a person may not grant an authorisation for the conduct or use of a covert human intelligence source unless he believes that arrangements exist that satisfy the requirements of section 29(5). For example, the arrangements must be adequate to ensure that the records relating to the source contain particulars of certain matters. Those matters are specified in these Regulations.

In some cases, the activities of the source will be for the benefit of more than one public authority. By virtue of section 29(9), the records relating to the source must be kept by one of those authorities. The matters specified in the Regulations, however, relate to the source's contact with each of them.

2000 No. 2793
Investigatory Powers

The Regulation of Investigatory Powers (Juveniles) Order 2000

Made 10th October 2000
Laid before Parliament 16th October 2000
Coming into force 6th November 2000

The Secretary of State, in exercise of the powers conferred on him by sections 29(2)(c), 29(7)(a) and (b) and 43(8) of the Regulation of Investigatory Powers Act 2000, hereby makes the following Order:

Citation and commencement

1. This Order may be cited as the Regulation of Investigatory Powers (Juveniles) Order 2000 and shall come into force on 6th November 2000.

Interpretation

2. In this Order–
    'the 2000 Act' means the Regulation of Investigatory Powers Act 2000;
    'guardian', in relation to a source, has the same meaning as is given to 'guardian of a child' by section 105 of the Children Act 1989;
    'relative' has the same meaning as it is given by section 105 of the Children Act 1989;
    'relevant investigating authority' has the meaning given by section 29(8) of the 2000 Act, and where the activities of a source are to be for the benefit of more than one public authority, each of these authorities is a relevant investigating authority;
    'source' means covert human intelligence source.

Sources under 16: prohibition

3. No authorisation may be granted for the conduct or use of a source if–
    (a) the source is under the age of sixteen; and
    (b) the relationship to which the conduct or use would relate is between the source and his parent or any person who has parental responsibility for him.

Sources under 16: arrangements for meetings

4.—(1) Where a source is under the age of sixteen, the arrangements referred to in section 29(2)(c) of the 2000 Act must be such that there is at all times a person holding an office, rank or position with a relevant investigating authority who has responsibility for ensuring that an appropriate adult is present at meetings to which this article applies.

(2) This article applies to all meetings between the source and a person representing any relevant investigating authority that take place while the source remains under the age of sixteen.

(3) In paragraph (1), 'appropriate adult' means–

    (a) the parent or guardian of the source;

    (b) any other person who has for the time being assumed responsibility for his welfare; or

    (c) where no person falling within paragraph (a) or (b) is available, any responsible person aged eighteen or over who is neither a member of nor employed by any relevant investigating authority.

Sources under 18: risk assessments etc.

5.   An authorisation for the conduct or use of a source may not be granted or renewed in any case where the source is under the age of eighteen at the time of the grant or renewal, unless–

    (a) a person holding an office, rank or position with a relevant investigating authority has made and, in the case of a renewal, updated a risk assessment sufficient to demonstrate that:

        (i) the nature and magnitude of any risk of physical injury to the source arising in the course of, or as a result of, carrying out the conduct described in the authorisation have been identified and evaluated; and

        (ii) the nature and magnitude of any risk of psychological distress to the source arising in the course of, or as a result of, carrying out the conduct described in the authorisation have been identified and evaluated;

    (b) the person granting or renewing the authorisation has considered the risk assessment and has satisfied himself that any risks identified in it are justified and, if they are, that they have been properly explained to and understood by the source; and

    (c) the person granting or renewing the authorisation knows whether the relationship to which the conduct or use would relate is between the source and a relative, guardian or person who has for the time being assumed responsibility for the source's welfare, and, if it is, has given particular consideration to whether the authorisation is justified in the light of that fact.

Sources under 18: duration of authorisations

6.   In relation to an authorisation for the conduct or the use of a source who is under the age of eighteen at the time the authorisation is granted or renewed, section 43(3) of the 2000 Act shall have effect as if the period specified in paragraph (b) of that subsection were one month instead of twelve months.

Charles Clarke
Minister of State

Home Office
10th October 2000

Explanatory Note

(This note is not part of the Order)

Section 29 of the Regulation of Investigatory Powers Act 2000 allows authorisations to be granted for the use or conduct of covert human intelligence sources.

This Order contains special provisions for the cases of covert human intelligence sources who are under eighteen.

2001 No. 1057
Investigatory Powers

The Regulation of Investigatory Powers
(British Broadcasting Corporation) Order 2001

Made 15th March 2001
Coming into force 16th March 2001

The Secretary of State, in exercise of the powers conferred on him by section 47(1) of the Regulation of Investigatory Powers Act 2000, hereby makes the following Order, of which a draft has, in accordance with section 47(2) of that Act, been laid before and approved by resolution of each House of Parliament:

Citation, commencement and interpretation

1.—(1) This Order may be cited as the Regulation of Investigatory Powers (British Broadcasting Corporation) Order 2001.
(2) This Order shall come into force on the day after the day on which it is made.
(3) In this Order 'the 2000 Act' means the Regulation of Investigatory Powers Act 2000.

Application of Part II of the 2000 Act to the detection of television receivers

2.—(1) Part II of the 2000 Act (surveillance and covert human intelligence sources) shall apply to surveillance which–
  (a) is carried out by means of apparatus designed or adapted for the purpose of detecting the installation or use in any residential or other premises of a television receiver (within the meaning of section 1 of the Wireless Telegraphy Act 1949), and
  (b) is carried out from outside those premises exclusively for that purpose,
and such surveillance is referred to in this Order as 'the detection of television receivers'.
(2) In its application to the detection of television receivers, Part II of the 2000 Act shall have effect as if–
  (a) the following provisions were omitted, namely, sections 28 to 42, in section 43, subsections (2), (6) to (8) and (10) and in subsection (4) the words 'Subject to subsection (6)', section 44, section 45(2) to (7) and section 46, and
  (b) the modifications set out in articles 3 to 5 were made.

New section 27A

3. In its application to the detection of television receivers, Part II of the 2000 Act shall have effect as if the following section were inserted after section 27–

'Authorisation of detection of television receivers

27A.—(1) Subject to the following provisions of this Part, the persons designated for the purposes of this section shall each have power to grant authorisations for the detection of television receivers, that is to say, surveillance which–

  (a) is carried out by means of apparatus designed or adapted for the purpose of detecting the installation or use in any residential or other premises of a television receiver (within the meaning of section 1 of the Wireless Telegraphy Act 1949), and

  (b) is carried out from outside those premises exclusively for that purpose.

(2) The persons designated for the purposes of this section are–

  (a) any person holding the position of head of sales or head of marketing within the Television Licence Management Unit of the British Broadcasting Corporation, and

  (b) any person holding a position within that Unit which is more senior than the positions mentioned in paragraph (a).

(3) A person shall not grant an authorisation for the detection of television receivers unless he believes–

  (a) that the authorisation is necessary–

    (i) for the purpose of preventing or detecting crime constituting an offence under section 1 or 1A of the Wireless Telegraphy Act 1949; or

    (ii) for the purpose of assessing or collecting sums payable to the British Broadcasting Corporation under regulations made under section 2 of the Wireless Telegraphy Act 1949; and

  (b) that the authorised surveillance is proportionate to what is sought to be achieved by carrying it out.

(4) The conduct that is authorised by an authorisation for the detection of television receivers is any conduct that–

  (a) consists in the carrying out of the detection of television receivers, and

  (b) is carried out by the persons described in the authorisation in the circumstances described in the authorisation.'.

Modifications of section 43

4. In its application to the detection of television receivers, section 43 of the 2000 Act (general rules about grant, renewal and duration) shall have effect as if–

  (a) in subsection (1), for paragraphs (a) and (b) there were substituted 'must be in writing';

  (b) for subsection (3) there were substituted–

    '(3) Subject to subsection (4), an authorisation under this Part shall cease to have effect–

      (a) in the case of an authorisation which has not been renewed and in which is specified a period of less than eight weeks beginning with the day on which the grant of the authorisation takes effect, at the end of that period;

(b) in the case of an authorisation which has not been renewed and to which paragraph (a) does not apply, at the end of the period of eight weeks beginning with the day on which the grant of the authorisation takes effect;

(c) in the case of an authorisation which has been renewed, and in which is specified a period of less than eight weeks beginning with the day on which the grant of the authorisation takes effect, at the end of a period of the same length beginning with the day on which the latest renewal takes effect;

(d) in the case of an authorisation which has been renewed, and to which paragraph (c) does not apply, at the end of the period of eight weeks beginning with the day on which the latest renewal takes effect.';

(c) for subsection (5) there were substituted–

'(5) Section 27A shall have effect in relation to the renewal of an authorisation under this Part as if references to the grant of an authorisation included references to its renewal.'; and

(d) in subsection (9) for paragraphs (a) to (c) there were substituted–

'(a) in the case of the grant of an authorisation, to the time at which or, as the case may be, day on which the authorisation is granted;

(b) in the case of the renewal of an authorisation, to the time at which or, as the case may be, day on which the authorisation would have ceased to have effect but for the renewal.'.

Modification of section 45(1)

5. In its application to the detection of television receivers, section 45 of the 2000 Act (cancellation of authorisations) shall have effect as if–

(a) in subsection (1) for the words from 'if' to the end there were substituted 'if he is satisfied that the authorisation is one in relation to which the requirements of section 27A(3)(a) and (b) are no longer satisfied'; and

(b) after subsection (1) there were inserted–

'(1A) Where any duty imposed by subsection (1) would otherwise fall on a person who is no longer available to perform it, that duty is to be performed by–

(a) the person, if any, appointed for the purpose of this subsection in accordance with subsection (1B);

(b) where no such person has been appointed, the person (if any) holding a position within the British Broadcasting Corporation who has taken over the responsibilities of the person who is no longer available, or most of them.

(1B) The person making an appointment for the purpose of subsection (1A), and the person appointed, must each be–

(a) a person designated for the purposes of section 27A, or

(b) a person holding a more senior position within the British Broadcasting Corporation than was held by the person who is no longer available.'.

Charles Clarke
Minister of State
Home Office
15th March 2001

Explanatory Note

(This note is not part of the Order)

This Order applies Part II of the Regulation of Investigatory Powers Act 2000, with modifications, to the carrying out of surveillance to detect whether a television receiver is being used in any residential or other premises (referred to in the Order as 'the detection of television receivers').

Part II of the 2000 Act provides for the grant of authorisations for certain forms of surveillance. By virtue of section 26(6), the detection of television receivers is not one of the kinds of surveillance regulated by Part II. However, section 47 provides for that Part to be applied, or applied with modifications, to surveillance not otherwise covered. This Order is made under that section, and provides for authorisations to be granted for the detection of television receivers under a modified version of Part II. Authorisations may cover such detection in any part of the United Kingdom.

Article 2 modifies Part II by providing that certain of its provisions are not to apply to the detection of television receivers. Article 3 modifies Part II so that it has effect in relation to such detection as if the 'section 27A' set out in that article were inserted in that Part. 'Section 27A' provides for authorisations to be granted by persons holding certain positions within the BBC, if they are satisfied that the authorisation is necessary for preventing or detecting certain offences under section 1 or 1A of the Wireless Telegraphy Act 1949, or for assessing or collecting sums payable in respect of television licences. Article 4 modifies the general rules in section 43 about the grant, renewal and duration of authorisations and provides (in particular) that authorisations for the detection of television receivers are to last for up to eight weeks. Article 5 modifies the duty imposed by section 45 to cancel an authorisation where the requirements that were necessary for its grant or renewal no longer apply.

Table of Statutory Instruments amending RIPA 2000

Number	Title
2000/2409	The Wireless Telegraphy (Interception and Disclosure of Messages) (Designation) Regulations 2000
2000/2417	The Regulation of Investigatory Powers (Prescription of Offices, Ranks and Positions) Order 2000
2000/2418	The Regulation of Investigatory Powers (Authorisations Extending to Scotland) Order 2000
2000/2543	The Regulation of Investigatory Powers Act 2000 (Commencement No. 1 and Transitional Provisions) Order 2000

2000/2563	The Regulation of Investigatory Powers (Notification of Authorizations etc.) Order 2000
2000/2665	The Investigatory Powers Tribunal Rules 2000
2000/2699	The Telecommunications (Lawful Business Practice) (Interception of Communications) Regulations 2000
2000/2725	The Regulation of Investigatory Powers (Source Records) Regulations 2000
2000/2793	The Regulation of Investigatory Powers (Juveniles) Order 2000
2000/2794	The Regulation of Investigatory Powers (Cancellation of Authorisations) Regulations 2000
2000/3252	The Scotland Act (Transfer of Functions to the Scottish Ministers etc.) (No. 2) Order 2000
2001/443	The Proscribed Organisations Appeal Commission (Procedure) Rules 2001
2001/1057	The Regulation of Investigatory Powers (British Broadcasting Corporation) Order 2001
2001/1126	The Regulation of Investigatory Powers (Designation of Public Authorities for the Purposes of Intrusive Surveillance) Order 2001
2001/2476	The Financial Services and Markets Tribunal Rules 2001
2001/2568	The Secretaries of State for Transport, Local Government and the Regions and for Environment, Food and Rural Affairs Order 2001
2001/2727	The Regulation of Investigatory Powers Act 2000 (Commencement No. 2) Order 2001
2001/3617	Postal Services Act 2000 (Disclosure of Information) Order 2001
2001/3686	The Intervention Board for Agricultural Produce (Abolition) Regulations 2001
2001/3734	The Regulation of Investigatory Powers (Technical Advisory Board) Order 2001
2002/794	The Ministry of Agriculture, Fisheries and Food (Dissolution) Order 2002
2002/1298	The Regulation of Investigatory Powers (Prescription of Offices, Ranks and Positions) (Amendment) Order 2002
2002/1397	The Secretaries of State for Education and Skills and for Work and Pensions Order 2002
2002/1693	The Regulation of Investigatory Powers (Interception of Communications: Code of Practice) Order 2002
2002/1931	The Regulation of Investigatory Powers (Maintenance of Interception Capability) Order 2002
2002/1932	The Regulation of Investigatory Powers (Covert Human Intelligence Sources: Code of Practice) Order 2002

2002/1933	The Regulation of Investigatory Powers (Covert Surveillance: Code of Practice) Order 2002
2002/2126	The Road Vehicles (Construction and Use) (Amendment) (No. 3) Regulations 2003
2002/2626	The Transfer of Functions (Transport, Local Government and the Regions) Order 2002
2003/335	The Proceeds of Crime Act 2002 (Disclosure of Information) Order 2003
2003/409	The Scottish Parliament (Disqualification) Order 2003
2003/1397	The Enterprise Act 2002 (Commencement No. 3 Transitional and Transitory Provisions and Savings) Order 2003
2003/1900	The Communications Act 2003 (Commencement No. 1) Order 2003
2003/1918	The Official Secrets Act (Prescription) (Amendment) Order 2003
2003/2498	The Copyright and Related Rights Regulations 2003
2003//2617	The Scotland Act 1998 (Transfer of Functions to the Scottish Ministers etc.) (No. 2) Order 2003
2003/3104	The Wireless Telegraphy (Interception and Disclosure of Messages) (Designation) Regulations 2003
2003/3140	The Regulation of Investigatory Powers Act 2000 (Commencement No. 3) Order 2003
2003/3171	The Regulation of Investigatory Powers (Directed Surveillance and Covert Human Intelligence Sources) Order 2003
2003/3172	The Regulation of Investigatory Powers (Communications Data) Order 2003
2003/3174	The Regulation of Investigatory Powers (Intrusive Surveillance) Order 2003
2004/157	The Regulation of Investigatory Powers (Conditions for the Lawful Interception of Persons outside the United Kingdom) Regulations 2004
2004/158	The Regulation of Investigatory Powers (Designation of an International Agreement) Order 2004
2004/815	The Independent Police Complaints Commission (Investigatory Powers) Order 2004
2004/1128	The Regulation of Investigatory Powers (Foreign Surveillance Operations) Order 2004
2004/2991	The Crown Court (Amendment No. 3) Rules 2004
2004/2993	The Magistrates Court (Amendment) Rules 2004

2005/384	The Criminal Procedure Rules 2005
2005/866	The Scotland Act 1998 (Modifications of Schedule 5) (No. 2) Order 2005
2005/1083	The Regulation of Investigatory Powers (Communications Data) (Amendment) Order 2005
2005/1085	The Regulations of Investigatory Powers (Directed Surveillance and Covert Human Intelligence Sources) (Amendment) Order 2005

Appendix D
The Covert Surveillance Code of Practice

1 Background

1.1 In this code the:
- '**1989 Act**' means the Security Service Act 1989;
- '**1994 Act**' means the Intelligence Services Act 1994;
- '**1997 Act**' means the Police Act 1997;
- '**2000 Act**' means the Regulation of Investigatory Powers Act 2000;
- '**RIP(S)A**' means the Regulation of Investigatory Powers (Scotland) Act 2000.

1.2 This code of practice provides guidance on the use of covert surveillance by public authorities under Part II of the 2000 Act and on entry on, or interference with, property (or with wireless telegraphy) under section 5 of the 1994 Act or Part III of the 1997 Act. This code replaces the code of practice issued in 1999 pursuant to section 101(3) of the 1997 Act.

1.3 General observation forms part of the duties of many law enforcement officers and other public authorities and is not usually regulated by the 2000 Act. For example, police officers will be on patrol to prevent and detect crime, maintain public safety and prevent disorder or trading standards, or HM Customs and Excise officers might covertly observe and then visit a shop as part of their enforcement function to verify the supply or level of supply of goods or services that may be liable to a restriction or tax. Such observation may involve the use of equipment to merely reinforce normal sensory perception, such as binoculars, or the use of cameras, where this does not involve systematic surveillance of an individual.

1.4 Although the provisions of the 2000 Act or of this code of practice do not normally cover the use of overt CCTV surveillance systems, since members of the public are aware that such systems are in use, there may be occasions when public authorities use overt CCTV systems for the purposes of a specific investigation or operation. In such cases, authorisation for intrusive or directed surveillance may be necessary.

1.5 The 2000 Act provides that all codes of practice relating to the 2000 Act are admissible as evidence in criminal and civil proceedings. If any provision of the code appears relevant to any court or tribunal considering any such proceedings, or to the Investigatory Powers Tribunal established under the 2000 Act, or to one of the Commissioners responsible for overseeing the powers conferred by the 2000 Act, it must be taken into account.

General extent of powers

1.6 Authorisations under the 2000 Act can be given for surveillance both inside and outside the United Kingdom. Authorisations for actions outside the United Kingdom can only validate them for the purposes of proceedings in the United Kingdom. An authorisation under Part II of the 2000 Act does not take into account the requirements of the country outside the United Kingdom in which the investigation or operation is taking place.

1.7 Where the conduct authorised is likely to take place in Scotland, authorisations should be granted under RIP(S)A, unless the authorisation is being obtained by those public authorities listed in section 46(3) of the 2000 Act and the Regulation of Investigatory Powers (Authorisations Extending to Scotland) Order 2000; SI No. 2418). Additionally any authorisation granted or renewed for the purposes of national security or the economic well-being of the United Kingdom must be made under the 2000 Act. This code of practice is extended to Scotland in relation to authorisations made under Part II of the 2000 Act which apply to Scotland. A separate code of practice applies in relation to authorisations made under RIP(S)A.

Use of material in evidence

1.8 Material obtained through covert surveillance may be used as evidence in criminal proceedings. The proper authorisation of surveillance should ensure the admissibility of such evidence under the common law, section 78 of the Police and Criminal Evidence Act 1984 and the Human Rights Act 1998. Furthermore, the product of the surveillance described in this code is subject to the ordinary rules for retention and disclosure of material under the Criminal Procedure and Investigations Act 1996, where those rules apply to the law enforcement body in question.

Directed surveillance, intrusive surveillance and entry on or interference with property or with wireless telegraphy

1.9 Directed surveillance is defined in section 26(2) of the 2000 Act as surveillance which is covert, but not intrusive, and undertaken:
(a) for the purposes of a specific investigation or specific operation;
(b) in such a manner as is likely to result in the obtaining of private information about a person (whether or not one specifically identified for the purposes of the investigation or operation); and
(c) otherwise than by way of an immediate response to events or circumstances the nature of which is such that it would not be reasonably practicable for an authorisation under Part II of the 2000 Act to be sought for the carrying out of the surveillance.

1.10 Directed surveillance investigations or operations can only be carried out by those public authorities who are listed in or added to Part I and Part II of schedule 1 of the 2000 Act.

1.11 intrusive surveillance is defined in section 26(3) of the 2000 Act as covert surveillance that:
(a) is carried out in relation to anything taking place on any residential premises or in any private vehicle; and
(b) involves the presence of an individual on the premises or in the vehicle or is carried out by means of a surveillance device.

1.12 Applications to carry out intrusive surveillance can only be made by the senior authorising officer of those public authorities listed in or added to section 32(6) of the 2000 Act or by a member or official of those public authorities listed in or added to section 41(1).

1.13 Applications to enter on or interfere with property or with wireless telegraphy can only be made by the authorising officers of those public authorities listed in or added to section 93(5) of the 1997 Act. Under section 5 of the 1994 Act only members of the intelligence services are able to make applications to enter on or interfere with property or with wireless telegraphy.

2 General Rules on Authorisations

2.1 An authorisation under Part II of the 2000 Act will provide lawful authority for a public authority to carry out surveillance. Responsibility for authorising surveillance investigations or operations will vary, depending on whether the authorisation is for intrusive surveillance or directed surveillance, and which public authority is involved. For the purposes of Chapter 2 and 3 of this code the authorising officer, senior authorising officer or the person who makes an application to the Secretary of State will be referred to as an 'authorising officer'.

2.2 Part II of the 2000 Act does not impose a requirement on public authorities to seek or obtain an authorisation where, under the 2000 Act, one is available (see section 80 of the 2000 Act). Nevertheless, where there is an interference by a public authority with the right to respect for private and family life guaranteed under Article 8 of the European Convention on Human Rights, and where there is no other source of lawful authority, the consequence of not obtaining an authorisation under the 2000 Act may be that the action is unlawful by virtue of section 6 of the Human Rights Act 1998.

2.3 Public authorities are therefore strongly recommended to seek an authorisation where the surveillance is likely to interfere with a person's Article 8 rights to privacy by obtaining private information about that person, whether or not that person is the subject of the investigation or operation. Obtaining an authorisation will ensure that the action is carried out in accordance with law and subject to stringent safeguards against abuse.

Necessity and proportionality

2.4 Obtaining an authorisation under the 2000 Act, the 1997 Act and 1994 Act will only ensure that there is a justifiable interference with an individual's Article 8 rights if it is necessary and proportionate for these activities to take place. The 2000 Act first requires that the person granting an authorisation believe that the authorisation is necessary in the circumstances of the particular case for one or more of the statutory grounds in section 28(3) of the 2000 Act for directed surveillance and in section 32(3) of the 2000 Act for intrusive surveillance.

2.5 Then, if the activities are necessary, the person granting the authorisation must believe that they are proportionate to what is sought to be achieved by carrying them out. This involves balancing the intrusiveness of the activity on the target and others who might be affected by it against the need for the activity in operational terms. The activity will not be proportionate if it is excessive in the circumstances of the case or if the information which is sought could reasonably be obtained by other less intrusive means. All such activity should be carefully managed to meet the objective in question and must not be arbitrary or unfair.

Collateral intrusion

2.6 Before authorising surveillance the authorising officer should also take into account the risk of intrusion into the privacy of persons other than those who are directly the subjects of the investigation or operation (collateral intrusion). Measures should be taken, wherever practicable, to avoid or minimise unnecessary intrusion into the lives of those not directly connected with the investigation or operation.

2.7 An application for an authorisation should include an assessment of the risk of any collateral intrusion. The authorising officer should take this into account, when considering the proportionality of the surveillance.

2.8 Those carrying out the surveillance should inform the authorising officer if the investigation or operation unexpectedly interferes with the privacy of individuals who are not covered by the authorisation. When the original authorisation may not be sufficient, consideration should be given to whether the authorisation needs to be amended and reauthorised or a new authorisation is required.

2.9 Any person granting or applying for an authorisation or warrant will also need to be aware of particular sensitivities in the local community where the surveillance is taking place and of similar activities being undertaken by other public authorities which could impact on the deployment of surveillance. In this regard, it is recommended that where the authorising officers in the National Criminal Intelligence Service (NCIS), the National Crime Squad (NCS) and HM Customs and Excise (HMCE) consider that conflicts might arise they should consult a senior officer within the police force area in which the investigation or operation takes place.

2.10 The matters in paragraphs 2.1–2.9 above must also be taken into account when applying for authorisations or warrants for entry on or interference with property or with wireless telegraphy. In particular they must be necessary in the circumstances of the particular case for one of the statutory ground listed in section 93(2)(a) of the 1997 Act and section 5(2)(c) of the 1994 Act, proportionate and when exercised steps should be taken to minimise collateral intrusion.

Combined authorisations

2.11 A single authorisation may combine:
- two or more different authorisations under Part II of the 2000 Act;
- an authorisation under Part II of the 2000 Act and an authorisation under Part III of the 1997 Act;
- a warrant for intrusive surveillance under Part II of the 2000 Act and a warrant under section 5 of the 1994 Act.

2.12 For example, a single authorisation may combine authorisations for directed and intrusive surveillance. The provisions applicable in the case of each of the authorisations must be considered separately. Thus, a police superintendent can authorise the directed surveillance but the intrusive surveillance needs the separate authorisation of a chief constable, and in certain cases the approval of a Surveillance Commissioner will also be necessary. Where an authorisation for directed surveillance or the use or conduct of a covert human intelligence source is combined with a Secretary of State authorisation for intrusive surveillance, the combined authorisation must be issued by the Secretary of State. However, this does not preclude public authorities from obtaining separate authorisations.

2.13 In cases where one agency is acting on behalf of another, it is usually for the tasking agency to obtain or provide the authorisation. For example, where surveillance is carried out by the Armed Forces on behalf of the police, authorisations would be sought by the police and granted by the appropriate authorising officer. In cases where the Security Service is acting in support of the police or other law enforcement agencies in the field of serious crime, the Security Service would normally seek authorisations.

Central record of all authorisations

2.14 A centrally retrievable record of all authorisations should be held by each public authority and regularly updated whenever an authorisation is granted, renewed or cancelled. The record should be made available to the relevant Commissioner or an Inspector from the Office of Surveillance Commissioners, upon request. These records should be retained for a period of at least three years from the ending of the authorisation and should contain the following information:
- the type of authorisation;
- the date the authorisation was given;
- name and rank/grade of the authorising officer;
- the unique reference number (URN) of the investigation or operation;
- the title of the investigation or operation, including a brief description and names of subjects, if known;
- whether the urgency provisions were used, and if so why.
- if the authorisation is renewed, when it was renewed and who authorised the renewal, including the name and rank/grade of the authorising officer;
- whether the investigation or operation is likely to result in obtaining confidential information as defined in this code of practice;
- the date the authorisation was cancelled.

2.15 In all cases, the relevant authority should maintain the following documentation which need not form part of the centrally retrievable record:
- a copy of the application and a copy of the authorisation together with any supplementary documentation and notification of the approval given by the authorising officer;
- a record of the period over which the surveillance has taken place;
- the frequency of reviews prescribed by the authorising officer;
- a record of the result of each review of the authorisation;
- a copy of any renewal of an authorisation, together with the supporting documentation submitted when the renewal was requested;
- the date and time when any instruction was given by the authorising officer.

Retention and destruction of the product

2.16 Where the product of surveillance could be relevant to pending or future criminal or civil proceedings, it should be retained in accordance with established disclosure requirements for a suitable further period, commensurate to any subsequent review.

2.17 In the cases of the law enforcement agencies (not including the Royal Navy Regulating Branch, the Royal Military Police and the Royal Air Force Police), particular attention is drawn to the requirements of the code of practice issued under the

Criminal Procedure and Investigations Act 1996. This requires that material which is obtained in the course of a criminal investigation and which may be relevant to the investigation must be recorded and retained.

2.18 There is nothing in the 2000 Act which prevents material obtained from properly authorised surveillance from being used in other investigations. Each public authority must ensure that arrangements are in place for the handling, storage and destruction of material obtained through the use of covert surveillance. Authorising officers must ensure compliance with the appropriate data protection requirements and any relevant codes of practice produced by individual authorities relating to the handling and storage of material.

The Intelligence Services, MOD and HM Forces

2.19 The heads of these agencies are responsible for ensuring that arrangements exist for securing that no information is stored by the authorities, except as necessary for the proper discharge of their functions. They are also responsible for arrangements to control onward disclosure. For the intelligence services, this is a statutory duty under the 1989 Act and the 1994 Act.

3 Special Rules on Authorisations

3.1 The 2000 Act does not provide any special protection for 'confidential information'. Nevertheless, particular care should be taken in cases where the subject of the investigation or operation might reasonably expect a high degree of privacy, or where confidential information is involved. Confidential information consists of matters subject to legal privilege, confidential personal information or confidential journalistic material. So, for example, extra care should be given where, through the use of surveillance, it would be possible to acquire knowledge of discussions between a minister of religion and an individual relating to the latter's spiritual welfare, or where matters of medical or journalistic confidentiality or legal privilege may be involved.

3.2 In cases where through the use of surveillance it is likely that knowledge of confidential information will be acquired, the use of surveillance is subject to a higher level of authorisation. Annex A lists the authorising officer for each public authority permitted to authorise such surveillance.

Communications subject to legal privilege

3.3 Section 98 of the 1997 Act describes those matters that are subject to legal privilege in England and Wales. In Scotland, the relevant description is contained in section 33 of the Criminal Law (Consolidation) (Scotland) Act 1995. With regard to Northern Ireland, Article 12 of the Police and Criminal Evidence (Northern Ireland) Order 1989 should be referred to.

3.4 Legal privilege does not apply to communications made with the intention of furthering a criminal purpose (whether the lawyer is acting unwittingly or culpably). Legally privileged communications will lose their protection if there are grounds to believe, for example, that the professional legal adviser is intending to hold or use them for a criminal purpose. But privilege is not lost if a professional legal adviser is properly advising a person who is suspected of having committed a criminal offence.

The concept of legal privilege applies to the provision of professional legal advice by any individual, agency or organisation qualified to do so.

3.5 The 2000 Act does not provide any special protection for legally privileged information. Nevertheless, such information is particularly sensitive and surveillance which acquires such material may engage Article 6 of the ECHR (right to a fair trial) as well as Article 8. Legally privileged information obtained by surveillance is extremely unlikely ever to be admissible as evidence in criminal proceedings. Moreover, the mere fact that such surveillance has taken place may lead to any related criminal proceedings being stayed as an abuse of process. Accordingly, action which may lead to such information being acquired is subject to additional safeguards under this code.

3.6 In general, an application for surveillance which is likely to result in the acquisition of legally privileged information should only be made in exceptional and compelling circumstances. Full regard should be had to the particular proportionality issues such surveillance raises. The application should include, in addition to the reasons why it is considered necessary for the surveillance to take place, an assessment of how likely it is that information subject to legal privilege will be acquired. In addition, the application should clearly state whether the purpose (or one of the purposes) of the surveillance is to obtain legally privileged information.

3.7 This assessment will be taken into account by the authorising officer in deciding whether the proposed surveillance is necessary and proportionate under section 28 of the 2000 Act for directed surveillance and under section 32 for intrusive surveillance. The authorising officer may require regular reporting so as to be able to decide whether the authorisation should continue. In those cases where legally privileged information has been acquired and retained, the matter should be reported to the relevant Commissioner or Inspector during his next inspection and the material be made available to him if requested.

3.8 A substantial proportion of the communications between a lawyer and his client(s) may be subject to legal privilege. Therefore, any case where a lawyer is the subject of an investigation or operation should be notified to the relevant Commissioner during his next inspection and any material which has been retained should be made available to him if requested.

3.9 Where there is any doubt as to the handling and dissemination of information which may be subject to legal privilege, advice should be sought from a legal adviser within the relevant public authority before any further dissemination of the material takes place. Similar advice should also be sought where there is doubt over whether information is not subject to legal privilege due to the 'in furtherance of a criminal purpose' exception. The retention of legally privileged information, or its dissemination to an outside body, should be accompanied by a clear warning that it is subject to legal privilege. It should be safeguarded by taking reasonable steps to ensure there is no possibility of it becoming available, or its contents becoming known, to any person whose possession of it might prejudice any criminal or civil proceedings related to the information. Any dissemination of legally privileged material to an outside body should be notified to the relevant Commissioner or Inspector during his next inspection.

Communications involving confidential personal information and confidential journalistic material

3.10 Similar consideration must also be given to authorisations that involve confidential personal information and confidential journalistic material. In those cases where confidential personal information and confidential journalistic material has been acquired and retained, the matter should be reported to the relevant Commissioner or Inspector during his next inspection and the material be made available to him if requested. Confidential personal information is information held in confidence relating to the physical or mental health or spiritual counselling concerning an individual (whether living or dead) who can be identified from it. Such information, which can include both oral and written communications, is held in confidence if it is held subject to an express or implied undertaking to hold it in confidence or it is subject to a restriction on disclosure or an obligation of confidentiality contained in existing legislation. Examples might include consultations between a health professional and a patient, or information from a patient's medical records.

3.11 Spiritual counselling means conversations between an individual and a Minister of Religion acting in his official capacity, where the individual being counselled is seeking or the Minister is imparting forgiveness, absolution or the resolution of conscience with the authority of the Divine Being(s) of their faith.

3.12 Confidential journalistic material includes material acquired or created for the purposes of journalism and held subject to an undertaking to hold it in confidence, as well as communications resulting in information being acquired for the purposes of journalism and held subject to such an undertaking.

4 Authorisation Procedures for Directed Surveillance

4.1 Directed surveillance is defined in section 26(2) of the 2000 Act as surveillance which is covert, but not intrusive, and undertaken:

a)   for the purposes of a specific investigation or specific operation;

b)   in such a manner as is likely to result in the obtaining of private information about a person (whether or not one specifically identified for the purposes of the investigation or operation); and

c)   otherwise than by way of an immediate response to events or circumstances the nature of which is such that it would not be reasonably practicable for an authorisation under Part II of the 2000 Act to be sought for the carrying out of the surveillance.

4.2 Covert surveillance is defined in section 26(9)(a) of the 2000 Act as any surveillance which is carried out in a manner calculated to ensure that the persons subject to the surveillance are unaware that it is or may be taking place.

4.3 Private information is defined in section 26(10) of the 2000 Act as including any information relating to a person's private or family life. The concept of private information should be broadly interpreted to include an individual's private or personal relationship with others. Family life should be treated as extending beyond the formal relationships created by marriage.

4.4 Directed surveillance does not include covert surveillance carried out by way of an immediate response to events or circumstances which, by their very nature, could not have been foreseen. For example, a police officer would not require an authorisation to conceal himself and observe a suspicious person that he came across in the course of a patrol.

4.5 By virtue of section 48(4) of the 2000 Act, surveillance includes the interception of postal and telephone communications where the sender or recipient consents to the reading of or listening to or recording of the communication (as the case may be). For further details see paragraphs 4.30–4.32 of this code.

4.6 Surveillance in residential premises or in private vehicles is defined as intrusive surveillance in section 26(3) of the 2000 Act and is dealt with in chapter 5 of this code. However, where surveillance is carried out by a device designed or adapted principally for the purpose of providing information about the location of a vehicle, the activity is directed surveillance and should be authorised accordingly.

4.7 Directed surveillance does not include entry on or interference with property or with wireless telegraphy. These activities are subject to a separate regime of authorisation or warranty, as set out in chapter 6 of this code.

4.8 Directed surveillance includes covert surveillance within office premises (as defined in paragraph 6.31 of this code). Authorising officers are reminded that confidential information should be afforded an enhanced level of protection. Chapter 3 of this code provides that in cases where the likely consequence of surveillance is to acquire confidential information, the authorisation should be given at a higher level.

Authorisation procedures

4.9 Under section 28(3) of the 2000 Act an authorisation for directed surveillance may be granted by an authorising officer where he believes that the authorisation is necessary in the circumstances of the particular case:

- in the interests of national security;[1,2]
- for the purpose of preventing and detecting[3] crime or of preventing disorder;
- in the interests of the economic well-being of the UK;
- in the interests of public safety;
- for the purpose of protecting public health;[4]

---

[1] One of the functions of the Security Service is the protection of national security and in particular the protection against threats from terrorism. These functions extend throughout the United Kingdom, save that, in Northern Ireland, where the lead responsibility for investigating the threat from terrorism related to the affairs of Northern Ireland lies with the Police Service of Northern Ireland. An authorising officer in another public authority should not issue an authorisation under Part II of the 2000 Act or under Part III of the 1997 Act where the operation or investigation falls within the responsibilities of the Security Service, as set out above, except where it is a directed surveillance investigation or operation that is to be carried out by a Special Branch or where the Security Service has agreed that another public authority can carry out a directed surveillance operation or investigation which would fall within the responsibilities of the Security Service.

[2] HM Forces may also undertake operations in connection with a military threat to national security and other operations in connection with national security in support of the Security Service, the Police Service of Northern Ireland or other Civil Powers.

[3] Detecting crime is defined in section 81(5) of the 2000 Act and is applied to the 1997 Act by section 134 of that Act (as amended).

[4] This could include investigations into infectious diseases, contaminated products or the illicit sale of pharmaceuticals.

- for the purpose of assessing or collecting any tax, duty, levy or other imposition, contribution or charge payable to a government department; or
- for any other purpose prescribed by an order made by the Secretary of State.[5]

4.10 The authorising officer must also believe that the surveillance is proportionate to what it seeks to achieve.

4.11 The public authorities entitled to authorise directed surveillance are listed in Schedule 1 to the 2000 Act. Responsibility for authorising the carrying out of directed surveillance rests with the authorising officer and requires the personal authority of the authorising officer. The Regulation of Investigatory Powers (Prescriptions of Offices, Ranks and Positions) Order 2000; SI No. 2417 designates the authorising officer for each different public authority and the officers entitled to act only in urgent cases. Where an authorisation for directed surveillance is combined with a Secretary of State authorisation for intrusive surveillance, the combined authorisation must be issued by the Secretary of State.

4.12 The authorising officer must give authorisations in writing, except that in urgent cases, they may be given orally by the authorising officer or the officer entitled to act in urgent cases. In such cases, a statement that the authorising officer has expressly authorised the action should be recorded in writing by the applicant as soon as is reasonably practicable.

4.13 A case is not normally to be regarded as urgent unless the time that would elapse before the authorising officer was available to grant the authorisation would, in the judgement of the person giving the authorisation, be likely to endanger life or jeopardise the investigation or operation for which the authorisation was being given. An authorisation is not to be regarded as urgent where the need for an authorisation has been neglected or the urgency is of the authorising officer's own making.

4.14 Authorising officers should not be responsible for authorising investigations or operations in which they are directly involved, although it is recognised that this may sometimes be unavoidable, especially in the case of small organisations, or where it is necessary to act urgently. Where an authorising officer authorises such an investigation or operation the central record of authorisations (see paragraphs 2.14–2.15) should highlight this and the attention of a Commissioner or Inspector should be invited to it during his next inspection.

4.15 Authorising officers within the Police, NCIS and NCS may only grant authorisations on application by a member of their own force, Service or Squad. Authorising officers in HMCE may only grant an authorisation on application by a customs officer.[6]

Information to be provided in applications for authorisation

4.16 A written application for authorisation for directed surveillance should describe any conduct to be authorised and the purpose of the investigation or operation. The application should also include:
- the reasons why the authorisation is necessary in the particular case and on the grounds (e.g. for the purpose of preventing or detecting crime) listed in Section 28(3) of the 2000 Act;

---

[5] This could only be for a purpose which satisfies the criteria set out in Article 8(2) of the ECHR.
[6] As defined in section 81(1) of the 2000 Act.

- the reasons why the surveillance is considered proportionate to what it seeks to achieve;
- the nature of the surveillance;
- the identities, where known, of those to be the subject of the surveillance;
- an explanation of the information which it is desired to obtain as a result of the surveillance;
- the details of any potential collateral intrusion and why the intrusion is justified;
- the details of any confidential information that is likely to be obtained as a consequence of the surveillance.
- the level of authority required (or recommended where that is different) for the surveillance; and
- a subsequent record of whether authority was given or refused, by whom and the time and date.

4.17 Additionally, in urgent cases, the authorisation should record (as the case may be):

- the reasons why the authorising officer or the officer entitled to act in urgent cases considered the case so urgent that an oral instead of a written authorisation was given; and/or
- the reasons why it was not reasonably practicable for the application to be considered by the authorising officer.

4.18 Where the authorisation is oral, the detail referred to above should be recorded in writing by the applicant as soon as reasonably practicable.

Duration of authorisations

4.19 A written authorisation granted by an authorising officer will cease to have effect (unless renewed) at the end of a period of **three months**, beginning with the day on which it took effect.

4.20 Urgent oral authorisations or written authorisations granted by a person who is entitled to act only in urgent cases will, unless renewed, cease to have effect after **seventy-two hours**, beginning with the time when the authorisation was granted or renewed.

Reviews

4.21 Regular reviews of authorisations should be undertaken to assess the need for the surveillance to continue. The results of a review should be recorded on the central record of authorisations (see paragraphs 2.14–2.15). Particular attention is drawn to the need to review authorisations frequently where the surveillance provides access to confidential information or involves collateral intrusion.

4.22 In each case the authorising officer within each public authority should determine how often a review should take place. This should be as frequently as is considered necessary and practicable.

Renewals

4.23 If at any time before an authorisation would cease to have effect, the authorising officer considers it necessary for the authorisation to continue for the purpose for which it was given, he may renew it in writing for a further period of **three**

months unless it is a case to which paragraph 4.25 applies. Renewals may also be granted orally in urgent cases and last for a period of **seventy-two hours**.

4.24 A renewal takes effect at the time at which, or day on which, the authorisation would have ceased to have effect but for the renewal. An application for renewal should not be made until shortly before the authorisation period is drawing to an end. Any person who would be entitled to grant a new authorisation can renew an authorisation. Authorisations may be renewed more than once, provided they continue to meet the criteria for authorisation.

4.25 If at any time before an authorisation for directed surveillance, granted on the grounds of it being in the interests of national security or in the interests of the economic well-being of the UK, would cease to have effect, an authorising officer who is a member of the intelligence services considers it necessary for it to continue, he may renew it for a further period of **six months**, beginning with the day on which it would have ceased to have effect but for the renewal.

4.26 All applications for the renewal of an authorisation for directed surveillance should record:

- whether this is the first renewal or every occasion on which the authorisation has been renewed previously;
- any significant changes to the information in paragraph 4.16;
- the reasons why it is necessary to continue with the directed surveillance;
- the content and value to the investigation or operation of the information so far obtained by the surveillance;
- the results of regular reviews of the investigation or operation.

4.27 Authorisations may be renewed more than once, if necessary, and the renewal should be kept/recorded as part of the central record of authorisations (see paragraphs 2.14–2.15).

Cancellations

4.28 The authorising officer who granted or last renewed the authorisation must cancel it if he is satisfied that the directed surveillance no longer meets the criteria upon which it was authorised. Where the authorising officer is no longer available, this duty will fall on the person who has taken over the role of authorising officer or the person who is acting as authorising officer (see the Regulation of Investigatory Powers (Cancellation of Authorisations) Order 2000; SI No. 2794).

Ceasing of surveillance activity

4.29 As soon as the decision is taken that directed surveillance should be discontinued, the instruction must be given to those involved to stop all surveillance of the subject(s). The date and time when such an instruction was given should be recorded in the central record of authorisations (see paragraphs 2.14–2.15) and the notification of cancellation where relevant.

Additional rules: Recording of telephone conversations

4.30 Subject to paragraph 4.31 below, the interception of communications sent by post or by means of public telecommunications systems or private telecommunications systems attached to the public network may be authorised only by the Secretary of State, in accordance with the terms of Part I of the 2000 Act. Nothing in this code should be taken as granting dispensation from the requirements of that Part of the 2000 Act.

4.31 Part I of the 2000 Act provides certain exceptions to the rule that interception of telephone conversations must be warranted under that Part. This includes, where one party to the communication consents to the interception, it may be authorised in accordance with section 48(4) of the 2000 Act provided that there is no interception warrant authorising the interception. In such cases, the interception is treated as directed surveillance.

4.32 The use of a surveillance device should not be ruled out simply because it may incidentally pick up one or both ends of a telephone conversation, and any such product can be treated as having been lawfully obtained. However, its use would not be appropriate where the sole purpose is to overhear speech which, at the time of monitoring, is being transmitted by a telecommunications system. In such cases an application should be made for an interception of communication warrant under section 5 of the 2000 Act.

5 Authorisation Procedures for Intrusive Surveillance

5.1 Intrusive surveillance is defined in section 26(3) of the 2000 Act as covert surveillance that:

(a) is carried out in relation to anything taking place on any residential premises or in any private vehicle; and

(b) involves the presence of an individual on the premises or in the vehicle or is carried out by means of a surveillance device.

5.2 Covert surveillance is defined in section 26(9)(a) of the 2000 Act as any surveillance which is carried out in a manner calculated to ensure that the persons subject to the surveillance are unaware that it is or may be taking place.

5.3 Where surveillance is carried out in relation to anything taking place on any residential premises or in any private vehicle by means of a device, without that device being present on the premises, or in the vehicle, it is not intrusive unless the device consistently provides information of the same quality and detail, as might be expected to be obtained from a device actually present on the premises or in the vehicle. Thus, an observation post outside premises, which provides a limited view and no sound of what is happening inside the premises, would not be considered as intrusive surveillance.

5.4 Residential premises are defined in section 48(1) of the 2000 Act. The definition includes hotel rooms, bedrooms in barracks, and police and prison cells, but not any common area to which a person is allowed access in connection with his occupation of such accommodation, e.g. a hotel lounge.

5.5 A private vehicle is defined in section 48(1) of the 2000 Act as any vehicle which is used primarily for the private purposes of the person who owns it or of a person otherwise having the right to use it. A person does not have a right to use a motor vehicle if his right to use it derives only from his having paid, or undertaken to pay, for the use of the vehicle and its driver for a particular journey.

5.6 In many cases, a surveillance investigation or operation may involve both intrusive surveillance and entry on or interference with property or with wireless telegraphy. In such cases, both activities need authorisation. This can be done as a combined authorisation (see paragraph 2.11).

5.7 An authorisation for intrusive surveillance may be issued by the Secretary of State (for the intelligence services, the Ministry of Defence, HM Forces and any other public authority designated under section 41(1)) or by a senior authorising officer (for police, NCIS, NCS and HMCE).

5.8 All authorisations require the personal authority of the Secretary of State or the senior authorising officer. Any members or officials of the intelligence services, the Ministry of Defence and HM Forces can apply to the Secretary of State for an intrusive surveillance warrant. Under section 32(2) of the 2000 Act neither the Secretary of State or the senior authorising officer may authorise intrusive surveillance unless he believes—

(a) that the authorisation is necessary in the circumstances of the particular case on the grounds that it is:
   • in the interests of national security;[7]
   • for the purpose of preventing or detecting serious crime; or
   • in the interests of the economic well-being of the UK;
and
(b) the authorising officer must also believe that the surveillance is proportionate to what it seeks to achieve.

5.9 A factor which must be taken into account in deciding whether an authorisation is necessary and proportionate is whether the information which it is thought necessary to obtain by means of the intrusive surveillance could reasonably be obtained by other less intrusive means.

Authorisation procedures for police, National Criminal Intelligence Service, the National Crime Squad and HM Customs and Excise

5.10 The senior authorising officer should generally give authorisations in writing. However, in urgent cases, they may be given orally. In an urgent oral case, a statement that the senior authorising officer has expressly authorised the conduct should be recorded in writing by the applicant as soon as is reasonably practicable.

5.11 If the senior authorising officer is absent then as provided for in section 12(4) of the Police Act 1996, section 5(4) of the Police (Scotland) Act 1967, section 25 of the City of London Police Act 1839, or sections 8 or 54 of the 1997 Act, an authorisation can be given in writing or, in urgent cases, orally by the designated deputy.

5.12 In an urgent case, where it is not reasonably practicable having regard to the urgency of the case for the designated deputy to consider the application, a written authorisation may be granted by a person entitled to act under section 34(4) of the 2000 Act.

5.13 A case is not normally to be regarded as urgent unless the time that would elapse before the authorising officer was available to grant the authorisation would,

---

[7] A senior authorising officer of a law enforcement agency should not issue an authorisation for intrusive surveillance or entry on or interference with property, or with wireless telegraphy where the operation is within the responsibilities of one of the intelligence services and properly falls to be authorised by warrant issued by the Secretary of State under Part II of the 2000 Act or the 1994 Act. Also see footnotes 1 and 2.

in the judgement of the person giving the authorisation, be likely to endanger life or jeopardise the investigation or operation for which the authorisation was being given. An authorisation is not to be regarded as urgent where the need for an authorisation has been neglected or the urgency is of the authorising officer's own making.

5.14 The consideration of an authorisation by the senior authorising officer is only to be regarded as not reasonably practicable (within the meaning of section 34(2) of the 2000 Act) if he is on annual leave, is absent from his office and his home, or is for some reason not able within a reasonable time to obtain access to a secure telephone or fax machine. Pressure of work is not normally to be regarded as rendering it impracticable for a senior authorising officer to consider an application. Where a designated deputy gives an authorisation this should be made clear and the reason for the absence of the senior authorising officer given.

5.15 A police, NCIS or NCS authorisation cannot be granted unless the application is made by a member of the same force, service or squad. For HMCE an authorisation cannot be granted unless the application is made by a customs officer. Where the surveillance is carried out in relation to any residential premises, the authorisation cannot be granted unless the residential premises are in the area of operation of the force, service, squad or organisation.

Information to be provided in applications for authorisation

5.16 Applications should be in writing and describe the conduct to be authorised and the purpose of the investigation or operation. The application should specify:
- the reasons why the authorisation is necessary in the particular case and on the grounds (e.g. for the purpose of preventing or detecting serious crime) listed in section 32(3) of the 2000 Act;
- the reasons why the surveillance is considered proportionate to what it seeks to achieve;
- the nature of the surveillance;
- the residential premises or private vehicle in relation to which the surveillance will take place;
- the identities, where known, of those to be the subject of the surveillance;
- an explanation of the information which it is desired to obtain as a result of the surveillance;
- details of any potential collateral intrusion and why the intrusion is justified;
- details of any confidential information that is likely to be obtained as a consequence of the surveillance.
- A subsequent record should be made of whether authority was given or refused, by whom and the time and date.

5.17 Additionally, in urgent cases, the authorisation should record (as the case may be):
- the reasons why the authorising officer or designated deputy considered the case so urgent that an oral instead of a written authorisation was given; and/or
- the reasons why it was not reasonably practicable for the application to be considered by the senior authorising officer or the designated deputy.

5.18 Where the application is oral, the detail referred to above should be recorded in writing as soon as is reasonably practicable.

Approval of Surveillance Commissioners

5.19 Except in urgent cases a police, NCIS, NCS or HMCE authorisation granted for intrusive surveillance will not take effect until it has been approved by a Surveillance Commissioner and written notice of the Commissioner's decision has been given to the person who granted the authorisation. This means that the approval will not take effect until the notice has been received in the office of the person who granted the authorisation within the relevant force, service, squad or HMCE.

5.20 When the authorisation is urgent it will take effect from the time it is granted provided notice is given to the Surveillance Commissioner in accordance with section 35(3)(b) (see section 36(3) of the 2000 Act).

5.21 There may be cases that become urgent after approval has been sought but before a response has been received from a Surveillance Commissioner. In such a case, the authorising officer should notify the Surveillance Commissioner that the case is now urgent (pointing out that it has become urgent since the notification). In these cases, the authorisation will take effect immediately.

Notifications to Surveillance Commissioners

5.22 Where a person grants, renews or cancels an authorisation, he must, as soon as is reasonably practicable, give notice in writing to a Surveillance Commissioner, in accordance with whatever arrangements have been made by the Chief Surveillance Commissioner.

5.23 In urgent cases, the notification must specify the grounds on which the case is believed to be one of urgency. The urgency provisions should not be used routinely. If the Surveillance Commissioner is satisfied that there were no grounds for believing the case to be one of urgency, he has the power to quash the authorisation.

5.24 The information to be included in the notification to the Surveillance Commissioner is set out in the Regulation of Investigatory Powers (Notification of Authorisations etc.) Order 2000; SI No. 2563.

Authorisation procedures for Secretary of State authorisations

Authorisations

5.25 An intrusive surveillance authorisation for any of the intelligence services, the Ministry of Defence, HM Forces or any other public authority designated for this purpose requires a Secretary of State authorisation/warrant, unless they are acting on behalf of another public authority that has obtained an authorisation. In this context, Secretary of State can mean any Secretary of State, although an authorisation or warrant should be obtained from the Secretary of State of the relevant department.

5.26 Intelligence services authorisations must be made by issue of a warrant. Such warrants will generally be given in writing by the Secretary of State. In urgent cases, a warrant may be signed (but not renewed) by a senior official, provided the Secretary of State has expressly authorised this.

5.27 Applications to the Secretary of State for authorisations should specify those matters listed in paragraph 5.16.

All intrusive surveillance authorisations

5.28 Paragraphs 5.29 to 5.42 deal with the duration, renewal and cancellation of authorisations. Unless otherwise specified the guidance below applies to all authorisations.

Duration of authorisations

All authorisations except Secretary of State intelligence services authorisations

5.29 A written authorisation granted by a Secretary of State, a senior authorising officer or a designated deputy will cease to have effect (unless renewed) at the end of a period of **three months**, beginning with the day on which it took effect.

5.30 Oral authorisations given in urgent cases by a Secretary of State, a senior authorising officer or their designated deputies, and written authorisations given by those only entitled to act in urgent cases (see paragraph 5.11), will cease to have effect (unless renewed) at the end of the period of **seventy-two hours**, beginning with the time when they took effect.

Secretary of State intelligence services authorisations

5.31 A warrant issued by the Secretary of State will cease to have effect at the end of a period of **six months**, beginning with the day on which it was issued.

5.32 Warrants expressly authorised by a Secretary of State, and signed on his behalf by a senior civil servant, will cease to have effect at the end of the **second working day** following the day of issue of the warrant unless renewed by the Secretary of State.

Renewals

All authorisations except Secretary of State intelligence services authorisations

5.33 If at any time before an authorisation expires the senior authorising officer or, in his absence, the designated deputy considers the authorisation should continue to have effect for the purpose for which it was issued, he may renew it in writing for a further period of **three months**.

5.34 As with the initial authorisation, the senior authorising officer must (unless it is a case to which the urgency procedure applies) seek the approval of a Surveillance Commissioner. This means that the renewal will not take effect until the notice of it has been received in the office of the person who granted the authorisation within the relevant force, service, squad or HMCE (but not before the day on which the authorisation would have otherwise ceased to have effect). In urgent cases, a renewal can take effect immediately (provided this is not before the day on which the authorisation would have otherwise ceased to have effect). See section 35 and 36 of the 2000 Act and the Regulation of Investigatory Powers (Notification of Authorisations etc.) Order 2000; SI No. 2563.

5.35 Subject to paragraph 5.36, if at any time before the day on which a Secretary of State authorisation expires, the Secretary of State considers it necessary for the warrant to be renewed for the purpose for which it was issued, he may renew it in writing for a further period of **three months**, beginning with the day on which it would have ceased to have effect but for the renewal.

Secretary of State intelligence services authorisations

5.36 If at any time before an intelligence service warrant expires, the Secretary of State considers it necessary for the warrant to be renewed for the purpose for which it was issued, he may renew it in writing for a further period of **six months**, beginning with the day on which it would have ceased to have effect but for the renewal.

5.37 All applications for a renewal of an authorisation or warrant should record:

- whether this is the first renewal or every occasion on which the warrant/ authorisation has been renewed previously;
- any significant changes to the information listed in paragraph 5.16;
- the reasons why it is necessary to continue with the intrusive surveillance;
- the content and value to the investigation or operation of the product so far obtained by the surveillance;
- the results of regular reviews of the investigation or operation.

5.38 Authorisations may be renewed more than once, if necessary, and the renewal should be kept/recorded as part of the central record of authorisations (see paragraphs 2.14–2.15).

Reviews

5.39 Regular reviews of authorisations should be undertaken to assess the need for the surveillance to continue. The results of a review should be recorded on the central record of authorisations (see paragraphs 2.14–2.15). Particular attention is drawn to the need to review authorisations frequently where the intrusive surveillance provides access to confidential information or involves collateral intrusion.

5.40 The senior authorising officer or, for those subject to Secretary of State authorisation, the member or official who made the application within each public authority should determine how often a review should take place. This should be as frequently as is considered necessary and practicable.

Cancellations

5.41 The senior authorising officer who granted or last renewed the authorisation must cancel it, or the person who made the application to the Secretary of State must apply for its cancellation, if he is satisfied that the surveillance no longer meets the criteria upon which it was authorised. Where the senior authorising officer or person who made the application to the Secretary of State is no longer available, this duty will fall on the person who has taken over the role of senior authorising officer or taken over from the person who made the application to the Secretary of State or the person who is acting as the senior authorising officer (see the Regulation of Investigatory Powers (Cancellation of Authorisations) Order 2000; SI No. 2794).

5.42 The Surveillance Commissioners must be notified where police, NCIS, NCS or HMCE authorisations are cancelled (see the Regulation of Investigatory Powers (Notification of Authorisations etc.) Order 2000; SI No. 2563).

Ceasing of surveillance activity

5.43 As soon as the decision is taken that the intrusive surveillance should be discontinued, instructions must be given to those involved to stop all surveillance of the subject(s). The date and time when such an instruction was given should be recorded in the central record of authorisations (see paragraphs 2.14–2.15) and the notification of cancellation where relevant.

Police, National Criminal Intelligence Service, the National Crime Squad and HM Customs and Excise authorisations

5.44 In cases where an authorisation is quashed or cancelled by a Surveillance Commissioner, the senior authorising officer must immediately instruct those carrying out the surveillance to stop monitoring, observing, listening or recording the activities of the subject of the authorisation. The date and time when such an instruction was given should be recorded on the central record of authorisations (see paragraphs 2.14–2.15).

6 Authorisation Procedures for Entry on or Interference with Property or with Wireless Telegraphy

6.1 The 1994 Act and 1997 Act provide lawful authority for entry on or interference with property or with wireless telegraphy by the intelligence services and the police, NCIS, NCS and HMCE.

6.2 In many cases a covert surveillance operation may involve both intrusive surveillance and entry on or interference with property or with wireless telegraphy. This can be done as a combined authorisation, although the criteria for authorisation of each activity must be considered separately (see paragraph 2.11).

Authorisations for entry on or interference with property or with wireless telegraphy by the police, National Criminal Intelligence Service, the National Crime Squad and HM Customs and Excise

6.3 Responsibility for such authorisations rests with the authorising officer as defined in section 93(5) of the 1997 Act, that is the chief constable or equivalent. Authorisations require the personal authority of the authorising officer (or his designated deputy) except in urgent situations, where it is not reasonably practicable for the application to be considered by such person. The person entitled to act in such cases is set out in section 94 of the 1997 Act.

6.4 Authorisations under the 1997 Act may not be necessary where the public authority is acting with the consent of a person able to give permission in respect of relevant property, although consideration should still be given to the need to obtain an authorisation under Part II of the 2000 Act.

6.5 Authorisations for the police, NCIS and NCS may only be given by an authorising officer on application by a member of his own force, Service or Squad for entry on or interference with property or with wireless telegraphy within the authorising officer's own area of operation. For HMCE an authorisation may only be given by an authorising officer on application by a customs officer. An authorising officer may authorise the taking of action outside the relevant area solely for the purpose of maintaining or retrieving any device, apparatus or equipment.

6.6 Any person giving an authorisation for entry on or interference with property or with wireless telegraphy under section 93(2) of the 1997 Act must believe that:

- it is necessary for the action specified to be taken for the purpose of preventing or detecting serious crime (or in the case of the Police Service of Northern Ireland, in the interests of national security);[8] and
- that the taking of the action is proportionate to what the action seeks to achieve.

6.7 The authorising officer must take into account whether what it is thought necessary to achieve by the authorised conduct could reasonably be achieved by other means.

6.8 Any person granting or applying for an authorisation or warrant to enter on or interfere with property or with wireless telegraphy will also need to be aware of particular sensitivities in the local community where the entry or interference is taking place and of similar activities being undertaken by other public authorities which could impact on the deployment. In this regard, it is recommended that the authorising officers in NCIS, NCS and HMCE should consult a senior officer within the police force in which the investigation or operation takes place where the authorising officer considers that conflicts might arise. The Chief Constable of the Police Service of Northern Ireland should be informed of any surveillance operation undertaken by another law enforcement agency which involve its officers in maintaining or retrieving equipment in Northern Ireland.

Authorisation procedures for entry on or interference with property or with wireless telegraphy by the police, National Criminal Intelligence Service, the National Crime Squad and HM Customs and Excise

6.9 Authorisations will generally be given in writing by the authorising officer. However, in urgent cases, they may be given orally by the authorising officer. In such cases, a statement that the authorising officer has expressly authorised the action should be recorded in writing by the applicant as soon as is reasonably practicable. This should be done by the person with whom the authorising officer spoke.

6.10 If the authorising officer is absent then as provided for in section 12(4) of the Police Act 1996, section 5(4) of the Police (Scotland) Act 1967, section 25 of the City of London Police Act 1839, or sections 8 or 54 of the 1997 Act, an authorisation can be given in writing or, in urgent cases, orally by the designated deputy.

6.11 Where, however, in an urgent case, it is not reasonably practicable for the designated deputy to consider an application, then written authorisation may be given by the following:

- in the case of the police, by an assistant chief constable (other than a designated deputy);
- in the case of the Metropolitan Police and City of London Police, by a commander;
- in the case of NCIS and NCS, by a person designated by the relevant Director General;[9]
- in the case of HMCE, by a person designated by the Commissioners of Customs and Excise.[10]

---

[8] See footnotes 1 and 2.

[9] For police members of NCIS or NCS, this will be an officer who holds the rank of assistant chief constable in that Service or Squad. Additionally, in the case of NCIS, this may be an assistant chief investigation officer of HMCE.

[10] This will be an officer of the rank of assistant chief investigation officer.

6.12 Applications to the authorising officer for authorisation must be made in writing by a police or customs officer or a member of NCIS or NCS (within the terms of section 93(3) of the 1997 Act) and should specify:

- the identity or identities of those to be targeted (where known);
- the property which the entry or interference with will affect;
- the identity of individuals and/or categories of people, where known, who are likely to be affected by collateral intrusion;
- details of the offence planned or committed;
- details of the intrusive surveillance involved;
- how the authorisation criteria (as set out in paragraphs 6.6 and 6.7) have been met;
- any action which may be necessary to retrieve any equipment used in the surveillance;
- in case of a renewal, the results obtained so far, or a full explanation of the failure to obtain any results; and
- whether an authorisation was given or refused, by whom and the time and date.

6.13 Additionally, in urgent cases, the authorisation should record (as the case may be):

- the reasons why the authorising officer or designated deputy considered the case so urgent that an oral instead of a written authorisation was given; and
- the reasons why (if relevant) the person granting the authorisation did not consider it reasonably practicable for the application to be considered by the senior authorising officer or the designated deputy.

6.14 Where the application is oral, the information referred to above should be recorded in writing by the applicant as soon as reasonably practicable.

Notifications to Surveillance Commissioners

6.15 Where a person gives, renews or cancels an authorisation, he must, as soon as is reasonably practicable, give notice of it in writing to a Surveillance Commissioner, in accordance with arrangements made by the Chief Surveillance Commissioner. In urgent cases which would otherwise have required the approval of a Surveillance Commissioner, the notification must specify the grounds on which the case is believed to be one of urgency.

6.16 There may be cases which become urgent after approval has been sought but before a response has been received from a Surveillance Commissioner. In such a case, the authorising officer should notify the Surveillance Commissioner that the case is urgent (pointing out that it has become urgent since the previous notification). In these cases, the authorisation will take effect immediately.

6.17 Notifications to Surveillance Commissioners in relation to the authorisation, renewal and cancellation of authorisations in respect of entry on or interference with property should be in accordance with the requirements of the Police Act 1997 (Notifications of Authorisations etc.) Order 1998; SI No. 3241.

Duration of authorisations

6.18 Written authorisations given by authorising officers will cease to have effect at the end of a period of **three months**, beginning with the day on which they took effect. In cases requiring prior approval by a Surveillance Commissioner this means from the time the Surveillance Commissioner has approved the authorisation and the person who gave the authorisation has been notified. This means that the approval will not take effect until the notice has been received in the office of the person who granted the authorisation within the relevant force, service, squad or HMCE. In cases not requiring prior approval, this means from the time the authorisation was given.

6.19 Oral authorisations given in urgent cases by:
- authorising officers;
- or designated deputies;

and written authorisations given by:
- assistant chief constables (other than a designated deputy);
- commanders in the Metropolitan Police and City of London Police;
- the person designated to act by the Director General of NCIS or of NCS;
- the person designated for the purpose by the Commissioners of Customs and Excise;

will cease at the end of the period of **seventy-two** hours, beginning with the time when they took effect.

Renewals

6.20 If at any time before the day on which an authorisation expires the authorising officer or, in his absence, the designated deputy considers the authorisation should continue to have effect for the purpose for which it was issued, he may renew it in writing for a period of **three months** beginning with the day on which the authorisation would otherwise have ceased to have effect. Authorisations may be renewed more than once, if necessary, and the renewal should be recorded on the authorisation record (see paragraph 6.27).

6.21 Commissioners must be notified of renewals of authorisations. The information to be included in the notification is set out in the Police Act 1997 (Notifications of Authorisations etc.) Order 1998; SI No. 3241.

6.22 If, at the time of renewal, the criteria in paragraph 6.30 exist, then the approval of a Surveillance Commissioner must be sought before the renewal can take effect. The fact that the initial authorisation required the approval of a Commissioner before taking effect does not mean that its renewal will automatically require such approval. It will only do so if, at the time of the renewal, it falls into one of the categories requiring approval (and is not urgent).

Reviews

6.23 Authorising officers should regularly review authorisations to assess the need for the entry on or interference with property or with wireless telegraphy to continue. This should be recorded on the authorisation record (see paragraph 6.27). The authorising officer should determine how often a review should take place when giving an authorisation. This should be as frequently as is considered necessary and practicable and at no greater interval than one month. Particular attention is drawn to the need to review authorisations and renewals regularly and frequently where the entry on or interference with property or with wireless telegraphy provides access to confidential information or involves collateral intrusion.

Cancellations

6.24 The senior authorising officer who granted or last renewed the authorisation must cancel it, or the person who made the application to the Secretary of State must apply for its cancellation, if he is satisfied that the authorisation no longer meets the criteria upon which it was authorised. Where the senior authorising officer or person who made the application to the Secretary of State is no longer available, this duty will fall on the person who has taken over the role of senior authorising officer or taken over from the person who made the application to the Secretary of State or the person who is acting as the senior authorising officer (see the Regulation of Investigatory Powers (Cancellation of Authorisations) Order 2000; SI No. 2794).

6.25 The Surveillance Commissioners must be notified of cancellations of authorisations. The information to be included in the notification is set out in the Police Act 1997 (Notifications of Authorisations etc.) Order 1998; SI No. 3421.

6.26 The Surveillance Commissioners have the power to cancel an authorisation if they are satisfied that, at any time after an authorisation was given or renewed, there were no reasonable grounds for believing the matters set out in paragraphs 6.6 and 6.7 above. In such circumstances, a Surveillance Commissioner may order the destruction of records, in whole or in part, other than any that are required for pending criminal or civil proceedings.

Authorisation record

6.27 An authorisation record should be created which records:
- the time and date when an authorisation is given;
- whether an authorisation is in written or oral form;
- the time and date when it was notified to a Surveillance Commissioner; and
- the time and date when the Surveillance Commissioner notified his approval (where appropriate).

The authorisation record should also record:
- every occasion when entry on or interference with property or with wireless telegraphy has occurred;
- the result of periodic reviews of the authorisation;
- the date of every renewal; and
- it should record the time and date when any instruction was given by the authorising officer to cease the interference with property or with wireless telegraphy.

Ceasing of entry on or interference with property or with wireless telegraphy

6.28 Once an authorisation or renewal expires or is cancelled or quashed, the authorising officer must immediately instruct those carrying out the surveillance to cease all the actions authorised for the entry on or interference with property or with wireless telegraphy. The time and date when such an instruction was given should be recorded on the authorisation record (see paragraph 6.27).

Retrieval of equipment

6.29 Where a Surveillance Commissioner quashes or cancels an authorisation or renewal, he will, if there are reasonable grounds for doing so, order that the authorisation remain effective for a specified period, to enable officers to retrieve anything left on the property by virtue of the authorisation. He can only do so if the authorisation or renewal makes provision for this. A decision by the Surveillance Commissioner not to give such an order can be the subject of an appeal to the Chief Surveillance Commissioner.

Special rules: Cases requiring prior approval of a Surveillance Commissioner

6.30 In certain cases, an authorisation for entry on or interference with property will not take effect until a Surveillance Commissioner has approved it and the notice has been received in the office of the person who granted the authorisation within the relevant force, service, squad or HMCE (unless the urgency procedures are used). These are cases where the person giving the authorisation believes that:
- any of the property specified in the authorisation:
  - is used wholly or mainly as a dwelling or as a bedroom in a hotel; or
  - constitutes office premises; or
- the action authorised is likely to result in any person acquiring knowledge of:
  - matters subject to legal privilege;
  - confidential personal information; or
  - confidential journalistic material.

6.31 Office premises are defined as any building or part of a building whose sole or principal use is as an office or for office purposes (which means purposes of administration, clerical work, handling money and telephone or telegraph operation).

Authorisations for entry on or interference with property or with wireless telegraphy by the intelligence services

6.32 Before granting a warrant, the Secretary of State must:
- think it necessary for the action to be taken for the purpose of assisting the relevant agency in carrying out its functions;
- be satisfied that the taking of the action is proportionate to what the action seeks to achieve;
- take into account in deciding whether an authorisation is necessary and proportionate whether the information which it is thought necessary to obtain by the conduct authorised by the warrant could reasonably be obtained by other means; and
- be satisfied that there are satisfactory arrangements in force under the 1994 Act or the 1989 Act in respect of disclosure of any material obtained by means of the warrant, and that material obtained will be subject to those arrangements.

6.33 An application for a warrant must be made by a member of the intelligence services for the taking of action in relation to that agency. In addition, the Security Service may make an application for a warrant to act on behalf of the Secret Intelligence Service (SIS) and the Governments Communication Headquarters (GCHQ). SIS and GCHQ may not be granted a warrant for action in support of the prevention or detection of serious crime which relates to property in the British Islands.

6.34 A warrant shall, unless renewed, cease to have effect if the warrant was under the hand of the Secretary of State, at the end of the period of **six months** beginning with the day on which it was issued. In any other case, at the end of the period ending with the **second working day** following that day.

6.35 If at any time before the day on which a warrant would cease to have effect the Secretary of State considers it necessary for the warrant to continue to have effect for the purpose for which it was issued, he may by an instrument under his hand renew it for a period of **six months** beginning with that day. The Secretary of State shall cancel a warrant if he is satisfied that the action authorised by it is no longer necessary.

6.36 The intelligence services should provide the same information as the police, as and where appropriate, when making applications, requests for renewal and requests for cancellation of property warrants.

Retrieval of equipment

6.37 Because of the time it can take to remove equipment from a person's property it may also be necessary to renew a property warrant in order to complete the retrieval. Applications to the Secretary of State for renewal should state why it is being or has been closed down, why it has not been possible to remove the equipment and any timescales for removal, where known.

7 Oversight by Commissioners

7.1 The 1997 and 2000 Acts require the Chief Surveillance Commissioner to keep under review (with the assistance of the Surveillance Commissioners and Assistant Surveillance Commissioners) the performance of functions under Part III of the 1997 Act and Part II of the 2000 Act by the police (including the Royal Navy Regulating Branch, the Royal Military Police and the Royal Air Force Police and the Ministry of Defence Police and the British Transport Police), NCIS, the NCS, HMCE and of the 2000 Act the other public authorities listed in Schedule 1 and in Northern Ireland officials of the Ministry of Defence and HM Forces.

7.2 The Intelligence Services Commissioner's remit is to provide independent oversight of the use of the powers contained within Part II of the 2000 Act and the 1994 Act by the Security Service, Secret Intelligence Service, GCHQ and the Ministry of Defence and HM Forces (excluding the Royal Navy Regulating Branch, the Royal Military Police and the Royal Air Force Police, and in Northern Ireland officials of the Ministry of Defence and HM Forces);

7.3 This code does not cover the exercise of any of the Commissioners' functions. It is the duty of any person who uses these powers to comply with any request made by a Commissioner to disclose or provide any information he requires for the purpose of enabling him to carry out his functions.

7.4 References in this code to the performance of review functions by the Chief Surveillance Commissioner and other Commissioners apply also to Inspectors and other members of staff to whom such functions have been delegated.

8 Complaints

8.1 The 2000 Act establishes an independent Tribunal. This Tribunal will be made up of senior members of the judiciary and the legal profession and is independent of the Government. The Tribunal has full powers to investigate and decide any case within its jurisdiction.

This code does not cover the exercise of the Tribunal's functions. Details of the relevant complaints procedure can be obtained from the following address:

Investigatory Powers Tribunal
PO Box 33220

London
SW1H 9ZQ

Annex A: Authorisation levels when knowledge of confidential information is likely to be acquired

Relevant public authorities	Authorisation level
Police forces–Any police force maintained under section 2 of the Police Act 1996 (police forces in England and Wales outside London)	Chief Constable
Police forces–Any police force maintained under or by virtue of section 1 of the Police (Scotland) Act 1967	Chief Constable
The Metropolitan police force	Assistant Commissioner
The City of London police force	Commissioner
The Police Service of Northern Ireland	Deputy Chief Constable
The Royal Navy Regulating Branch The Royal Military Police The Royal Air Force Police	Provost Marshal Provost Marshal Provost Marshal
National Criminal Intelligence Service (NCIS)	Director General
National Crime Squad (NCS)	Director General or Deputy Director General
Serious Fraud Office	Director or Assistant Director

The intelligence services
    Government Communications Headquarters
    Security Service
    Secret Intelligence Service
	
	A Director of GCHQ
	Deputy Director General
	A Director of the Secret Intelligence Service

HM Forces
    Royal Navy
    Army
    Royal Air Force
	
	Rear Admiral
	Major General
	Air-Vice Marshall

HM Customs and Excise	Director Investigation or Regional Heads of Investigation
Inland Revenue	Deputy Chairman of Inland Revenue

Department for Environment, Food and Rural Affairs
    DEFRA Investigation Branch
 	
    Horticultural Marketing Inspectorate
	
	Immediate Senior Officer of Head of DEFRA Prosecution Division
	Immediate Senior Officer of Head of DEFRA Prosecution Division

Plant Health and Seed Inspectorate	Immediate Senior Officer of Head of DEFRA Prosecution Division
Egg Marketing Inspectorate	Immediate Senior Officer of Head of DEFRA Prosecution Division
Sea Fisheries Inspectorate (SFI)	Immediate Senior Officer of Head of DEFRA Prosecution Division
Centre for Environment, Fisheries and Aquaculture Science (CEFAS)	Immediate Senior Officer of Head of DEFRA Prosecution Division
Ministry of Defence	Director General or equivalent
Department for Transport, Local Government and Regions	
Vehicle Inspectorate	No
Transport Security (Transec)	Director of Transport Security
Department of Health	
Medical Devices Agency	Chief Executive
Medicine Control Agency	Chief Executive
Welfare Foods Policy Unit	Deputy Chief Medical Officer
Directorate of Counter Fraud Services (DFCS)	Director of Counter Fraud Services
Home Office	
HM Prison Service	Deputy Director General of the Prison Service
Immigration Service	Chief Inspector of the Immigration Service
Department of Work and Pensions	
Benefits Agency	Chief Executive of the Benefits Agency
Department of Trade and Industry	
Radiocommunications Agency	No
British Trade International	No
Coal Health Claims Unit	Director of Coal Health Claims unit
Companies Investigation Branch	The Inspector of Companies
Legal Services Directorate D	The Director of Legal Service D
National Assembly for Wales	Head of NHS Directorate in the National Assembly for Wales
	Head of NHS Finance Division in the National Assembly for Wales
	Head of Common Agricultural Policy Management Division in the National Assembly for Wales
Local Authorities	The Head of Paid Service or (in his absence) a Chief Officer
Environment Agency	Chief Executive of the Environment Agency
Financial Services Authority	Chairman of the Financial Services Authority
Food Standards Agency	Head of Group, Deputy Chief Executive and Chief Executive of the Foods Standards Agency

The Intervention Board for Agricultural Produce	Chief Executive of the Intervention Board for Agricultural Produce
Personal Investment Authority	Chairman of the Personal Investment Authority
Post Office	Director of Security
Health & Safety Executive	Director of Field Operations, Director of Hazardous Installations Directorate, Her Majesty's Chief Inspector of Nuclear Installations.
NHS bodies in England and Wales	
A health authority established under section 8 of the National Health Service Act 1977	Chief Executive
A Special Health Authority established under section 11 of the National Health Service 1977	Chief Executive
A National Health Service Trust established under section 5 of the National Health Service and Community Care Act 1990	Chief Executive
Royal Pharmaceutical Society of Great Britain	Director of Professional Standards

Appendix E
Covert Human Intelligence Sources (CHIS) Code of Practice

1 General

1.1 In this code the:

- **'1989 Act'** means the Security Service Act 1989;
- **'1994 Act'** means the Intelligence Services Act 1994;
- **'1997 Act'** means the Police Act 1997;
- **'2000 Act'** means the Regulation of Investigatory Powers Act 2000;
- **'RIP(S)A'** means the Regulation of Investigatory Powers (Scotland) Act 2000;

1.2 This code of practice provides guidance on the authorisation of the use or conduct of covert human intelligence sources ('a source') by public authorities under Part II of the 2000 Act.

1.3 The provisions of the 2000 Act are not intended to apply in circumstances where members of the public volunteer information to the police or other authorities, as part of their normal civic duties, or to contact numbers set up to receive information (such as Crimestoppers, Customs Confidential, the Anti Terrorist Hotline, or the Security Service Public Telephone Number). Members of the public acting in this way would not generally be regarded as sources.

1.4 Neither Part II of the 2000 Act or this code of practice is intended to affect the practices and procedures surrounding criminal participation of sources.

1.5 The 2000 Act provides that all codes of practice relating to the 2000 Act are admissible as evidence in criminal and civil proceedings. If any provision of the code appears relevant to any court or tribunal considering any such proceedings, or to the Investigatory Powers Tribunal established under the 2000 Act, or to one of the Commissioners responsible for overseeing the powers conferred by the 2000 Act, it must be taken into account.

General extent of powers

1.6 Authorisations can be given for the use or conduct of a source both inside and outside the United Kingdom. Authorisations for actions outside the United Kingdom can only validate them for the purposes of proceedings in the United Kingdom. An authorisation under Part II of the 2000 Act does not take into account the requirements of the country outside the United Kingdom in which the investigation or operation is taking place.

1.7 Members of foreign law enforcement or other agencies or sources of those agencies may be authorised under the 2000 Act in the UK in support of domestic and international investigations.

1.8 Where the conduct authorised is likely to take place in Scotland, authorisations should be granted under RIP(S)A, unless the authorisation is being obtained by those public authorities listed in section 46(3) of the 2000 Act and the Regulation of Investigatory Powers (Authorisations Extending to Scotland) Order 2000. Additionally, any authorisation granted or renewed for the purposes of national security or the economic well-being of the UK must be made under the 2000 Act. This code of practice is extended to Scotland in relation to authorisations made under Part II of the 2000 Act which apply to Scotland. A separate code of practice applies in relation to authorisations made under RIP(S)A.

Use of material in evidence

1.9 Material obtained from a source may be used as evidence in criminal proceedings. The proper authorisation of a source should ensure the suitability of such evidence under the common law, section 78 of the Police and Criminal Evidence Act 1984 and the Human Rights Act 1998. Furthermore, the product obtained by a source described in this code is subject to the ordinary rules for retention and disclosure of material under the Criminal Procedure and Investigations Act 1996, where those rules apply to the law enforcement body in question. There are also well-established legal procedures that will protect the identity of a source from disclosure in such circumstances.

2 General Rules on Authorisations

2.1 An authorisation under Part II of the 2000 Act will provide lawful authority for the use of a source. Responsibility for giving the authorisation will depend on which public authority is responsible for the source.

2.2 Part II of the 2000 Act does not impose a requirement on public authorities to seek or obtain an authorisation where, under the 2000 Act, one is available (see section 80 of the 2000 Act). Nevertheless, where there is an interference by a public authority with the right to respect for private and family life guaranteed under Article 8 of the European Convention on Human Rights, and where there is no other lawful authority, the consequences of not obtaining an authorisation under the 2000 Act may be that the action is unlawful by virtue of section 6 of the Human Rights Act 1998.

2.3 Public authorities are therefore strongly recommended to seek an authorisation where the use or conduct of a source is likely to interfere with a person's Article 8 rights to privacy by obtaining information from or about a person, whether or not that person is the subject of the investigation or operation. Obtaining an authorisation will ensure that the action is carried out in accordance with law and subject to stringent safeguards against abuse.

Necessity and proportionality

2.4 Obtaining an authorisation under the 2000 Act will only ensure that the authorised use or conduct of a source is a justifiable interference with an individual's Article 8 rights if it is necessary and proportionate for the source to be used. The 2000 Act first requires that the person granting an authorisation believes that the authorisation is necessary in the circumstances of the particular case for one or more of the statutory grounds in section 29(3) of the 2000 Act.

2.5 Then, if the use of the source is necessary, the person granting the authorisation must believe that the use of a source is proportionate to what is sought to be achieved by the conduct and use of that source. This involves balancing the intrusiveness of the use of the source on the target and others who might be affected by it against the need for the source to be used in operational terms. The use of a source will not be proportionate if it is excessive in the circumstances of the case or if the information which is sought could reasonably be obtained by other less intrusive means. The use of a source should be carefully managed to meet the objective in question and sources must not be used in an arbitrary or unfair way.

Collateral intrusion

2.6 Before authorising the use or conduct of a source, the authorising officer should also take into account the risk of intrusion into the privacy of persons other than those who are directly the subjects of the operation or investigation (collateral intrusion). Measures should be taken, wherever practicable, to avoid unnecessary intrusion into the lives of those not directly connected with the operation.

2.7 An application for an authorisation should include an assessment of the risk of any collateral intrusion. The authorising officer should take this into account, when considering the proportionality of the use and conduct of a source.

2.8 Those tasking a source should inform the authorising officer if the investigation or operation unexpectedly interferes with the privacy of individuals who are not covered by the authorisation. When the original authorisation may not be sufficient, consideration should be given to whether the authorisation needs to be amended and reauthorised or a new authorisation is required.

2.9 Any person granting or applying for an authorisation will also need to be aware of any particular sensitivities in the local community where the source is being used and of similar activities being undertaken by other public authorities which could impact on the deployment of the source. Consideration should also be given to any adverse impact on community confidence or safety that may result from the use or conduct of a source or of information obtained from that source. In this regard, it is recommended that where the authorising officers in the National Criminal Intelligence Service (NCIS), the National Crime Squad (NCS) and HM Customs and Excise (HMCE) consider that conflicts might arise they should consult a senior officer within the police force area in which the source is deployed. Additionally, the authorising officer should make an assessment of any risk to a source in carrying out the conduct in the proposed authorisation.

2.10 In a very limited range of circumstances an authorisation under Part II may, by virtue of sections 26(7) and 27 of the 2000 Act, render lawful conduct which would otherwise be criminal, if it is incidental to any conduct falling within section 26(8) of the 2000 Act which the source is authorised to undertake. This would depend on the circumstances of each individual case, and consideration should always be given to seeking advice from the legal adviser within the relevant public authority when such activity is contemplated. A source that acts beyond the limits recognised by the law will be at risk from prosecution. The need to protect the source cannot alter this principle.

Combined authorisations

2.11 A single authorisation may combine two or more different authorisations under Part II of the 2000 Act. For example, a single authorisation may combine authorisations for intrusive surveillance and the conduct of a source. In such cases the provisions applicable to each of the authorisations must be considered separately. Thus, a police superintendent can authorise the conduct of a source but an authorisation for intrusive surveillance by the police needs the separate authority of a chief constable, and in certain cases the approval of a Surveillance Commissioner will also be necessary. Where an authorisation for the use or conduct of a covert human intelligence source is combined with a Secretary of State authorisation for intrusive surveillance, the combined authorisation must be issued by the Secretary of State. However, this does not preclude public authorities from obtaining separate authorisations.

Directed surveillance against a potential source

2.12 It may be necessary to deploy directed surveillance against a potential source as part of the process of assessing their suitability for recruitment, or in planning how best to make the approach to them. An authorisation under this code authorising an officer to establish a covert relationship with a potential source could be combined with a directed surveillance authorisation so that both the officer and potential source could be followed. Directed surveillance is defined in section 26(2) of the 2000 Act. See the code of practice on Covert Surveillance.

Central record of all authorisations

2.13 A centrally retrievable record of all authorisations should be held by each public authority and regularly updated whenever an authorisation is granted, renewed or cancelled. The record should be made available to the relevant Commissioner or an Inspector from the Office of Surveillance Commissioners, upon request. These records should be retained for a period of at least three years from the ending of the authorisation.

2.14 Proper records must be kept of the authorisation and use of a source. Section 29(5) of the 2000 Act provides that an authorising officer must not grant an authorisation for the use or conduct of a source unless he believes that there are arrangements in place for ensuring that there is at all times a person with the responsibility for maintaining a record of the use made of the source. The Regulation of Investigatory Powers (Source Records) Regulations 2000; SI No. 2725 details the particulars that must be included in the records relating to each source.

2.15 In addition, records or copies of the following, as appropriate, should be kept by the relevant authority:
- a copy of the authorisation, together with any supplementary documentation and notification of the approval given by the authorising officer;
- a copy of any renewal of an authorisation, together with the supporting documentation submitted when the renewal was requested;
- the reason why the person renewing an authorisation considered it necessary to do so;

- any authorisation which was granted or renewed orally (in an urgent case) and the reason why the case was considered urgent;
- any risk assessment made in relation to the source;
- the circumstances in which tasks were given to the source;
- the value of the source to the investigating authority;
- a record of the results of any reviews of the authorisation;
- the reasons, if any, for not renewing an authorisation;
- the reasons for cancelling an authorisation;
- the date and time when any instruction was given by the authorising officer to cease using a source.

2.16 The records kept by public authorities should be maintained in such a way as to preserve the confidentiality of the source and the information provided by that source. There should, at all times, be a designated person within the relevant public authority who will have responsibility for maintaining a record of the use made of the source.

Retention and destruction of the product

2.17 Where the product obtained from a source could be relevant to pending or future criminal or civil proceedings, it should be retained in accordance with established disclosure requirements for a suitable further period, commensurate to any subsequent review.

2.18 In the cases of the law enforcement agencies (not including the Royal Navy Regulating Branch, the Royal Military Police and the Royal Air Force Police), particular attention is drawn to the requirements of the code of practice issued under the Criminal Procedure and Investigations Act 1996. This requires that material which is obtained in the course of a criminal investigation and which may be relevant to the investigation must be recorded and retained.

2.19 There is nothing in the 2000 Act which prevents material obtained from properly authorised use of a source being used in other investigations. Each public authority must ensure that arrangements are in place for the handling, storage and destruction of material obtained through the use of a source. Authorising officers must ensure compliance with the appropriate data protection requirements and any relevant codes of practice produced by individual authorities in the handling and storage of material.

The intelligence services, MOD and HM Forces

2.20 The heads of these agencies are responsible for ensuring that arrangements exist to ensure that no information is stored by the authorities, except as necessary for the proper discharge of their functions. They are also responsible for arrangements to control onward disclosure. For the intelligence services, this is a statutory duty under the 1989 Act and the 1994 Act.

3 Special Rules on Authorisations

Confidential information

3.1 The 2000 Act does not provide any special protection for 'confidential information'. Nevertheless, particular care should be taken in cases where the subject of the investigation or operation might reasonably expect a high degree of privacy, or where confidential information is involved. Confidential information consists of matters subject to legal privilege, confidential personal information or confidential journalistic material.

3.2 In cases where through the use or conduct of a source it is likely that knowledge of confidential information will be acquired, the deployment of the source is subject to a higher level of authorisation. Annex A lists the authorising officer for each public authority permitted to authorise such use or conduct of a source.

Communications subject to legal privilege

3.3 Section 98 of the 1997 Act describes those matters that are subject to legal privilege in England and Wales. In Scotland, the relevant description is contained in section 33 of the Criminal Law (Consolidation) (Scotland) Act 1995. With regard to Northern Ireland, Article 12 of the Police and Criminal Evidence (Northern Ireland) Order 1989 should be referred to.

3.4 Legal privilege does not apply to communications made with the intention of furthering a criminal purpose (whether the lawyer is acting unwittingly or culpably). Legally privileged communications will lose their protection if there are grounds to believe, for example, that the professional legal adviser is intending to hold or use them for a criminal purpose. But privilege is not lost if a professional legal adviser is properly advising a person who is suspected of having committed a criminal offence. The concept of legal privilege applies to the provision of professional legal advice by any individual, agency or organisation qualified to do so.

3.5 The 2000 Act does not provide any special protection for legally privileged information. Nevertheless, such information is particularly sensitive and any source which acquires such material may engage Article 6 of the ECHR (right to a fair trial) as well as Article 8. Legally privileged information obtained by a source is extremely unlikely ever to be admissible as evidence in criminal proceedings. Moreover, the mere fact that use has been made of a source to obtain such information may lead to any related criminal proceedings being stayed as an abuse of process. Accordingly, action which may lead to such information being obtained is subject to additional safeguards under this code.

3.6 In general, an application for the use or conduct of a source which is likely to result in the acquisition of legally privileged information should only be made in exceptional and compelling circumstance. Full regard should be had to the particular proportionality issues such a use or conduct of a source raises. The application should include, in addition to the reasons why it is considered necessary for the use or conduct of a source to be used, an assessment of how likely it is that information subject to legal privilege will be acquired. The application should clearly state whether the purpose (or one of the purposes) of the use or conduct of the source is to obtain legally privileged information.

3.7 This assessment will be taken into account by the authorising officer in deciding whether the proposed use or conduct of a source is necessary and proportionate for a purpose under section 29 of the 2000 Act. The authorising officer may require regular reporting so as to be able to decide whether the authorisation should continue. In those cases where legally privileged information has been acquired and retained, the matter should be reported to the relevant Commissioner or Inspector during his next inspection and the material should be made available to him if requested.

3.8 A substantial proportion of the communications between a lawyer and his client(s) may be subject to legal privilege. Therefore, any case where a lawyer is the subject of an investigation or operation should be notified to the relevant Commissioner or Inspector during his next inspection and any material which has been retained should be made available to him if requested.

3.9 Where there is any doubt as to the handling and dissemination of information which may be subject to legal privilege, advice should be sought from a legal adviser within the relevant public authority before any further dissemination of the material takes place. Similar advice should also be sought where there is doubt over whether information is not subject to legal privilege due to the 'in furtherance of a criminal purpose' exception. The retention of legally privileged information, or its dissemination to an outside body, should be accompanied by a clear warning that it is subject to legal privilege. It should be safeguarded by taking reasonable steps to ensure there is no possibility of it becoming available, or its contents becoming known to any person whose possession of it might prejudice any criminal or civil proceedings related to the information. Any dissemination of legally privileged material to an outside body should be notified to the relevant Commissioner or Inspector during his next inspection.

Communications involving confidential personal information and confidential journalistic material

3.10 Similar consideration must also be given to authorisations that involve confidential personal information and confidential journalistic material. In those cases where confidential personal information and confidential journalistic material has been acquired and retained, the matter should be reported to the relevant Commissioner or Inspector during his next inspection and the material be made available to him if requested. Confidential personal information is information held in confidence relating to the physical or mental health or spiritual counselling concerning an individual (whether living or dead) who can be identified from it. Such information, which can include both oral and written communications, is held in confidence if it is held subject to an express or implied undertaking to hold it in confidence, or it is subject to a restriction on disclosure or an obligation of confidentiality contained in existing legislation. Examples might include consultations between a health professional and a patient, or information from a patient's medical records.

3.11 Spiritual counselling means conversations between an individual and a Minister of Religion acting in his official capacity, where the individual being counselled is seeking or the Minister is imparting forgiveness, absolution or the resolution of conscience with the authority of the Divine Being(s) of their faith.

3.12 Confidential journalistic material includes material acquired or created for the purposes of journalism and held subject to an undertaking to hold it in confidence, as well as communications resulting in information being acquired for the purposes of journalism and held subject to such an undertaking.

Vulnerable individuals

3.13 A 'vulnerable individual' is a person who is or may be in need of community care services by reason of mental or other disability, age or illness and who is or may be unable to take care of himself, or unable to protect himself against significant harm or exploitation. Any individual of this description should only be authorised to act as a source in the most exceptional circumstances. In these cases, the attached table in Annex A lists the authorising officer for each public authority permitted to authorise the use of a vulnerable individual as a source.

Juvenile sources

3.14 Special safeguards also apply to the use or conduct of juvenile sources; that is, sources under the age of 18 years. **On no occasion should the use or conduct of a source under 16 years of age be authorised to give information against his parents or any person who has parental responsibility for him.** In other cases, authorisations should not be granted unless the special provisions contained within The Regulation of Investigatory Powers (Juveniles) Order 2000; SI No. 2793 are satisfied. Authorisations for juvenile sources should be granted by those listed in the attached table at Annex A. The duration of such an authorisation is **one month** instead of twelve months.

4 Authorisation Procedures for Covert Human Intelligence Sources

4.1 Under section 26(8) of the 2000 Act a person is a source if:

(a) he establishes or maintains a personal or other relationship with a person for the covert purpose of facilitating the doing of anything falling within paragraph (b) or (c);

(b) he covertly uses such a relationship to obtain information or to provide access to any information to another person; or

(c) he covertly discloses information obtained by the use of such a relationship or as a consequence of the existence of such a relationship.

4.2 A source may include those referred to as agents, informants and officers working undercover.

4.3 By virtue of section 26(9)(b) of the 2000 Act a purpose is covert, in relation to the establishment or maintenance of a personal or other relationship, if and only if, the relationship is conducted in a manner that is calculated to ensure that one of the parties to the relationship is unaware of the purpose.

4.4 By virtue of section 26(9)(c) of the 2000 Act a relationship is used covertly, and information obtained as mentioned in paragraph 4.1(c) above is disclosed covertly, if and only if it is used or, as the case may be, disclosed in a manner that is calculated to ensure that one of the parties to the relationship is unaware of the use or disclosure in question.

4.5 The use of a source involves inducing, asking or assisting a person to engage in the conduct of a source or to obtain information by means of the conduct of such a source.

4.6 The conduct of a source is any conduct falling within section 29(4) of the 2000 Act, or which is incidental to anything falling within section 29(4) of the 2000 Act.

Authorisation procedures

4.7 Under section 29(3) of the 2000 Act an authorisation for the use or conduct of a source may be granted by the authorising officer where he believes that the authorisation is necessary:

- in the interests of national security;[1,2]
- for the purpose of preventing and detecting[3] crime or of preventing disorder;
- in the interests of the economic well-being of the UK;
- in the interests of public safety;
- for the purpose of protecting public health;[4]
- for the purpose of assessing or collecting any tax, duty, levy or other imposition, contribution or charge payable to a government department; or
- for any other purpose prescribed in an order made by the Secretary of State.[5]

4.8 The authorising officer must also believe that the authorised use or conduct of a source is proportionate to what is sought to be achieved by that use or conduct.

4.9 The public authorities entitled to authorise the use or conduct of a source are those listed in Schedule 1 to the 2000 Act. Responsibility for authorising the use or conduct of a source rests with the authorising officer and all authorisations require the personal authority of the authorising officer. An authorising officer is the person designated under section 29 of the 2000 Act to grant an authorisation for the use or conduct of a source. The Regulation of Investigatory Powers (Prescriptions of Offices, Ranks and Positions) Order 2000; SI No. 2417 designates the authorising officer for each different public authority and the officers entitled to act only in urgent cases. In certain circumstances the Secretary of State will be the authorising officer (see section 30(2) of the 2000 Act).

4.10 The authorising officer must give authorisations in writing, except that in urgent cases, they may be given orally by the authorising officer or the officer entitled to act in urgent cases. In such cases, a statement that the authorising officer has expressly authorised the action should be recorded in writing by the applicant as soon as is reasonably practicable.

4.11 A case is not normally to be regarded as urgent unless the time that would elapse before the authorising officer was available to grant the authorisation would,

---

[1] One of the functions of the Security Service is the protection of national security and in particular the protection against threats from terrorism. These functions extend throughout the United Kingdom, save that, in Northern Ireland, where the lead responsibility for investigating the threat from terrorism related to the affairs of Northern Ireland lies with the Police Service of Northern Ireland. An authorising officer in another public authority should not issue an authorisation under Part II of the 2000 Act where the operation or investigation falls within the responsibilities of the Security Service, as set out above, except where it is to be carried out by a Special Branch or where the Security Service has agreed that another public authority can authorise the use or conduct of a source which would normally fall within the responsibilities of the Security Service.

[2] HM Forces may also undertake operations in connection with a military threat to national security and other operations in connection with national security in support of the Security Service, the Police Service of Northern Ireland or other Civil Powers.

[3] Detecting crime is defined in section 81(5) of the 2000 Act.

[4] This could include investigations into infectious diseases, contaminated products or the illicit sale of pharmaceuticals.

[5] This could only be for a purpose which satisfies the criteria set out in Article 8(2) of the ECHR.

in the judgement of the person giving the authorisation, be likely to endanger life or jeopardise the operation or investigation for which the authorisation was being given. An authorisation is not to be regarded as urgent where the need for an authorisation has been neglected or the urgency is of the authorising officer's own making.

4.12 Authorising officers should not be responsible for authorising their own activities, e.g. those in which they, themselves, are to act as the source or in tasking the source. However, it is recognised that this is not always possible, especially in the cases of small organisations. Where an authorising officer authorises his own activity the authorisation record (see paragraphs 2.13–2.15) should highlight this and the attention of a Commissioner or Inspector should be invited to it during his next inspection.

4.13 The authorising officers within the police, NCIS and NCS may only grant authorisations on application by a member of their own force, Service or Squad. Authorising officers in HMCE may only grant authorisations on application by a customs officer.[6]

Information to be provided in applications for authorisation

4.14 An application for authorisation for the use or conduct of a source should be in writing and record:
- the reasons why the authorisation is necessary in the particular case and on the grounds (e.g. for the purpose of preventing or detecting crime) listed in section 29(3) of the 2000 Act;
- the reasons why the authorisation is considered proportionate to what it seeks to achieve;
- the purpose for which the source will be tasked or deployed (e.g. in relation to an organised serious crime, espionage, a series of racially motivated crimes etc.);
- where a specific investigation or operation is involved, nature of that investigation or operation;
- the nature of what the source will be tasked to do;
- the level of authority required (or recommended, where that is different);
- the details of any potential collateral intrusion and why the intrusion is justified;
- the details of any confidential information that is likely to be obtained as a consequence of the authorisation; and
- a subsequent record of whether authority was given or refused, by whom and the time and date.

4.15 Additionally, in urgent cases, the authorisation should record (as the case may be):
- the reasons why the authorising officer or the officer entitled to act in urgent cases considered the case so urgent that an oral instead of a written authorisation was given; and/or
- the reasons why it was not reasonably practicable for the application to be considered by the authorising officer.

---

[6] As defined in section 81(1) of the 2000 Act.

4.16 Where the authorisation is oral, the detail referred to above should be recorded in writing by the applicant as soon as reasonably practicable.

Duration of authorisations

4.17 A written authorisation will, unless renewed, cease to have effect at the end of a period of **twelve months**, beginning with the day on which it took effect.

4.18 Urgent oral authorisations or authorisations granted or renewed by a person who is entitled to act only in urgent cases will, unless renewed, cease to have effect after **seventy-two hours**, beginning with the time when the authorisation was granted or renewed.

Reviews

4.19 Regular reviews of authorisations should be undertaken to assess the need for the use of a source to continue. The review should include the use made of the source during the period authorised, the tasks given to the source and the information obtained from the source. The results of a review should be recorded on the authorisation record (see paragraphs 2.13–2.15). Particular attention is drawn to the need to review authorisations frequently where the use of a source provides access to confidential information or involves collateral intrusion.

4.20 In each case the authorising officer within each public authority should determine how often a review should take place. This should be as frequently as is considered necessary and practicable.

Renewals

4.21 Before an authorising officer renews an authorisation, he must be satisfied that a review has been carried out of the use of a source as outlined in paragraph 4.19.

4.22 If at any time before an authorisation would cease to have effect, the authorising officer considers it necessary for the authorisation to continue for the purpose for which it was given, he may renew it in writing for a further period of **twelve months**. Renewals may also be granted orally in urgent cases and last for a period of **seventy-two hours**.

4.23 A renewal takes effect at the time at which, or day on which, the authorisation would have ceased to have effect but for the renewal. An application for renewal should not be made until shortly before the authorisation period is drawing to an end. Any person who would be entitled to grant a new authorisation can renew an authorisation. Authorisations may be renewed more than once, if necessary, provided they continue to meet the criteria for authorisation. The renewal should be kept/recorded as part of the authorisation record (see paragraphs 2.13–2.15).

4.24 All applications for the renewal of an authorisation should record:
- whether this is the first renewal or every occasion on which the authorisation has been renewed previously;
- any significant changes to the information in paragraph 4.14;
- the reasons why it is necessary to continue to use the source;
- the use made of the source in the period since the grant or, as the case may be, latest renewal of the authorisation;

- the tasks given to the source during that period and the information obtained from the conduct or use of the source;
- the results of regular reviews of the use of the source.

Cancellations

4.25 The authorising officer who granted or renewed the authorisation must cancel it if he is satisfied that the use or conduct of the source no longer satisfies the criteria for authorisation or that satisfactory arrangements for the source's case no longer exist. Where the authorising officer is no longer available, this duty will fall on the person who has taken over the role of authorising officer or the person who is acting as authorising officer (see the Regulation of Investigatory Powers (Cancellation of Authorisations) Order 2000; SI No. 2794). Where necessary, the safety and welfare of the source should continue to be taken into account after the authorisation has been cancelled.

Management of sources

Tasking

4.26 Tasking is the assignment given to the source by the persons defined at sections 29(5)(a) and (b) of the 2000 Act, asking him to obtain information, to provide access to information or to otherwise act, incidentally, for the benefit of the relevant public authority. Authorisation for the use or conduct of a source is required prior to any tasking where such tasking requires the source to establish or maintain a personal or other relationship for a covert purpose.

4.27 The person referred to in section 29(5)(a) of the 2000 Act will have day to day responsibility for:
- dealing with the source on behalf of the authority concerned;
- directing the day to day activities of the source;
- recording the information supplied by the source; and
- monitoring the source's security and welfare.

4.28 The person referred to in section 29(5)(b) of the 2000 Act will be responsible for the general oversight of the use of the source.

4.29 In some instances, the tasking given to a person will not require the source to establish a personal or other relationship for a covert purpose. For example, a source may be tasked with finding out purely factual information about the layout of commercial premises. Alternatively, a trading standards officer may be involved in the test purchase of items which have been labelled misleadingly or are unfit for consumption. In such cases, it is for the relevant public authority to determine where, and in what circumstances, such activity may require authorisation.

4.30 It is not the intention that authorisations be drawn so narrowly that a separate authorisation is required each time the source is tasked. Rather, an authorisation might cover, in broad terms, the nature of the source's task. If this changes, then a new authorisation may need to be sought.

4.31 It is difficult to predict exactly what might occur each time a meeting with a source takes place, or the source meets the subject of an investigation. There may be occasions when unforeseen action or undertakings occur. When this happens, the occurrence must be recorded as soon as is practicable after the event and, if the existing authorisation is insufficient, it should either be updated and reauthorised (for minor amendments only) or it should be cancelled and a new authorisation should be obtained before any further such action is carried out.

4.32 Similarly, where it is intended to task a source in a new way or significantly greater way than previously identified, the persons defined at section 29(5)(a) or (b) of the 2000 Act must refer the proposed tasking to the authorising officer, who should consider whether a separate authorisation is required. This should be done in advance of any tasking and the details of such referrals must be recorded.

Management responsibility

4.33 Public authorities should ensure that arrangements are in place for the proper oversight and management of sources, including appointing individual officers as defined in section 29(5)(a) and (b) of the 2000 Act for each source.

4.34 The person responsible for the day-to-day contact between the public authority and the source will usually be of a rank or position below that of the authorising officer.

4.35 In cases where the authorisation is for the use or conduct of a source whose activities benefit more than a single public authority, responsibilities for the management and oversight of that source may be taken up by one authority or can be split between the authorities.

Security and welfare

4.36 Any public authority deploying a source should take into account the safety and welfare of that source, when carrying out actions in relation to an authorisation or tasking, and to foreseeable consequences to others of that tasking. Before authorising the use or conduct of a source, the authorising officer should ensure that a risk assessment is carried out to determine the risk to the source of any tasking and the likely consequences should the role of the source become known. The ongoing security and welfare of the source, after the cancellation of the authorisation, should also be considered at the outset.

4.37 The person defined at section 29(5)(a) of the 2000 Act is responsible for bringing to the attention of the person defined at section 29(5)(b) of the 2000 Act any concerns about the personal circumstances of the source, insofar as they might affect:
• the validity of the risk assessment;
• the conduct of the source; and
• the safety and welfare of the source.

4.38 Where deemed appropriate, concerns about such matters must be considered by the authorising officer, and a decision taken on whether or not to allow the authorisation to continue.

Additional rules

Recording of telephone conversations

4.39 Subject to paragraph 4.40 below, the interception of communications sent by post or by means of public telecommunications systems or private telecommunications systems attached to the public network may be authorised only by the Secretary of State, in accordance with the terms of Part I of the 2000 Act. Nothing in this code should be taken as granting dispensation from the requirements of that Part of the 2000 Act.

4.40 Part I of the 2000 Act provides certain exceptions to the rule that interception of telephone conversations must be warranted under that Part. This includes, where one party to the communication consents to the interception, that it may be authorised in accordance with section 48(4) of the 2000 Act provided that there is no interception warrant authorising the interception. In such cases, the interception is treated as directed surveillance (see chapter 4 of the Covert Surveillance code of practice).

Use of a covert human intelligence source with technical equipment

4.41 A source, whether or not wearing or carrying a surveillance device and invited into residential premises or a private vehicle, does not require additional authorisation to record any activity taking place inside those premises or vehicle which take place in his presence. This also applies to the recording of telephone conversations other than by interception which takes place in the source's presence. Authorisation for the use or conduct of that source may be obtained in the usual way.

4.42 However, if a surveillance device is to be used, other than in the presence of the source, an intrusive surveillance authorisation and if applicable an authorisation for interference with property should be obtained.

5 Oversight by Commissioners

5.1 The 2000 Act requires the Chief Surveillance Commissioner to keep under review (with the assistance of the Surveillance Commissioners and Assistant Surveillance Commissioners) the performance of functions under Part III of the 1997 Act and Part II of the 2000 Act by the police (including the Royal Navy Regulating Branch, the Royal Military Police and the Royal Air Force Police and the Ministry of Defence Police and the British Transport Police), NCIS, NCS, HMCE and of the 2000 Act the other public authorities listed in Schedule 1 and in Northern Ireland officials of the Ministry of Defence and HM Forces.

5.2 The Intelligence Services Commissioner's remit is to provide independent oversight of the use of the powers contained within Part II of the 2000 Act by the Security Service, Secret Intelligence Service (SIS), the Governments Communication Headquarters (GCHQ) and the Ministry of Defence and HM Forces (excluding the Royal Navy Regulating Branch, the Royal Military Police and the Royal Air Force Police, and in Northern Ireland officials of the Ministry of Defence HM Forces).

5.3 This code does not cover the exercise of any of the Commissioners' functions. It is the duty of any person who uses these powers to comply with any request made by a Commissioner to disclose or provide any information he requires for the purpose of enabling him to carry out his functions.

5.4 References in this code to the performance of review functions by the Chief Surveillance Commissioner and other Commissioners apply also to Inspectors and other members of staff to whom such functions have been delegated.

6 Complaints

6.1 The 2000 Act establishes an independent Tribunal. This Tribunal will be made up of senior members of the judiciary and the legal profession and is independent of the Government. The Tribunal has full powers to investigate and decide any case within its jurisdiction.

6.2 This code does not cover the exercise of the Tribunal's functions. Details of the relevant complaints procedure can be obtained from the following address:

Investigatory Powers Tribunal

PO Box 33220

London

SW1H 9ZQ

Annex A: Authorisation levels when knowledge of confidential information is likely to be acquired or when a vulnerable individual or juvenile is to be used as a source

Government department/ public authority	Authorisation level for when knowledge of confidential information is likely to be acquired	Authorisation level for when a vulnerable individual or a juvenile is to be used as a source
Police forces—Any police force maintained under section 2 of the Police Act 1996 (police forces in England and Wales outside London).	Chief Constable	Assistant Chief Constable
Police forces—Any police force maintained under or by virtue of section 1 of the Police (Scotland) Act 1967.	Chief Constable	Assistant Chief Constable
The Metropolitan police force	Assistant Commissioner	Commander
The City of London police force	Commissioner	Commander
The Police Service of Northern Ireland	Deputy Chief Constable	Assistant Chief Constable
The Royal Navy Regulating Branch	Provost Marshal	Provost Marshal
Royal Military Police	Provost Marshal	Provost Marshal
Royal Air Force Police	Provost Marshal	Provost Marshal
National Criminal Intelligence Service (NCIS)	Director General	Assistant Chief Constable or Assistant Chief Investigation Officer
National Crime Squad (NCS)	Director General or Deputy Director General	Assistant Chief Constable
Serious Fraud Office	Director or Assistant Director	Director or Assistant Director
The intelligence services		
Government Communications Headquarters	A Director of GCHQ	A Director of GCHQ
Security Service	Deputy Director General	Deputy Director General

Secret Intelligence Service	A Director of the Secret Intelligence Service	A member of the Secret Intelligence Service not below the equivalent rank to that of a Grade 5 in the Home Civil Service
HM Forces		
Royal Navy	Rear Admiral	Rear Admiral
Army	Major General	Major General
Royal Air Force	Air-Vice Marshall	Air-Vice Marshall
HM Customs and Excise	Director Investigation or Regional Heads of Investigation	Band 11 (Intelligence)
Inland Revenue	Deputy Chairman of Inland Revenue	Head of Special Compliance Office
Department for the Environment, Food and Rural Affairs		
DEFRA Investigation Branch	Immediate Senior Officer of Head of DEFRA Prosecution Division	Head of DEFRA Prosecution Division
Horticultural Marketing Inspectorate	Immediate Senior Officer of Head of DEFRA Prosecution Division	No
Plant Health and Seed Inspectorate	Immediate Senior Officer of Head of DEFRA Prosecution Division	No
Egg Marketing Inspectorate	Immediate Senior Officer of Head of DEFRA Prosecution Division	No
Sea Fisheries Inspectorate (SFI)	Immediate Senior Officer of Head of DEFRA Prosecution Division	No
Centre for Environment, Fisheries and Aquaculture Science (CEFAS)	Immediate Senior Officer of Head of DEFRA Prosecution Division	Head of DEFRA Prosecution Division
Ministry of Defence	Director General or equivalent	Director General or equivalent
Department for Transport, Local Government and the Regions		
Vehicle Inspectorate	No	No
Transport Security (Transec)	Director of Transport Security	Deputy Director of Transport Security
Department of Health		
Medical Devices Agency	Chief Executive	No
Medicine Control Agency	Chief Executive	Head of Division for Inspection and Enforcement
Welfare Foods Policy Unit	Deputy Chief Medical Officer	No
Directorate of Counter Fraud Services (DFCS)	Director of Counter Fraud Services	Director of Counter Fraud Services
Home Office		
HM Prison Service	Deputy Director General	Area Managers
Immigration Service	Chief Inspector	Director

Department of Work and Pensions		
Benefits Agency	Chief Executive	Head of Fraud Investigation
Department of Trade and Industry		
Radiocommunications Agency	No	No
British Trade International	No	No
Coal Health Claims Unit	Director of Coal Health Claims unit	No
Companies Investigation Branch	The Inspector of Companies	The Inspector of Companies
Legal Services Directorate D	The Director of Legal Service D	The Director of Legal Service D
National Assembly for Wales	Health—Director, NHS Wales	Health—Director, NHS Wales
Local authorities	Agriculture—Head, National Assembly for Wales Agriculture Department The Head of Paid Service or (in his absence) a Chief Officer	Agriculture—Head, National Assembly for Wales Agriculture Department The Head of Paid Service or (in his absence) a Chief Officer
Environment Agency	Chief Executive	Executive Managers
Financial Services Authority	Chairman	Chairman
Food Standards Agency	Head of Group, Deputy Chief Executive and Chief Executive	Head of Group, Deputy Chief Executive and Chief Executive
The Intervention Board for Agricultural Produce	Chief Executive	Legal Director
Personal Investment Authority	Chairman	Chairman
Post Office	Director of Security	Head of Corporate Security/Head of Security for the Royal Mail/Head of Security for Counter Business

Appendix F
Interception of Communications Code of Practice

1 General

1.1 This code of practice relates to the powers and duties conferred or imposed under Chapter I of Part I of the Regulation of Investigatory Powers Act 2000 ('the Act'). It provides guidance on the procedures that must be followed before interception of communications can take place under those provisions. It is primarily intended for use by those public authorities listed in section 6(2) of the Act. It will also prove useful to postal and telecommunication operators and other interested bodies to acquaint themselves with the procedures to be followed by those public authorities.

1.2 The Act provides that all codes of practice relating to the Act are admissible as evidence in criminal and civil proceedings. If any provision of this code appears relevant before any court or tribunal considering any such proceedings, or to the Tribunal established under the Act, or to one of the Commissioners responsible for overseeing the powers conferred by the Act, it must be taken into account.

2 General Rules on Interception with a Warrant

2.1 There are a limited number of persons by whom, or on behalf of whom, applications for interception warrants may be made. These persons are:
- The Director-General of the Security Service
- The Chief of the Secret Intelligence Service
- The Director of GCHQ
- The Director General of the National Criminal Intelligence Service (NCIS handle interception on behalf of police forces in England and Wales)
- The Commissioner of the Police of the Metropolis (the Metropolitan Police Special Branch handle interception on behalf of Special Branches in England and Wales)
- The Chief Constable of the Police Service of Northern Ireland
- The Chief Constable of any police force maintained under or by virtue of section 1 of the Police (Scotland) Act 1967
- The Commissioners of Customs and Excise
- The Chief of Defence Intelligence

A person who, for the purposes of any international mutual assistance agreement, is the competent authority of a country or territory outside the United Kingdom.

Any application made on behalf of one of the above must be made by a person holding office under the Crown.

2.2 All interception warrants are issued by the Secretary of State. Even where the urgency procedure is followed, the Secretary of State personally authorises the warrant, although it is signed by a senior official.

2.3 Before issuing an interception warrant, the Secretary of State must believe that what the action seeks to achieve is necessary for one of the following section 5(3) purposes:
- in the interests of national security;
- for the purpose of preventing or detecting serious crime; or
- for the purpose of safeguarding the economic well-being of the UK;

and that the conduct authorised by the warrant is proportionate to what is sought to be achieved by that conduct.

Necessity and proportionality

2.4 Obtaining a warrant under the Act will only ensure that the interception authorised is a justifiable interference with an individual's rights under Article 8 of the European Convention of Human Rights (the right to privacy) if it is necessary and proportionate for the interception to take place. The Act recognises this by first requiring that the Secretary of State believes that the authorisation is necessary on one or more of the statutory grounds set out in section 5(3) of the Act. This requires him to believe that it is necessary to undertake the interception which is to be authorised for a particular purpose falling within the relevant statutory ground.

2.5 Then, if the interception is necessary, the Secretary of State must also believe that it is proportionate to what is sought to be achieved by carrying it out. This involves balancing the intrusiveness of the interference, against the need for it in operational terms. Interception of communications will not be proportionate if it is excessive in the circumstances of the case or if the information which is sought could reasonably be obtained by other means. Further, all interception should be carefully managed to meet the objective in question and must not be arbitrary or unfair.

Implementation of warrants

2.6 After a warrant has been issued it will be forwarded to the person to whom it is addressed, in practice the intercepting agency which submitted the application. The Act (section 11) then permits the intercepting agency to carry out the interception, or to require the assistance of other persons in giving effect to the warrant. Warrants cannot be served on those outside the jurisdiction of the UK.

Provision of reasonable assistance

2.7 Any postal or telecommunications operator (referred to as communications service providers) in the United Kingdom may be required to provide assistance in giving effect to an interception. The Act places a requirement on postal and telecommunications operators to take all such steps for giving effect to the warrant as are notified to them (section 11(4) of the Act). But the steps which may be required are limited to those which it is reasonably practicable to take (section 11(5)). What is reasonably practicable should be agreed after consultation between the postal or telecommunications operator and the Government. If no agreement can be reached it will be for the Secretary of State to decide whether to press forward with civil proceedings. Criminal proceedings may also be instituted by or with the consent of the Director of Public Prosecutions.

2.8 Where the intercepting agency requires the assistance of a communications service provider in order to implement a warrant, they should provide the following to the communications service provider:

- A copy of the warrant instrument signed and dated by the Secretary of State (or in an urgent case, by a senior official).
- The relevant schedule for that service provider setting out the numbers, addresses or other factors identifying the communications to be intercepted.
- A covering document from the intercepting agency requiring the assistance of the communications service provider and specifying any other details regarding the means of interception and delivery as may be necessary. Contact details with respect to the intercepting agency will either be provided in this covering document or will be available in the handbook provided to all postal and telecommunications operators who maintain an intercept capability.

Provision of intercept capability

2.9 Whilst all persons who provide a postal or telecommunications service are obliged to provide assistance in giving effect to an interception, persons who provide a public postal or telecommunications service, or plan to do so, may also be required to provide a reasonable intercept capability. The obligations the Secretary of State considers reasonable to impose on such persons to ensure they have such a capability will be set out in an order made by the Secretary of State and approved by Parliament. The Secretary of State may then serve a notice upon a communications service provider setting out the steps they must take to ensure they can meet these obligations. A notice will not be served without consultation over the content of the notice between the Government and the service provider having previously taken place. When served with such a notice, a communications service provider, if he feels it unreasonable, will be able to refer that notice to the Technical Advisory Board (TAB) on the reasonableness of the technical requirements and capabilities that are being sought. Details of how to submit a notice to the TAB will be provided either before or at the time the notice is served.

2.10 Any communications service provider obliged to maintain a reasonable intercept capability will be provided with a handbook which will contain the basic information they require to respond to requests for reasonable assistance for the interception of communications.

Duration of interception warrants

2.11 All interception warrants are valid for an initial period of three months. Upon renewal, warrants issued on serious crime grounds are valid for a further period of three months. Warrants renewed on national security/economic well-being grounds are valid for a further period of six months. Urgent authorisations are valid for five working days following the date of issue unless renewed by the Secretary of State.

2.12 Where modifications take place, the warrant expiry date remains unchanged. However, where the modification takes place under the urgency provisions, the modification instrument expires after five working days following the date of issue unless renewed following the routine procedure.

2.13 Where a change in circumstance prior to the set expiry date leads the intercepting agency to consider it no longer necessary or practicable for the warrant to be in force, it should be cancelled with immediate effect.

Stored communications

2.14 Section 2(7) of the Act defines a communication in the course of its transmission as also encompassing any time when the communication is being stored on the communication system in such a way as to enable the intended recipient to have access to it. This means that a warrant can be used to obtain both communications that are in the process of transmission and those that are being stored on the transmission system.

2.15 Stored communications may also be accessed by means other than a warrant. If a communication has been stored on a communication system it may be obtained with lawful authority by means of an existing statutory power such as a production order (under the Police and Criminal Evidence Act 1984) or a search warrant.

3 Special Rules on Interception with a Warrant

Collateral intrusion

3.1 Consideration should be given to any infringement of the privacy of individuals who are not the subject of the intended interception, especially where communications relating to religious, medical, journalistic or legally privileged material may be involved. An application for an interception warrant should draw attention to any circumstances which give rise to an unusual degree of collateral infringement of privacy, and this will be taken into account by the Secretary of State when considering a warrant application. Should an interception operation reach the point where individuals other than the subject of the authorisation are identified as directly relevant to the operation, consideration should be given to applying for separate warrants covering those individuals.

Confidential information

3.2 Particular consideration should also be given in cases where the subject of the interception might reasonably assume a high degree of privacy, or where confidential information is involved. Confidential information consists of matters subject to legal privilege, confidential personal information or confidential journalistic material (see paragraphs 3.9–3.11). For example, extra consideration should be given where interception might involve communications between a minister of religion and an individual relating to the latter's spiritual welfare, or where matters of medical or journalistic confidentiality or legal privilege may be involved.

Communications subject to legal privilege

3.3 Section 98 of the Police Act 1997 describes those matters that are subject to legal privilege in England and Wales. In relation to Scotland, those matters subject to legal privilege contained in section 33 of the Criminal Law (Consolidation) (Scotland) Act 1995 should be adopted. With regard to Northern Ireland, Article 12 of the Police and Criminal Evidence (Northern Ireland) Order 1989 should be referred to.

3.4 Legal privilege does not apply to communications made with the intention of furthering a criminal purpose (whether the lawyer is acting unwittingly or culpably). Legally privileged communications will lose their protection if there are grounds to believe, for example, that the professional legal advisor is intending to hold or use the information for a criminal purpose. But privilege is not lost if a professional legal advisor is properly advising a person who is suspected of having committed a criminal offence. The concept of legal privilege applies to the provision of professional legal advice by any individual, agency or organisation qualified to do so.

3.5 The Act does not provide any special protection for legally privileged communications. Nevertheless, intercepting such communications is particularly sensitive and is therefore subject to additional safeguards under this Code. The guidance set out below may in part depend on whether matters subject to legal privilege have been obtained intentionally or incidentally to some other material which has been sought.

3.6 In general, any application for a warrant which is likely to result in the interception of legally privileged communications should include, in addition to the reasons why it is considered necessary for the interception to take place, an assessment of how likely it is that communications which are subject to legal privilege will be intercepted. In addition, it should state whether the purpose (or one of the purposes) of the interception is to obtain privileged communications. This assessment will be taken into account by the Secretary of State in deciding whether an interception is necessary under section 5(3) of the Act and whether it is proportionate. In such circumstances, the Secretary of State will be able to impose additional conditions such as regular reporting arrangements so as to be able to exercise his discretion on whether a warrant should continue to be authorised. In those cases where communications which include legally privileged communications have been intercepted and retained, the matter should be reported to the Interception of Communications Commissioner during his inspections and the material be made available to him if requested.

3.7 Where a lawyer is the subject of an interception, it is possible that a substantial proportion of the communications which will be intercepted will be between the lawyer and his client(s) and will be subject to legal privilege. Any case where a lawyer is the subject of an investigation should be notified to the Interception of Communications Commissioner during his inspections and any material which has been retained should be made available to him if requested.

3.8 In addition to safeguards governing the handling and retention of intercept material as provided for in section 15 of the Act, caseworkers who examine intercepted communications should be alert to any intercept material which may be subject to legal privilege. Where there is doubt as to whether the communications are subject to legal privilege, advice should be sought from a legal adviser within the intercepting agency. Similar advice should also be sought where there is doubt over whether communications are not subject to legal privilege due to the 'in furtherance of a criminal purpose' exception.

Communications involving confidential personal information and confidential journalistic material

3.9 Similar consideration to that given to legally privileged communications must also be given to the interception of communications that involve confidential personal information and confidential journalistic material. Confidential personal information is information held in confidence concerning an individual (whether living or dead) who can be identified from it, and the material in question relates to his physical or mental health or to spiritual counselling. Such information can include both oral and written communications. Such information as described above is held in confidence if it is held subject to an express or implied undertaking to hold it in confidence, or it is subject to a restriction on disclosure or an obligation of confidentiality contained in existing legislation. For example, confidential personal information might include consultations between a health professional and a patient, or information from a patient's medical records.

3.10 Spiritual counselling is defined as conversations between an individual and a Minister of Religion acting in his official capacity, and where the individual being counselled is seeking or the Minister is imparting forgiveness, absolution or the resolution of conscience with the authority of the Divine Being(s) of their faith.

3.11 Confidential journalistic material includes material acquired or created for the purposes of journalism and held subject to an undertaking to hold it in confidence, as well as communications resulting in information being acquired for the purposes of journalism and held subject to such an undertaking.

4 Interception Warrants (section 8(1))

4.1 This section applies to the interception of communications by means of a warrant complying with section 8(1) of the Act. This type of warrant may be issued in respect of the interception of communications carried on any postal service or telecommunications system, as defined in section 2(1) of the Act (including a private telecommunications system). Responsibility for the issuing of interception warrants rests with the Secretary of State.

Application for a section 8(1) warrant

4.2 An application for a warrant is made to the Secretary of State. Interception warrants, when issued, are addressed to the person who submitted the application. This person may then serve a copy upon any person who may be able to provide assistance in giving effect to that warrant. Each application, a copy of which must be retained by the applicant, should contain the following information:

- Background to the operation in question
- Person or premises to which the application relates (and how the person or premises feature in the operation)
- Description of the communications to be intercepted, details of the communications service provider(s) and an assessment of the feasibility of the interception operation where this is relevant
- Description of the conduct to be authorised as considered necessary in order to carry out the interception, where appropriate

- An explanation of why the interception is considered to be necessary under the provisions of section 5(3)
- A consideration of why the conduct to be authorised by the warrant is proportionate to what is sought to be achieved by that conduct
- A consideration of any unusual degree of collateral intrusion and why that intrusion is justified in the circumstances. In particular, where the communications in question might affect religious, medical or journalistic confidentiality or legal privilege, this must be specified in the application
- Where an application is urgent, supporting justification should be provided
- An assurance that all material intercepted will be handled in accordance with the safeguards required by section 15 of the Act.

Authorisation of a section 8(1) warrant

4.3 Before issuing a warrant under section 8(1), the Secretary of State must believe the warrant is necessary

- in the interests of national security;
- for the purpose of preventing or detecting serious crime; or
- for the purpose of safeguarding the economic well-being of the United Kingdom.

4.4 In exercising his power to issue an interception warrant for the purpose of safeguarding the economic well-being of the United Kingdom (as provided for by section 5(3)(c) of the Act), the Secretary of State will consider whether the economic well-being of the United Kingdom which is to be safeguarded is, on the facts of each case, directly related to state security. The term 'state security', which is used in Directive 97/66/EC (concerning the processing of personal data and the protection of privacy in the telecommunications sector), should be interpreted in the same way as the term 'national security' which is used elsewhere in the Act and this Code. The Secretary of State will not issue a warrant on section 5(3)(c) grounds if this direct link between the economic well-being of the United Kingdom and state security is not established. Any application for a warrant on section 5(3)(c) grounds should therefore explain how, in the applicant's view, the economic well-being of the United Kingdom which is to be safeguarded is directly related to state security on the facts of the case.

4.5 The Secretary of State must also consider that the conduct authorised by the warrant is proportionate to what it seeks to achieve (section 5(2)(b)). In considering necessity and proportionality, the Secretary of State must take into account whether the information sought could reasonably be obtained by other means (section 5(4)).

Urgent authorisation of a section 8(1) warrant

4.6 The Act makes provision (section 7(1)(b)) for cases in which an interception warrant is required urgently, yet the Secretary of State is not available to sign the warrant. In these cases the Secretary of State will still personally authorise the interception but the warrant is signed by a senior official, following discussion of the case between officials and the Secretary of State. The Act restricts issue of warrants in this way to urgent cases where the Secretary of State has himself expressly authorised the issue of the warrant (section 7(2)(a)), and requires the warrant to contain a statement to that effect (section 7(4)(a)). A warrant issued under the urgency procedure lasts for five working days following the day of issue unless renewed by the Secretary of State, in which case it expires after three months in the case of serious crime or six months in the case of national security or economic well-being in the same way as other non-urgent section 8(1) warrants. An urgent case is one in which interception authorisation is required within a twenty-four hour period.

Format of a section 8(1) warrant

4.7 Each warrant comprises two sections, a warrant instrument signed by the Secretary of State listing the subject of the interception or set of premises, a copy of which each communications service provider will receive, and a schedule or set of schedules listing the communications to be intercepted. Only the schedule relevant to the communications that can be intercepted by the specified communications service provider will be provided to that service provider.

4.8 The warrant instrument should include:

• The name or description of the interception subject or of a set of premises in relation to which the interception is to take place
• A warrant reference number
• The persons who may subsequently modify the scheduled part of the warrant in an urgent case (if authorised in accordance with section 10(8) of the Act).

4.9 The scheduled part of the warrant will comprise one or more schedules. Each schedule should contain:

• The name of the communication service provider, or the other person who is to take action
• A warrant reference number
• A means of identifying the communications to be intercepted.

Modification of section 8(1) warrant

4.10 Interception warrants may be modified under the provisions of section 10 of the Act. The unscheduled part of a warrant may only be modified by the Secretary of State or, in an urgent case, by a senior official with the express authorisation of the Secretary of State. In these cases, a statement of that fact must be endorsed on the modifying instrument, and the modification ceases to have effect after five working days following the day of issue unless it is renewed by the Secretary of State. The modification will then expire upon the expiry date of the warrant.

4.11 Scheduled parts of a warrant may be modified by the Secretary of State, or by a senior official acting upon his behalf. A modification to the scheduled part of the warrant may include the addition of a new schedule relating to a communication service provider on whom a copy of the warrant has not been previously served. Modifications made in this way expire at the same time as the warrant expires. There also exists a duty to modify a warrant by deleting a communication identifier if it is no longer relevant. When a modification is sought to delete a number or other communication identifier, the relevant communications service provider must be advised and interception suspended before the modification instrument is signed.

4.12 In an urgent case, and where the warrant specifically authorises it, scheduled parts of a warrant may be modified by the person to whom the warrant is addressed (the person who submitted the application) or a subordinate (where the subordinate is identified in the warrant). Modifications of this kind are valid for five working days following the day of issue unless the modification instrument is endorsed by a senior official acting on behalf of the Secretary of State. Where the modification is endorsed in this way, the modification expires upon the expiry date of the warrant.

Renewal of a section 8(1) warrant

4.13 The Secretary of State may renew a warrant at any point before its expiry date. Applications for renewals must be made to the Secretary of State and should contain an update of the matters outlined in paragraph 4.2 above. In particular, the applicant should give an assessment of the value of interception to the operation to date and explain why he considers that interception continues to be necessary for one or more of the purposes in section 5(3).

4.14 Where the Secretary of State is satisfied that the interception continues to meet the requirements of the Act he may renew the warrant. Where the warrant is issued on serious crime grounds, the renewed warrant is valid for a further three months. Where it is issued on national security/economic well-being grounds, the renewed warrant is valid for six months. These dates run from the date of signature on the renewal instrument.

4.15 A copy of the warrant renewal instrument will be forwarded by the intercepting agency to all relevant communications service providers on whom a copy of the original warrant instrument and a schedule have been served, providing they are still actively assisting. A warrant renewal instrument will include the reference number of the warrant and description of the person or premises described in the warrant.

Warrant cancellation

4.16 The Secretary of State is under a duty to cancel an interception warrant if, at any time before its expiry date, he is satisfied that the warrant is no longer necessary on grounds falling within section 5(3) of the Act. Intercepting agencies will therefore need to keep their warrants under continuous review. In practice, cancellation instruments will be signed by a senior official on his behalf.

4.17 The cancellation instrument should be addressed to the person to whom the warrant was issued (the intercepting agency) and should include the reference number of the warrant and the description of the person or premises specified in the warrant. A copy of the cancellation instrument should be sent to those communications service providers who have held a copy of the warrant instrument and accompanying schedule during the preceding twelve months.

Records

4.18 The intercepting agency should keep the following to be made available for scrutiny by the Commissioner as he may require:
- all applications made for warrants complying with section 8(1) and applications made for the renewal of such warrants;
- all warrants, and renewals and copies of schedule modifications (if any);
- where any application is refused, the grounds for refusal as given by the Secretary of State;
- the dates on which interception is started and stopped.

4.19 Records shall also be kept of the arrangements by which the requirements of section 15(2) (minimisation of copying and destruction of intercepted material) and section 15(3) (destruction of intercepted material) are to be met. For further details see section on 'Safeguards'.

4.20 The term 'intercepted material' is used throughout to embrace copies, extracts or summaries made from the intercepted material as well as the intercept material itself.

5 Interception Warrants (section 8(4))

5.1 This section applies to the interception of external communications by means of a warrant complying with section 8(4) of the Act. External communications are defined by the Act to be those which are sent or received outside the British Islands. They include those which are both sent and received outside the British Islands, whether or not they pass through the British Islands in course of their transit. They do not include communications both sent and received in the British Islands, even if they pass outside the British Islands en route. Responsibility for the issuing of such interception warrants rests with the Secretary of State.

Application for a section 8(4) warrant

5.2 An application for a warrant is made to the Secretary of State. Interception warrants, when issued, are addressed to the person who submitted the application. This person may then serve a copy upon any person who may be able to provide assistance in giving effect to that warrant. Each application, a copy of which must be retained by the applicant, should contain the following information:

- Background to the operation in question
- Description of the communications to be intercepted, details of the communications service provider(s) and an assessment of the feasibility of the operation where this is relevant
- Description of the conduct to be authorised, which must be restricted to the interception of external communications, or to conduct necessary in order to intercept those external communications, where appropriate
- The certificate that will regulate examination of intercepted material
- An explanation of why the interception is considered to be necessary for one or more of the section 5(3) purposes
- A consideration of why the conduct to be authorised by the warrant is proportionate to what is sought to be achieved by that conduct
- A consideration of any unusual degree of collateral intrusion, and why that intrusion is justified in the circumstances. In particular, where the communications in question might affect religious, medical or journalistic confidentiality or legal privilege, this must be specified in the application
- Where an application is urgent, supporting justification should be provided
- An assurance that intercepted material will be read, looked at or listened to only so far as it is certified, and it meets the conditions of sections 16(2)–16(6) of the Act
- An assurance that all material intercepted will be handled in accordance with the safeguards required by sections 15 and 16 of the Act.

Authorisation of a section 8(4) warrant

5.3 Before issuing a warrant under section 8(4), the Secretary of State must believe that the warrant is necessary:

- in the interests of national security;
- for the purpose of preventing or detecting serious crime; or
- for the purpose of safeguarding the economic well-being of the United Kingdom.

5.4 In exercising his power to issue an interception warrant for the purpose of safeguarding the economic well-being of the United Kingdom (as provided for by section 5(3)(c) of the Act), the Secretary of State will consider whether the economic well-being of the United Kingdom which is to be safeguarded is, on the facts of each case, directly related to state security. The term 'state security', which is used in Directive 97/66/EC (concerning the processing of personal data and the protection of privacy in the telecommunications sector), should be interpreted in the same way as the term 'national security' which is used elsewhere in the Act and this Code. The Secretary of State will not issue a warrant on section 5(3)(c) grounds if this direct link between the economic well-being of the United Kingdom and state security is not established. Any application for a warrant on section 5(3)(c) grounds should therefore explain how, in the applicant's view, the economic well-being of the United Kingdom which is to be safeguarded is directly related to state security on the facts of the case.

5.5 The Secretary of State must also consider that the conduct authorised by the warrant is proportionate to what it seeks to achieve (section 5(2)(b)). In considering necessity and proportionality, the Secretary of State must take into account whether the information sought could reasonably be obtained by other means (section 5(4)).

5.6 When the Secretary of State issues a warrant of this kind, it must be accompanied by a certificate in which the Secretary of State certifies that he considers examination of the intercepted material to be necessary for one or more of the section 5(3) purposes. The Secretary of State has a duty to ensure that arrangements are in force for securing that only that material which has been certified as necessary for examination for a section 5(3) purpose, and which meets the conditions set out in section 16(2) to section 16(6) is, in fact, read, looked at or listened to. The Interception of Communications Commissioner is under a duty to review the adequacy of those arrangements.

Urgent authorisation of a section 8(4) warrant

5.7 The Act makes provision (section 7(1)(b)) for cases in which an interception warrant is required urgently, yet the Secretary of State is not available to sign the warrant. In these cases the Secretary of State will still personally authorise the interception but the warrant is signed by a senior official, following discussion of the case between officials and the Secretary of State. The Act restricts issue of warrants in this way to urgent cases where the Secretary of State has himself expressly authorised the issue of the warrant (section 7(2)(a)), and requires the warrant to contain a statement to that effect (section 7(4)(a)).

5.8 A warrant issued under the urgency procedure lasts for five working days following the day of issue unless renewed by the Secretary of State, in which case it expires after three months in the case of serious crime or six months in the case of national security or economic well-being in the same way as other section 8(4) warrants.

Format of a section 8(4) warrant

5.9 Each warrant is addressed to the person who submitted the application. This person may then serve a copy upon such providers of communications services as he believes will be able to assist in implementing the interception. Communications service providers will not receive a copy of the certificate.

The warrant should include the following:
- A description of the communications to be intercepted
- The warrant reference number
- The persons who may subsequently modify the scheduled part of the warrant in an urgent case (if authorised in accordance with section 10(8) of the Act).

Modification of a section 8(4) warrant

5.10 Interception warrants may be modified under the provisions of section 10 of the Act. The warrant may only be modified by the Secretary of State or, in an urgent case, by a senior official with the express authorisation of the Secretary of State. In these cases a statement of that fact must be endorsed on the modifying instrument, and the modification ceases to have effect after five working days following the day of issue unless it is endorsed by the Secretary of State.

5.11 The certificate must be modified by the Secretary of State, save in an urgent case where a certificate may be modified under the hand of a senior official provided that the official holds a position in respect of which he is expressly authorised by provisions contained in the certificate to modify the certificate on the Secretary of State's behalf, or the Secretary of State has himself expressly authorised the modification and a statement of that fact is endorsed on the modifying instrument. Again the modification shall cease to have effect after five working days following the day of issue unless it is endorsed by the Secretary of State.

Renewal of a section 8(4) warrant

5.12 The Secretary of State may renew a warrant at any point before its expiry date. Applications for renewals are made to the Secretary of State and contain an update of the matters outlined in paragraph 5.2 above. In particular, the applicant must give an assessment of the value of interception to the operation to date and explain why he considers that interception continues to be necessary for one or more of purposes in section 5(3).

5.13 Where the Secretary of State is satisfied that the interception continues to meet the requirements of the Act he may renew the warrant. Where the warrant is issued on serious crime grounds, the renewed warrant is valid for a further three months. Where it is issued on national security/economic well-being grounds the renewed warrant is valid for six months. These dates run from the date of signature on the renewal instrument.

5.14 In those circumstances where the assistance of communications service providers has been sought, a copy of the warrant renewal instrument will be forwarded by the intercepting agency to all those on whom a copy of the original warrant instrument has been served, providing they are still actively assisting. A warrant renewal instrument will include the reference number of the warrant and description of the communications to be intercepted.

Warrant cancellation

5.15 The Secretary of State shall cancel an interception warrant if, at any time before its expiry date, he is satisfied that the warrant is no longer necessary on grounds falling within Section 5(3) of the Act. In practice, cancellation instruments will be signed by a senior official on his behalf.

5.16 The cancellation instrument will be addressed to the person to whom the warrant was issued (the intercepting agency). A copy of the cancellation instrument should be sent to those communications service providers, if any, who have given effect to the warrant during the preceding twelve months.

Records

5.17 The oversight regime allows the Interception of Communications Commissioner to inspect the warrant application upon which the Secretary of State based his decision, and the applicant may be required to justify the content. Each intercepting agency should keep, so to be made available for scrutiny by the Interception of Communications Commissioner, the following:

- all applications made for warrants complying with section 8(4), and applications made for the renewal of such warrants;
- all warrants and certificates, and copies of renewal and modification instruments (if any);
- where any application is refused, the grounds for refusal as given by the Secretary of State;
- the dates on which interception is started and stopped.

Records shall also be kept of the arrangements in force for securing that only material which has been certified for examination for a purpose under section 5(3) and which meets the conditions set out in sections 16(2)–16(6) of the Act in accordance with section 15 of the Act. Records shall be kept of the arrangements by which the requirements of section 15(2) (minimisation of copying and distribution of intercepted material) and section 15(3) (destruction of intercepted material) are to be met. For further details see section on 'Safeguards'.

6 Safeguards

6.1 All material (including related communications data) intercepted under the authority of a warrant complying with section 8(1) or section 8(4) of the Act must be handled in accordance with safeguards which the Secretary of State has approved in conformity with the duty imposed upon him by the Act. These safeguards are made available to the Interception of Communications Commissioner, and they must meet the requirements of section 15 of the Act which are set out below. In addition, the safeguards in section 16 of the Act apply to warrants complying with section 8(4). Any breach of these safeguards must be reported to the Interception of Communications Commissioner.

6.2 Section 15 of the Act requires that disclosure, copying and retention of intercept material be limited to the minimum necessary for the authorised purposes. The authorised purposes defined in section 15(4) of the Act include:

- if the material continues to be, or is likely to become, necessary for any of the purposes set out in section 5(3)—namely, in the interests of national security, for the purpose of preventing or detecting serious crime, for the purpose of safeguarding the economic well-being of the United Kingdom;
- if the material is necessary for facilitating the carrying out of the functions of the Secretary of State under Chapter I of Part I of the Act;
- if the material is necessary for facilitating the carrying out of any functions of the Interception of Communications Commissioner or the Tribunal;
- if the material is necessary to ensure that a person conducting a criminal prosecution has the information he needs to determine what is required of him by his duty to secure the fairness of the prosecution;
- if the material is necessary for the performance of any duty imposed by the Public Record Acts.

6.3 Section 16 provides for additional safeguards in relation to material gathered under section 8(4) warrants, requiring that the safeguards:
- ensure that intercepted material is read, looked at or listened to by any person only to the extent that the material is certified;
- regulate the use of selection factors that refer to individuals known to be for the time being in the British Islands.

The Secretary of State must ensure that the safeguards are in force before any interception under warrants complying with section 8(4) can begin. The Interception of Communications Commissioner is under a duty to review the adequacy of the safeguards.

Dissemination of intercepted material

6.4 The number of persons to whom any of the material is disclosed, and the extent of disclosure, must be limited to the minimum that is necessary for the authorised purposes set out in section 15(4) of the Act. This obligation applies equally to disclosure to additional persons within an agency, and to disclosure outside the agency. It is enforced by prohibiting disclosure to persons who do not hold the required security clearance, and also by the need-to-know principle: intercepted material must not be disclosed to any person unless that person's duties, which must relate to one of the authorised purposes, are such that he needs to know about the material to carry out those duties. In the same way only so much of the material may be disclosed as the recipient needs; for example, if a summary of the material will suffice, no more than that should be disclosed.

6.5 The obligations apply not just to the original interceptor, but also to anyone to whom the material is subsequently disclosed. In some cases this will be achieved by requiring the latter to obtain the originator's permission before disclosing the material further. In others, explicit safeguards are applied to secondary recipients.

Copying

6.6 Intercepted material may only be copied to the extent necessary for the identities of the persons to or by whom the intercepted material was sent. The restrictions are implemented by requiring special treatment of such copies, extracts and summaries that are made by recording their making, distribution and destruction.

Storage

6.7 Intercepted material, and all copies, extracts and summaries of it, must be handled and stored securely, so as to minimise the risk of loss or theft. It must be held so as to be inaccessible to persons without the required level of security clearance. This requirement to store intercept product securely applies to all those who are responsible for the handling of this material, including communications service providers. The details of what such a requirement will mean in practice for communications service providers will be set out in the discussions they will be having with the Government before a Section 12 Notice is served (see paragraph 2.9).

Destruction

6.8 Intercepted material, and all copies, extracts and summaries which can be identified as the product of an interception, must be securely destroyed as soon as it is no longer needed for any of the authorised purposes. If such material is retained, it should be reviewed at appropriate intervals to confirm that the justification for its retention is still valid under section 15(3) of the Act.

Personnel security

6.9 Each intercepting agency maintains a distribution list of persons who may have access to intercepted material or need to see any reporting in relation to it. All such persons must be appropriately vetted. Any person no longer needing access to perform his duties should be removed from any such list. Where it is necessary for an officer of one agency to disclose material to another, it is the former's responsibility to ensure that the recipient has the necessary clearance.

7 Disclosure to Ensure Fairness in Criminal Proceedings

7.1 Section 15(3) of the Act states the general rule that intercepted material must be destroyed as soon as its retention is no longer necessary for a purpose authorised under the Act. Section 15(4) specifies the authorised purposes for which retention is necessary.

7.2 This part of the Code applies to the handling of intercepted material in the context of criminal proceedings where the material has been retained for one of the purposes authorised in section 15(4) of the Act. For those who would ordinarily have had responsibility under the Criminal Procedure and Investigations Act 1996 to provide disclosure in criminal proceedings, this includes those rare situations where destruction of intercepted material has not taken place in accordance with section 15(3) and where that material is still in existence after the commencement of a criminal prosecution, retention having been considered necessary to ensure that a person conducting a criminal prosecution has the information he needs to discharge his duty of ensuring its fairness (section 15(4)(d)).

Exclusion of matters from legal proceedings

7.3 The general rule is that neither the possibility of interception nor intercepted material itself plays any part in legal proceedings. This rule is set out in section 17 of the Act, which excludes evidence, questioning, assertion or disclosure in legal proceedings likely to reveal the existence (or the absence) of a warrant issued under this Act (or the Interception of Communications Act 1985). This rule means that the intercepted material cannot be used either by the prosecution or the defence. This preserves 'equality of arms' which is a requirement under Article 6 of the European Convention on Human Rights.

7.4 Section 18 contains a number of tightly-drawn exceptions to this rule. This part of the Code deals only with the exception in subsections (7) to (11).

Disclosure to a prosecutor

7.5 Section 18(7)(a) provides that intercepted material obtained by means of a warrant and which continues to be available, may, for a strictly limited purpose, be disclosed to a person conducting a criminal prosecution.

7.6 This may only be done for the purpose of enabling the prosecutor to determine what is required of him by his duty to secure the fairness of the prosecution. The prosecutor may not use intercepted material to which he is given access under section 18(7)(a) to mount a cross-examination, or to do anything other than ensure the fairness of the proceedings.

7.7 The exception does not mean that intercepted material should be retained against a remote possibility that it might be relevant to future proceedings. The normal expectation is, still, for the intercepted material to be destroyed in accordance with the general safeguards provided by section 15. The exceptions only come into play if such material has, in fact, been retained for an authorised purpose. Because the authorised purpose given in section 5(3)(b) ('for the purpose of preventing or detecting serious crime') does not extend to gathering evidence for the purpose of a prosecution, material intercepted for this purpose may not have survived to the prosecution stage, as it will have been destroyed in accordance with the section 15(3) safeguards. There is, in these circumstances, no need to consider disclosure to a prosecutor if, in fact, no intercepted material remains in existence.

7.8 Be that as it may, section 18(7)(a) recognises the duty on prosecutors, acknowledged by common law, to review all available material to make sure that the prosecution is not proceeding unfairly. 'Available material' will only ever include intercepted material at this stage if the conscious decision has been made to retain it for an authorised purpose.

7.9 If intercepted material does continue to be available at the prosecution stage, once this information has come to the attention of the holder of this material the prosecutor should be informed that a warrant has been issued under section 5 and that material of possible relevance to the case has been intercepted.

7.10 Having had access to the material, the prosecutor may conclude that the material affects the fairness of the proceedings. In these circumstances, he will decide how the prosecution, if it proceeds, should be presented.

Disclosure to a judge

7.11 Section 18(7)(b) recognises that there may be cases where the prosecutor, having seen intercepted material under subsection (7)(a), will need to consult the trial judge. Accordingly, it provides for the judge to be given access to intercepted material, where there are exceptional circumstances making that disclosure essential in the interests of justice.

7.12 This access will be achieved by the prosecutor inviting the judge to make an order for disclosure to him alone, under this subsection. This is an exceptional procedure; normally, the prosecutor's functions under subsection (7)(a) will not fall to be reviewed by the judge. To comply with section 17(1), any consideration given to, or exercise of, this power must be carried out without notice to the defence. The purpose of this power is to ensure that the trial is conducted fairly.

7.13 The judge may, having considered the intercepted material disclosed to him, direct the prosecution to make an admission of fact. The admission will be abstracted from the interception; but, in accordance with the requirements of section 17(1), it must not reveal the fact of interception. This is likely to be a very unusual step. The Act only allows it where the judge considers it essential in the interests of justice.

7.14 Nothing in these provisions allows intercepted material, or the fact of interception, to be disclosed to the defence.

8 Oversight

8.1 The Act provides for an Interception of Communications Commissioner whose remit is to provide independent oversight of the use of the powers contained within the warranted interception regime under Chapter I of Part I of the Act.

8.2 This Code does not cover the exercise of the Commissioner's functions. However, it will be the duty of any person who uses the above powers to comply with any request made by the Commissioner to provide any information as he requires for the purpose of enabling him to discharge his functions.

9 Complaints

9.1 The Act establishes an independent Tribunal. This Tribunal will be made up of senior members of the judiciary and the legal profession and is independent of the Government. The Tribunal has full powers to investigate and decide any case within its jurisdiction.

9.2 This code does not cover the exercise of the Tribunal's functions. Details of the relevant complaints procedure can be obtained from the following address:

The Investigatory Powers Tribunal
PO Box 33220
London
SW1H 9ZQ

10 Interception without a Warrant

10.1 Section 1(5) of the Act permits interception without a warrant in the following circumstances:
- where it is authorised by or under sections 3 or 4 of the Act (see below);
- where it is in exercise, in relation to any stored communication, of some other statutory power exercised for the purpose of obtaining information or of taking possession of any document or other property, for example, the obtaining of a production order under Schedule 1 to the Police and Criminal Evidence Act 1984 for stored data to be produced.

Interception in accordance with a warrant under section 5 of the Act is dealt with under parts 2, 3, 4 and 5 of this Code.

10.2 For lawful interception which takes place without a warrant, pursuant to sections 3 or 4 of the Act or pursuant to some other statutory power, there is no prohibition in the Act on the evidential use of any material that is obtained as a result. The matter may still, however, be regulated by the exclusionary rules of evidence to be found in the common law, section 78 of the Police and Criminal Evidence Act 1984, and/or pursuant to the Human Rights Act 1998.

Interception with the consent of both parties

10.3 Section 3(1) of the Act authorises the interception of a communication if both the person sending the communication and the intended recipient(s) have consented to its interception, or where the person conducting the interception has reasonable grounds for believing that all parties have consented to the interception.

Interception with the consent of one party

10.4 Section 3(2) of the Act authorises the interception of a communication if either the sender or intended recipient of the communication has consented to its interception, and directed surveillance by means of that interception has been authorised under Part II of the Act. Further details can be found in chapter 4 of the Covert Surveillance Code of Practice and in chapter 2 of the Covert Human Intelligence Sources Code of Practice.

Interception for the purposes of a communication service provider

10.5 Section 3(3) of the Act permits a communication service provider or a person acting upon their behalf to carry out interception for purposes connected with the operation of that service or for purposes connected with the enforcement of any enactment relating to the use of the communication service.

Lawful business practice

10.6 Section 4(2) of the Act enables the Secretary of State to make regulations setting out those circumstances where it is lawful to intercept communications for the purpose of carrying on a business. These regulations apply equally to public authorities.

These Lawful Business Practice Regulations can be found on the following Department of Trade and Industry website <http://www.dti.gov.uk/cii/regulation.html>.

Index

abroad, covert investigation 273–4
  authority regime 156–7
  case law 157–9
  checklist 161–2
  diplomatic negotiation 154
  EU Convention on Mutual Assistance
    in Criminal Matters 153–5
  generally 152
  international 152
  International Criminal Court 152
  joint investigation teams (JITs) 154,
    156–7
  mutual legal assistance 152, 154–5
  non-EU states 155
  planning actions 162
  powers 153–6
  public authorities carrying out 153
  Schengen Convention 1990 153–4
  sources of advice 159–60
  transnational 152
  vehicle tracking devices 156
admissibility of evidence
  malpractice by investigator 19–20
agents provocateurs 138–9
appeals
  Office of Surveillance Commissioners
    (OSC) 186–7
audio devices
  police cells, in 54–5

billing data
  communications data 108
Birkett Report 7
British Broadcasting
  Corporation 278–81

cancellation of authorities
  directed surveillance 34–6
car parks
  theft of motor vehicles from 12–13
case law
  abroad, covert investigation 157–9
  communications data 111
  covert human intelligence source
    (CHIS) 137–42

  directed surveillance 36–42
  entry onto land 73
  interception of communications 126
  intrusive surveillance 54–6
  legality, principle of 14
  mobile phone examination 100
  property or wireless telegraphy
    interference 73
CCTV
  directed surveillance 36
  use 3
CDRPs *see* **Crime and Disorder**
  Reduction Partnerships (CDRP)
CHIS *see* **covert human intelligence**
  source (CHIS)
codes of practice
  Covert Human Intelligence Sources: Codes
    of Practice 16, 313–29
  Covert Surveillance: Codes of Practice 16,
    28, 48, 285–312
  generally 7
  interception of
    communications 331–48
  legality, principle of 14–15
  National Intelligence Model: Code of
    Practice 16
communications data 214–19, 262–4
  assessment or collection of taxes, duties
    or levies 107
  authority regime 109–10
  billing data 108
  case law 111
  checklist 111
  crime prevention 107
  definition 108
  detection of crime 107
  economic well-being of UK 107
  emergencies 107
  errors 108
  evidence 106
  generally 106
  national security 107
  necessity 107
  planning actions 112
  powers 107–9

communications data (*cont.*):
  proportionality 107
  public authorities 106–7, 267–9
  public authorities capable of
    investigating 106–7
  public health, protection of 107
  public safety 107
  service use information 108–9
  single point of contact (SPOC) 106
  subscriber information 108–9
  traffic data 108
  types 108
computers
  appropriate authority for accessing
    stored data 90
  checklist 92–3
  collateral intrusion 84
  data protection 91
  directed surveillance 85–8
  generally 84
  geographical location of computer 91
  good practice 90–1
  interception warrant 84, 89–90
  internet service providers 91
  intrusive surveillance 84–5, 88
  issues 91–2
  jurisdiction 91
  legal authorities required 84–6
  planning actions 93–4
  private information 92
  property, interference with 84, 88–9
  proportionality 84
  public authorities capable of
    investigating 84–7
  scenario 92
  warrantor production order 90
covert human intelligence source
  (CHIS) 219–44
  acquisition of confidential information
    by 136–7, 183–4
  agents provocateurs 138–9
  assessment or collection of tax, duty,
    levy, etc. 135
  authority regime 135–6
  authorizing officers 135–6
  case law 137–42
  checklist 146–7
  combined authorization 136
  confidential contact 134
  confidential source 134
  *Covert Human Intelligence Sources: Codes
    of Practice* 16, 132, 313–30

  crime prevention 135
  definition 132
  detection of crime 135
  directed surveillance 251–62
  economic well-being of the UK 135
  entrapment 140
  good practice 142–3
  handler 137
  infiltration 135
  juveniles 136, 276–7
  management regime 137
  meaning 133–4
  national security 135
  necessity 135
  planning actions 147–8
  powers 134–5
  proportionality 135
  protection 21, 141–2
  public authorities deploying 132–3
  public health, protection of 135
  public safety 135
  records of use 137
  registers 134
  risk management 137
  scenarios 144–5
  securing evidence 140–1
  source records 274–6
  test for 133–4
  test purchase operatives 143–4
  vulnerable persons 136
covert investigation
  advantage 4
  benefits of UK regulatory regime 9–12
  checklist for decision to deploy 22
  Codes of Practice 7
  computers *see* computers
  criteria for management 4–5
  disadvantages of UK regulatory
    regime 9–12
  historical development 6–9
  intrusive aspect 5
  issues arising from 4–6
  meaning 2
  methodology, protecting 21–3
  reasons for using 2–4
  *Covert Surveillance: Codes of
    Practice* 16, 28
**Crime and Disorder Reduction
  Partnerships (CDRP)**
  establishment 12
crime prevention 2
  communications data 107

covert human intelligence source
(CHIS) 135
intrusive surveillance 50

delegated legislation
legality, principle of 14
directed surveillance
see also surveillance
action going beyond 32
application to conduct 28
authority 31–3
authorizing officers 33–4
cancellation of authorities 34–6
direct involvement of authorizing
officers 35
disclosure 38
duration 36
lack of precise wording in 35–6
more than applied for, authorization
of 36
necessity 35
power to grant 33
proportionality 35
regime 33–4
renewal 36
tests for grant 35
urgent authority procedure 34–5
authorizing officers 33–4
cancellation of authorities 34–6
case law 36–42
CCTV 36
checklist on decision whether to
employ 41–2
combined authority 50
computers 85–8
covert human intelligence source
(CHIS) 251–62
covert observation 31
definition 31
direct involvement of authorizing
officers 35
disclosure of surveillance
authorizations 38
duration of authority 36
economic well-being of UK 31
fiscal levies, assessing or collecting 31
flowchart 43–4
immediate response to spontaneous
events 31–3
Local Health Boards 4
meaning of surveillance 28
national security 31

necessity 35
NHS Trusts 4
observation posts, protection of
37
offices 32
permitted purposes 31
place of 32
planning actions 42
postponing operation 34
powers 31–3
premises 32
private information 31, 33
private life, respect for 36
proportionality 35
public authorities capable of
deploying 29–31
public health, protection of 31
public safety 31
purpose 31
remote technical means 32
renewal of authority 36
scenarios 31–2, 35, 38–41
Special Health Authorities 4
specific investigation or operation, for
purpose of 31
urgent authority procedure 34–5
vehicles 32
disclosure
directed surveillance authorizations 38
intercept product 125
intrusive surveillance authorizations 56
drug trafficking 3
due process 4

economic well-being of the UK
communications data 107
covert human intelligence source
(CHIS) 135
directed surveillance 31
intrusive surveillance 50
entrapment 140
entry onto land
authority
cancellation 72–3
drafting applications 71
duration 71
prior approval of OSC 70, 72
regime 70–2
timescales 70
cancellation of authorities
72–3
case law 73

entry onto land (*cont.*):
  checklist 75–6
  duration of authority 71
  flowchart 77
  generally 68
  planning actions 76
  powers 69–70
  prior approval of OSC 70, 72
  public authorities capable of carrying
    out 68–9
  scenarios 74–5
  serious crime 69–70
**EU Convention on Mutual Assistance
  in Criminal Matters** 153
European Community law
  legality, principle of 14
**European Convention on Human
  Rights**
  intention 5
  private life, respect for *see* private life,
    respect for
**exclusion of unfairly obtained
  evidence**
  malpractice by investigator 19–20

fiscal levies, assessing or collecting
  directed surveillance 31

hot-spots, crime 12
Human Rights Act 1998
  incompatible acts 5
  public authorities 14
  scope 14

**immediate response to spontaneous
  events**
  directed surveillance 31–3
informants *see* **covert human
  intelligence source (CHIS)**
**interception of
  communications** 191–214, 269–72
  authority regime
    business purposes 119
    one-sided consent 119
    two-party consent 119
    wireless telegraphy, in connection
      with 120
  case law 126
  checklist 126–8
  codes of practice 331–48
  computers 84, 89–90
  confidential information 123, 183–4
  definitions
    in the course of transmission 117
    interception 117
  disclosure of intercept product 125
  evidence 116
  existing statutory power 120
  generally 116–17
  handling intercept product 124–5
  intelligence purposes 116
  journalistic material, confidential 124,
    184
  legal privilege 123, 183
  personal information 123
  planning actions 128
  postal items 124
  powers 118
  practical difficulties with use as
    evidence 117
  'Preston' briefing 125
  prisons 122–3
  public authorities that can
    intercept 117–18
  warrant 120–1
International Criminal Court 152
internet service providers 91
intrusive surveillance
  see also surveillance
  application to conduct 28
  audio devices in police cells 54–5
  authority
    cancellation 53
    combined 50
    disclosure of authorizations 56
    duration 51
    key points 51–2
    persons authorised to grant 51
    prior approval from Office of
      Surveillance Commissioners 52–3
    regime 51–2
    renewal 51
  case law 54–6
  checklist 60–1
  combined authority 50
  computers 84–5, 88
  crime prevention 50
  definition 49
  detecting serious crime 50
  disclosure of authorizations 56
  duration of authority 51
  economic well-being of UK
    50
  flowchart 62–3

key points
  applicants 51
  authorizing officers 51–2
meaning 32
national security 50
notification of authorizations 249–51
observation posts, protection of
  55–6
permitted purposes 50
planning actions 61
powers 49–50
prior approval from Office of
  Surveillance Commissioners 52–3
private life, respect for 54
public authorities capable of
  deploying 49, 51
purpose 50
renewal of authority 51
scenarios 56–60
serious crime 50

joint investigation teams (JITs) 154
journalistic material, confidential
  interception of communications 124,
  184
juveniles
  covert human intelligence source
  (CHIS) 136, 276–7

legal privilege
  interception of communications 123,
  183
legality, principle of
  case law 14–15
  codes of practice 14–15
  delegated legislation 14
  European Community law 14
  satisfying 14–15
  statute 14
Local Health Boards
  directed surveillance 4

malpractice by investigator
  admissibility of evidence 19–20
  consequences 19–21
  exclusion of unfairly obtained
    evidence 19–20
  fair trial requirements 20
  New Zealand 19
  stay of proceedings 19
mobile phone examination
  authority regime 99–100

case law 100
checklist 101–2
generally 98
methods of data storage 99
planning actions 102
powers 99
public authorities capable of 98
scenarios 100–1

National Crime Squad
  authorizing officers 11
National Intelligence Model (NIM) 2
  code of practice 16
  hotspots, policing of 12
National Policing Plans
  2004–2007 12
national security
  communications data 107
  covert human intelligence source
    (CHIS) 135
  directed surveillance 31
  intrusive surveillance 50
necessity
  communications data 107
  covert human intelligence source
    (CHIS) 135
  directed surveillance 35
negligence
  risk management 166
New Zealand
  malpractice by investigator 19
NHS Trusts
  directed surveillance 4

observation posts, protection of
  directed surveillance 37
  intrusive surveillance 55–6
Office of Surveillance Commissioners
  (OSC)
  annual reports 11, 17–18
  appeals 186–7
  approval
    entry onto land 70, 72
    intrusive surveillance 52–3
  Assistant Commissioners 9
  authorizations 176–83
  Chief Surveillance Commissioner 9
    annual reports 17–18
    duties 17
  Commissioners 9, 175–6, 187–8
  complaints 184–6
  deficiencies identified by 18–19

**Office of Surveillance Commissioners
(OSC)** (*cont.*):
establishment 9, 17
intrusive surveillance, prior approval
for 52–3
issues arising from inspections
by 17–19
property or wireless telegraphy,
interference with 70, 72
role 4
offices
directed surveillance 32
OSC *see* **Office of Surveillance
Commissioners (OSC)**

partnership protocols
use 3–4
personal information
interception of communications 123
Police Act 1997
Part III, extracts from 175–89
police cells
audio devices in 54–5
postal items
interception of communications 124
PPPLEM model 168–70
'Preston' briefing 125
principle of legality *see* **legality,
principle of**
prisons
interception of communications
122–3
private information
computers 92
definition 33
directed surveillance 31, 33
likelihood of obtaining 13
private life, respect for
see also Human Rights Act 1998
Convention right 5
directed surveillance 36
ECtHR tests *see* tests *below*
generally 5
intrusive surveillance 54
qualified right 5–6
tests 6
interference in accordance with the
law 14–15
investigative act falls within scope of
Article 8, whether 12–13
legitimate aim of interference 15
meaning 12–17

necessary and proportionate in a
democratic society, interference
being 15–17
public authority, interference of
Article 8 right by 14
production order
computers 90
**property or wireless telegraphy
interference**
authority
cancellation 72–3
drafting applications 71
duration 71
prior approval of OSC 70
regime 70–2
timescales 70
cancellation of authorities 72–3
case law 73
checklist 75–6
computers 84, 88–9
duration of authorization 71
flowchart 77, 79
generally 68
planning actions 76
powers 69–70
public authorities capable of carrying
out 68–9
scenarios 74–5
serious crime 69–70
proportionality
communications data 107
covert human intelligence source
(CHIS) 135
directed surveillance 35
test 15–17
proportionality
computers 84
public authorities 244–7
abroad, covert investigation 153
communications data 106–7, 267–9
computers 84–7
covert human intelligence source
(CHIS) 132–3
directed surveillance 29–31
entry onto land 68–9
Human Rights Act 1998 14
individuals in 265–7
interception of
communications 117–18
mobile phone examination 98
property or wireless telegraphy
interference 68–9

public health, protection of
communications data 107
covert human intelligence source
(CHIS) 135
directed surveillance 31
public interest immunity (PII)
exemption 21–2
case law criteria 22
public safety
communications data 107
covert human intelligence source
(CHIS) 135
directed surveillance 31

RARA model 168–9,171–2
Regulation of Investigatory Powers Act
2000, extracts from 191–247
remote technical means
directed surveillance 32
rights culture
promotion 11–12
risk management
assessment, risk 168
benefits of 167–8
covert human intelligence source
(CHIS) 137
definitions 167–8
European Convention on Human
Rights 166
generally 166
identification of risks 168–9
inadequacies 166–7
initial application 167
management of risks 168–9
negligence 166
positive obligations on
investigators 166–7
PPPLEM model 168–70
RARA model 168–9, 171–2
risk 167
strategy 166
threat distinguished 167

vulnerability 167–9
Schengen Convention 1990 153–4
search warrants
limitations 11
self-incrimination 4
serious crime
definition 50, 69–70
entry onto land 69–70
intrusive surveillance 50
property or wireless telegraphy
interference 69–70
service use information
communications data 108–9
single point of contact (SPOC)
communications data 106
Special Health Authorities
directed surveillance 4
statute
legality, principle of 14
subscriber information
communications data 108–9
surveillance
application to conduct 28, 48
controversial 2
covert 2
definition 28, 48
directed *see* directed surveillance
intrusive *see* intrusive surveillance

traffic data
communications data 108

urgent authority procedure
directed surveillance 34–5

warrant
interception of communications
120–1
computers 90
wireless telegraphy
interference *see* property or wireless
telegraphy interference